Cueva Blanca

PREHISTORY AND HUMAN ECOLOGY OF THE VALLEY OF OAXACA

Kent V. Flannery and Joyce Marcus
General Editors

Volume 1   *The Use of Land and Water Resources in the Past and Present Valley of Oaxaca, Mexico*, by Anne V.T. Kirkby. Memoirs of the Museum of Anthropology, University of Michigan, No. 5. 1973.

Volume 2   *Sociopolitical Aspects of Canal Irrigation in the Valley of Oaxaca*, by Susan H. Lees. Memoirs of the Museum of Anthropology, University of Michigan, No. 6. 1973.

Volume 3   *Formative Mesoamerican Exchange Networks with Special Reference to the Valley of Oaxaca*, by Jane W. Pires-Ferreira. Memoirs of the Museum of Anthropology, University of Michigan, No. 7. 1975.

Volume 4   *Fábrica San José and Middle Formative Society in the Valley of Oaxaca*, by Robert D. Drennan. Memoirs of the Museum of Anthropology, University of Michigan, No. 8. 1976.

Volume 5   Part 1. *The Vegetational History of the Oaxaca Valley*, by C. Earle Smith, Jr. Part 2. *Zapotec Plant Knowledge: Classification, Uses and Communication*, by Ellen Messer. Memoirs of the Museum of Anthropology, University of Michigan, No. 10. 1978.

Volume 6   *Excavations at Santo Domingo Tomaltepec: Evolution of a Formative Community in the Valley of Oaxaca, Mexico*, by Michael E. Whalen. Memoirs of the Museum of Anthropology, University of Michigan, No. 12. 1981.

Volume 7   *Monte Albán's Hinterland, Part 1: The Prehispanic Settlement Patterns of the Central and Southern Parts of the Valley of Oaxaca, Mexico*, by Richard E. Blanton, Stephen Kowalewski, Gary Feinman, and Jill Appel. Memoirs of the Museum of Anthropology, University of Michigan, No. 15. 1982.

Volume 8   *Chipped Stone Tools in Formative Oaxaca, Mexico: Their Procurement, Production and Use*, by William J. Parry. Memoirs of the Museum of Anthropology, University of Michigan, No. 20. 1987.

Volume 9   *Agricultural Intensification and Prehistoric Health in the Valley of Oaxaca, Mexico*, by Denise C. Hodges. Memoirs of the Museum of Anthropology, University of Michigan, No. 22. 1989.

Volume 10   *Early Formative Pottery of the Valley of Oaxaca*, by Kent V. Flannery and Joyce Marcus, with ceramic analysis by William O. Payne. Memoirs of the Museum of Anthropology, University of Michigan, No. 27. 1994.

Volume 11   *Women's Ritual in Formative Oaxaca: Figurine-Making, Divination, Death and the Ancestors*, by Joyce Marcus. Memoirs of the Museum of Anthropology, University of Michigan, No. 33. 1998.

Volume 12   *The Sola Valley and the Monte Albán State: A Study of Zapotec Imperial Expansion*, by Andrew K. Balkansky. Memoirs of the Museum of Anthropology, University of Michigan, No. 36. 2002.

Volume 13   *Excavations at San José Mogote 1: The Household Archaeology*, by Kent V. Flannery and Joyce Marcus. Memoirs of the Museum of Anthropology, University of Michigan, No. 40. 2005.

Volume 14   *Excavations at Cerro Tilcajete: A Monte Albán II Administrative Center in the Valley of Oaxaca*, by Christina Elson. Memoirs of the Museum of Anthropology, University of Michigan, No. 42. 2007.

Volume 15   *Cerro Danush: Excavations at a Hilltop Community in the Eastern Valley of Oaxaca, Mexico*, by Ronald K. Faulseit. Memoirs of the Museum of Anthropology, University of Michigan, No. 54. 2013.

Volume 16   *Excavations at San José Mogote 2: The Cognitive Archaeology*, by Kent V. Flannery and Joyce Marcus. Memoirs of the Museum of Anthropology, University of Michigan, No. 58. 2015.

Volume 17   *Cueva Blanca: Social Change in the Archaic of the Valley of Oaxaca*, by Kent V. Flannery and Frank Hole. Memoirs of the Museum of Anthropology, University of Michigan, No. 60. 2019.

Related Volumes

Flannery, Kent V.
    2009 *Guilá Naquitz: Archaic Foraging and Early Agriculture in Oaxaca, Mexico*. Walnut Creek, CA: Left Coast Press.

Flannery, Kent V., and Joyce Marcus
    2003 *The Cloud People: Divergent Evolution of the Zapotec and Mixtec Civilizations*. Clinton Corners, New York: Percheron Press.

Marcus, Joyce, and Kent V. Flannery
    1996 *Zapotec Civilization: How Urban Society Evolved in Mexico's Oaxaca Valley*. London: Thames and Hudson.

Typical projectile points of Oaxaca's Late Archaic. Illustration by John Klausmeyer.

Memoirs of the Museum of Anthropology
University of Michigan
Number 60

PREHISTORY AND HUMAN ECOLOGY OF THE VALLEY OF OAXACA
Kent V. Flannery and Joyce Marcus, General Editors
Volume 17

Cueva Blanca

Social Change in the Archaic of the Valley of Oaxaca

Kent V. Flannery and Frank Hole

with contributions by
Robert G. Reynolds, Charles S. Spencer, and Jane C. Wheeler

Ann Arbor, Michigan
2019

©2019 by the Regents of the University of Michigan
The Museum of Anthropology
All rights reserved

Printed in the United States of America
ISBN 978-0-915703-91-3 (print)
ISBN 978-0-915703-94-4 (ebook)

Cover design by John Klausmeyer

The Museum currently publishes two monograph series: Anthropological Papers and Memoirs. For permissions, questions, or manuscript queries, contact Museum publications in Ann Arbor, Michigan by email at umma-pubs@umich.edu or visit our websites at lsa.umich.edu/ummaa (the Museum) and sites.lsa.umich.edu/archaeology-books (our books).

Library of Congress Cataloging-in-Publication Data

Names: Flannery, Kent V., author. | Hole, Frank, author.
Title: Cueva Blanca : Social Change in the Archaic of the Valley of Oaxaca / Kent V. Flannery and Frank Hole ; with contributions by Robert G. Reynolds, Charles S. Spencer, and Jane C. Wheeler.
Description: Ann Arbor, Michigan : Museum of Anthropology, University of Michigan, 2019. | Series: Memoirs of the Museum of Anthropology, University of Michigan ; Number 60 | Includes bibliographical references. | Identifiers: LCCN 2019008170 (print) | LCCN 2019010744 (ebook) | ISBN 9780915703944 () | ISBN 9780915703913 (pbk. : alk. paper)
Subjects: LCSH: Indians of Mexico--Mexico--Oaxaca Valley--Antiquities. | Excavations (Archaeology)--Mexico--Oaxaca Valley | Oaxaca Valley (Mexico)--Antiquities. | Oaxaca Valley (Mexico)--Social life and customs. | Indians of Mexico--Mexico--San José Mogote--Antiquities. | Excavations (Archaeology)--Mexico--San José Mogote. | San José Mogote (Mexico)--Antiquities. | Mixtec Indians--Antiquities. | Zapotec Indians--Antiquities.
Classification: LCC F1219.1.O11 (ebook) | LCC F1219.1.O11 F55 2019 (print) | DDC 972/.74--dc23
LC record available at https://lccn.loc.gov/2019008170

The paper used in this publication meets the requirements of the ANSI Standard Z39.48-1984 (Permanence of Paper).

Dedicated to the memory of Richard J. Orlandini

archaeologist, civil rights activist, anti-war protester,
and discoverer of Archaic and Paleoindian sites

Table of Contents

List of Illustrations — xi
List of Tables — xv
Acknowledgments — xvi

Part I. Discovery and Excavation

Chapter 1. The Research Questions — 3
Kent V. Flannery

Chapter 2. The Discovery of Cueva Blanca — 14
Kent V. Flannery

Chapter 3. The Excavation of Cueva Blanca — 26
Kent V. Flannery and Frank Hole

Chapter 4. The Radiocarbon Dates from Cueva Blanca — 52
Kent V. Flannery

Part II. The Artifacts

Chapter 5. The Chipped Stone Tools — 59
Frank Hole

Chapter 6. The Archaic Projectile Points — 101
Kent V. Flannery and Frank Hole

Chapter 7. The Ground Stone Tools — 126
Kent V. Flannery

Chapter 8. Artifacts of Bone and Shell — 129
Kent V. Flannery

Part III. Environment and Subsistence

Chapter 9. Animal Bones from the Archaic Living Floors — 133
Kent V. Flannery and Jane C. Wheeler

Chapter 10. The Microfauna from Cueva Blanca 143
Kent V. Flannery and Jane C. Wheeler

Chapter 11. The Late Archaic Plant Evidence 146
Kent V. Flannery

Part IV. Analysis of the Living Floors

Chapter 12. Distributional Variability in Zones E–C of Cueva Blanca: 149
  A Local Analysis of Grid-Density Data
Charles S. Spencer and Kent V. Flannery

Chapter 13. The Search for Tool Kits at Cueva Blanca: Two Statistical Approaches 168
Robert G. Reynolds

Chapter 14. The Search for "Drop Zones" at Cueva Blanca: An Approach Drawn 185
  from Artificial Intelligence
Robert G. Reynolds

Part V. Summary and Conclusions

Chapter 15. The Place of Cueva Blanca in Oaxaca's Archaic Sequence 197
Kent V. Flannery and Frank Hole

Appendix A. Resumen en Español 202
Soren Frykholm

References 204

List of Illustrations

Frontispiece: Typical projectile points of Oaxaca's Late Archaic.

Figure 1.1. Caves, rockshelters, and open-air sites in the eastern Valley of Oaxaca, *4*
Figure 1.2. The eastern Valley of Oaxaca, showing the cave study area, *7*
Figure 1.3. Lands of the ex-hacienda El Fuerte, showing Archaic sites, watercourses, and elevations in meters, *8*
Figure 1.4. Environmental zones on the ex-hacienda El Fuerte and location of Archaic sites, *9*
Figure 1.5. Primitive maize cobs found in ash lenses above Zone B1 at Guilá Naquitz, *11*
Figure 1.6. Valleys of Tehuacán, Cuicatlán, Nochixtlán, Oaxaca, and Miahuatlán, showing excavated Archaic sites and surface finds, *13*

Figure 2.1. A view of Cueva Blanca from the northwest, showing its location relative to the Mitla Fortress, the town of Mitla, the Tlacolula subvalley, and Cerro Nueve Puntas, *15*
Figure 2.2. A broken atlatl point from the talus slope below Cueva Blanca, *16*
Figure 2.3. A cross-section of the El Fuerte caves region, from Guilá Naquitz Cave to Cueva Blanca, *17*
Figure 2.4. The Cueva Blanca group (OC-29, OC-30, and OC-31) in its thorn forest setting, *18*
Figure 2.5. West-to-east cross-section through Cueva Blanca and the agricultural terraces on the talus below it, *19*
Figure 2.6. Plan view of Cueva Blanca, showing the 1 x 1 m squares that were excavated, *20*
Figure 2.7. Fragments of Texas gopher tortoise from Zone F of Cueva Blanca, *21*
Figure 2.8. Fluted points from sites within walking distance of Cueva Blanca, *21*
Figure 2.9. Eligio Martínez is exposing the thick layer of firecracked rocks that comprised Zone B, *22*
Figure 2.10. The talus slope below Cueva Blanca, *23*
Figure 2.11. Plan view of Feature 8, a two-chambered pottery kiln found in Squares F2–F5 and G2–G5 of Zone A, *24*
Figure 2.12. A blob of pottery clay from Zone A of Cueva Blanca, showing signs of squeezing and kneading, *24*

Figure 3.1. The east profile of Square D9, showing Zones A–F, *28*
Figure 3.2. The north profile of Squares H9–B9, *29*
Figure 3.3. Félix trowels his way through the Archaic levels in Square E5, *31*
Figure 3.4. The east profile of Squares E3–E13, *32*
Figure 3.5. Eligio supervises excavation of Squares E3 and E4, *33*
Figure 3.6. Work beginning on Zone A of Square E12, *34*
Figure 3.7. Plan view of Cueva Blanca, showing (1) squares excavated and (2) the location of the four longest stratigraphic profiles, *35*
Figure 3.8. An ornament made from olive shell (*Agaronia testacea*) from Zone C, 35
Figure 3.9. The excavation of Squares D5 and D7, *36*
Figure 3.10. The east profile of Squares D3–D12, *37*
Figure 3.11. The excavation of alternate Squares D4, D6, and D8, *38*
Figure 3.12. Looking north down the "D" and "E" rows of squares, *39*
Figure 3.13. Coxcatlán point found *in situ* in Zone C of Square D8, *40*
Figure 3.14. Sweeping the completed "E" row of squares and shaving the east profile of the "D" row, *41*
Figure 3.15. Work begins on a stratigraphic test in Terrace 3 of the agricultural terrace system below Cueva Blanca, *42*
Figure 3.16. The stratigraphic test in Terrace 3 carried to sterile soil, *43*
Figure 3.17. Plan view of Feature 18, a hearth originating in Zone D, *44*
Figure 3.18. Left metatarsal of *Odocoileus* recovered from Zone F, *45*
Figure 3.19. The south profile of Squares F13–J13, *46*
Figure 3.20. Plan view of Feature 15, a large but shallow hearth apparently originating in Zone E, *47*
Figure 3.21. Squares F2–F4 and G2–G4, showing Feature 8, a Monte Albán V pottery kiln, *48*
Figure 3.22. Frank Hole supervises don Juan and Félix while they excavate Square C11, *50*

xii

Figure 4.1. Left distal humerus of a white-tailed deer from Zone F of Cueva Blanca (Square G11), *53*

Figure 5.1. A hammerstone from Zone D (Square H9), *60*
Figure 5.2. A typical Archaic hammerstone, *60*
Figure 5.3. A typical Archaic flake core from Zone C (Square D11), *61*
Figure 5.4. A typical Archaic flake core, redeposited in Zone B, *61*
Figure 5.5. A discoidal core from Zone D (Square D6), *61*
Figure 5.6. Fragments of Archaic cores, redeposited in Zone B, *62*
Figure 5.7. A large utilized flake, *63*
Figure 5.8. Small to medium-sized utilized flakes, *64*
Figure 5.9. A large notched flake, discovered *in situ* in Zone D (Square D5), *64*
Figure 5.10. A large notched flake, redeposited in Zone B, *65*
Figure 5.11. Small to medium-sized notched flakes, *65*
Figure 5.12. Notched flakes, *66*
Figure 5.13. Crude blades, plain, discovered *in situ* in Zones E, D, and C, *66*
Figure 5.14. Crude blades from Archaic strata, *66*
Figure 5.15. Crude blades, retouched, *67*
Figure 5.16. Flakes with sheen, discovered *in situ* in Zones E, D, and F, *67*
Figure 5.17. Typical Archaic flakes with sheen, redeposited in Zone B, *68*
Figure 5.18. A flake with sheen, found *in situ* in Zone C (Square C7), *69*
Figure 5.19. Choppers/knives, found *in situ* in Archaic strata, *70*
Figure 5.20. Bifacial Archaic scraper/knife, redeposited in Zone B, *71*
Figure 5.21. Bifacial Archaic chopper/knife, redeposited in Zone B, *71*
Figure 5.22. Large bifacial Archaic chopper/knife, redeposited in Zone B, *72*
Figure 5.23. Large bifacial Archaic chopper/knife, redeposited in Zone B, *73*
Figure 5.24. Large Archaic chopper/knife, redeposited in Zone B, showing evidence of battering on its edges, *74*
Figure 5.25. End scrapers, found *in situ* in Archaic strata, *75*
Figure 5.26. An end scraper, found *in situ* in Zone D (Square D7), *76*
Figure 5.27. Sidescrapers/knives, found *in situ* in Archaic strata, *76*
Figure 5.28. Typical Archaic sidescrapers/knives, redeposited in Zone B, *77*
Figure 5.29. A sidescraper/knife found in Zone E (Square E4), *77*
Figure 5.30. Ovoid scrapers, found *in situ* in Archaic strata, *78*
Figure 5.31. Typical Archaic ovoid scrapers, redeposited in Zone B, *79*
Figure 5.32. Typical Archaic ovoid scraper, redeposited in Zone B, *79*
Figure 5.33. A steep denticulate scraper, found *in situ* in Zone D (Square E8), *80*
Figure 5.34. Steep denticulate scrapers, found *in situ* in Archaic strata, *81*
Figure 5.35. A steep denticulate scraper found in Zone D (Square D7), *82*
Figure 5.36. Typical Archaic steep denticulate scraper, redeposited in Zone B, *82*
Figure 5.37. Two typical Archaic steep denticulate scrapers, redeposited in Zone B, *83*
Figure 5.38. Two steep denticulate scrapers found *in situ* in Zone D, showing the range of variation in size, *84*
Figure 5.39. Two typical Archaic steep denticulate scrapers, redeposited in Zone B, *85*
Figure 5.40. A burin, discovered *in situ* in Zone D (Square D11), *85*
Figure 5.41. Typical Archaic burins, redeposited in Zone B, *86*
Figure 5.42. A burin found in Zone D (Square D11), *86*
Figure 5.43. Archaic drills, *87*
Figure 5.44. Archaic drills, *87*
Figure 5.45. Variety A biface found *in situ* in Zone D (Square C6), *88*
Figure 5.46. A Variety A ("Martínez") biface from Zone D (Square C6), *88*
Figure 5.47. A broken Variety A biface, redeposited in Zone B, *89*
Figure 5.48. A Variety B biface, discovered *in situ* in Zone D (Square D7), *89*
Figure 5.49. A broken Variety B biface, redeposited in Zone B, *90*
Figure 5.50. A Variety C biface, redeposited in Zone B, *90*
Figure 5.51. Typical Archaic bifaces, redeposited in Zone B, *91*

Figure 5.52. Biface fragments, redeposited in Zone B, *92*
Figure 5.53. This flake with a chipped base was a unique tool at Cueva Blanca discovered *in situ* in Zone C, *92*
Figure 5.54. Two chipped stone artifacts in Zone A were unique at Cueva Blanca, *93*

Figure 6.1. The effect of rejuvenation on damaged Elko points, *104*
Figure 6.2. Two Palmillas points recovered from Zone D of Cueva Blanca, *105*
Figure 6.3. La Mina points from Cueva Blanca, *106*
Figure 6.4. When La Mina points were damaged and rejuvenated, the stem often remained the same while the body became shorter, *107*
Figure 6.5. Trinidad points from Cueva Blanca, *107*
Figure 6.6. Tilapa points recovered in Zone D, *108*
Figure 6.7. San Nicolás points, *109*
Figure 6.8. Coxcatlán points from Cueva Blanca, *110*
Figure 6.9. Many points assigned to the type "Hidalgo" appear to have been rejuvenated, *111*
Figure 6.10. Stemless Archaic points redeposited in later levels at Cueva Blanca, *112*
Figure 6.11. A Gary point redeposited in Zone B, *112*
Figure 6.12. This point, discovered *in situ* in Zone D, does not readily conform to any Tehuacán Valley types, *113*
Figure 6.13. An unusually large point recovered from Zone C (Square F8), *114*
Figure 6.14. Unclassified point fragments redeposited in Zone A features, *115*
Figure 6.15. Two atlatl points from Zone E, *115*
Figure 6.16. The distribution of projectile points in Zone E, *116*
Figure 6.17. Atlatl points from Zone D, *117*
Figure 6.18. The distribution of projectile points in Zone D, *118*
Figure 6.19. Projectile points from Zone C, *120*
Figure 6.20. Distribution of projectile points in Zone C, *121*
Figure 6.21. Representative Archaic points redeposited in Zone B, *122*
Figure 6.22. Representative Archaic points redeposited in Zone A, *123*
Figure 6.23. Hypothetical series of modifications of a Type A biface, *125*

Figure 7.1. Examples of Archaic ground stone tools from Cueva Blanca, *127*

Figure 8.1. Archaic artifacts carved from deer bone, *130*

Figure 9.1. The skeleton of a white-tailed deer, with the skeletal elements present in Zone E, *135*
Figure 9.2. The skeleton of a white-tailed deer, with the skeletal elements present in Zone D, *138*
Figure 9.3. The skeleton of a white-tailed deer, with the skeletal elements present in Zone C, *141*

Figure 12.1. Cartesian grid of 126 squares used for density contour study, with excavated squares indicated, *151*
Figure 12.2. Feature 15, a hearth that might have influenced the distribution of items in Zone E, *153*
Figure 12.3. Density contours for total tools, Zone E, *153*
Figure 12.4. Density contours for notched flakes, Zone E, *154*
Figure 12.5. Density contours for identified deer bone, Zone E, *154*
Figure 12.6. Density contours for identified cottontail rabbit bones, Zone E, *155*
Figure 12.7. Density contours for bird bones, Zone E, *155*
Figure 12.8. Feature 18, a hearth that might have influenced the distribution of items in Zone D, *156*
Figure 12.9. Density contours for debitage, Zone D, *156*
Figure 12.10. Density contours for total tools, Zone D, *157*
Figure 12.11. Density contours for steep denticulate scrapers, Zone D, *158*
Figure 12.12. Density contours for utilized flakes, Zone D, *158*
Figure 12.13. Density contours for notched flakes, Zone D, *159*

Figure 12.14. Density contours for identified deer bone, Zone D, *159*
Figure 12.15. Density contours for identified cottontail rabbit bones, Zone D, *160*
Figure 12.16. Density contours for unidentified fragments of small mammal bone, Zone D, *161*
Figure 12.17. Density contours for bird bones, Zone D, *161*
Figure 12.18. Results of multidimensional scaling of eight categories of items found in Zone D, *162*
Figure 12.19. Density contours for debitage, Zone C, *163*
Figure 12.20. Density contours for total tools, Zone C, *163*
Figure 12.21. Density contours for utilized flakes, Zone C, *164*
Figure 12.22. Density contours for notched flakes, Zone C, *164*
Figure 12.23. Density contours for identified deer bone, Zone C, *165*
Figure 12.24. Density contours for identified cottontail rabbit bones, Zone C, *165*
Figure 12.25. Density contours for unidentified fragments of small mammal bone, *166*
Figure 12.26. Density contours for identified mud turtle bones and scutes, Zone C, *166*
Figure 12.27. Results of multidimensional scaling of seven categories of items found in Zone C, *167*

Figure 14.1. Zone E of Cueva Blanca, showing cells in States 5, 6, and 7, *190*
Figure 14.2. Zone D of Cueva Blanca, showing cells in States 5, 6, and 7, *191*
Figure 14.3. Zone C of Cueva Blanca, showing cells in States 5, 6, and 7, *192*

Figure 15.1. A typical Pedernales point, *200*

List of Tables

Table 5.1. Distribution of tool categories by 1 x 1 m square, Stratigraphic Zone E, *94*
Table 5.2. Distribution of tool categories by 1 x 1 m square, Stratigraphic Zone D, *96*
Table 5.3. Distribution of tool categories by 1 x 1 m square, Stratigraphic Zone C, *98*
Table 5.4. Tool category totals for Zones E, D, and C, *100*

Table 9.1. Distribution of animal bones by square in Zone E, Cueva Blanca, *134*
Table 9.2. Distribution of animal bones by square in Zone D, Cueva Blanca, *137*
Table 9.3. Distribution of animal bones by square in Zone C, Cueva Blanca, *140*

Table 10.1. Rodents and shrews from owl pellets on the surface of Cueva Blanca, 1966, *144*

Table 13.1. The maximum number and average number of chipped stone tools per square in Zones E, D, and C of Cueva Blanca, *170*
Table 13.2. Rank-order table showing the strength of association of all chipped stone tools with projectile points over all squares, Zones E through C, *171*
Table 13.3. Rank-order table showing the strength of association of all chipped stone tools with flakes with sheen over all squares, Zones E through C, *172*
Table 13.4. Rank-order table showing the strength of association of all chipped stone tools with projectile points over all squares, Zone E, *173*
Table 13.5. Rank-order table showing the strength of association of all chipped stone tools with flakes with sheen over all squares, Zone E, *174*
Table 13.6. Rank-order table showing the strength of association of all chipped stone tools with projectile points over all squares, Zone D, *175*
Table 13.7. Rank-order table showing the strength of association of all chipped stone tools with flakes with sheen over all squares, Zone D, *176*
Table 13.8. Rank-order table showing the strength of association of all chipped stone tools with projectile points over all squares, Zone C, *177*
Table 13.9. Rank-order table showing the strength of association of all chipped stone tools with flakes with sheen over all squares, Zone C, *178*
Table 13.10. Dendrogram resulting from a cluster analysis of chipped stone tools from Zones E, D, and C of Cueva Blanca, *180*
Table 13.11. Dendrogram resulting from a cluster analysis of chipped stone tools from Zone E, Cueva Blanca, *181*
Table 13.12. Dendrogram resulting from a cluster analysis of chipped stone tools from Zone D, Cueva Blanca, *182*
Table 13.13. Dendrogram resulting from a cluster analysis of chipped stone tools from Zone C, Cueva Blanca, *184*

Acknowledgments

The excavation of Cueva Blanca was supported by Smithsonian Institution Grant 019. The costs of analysis were covered partly by National Science Foundation Grant GS-1616 and partly by the University of Michigan and Rice University.

The excavators were provided with lodging and laboratory space by the Frissell Museum of Zapotec Art in Mitla, Oaxaca, a facility operated by the Universidad de las Américas (then called Mexico City College). We are grateful to the late Dr. John Paddock of Mexico City College and the late Sr. Darío Quero, manager of the Museum, for their hospitality. We also have fond memories of our team of Zapotec workmen, whose names and photographs can be found in Chapter 3.

The final volume owes a great deal to the Museum of Anthropological Archaeology's editor, Elizabeth Noll, and its staff artist, John Klausmeyer, who did most of the art, including the cover and frontispiece. In Mitla, project artist Nancy Hansen drew the chipped stone tools as fast as Hole analyzed them, and project photographer Chris L. Moser developed all our negatives in a small bathroom converted to a darkroom. Geologist Michael Kirkby identified the raw material used for every atlatl point.

We extend our thanks to Bruce D. Smith, who provided funding for many of our radiocarbon dates; to Darden Hood of Beta Analytic, who calibrated all our dates; to Matthew P. Linke of the Ruthven Natural History Museum, who determined the seasons during which certain areas of the cave chamber would be illuminated by the sun; to Nelly Robles García, who convinced UNESCO to declare the region of Mitla's Archaic sites a World Heritage Protected Zone; and to Leonardo López Luján, whose valuable advice improved the book.

Finally, it is fair to say that this book would not exist without the relentless encouragement, pre-production editing, quality control, and bibliographic detective work of our colleague Joyce Marcus. Her efforts were herculean, and we would have been unable to face her had we not seen the book through to completion.

Part I

Discovery and Excavation

1

The Research Questions

Kent V. Flannery

We still have a great deal to learn about the Archaic period of the Mexican highlands. That period began with the transition from Pleistocene to Holocene environmental conditions (ca. 11,000 years ago) and ended with Mexico's first pottery-making villages (ca. 3,500 years ago). Archaic subsistence combined the hunting of wild animals, the harvesting of wild plants, the planting of early cultivars, and the raising of domestic dogs. The rhythm of life was seminomadic at first, but became more sedentary as cultivated plants increased in importance.

One region with the potential to increase our knowledge of the Archaic is the eastern Valley of Oaxaca (Flannery 2009a). Archaeological surveys in this region between 1964 and 1966 brought to light more than 60 caves and rockshelters (Figure 1.1; Finsten et al. 1989). My colleagues and I selected ten of these sites for testing and, based on the test results, chose three of them for more extensive excavation. We soon realized that digging caves alone would likely provide us with a biased view of the Archaic, which meant that we needed to make an effort to find open-air sites. A new survey, begun in 1967, revealed several Archaic open-air sites that could be used to complement our caves and rockshelters.

The most productive area of survey for Archaic sites was bounded on the east by the village of Xaagá, on the west by the *agencia* of Unión Zapata ("Loma Larga"), and on the north by the mountain range known in Zapotec as Dan Ro'. Recently—thanks to the extraordinary efforts of Mexican archaeologist Nelly Robles García—UNESCO has declared this area a World Heritage Protected Zone. As a result, the Archaic sites of the Mitla region will be protected from future looting or highway building.

Most of the promising Archaic sites lie on the former lands of the ex-Hacienda El Fuerte, which took its name from a site called the Fortress of Mitla. This fortified mesa features veins of silicified ignimbrite (volcanic tuff), which provided raw material for thousands of chipped stone tools (Williams and Heizer 1965).

The Paleoenvironment of the Mitla Region

The Archaic of the Mitla region is inextricably linked to the transition from Pleistocene to Holocene environmental conditions. In many parts of the world—Europe, for example—there have been revolutionary advances in our knowledge of that transition (Kohler et al. 2018). Unfortunately, the Valley of Oaxaca has not been one of the areas on which paleoclimatologists have concentrated their efforts. As a result, we must extrapolate from studies done in the Trans-Mexican Volcanic Belt (Metcalfe 2006,

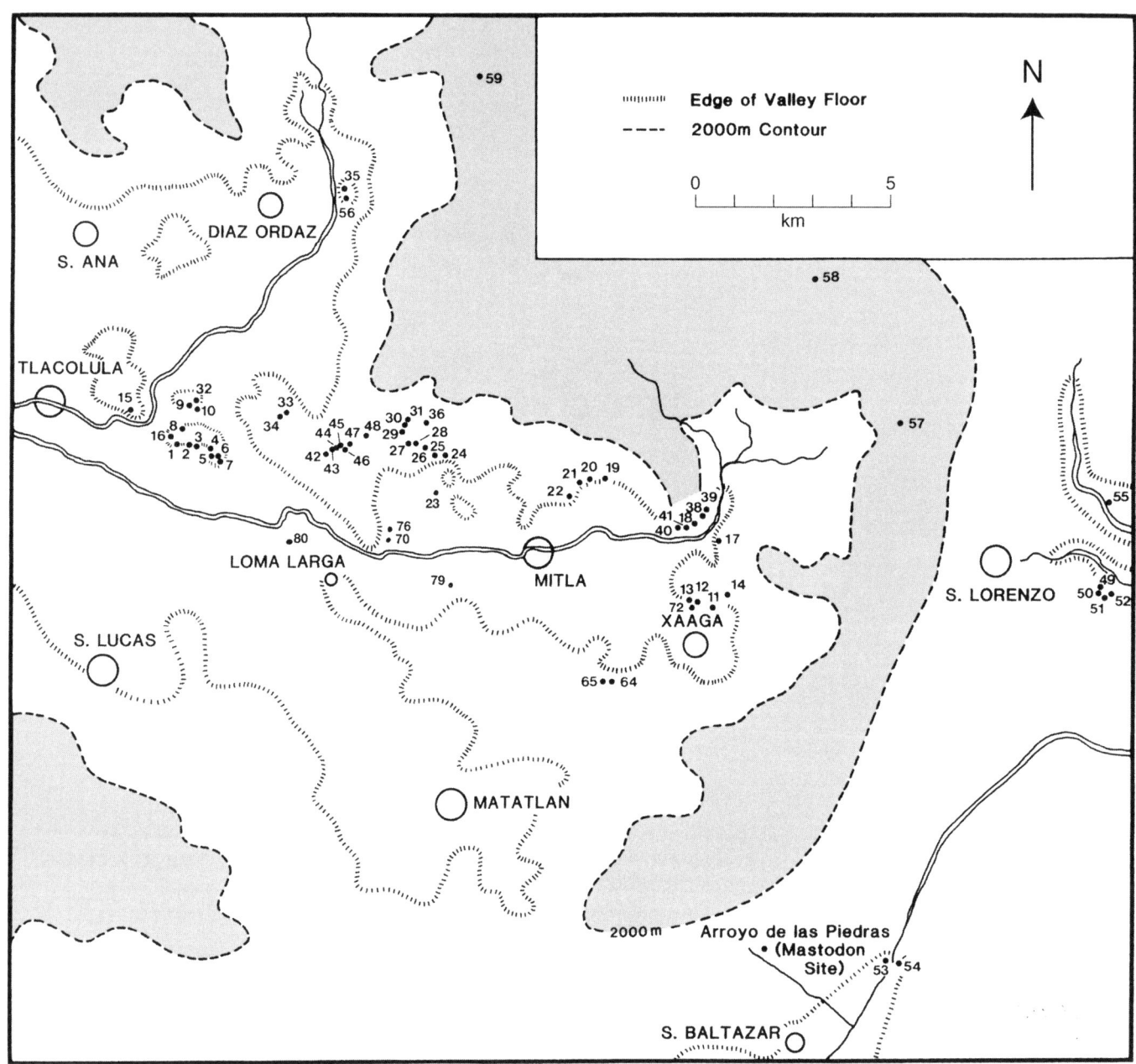

Figure 1.1. Caves, rockshelters, and open-air sites in the eastern Valley of Oaxaca and nearby canyons. (Site descriptions in Finsten et al. 1989).

Bradbury 1997), the Tehuacán Valley of Puebla (Flannery 1966, 1967), and the neighboring state of Guerrero (Bernal et al. 2011, Lachniet et al. 2013).

The Basin of Mexico lies in the eastern half of the Trans-Mexican Volcanic Belt. According to Metcalfe (2006), the glacial maximum for the Late Pleistocene occurred about 18,000 years ago. The Basin of Mexico was significantly cooler and drier during the Late Pleistocene. Today's monsoonal summer rains had not yet been established, and the region "saw more winter precipitation derived from midlatitude frontal systems" (Metcalfe 2006:258).

This conclusion reinforces an earlier model by Spaulding (1989), in which the Late Pleistocene saw colder winters and a suppression of the summer rainy season that is typical of today's central and southern Mexican highlands. Areas of spruce and pinyon-juniper woodlands extended farther south into central Mexico than they do today; stated differently, the lower temperatures of the Late Pleistocene caused some species typical of Chihuahua today to extend their ranges much farther to the south (Shafer 1986:40–41). This observation helps to explain why there were pinyon nuts in the earliest levels at Guilá Naquitz

Cave (Flannery 2009a) and grains of spruce pollen in the Late Pleistocene stratum at Cueva Blanca (see below).

After the Younger Dryas cooling event (roughly 11,000–10,000 years ago), glacial meltwater was re-routed into the Gulf of Mexico and the modern summer rainfall regime was established. Spruce trees disappeared and the pinyon-juniper woodlands retreated to the north.

Today's rainfall regime depends on a system called the Intertropical Convergence Zone, which moves north during the summer to cause Oaxaca's monsoonal rains. During the winter it moves south, creating dry conditions in central and southern Mexico.

Once we proceed from the Basin of Mexico to the Tehuacán Valley of Puebla, we are forced to glean our environmental data from the faunal remains in Coxcatlán Cave (Flannery 1967). The four oldest stratigraphic levels in that cave, which date to the Late Pleistocene, provide further evidence that the climate of that era was cooler and drier than today's. They produced the remains of Pleistocene horse, pronghorn antelope, and the Texas gopher tortoise (*Gopherus berlandieri*), all species that can no longer be found in Tehuacán. There were also more than 700 bones of rabbits on those four living floors, along with evidence that jackrabbits were being hunted by means of large communal drives (Flannery 1966). The Pleistocene horse is now extinct everywhere, but pronghorns and jackrabbits are still common in cooler and drier northern Mexico. Once the Pleistocene had ended, many creatures disappeared from the Tehuacán region and the Coxcatlán Cave area became semitropical thorn forest.

Let us turn next to Guerrero, the state that borders Oaxaca on the west. Here our paleoclimatic reconstructions are based on oxygen isotope variations in the growth of speleothems (cave stalagmites), fixed in time by thorium-uranium dates. The speleothems involved are Stalagmite JX-2 from Juxtlahuaca Cave, which is 100 km from Chilpancingo (Lachniet et al. 2013), and Stalagmite CBD-2 from Cueva del Diablo, which is 150 km from Acapulco (Bernal et al. 2011).

The stalagmite from Juxtlahuaca Cave provided a 22,000-year-long series of oxygen isotope changes. Lachniet et al. (2013) report that Guerrero's climate was drier from the period of the glacial maximum to Heinrich Stadial 1 (about 17,000 years ago), and again during the Younger Dryas. The Cueva del Diablo stalagmite was growing some 11,000 years ago, and recorded an abrupt change to wetter conditions between 7,300 and 7,100 years ago (Bernal et al. 2011).

All these data from neighboring regions lead us to suspect that the Valley of Oaxaca was probably cooler and drier during the Late Pleistocene. We are presented with a glimpse of that period by Cueva Blanca, the site that is the subject of this volume. Zone F, the oldest stratigraphic level at Cueva Blanca, produced specimens of the Texas gopher tortoise, a species present in Texas and Chihuahua but unknown in Oaxaca today. This is the same tortoise that was present in Late Pleistocene levels at Coxcatlán Cave.

Pollen grains from Zone F of Cueva Blanca, analyzed by Schoenwetter and Smith (2009: Table 15.27), reflect a cooler climate than today's. The sample from Zone F is dominated by pine pollen—very likely that of the pinyon pine, whose nuts were well represented in the oldest levels at nearby Guilá Naquitz Cave (C. E. Smith 2009). There were also occasional examples of spruce, fir, oak, and alder pollen.

To be sure, the Late Pleistocene vegetation near Cueva Blanca and Coxcatlán Cave would not have been identical; the two caves, after all, differ in elevation by at least 1000 meters. During the subsequent Holocene, the Cueva Blanca area featured an early version of the thorn forest/mesquite grassland vegetation described by Kirkby et al. (2009), while the warmer Coxcatlán area became tropical deciduous thorn-cactus-scrub (Flannery 1966).

The Transition from Pleistocene to Holocene Climate

The transition from Pleistocene to Holocene conditions had a profound effect on the hunters and gatherers of the Puebla-Oaxaca highlands. The cool-temperate Pleistocene steppe was gone, and their strategy of traveling long distances to take advantage of periodic abundances of jackrabbits, pronghorn, or mammoths would no longer be effective (Marcus and Flannery 1996:49–50). Now foragers had to adapt to thorn forests with a complex assemblage of seasonally available plant foods. Their new adaptation featured a process called "ecological niche construction" (Rowley-Conwy and Layton 2011, B. D. Smith 2015), which ultimately led to the domestication of gourds, squash, beans, maize, chile peppers, and husk tomatoes (Byers 1967).

The transition from Pleistocene to Holocene conditions was accompanied by a transition from Paleoindian to Archaic tool assemblages. The relevant questions asked by archaeologists include these two: (1) How long did the transition from a Late Pleistocene environment to a Holocene environment take, and (2) How long did it take foragers to develop their new Archaic tool kits?

Paleoclimatologists have been working on the first question, and some of their answers may come as a surprise. Perhaps most surprising is the rapidity with which climate change is now thought to have taken place.

> Until recently, ice ages were thought to come and go gradually, over thousands or tens of thousands of years, and rapid climate changes were believed to require external causes such as changes in the summertime earth-sun distance. Interpretation of climate indicators from ocean-sediment cores, ice cores, and other archives has now shown that these beliefs have been wrong for some times and places. The Earth's climate contains "switches" as well as "dials." Hemispheric to global climate changes

larger than any experienced by agricultural or industrial humans have occurred repeatedly, in as little as decades to years, apparently without globally significant causes. (Richard B. Alley, 1998)

According to data from the Greenland ice core drilling program, the Pleistocene-Holocene change may have involved a "switch." "The earth's climate warmed abruptly, in less than a decade and perhaps as little as three years, during and at the end of the last ice age some 11,000 years ago" (Severinghaus 1998; see also Alley et al. 1993, Alley et al. 1999). Needless to say, such an abrupt change would be difficult for archaeologists to document, given their dating methods.

This ice core evidence for rapid Pleistocene-Holocene warming raises additional questions: (1) How long did it actually take for the vegetation to change, and (2) How long did it take hunter-gatherers to adapt to their new environment? Even if the temperature itself rose in a mere three years, we find it unlikely that the native vegetation could have changed at such a rapid rate. It is well documented that there may be a time lag between climate change and subsequent species disappearance (O'Dea et al. 2007).

A partial answer to the first of these questions can be derived from the gradual disappearance of pinyon pines from the El Fuerte region. These trees—seemingly well represented in Mitla's Late Pleistocene pollen record—can no longer be found in the Valley of Oaxaca. Their gradual disappearance is probably reflected in the decreasing pinyon nut counts from Early Archaic levels at Guilá Naquitz (C. E. Smith 2009: Table 19.1).

The largest quantity of pinyon nuts, 155, was recovered from Zone E of Guilá Naquitz. These nuts decreased in number in Zone D (94) and Zone C (80). Only four pinyon nuts were recovered from Zone B3, and there were none at all in Zone B2+3. We found small numbers of nuts in Zones B2 and B1, but their period of abundance was clearly over by then.

To determine what this meant in real time we must turn to the calibrated dates from Guilá Naquitz, presented in Table 1 of Flannery (2009b). Perhaps our most consistent dates are the six from Zone D, which range from 9005 BC to 7695 BC. Five calibrated dates from Zone C range from 9150 BC to 6535 BC. Zone B2+3—the oldest level to produce no pinyon nuts—has a single calibrated date of 8235–7565 BC. Zone B1 yielded five dates with a calibrated range of 6610 BC to 6220 BC.

These dates allow us to suggest the following. Even if Late Pleistocene temperatures warmed to Holocene levels with "switch-like" rapidity some 11,000 years ago, pinyon trees evidently continued to grow within walking distance of Guilá Naquitz Cave until at least 7000 BC. While we cannot determine with any accuracy when the last pinyon tree vanished, our suspicion is that it was gone by 6000 BC. By then, of course, many plants typical of today's El Fuerte region were present in the deposits at Guilá Naquitz (C. E. Smith 2009).

How long did it take for the Paleoindian tool assemblage to give way to an Archaic tool assemblage? Apparently, we must consider the possibility that this process also took place with relatively switch-like speed. Our youngest Paleoindian projectile point—an unfinished Lerma—was found in Zone E of Guilá Naquitz (Hole 2009: Figures 6.26–6.27), a level dated to 8995–8495 BC (Flannery 2009b: Table 1). Our oldest corner-notched Archaic point—an unfinished Palmillas—was found in Zone E of Cueva Blanca, a level dated somewhere between 10,718 BC and 8304 BC (see Chapter 4). Given these calibrated dates, we are currently unable to argue that the period of transition from Paleoindian tools to Archaic tools was long and slow.

The Place of Cueva Blanca Among Neighboring Archaic Sites

The lands of the ex-hacienda El Fuerte lie in a region of volcanic tuff cliffs and ephemeral freshwater streams, some 4–5 km northwest of Mitla and 2–3 km west of the Mitla Fortress (Figure 1.2). A seasonal stream called Gheo-Loh divides the most promising caves into two groups (Figure 1.3). The larger group, including Guilá Naquitz (Site OC-43), the Martínez Rockshelter (OC-48), Silvia's Cave (OC-47), and Cueva de los Afligidos (OC-45), is situated along a continuous cliff at an elevation of roughly 1900 m. The smaller group, including Cueva Blanca (OC-30) and Cueva Redonda (OC-27), lies 1.5 km to the northeast along another continuous cliff at an elevation of roughly 1800 m. The Archaic open-air site of Gheo-Shih (OS-70) lies 2.8 km to the south of Cueva Blanca, near the right bank of the Río Mitla.

Kirkby et al. (2009) have defined four vegetation zones for the El Fuerte region, each zone comprised of two facies (Figure 1.4). Each facies was described in detail in the Guilá Naquitz report, and those descriptions need not be repeated here. Suffice it to say that Guilá Naquitz and the Martínez Rockshelter lie in the *Cassia* facies of the Thorn Forest A Zone, while Cueva Blanca lies near the border between two facies—the *Quercus* facies of Thorn Forest A and the *Bursera* facies of Thorn Forest B.

The nearest water source for Cueva Blanca is a stream 60 m away, which—although it carries running water only during the May-September rainy season—usually leaves behind a series of standing-water pools that can be visited even after the rains have ceased.

Resources near Cueva Blanca would have included acorns (*Quercus* sp.), guajes and tepeguajes (*Leucaena* sp., *Conzatia* sp.), huizache (*Acacia* sp.), prickly pear (*Opuntia* spp.), organ cactus (*Myrtillocactus* sp., *Lemaireocereus* sp.), agaves, wild black zapote (*Diospyros* sp.), hawthorn (*Crataegus* sp.), West Indian cherry (*Malpighia* sp.), and *yak susí* (*Jatropha neodioica*). Present in the region today are at least three species of wild beans (*Phaseolus anisotrichos, P. heterophyllus,* and *P. atropurpureus*), the coyote melon (*Apodanthera aspera*), and numerous wild onions (*Allium* sp.) that grow near springs and freshwater seeps. At lower elevations, only a half-hour's walk from Cueva Blanca, were areas where mesquite pods (*Prosopis juliflora*) and desert hackberry fruits (*Celtis pallida*) could be collected.

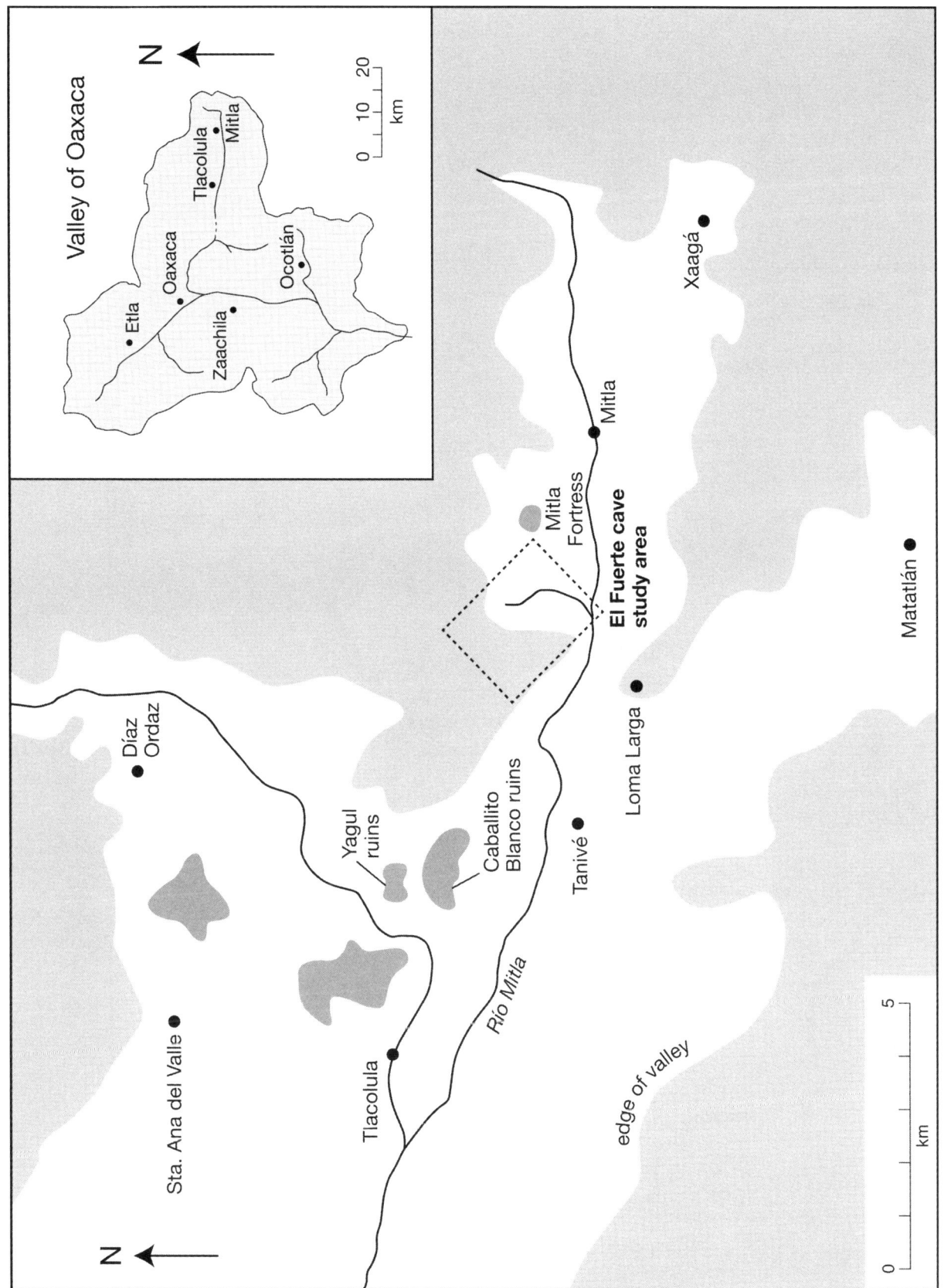

Figure 1.2. The eastern Valley of Oaxaca, showing the cave study area on lands of the ex-hacienda El Fuerte.

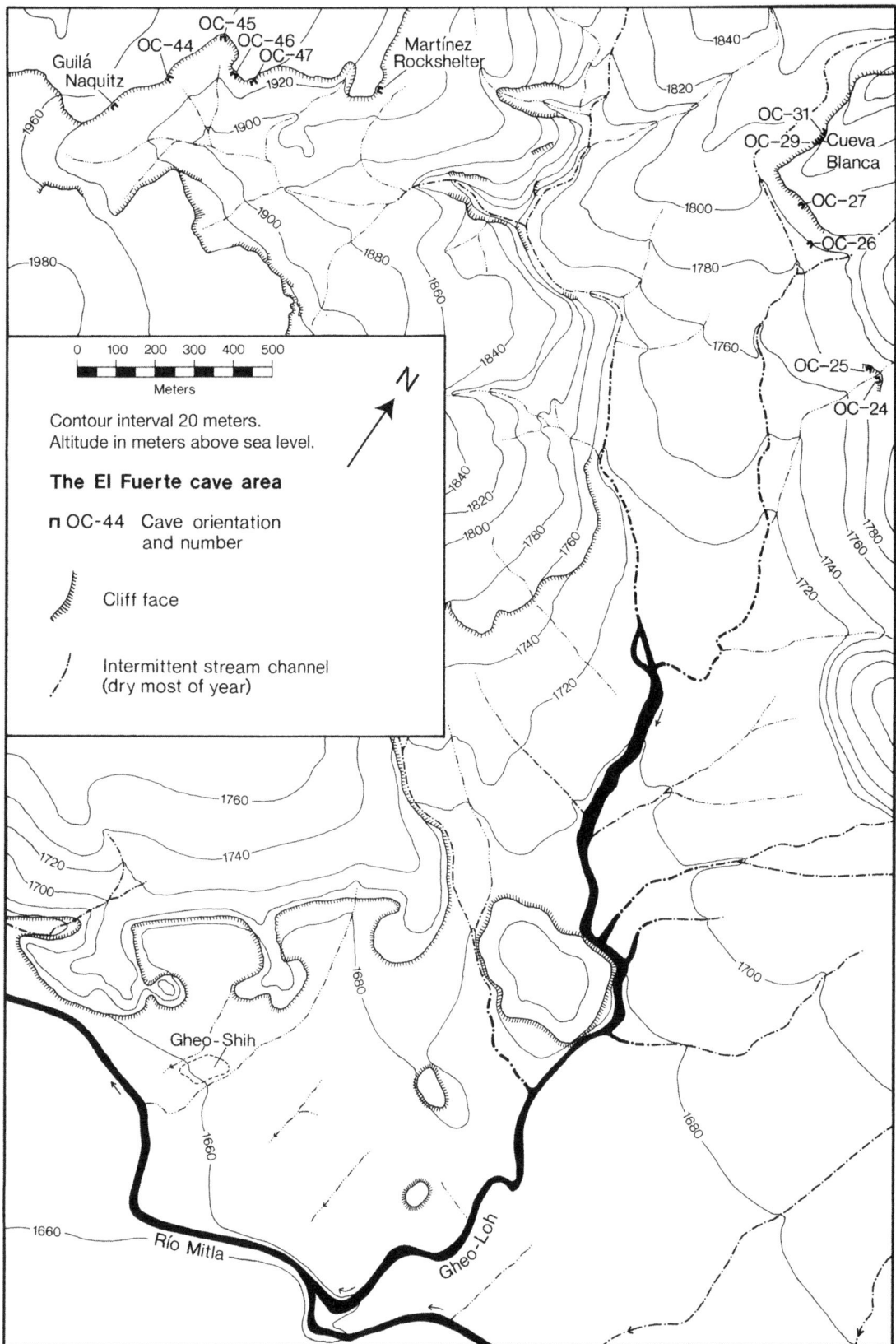

Figure 1.3. The lands of the ex-hacienda El Fuerte, showing Archaic sites, watercourses, and elevations in meters.

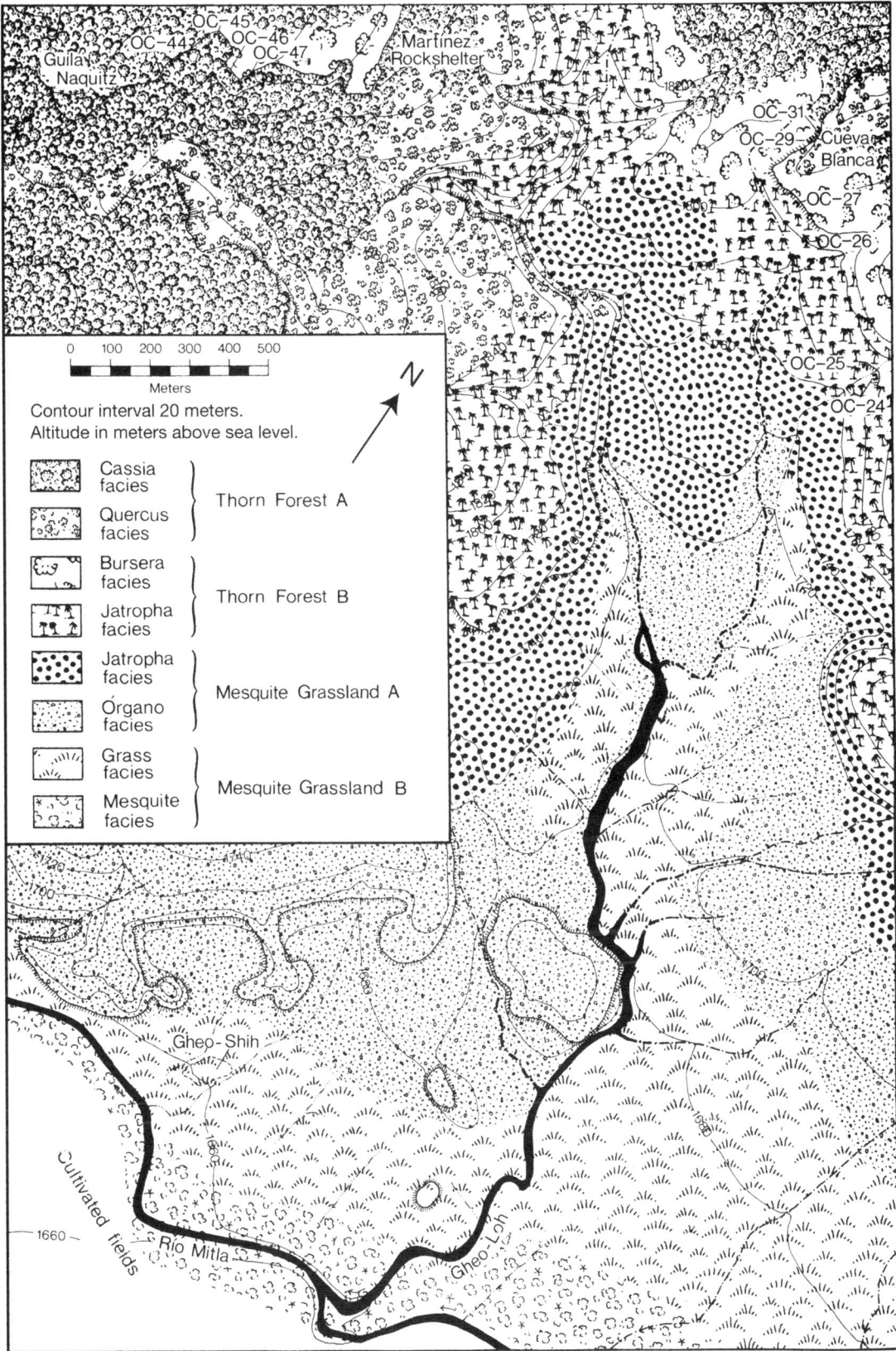

Figure 1.4. Environmental zones and their vegetational facies on the lands of the ex-hacienda El Fuerte. Also shown are the known Archaic sites.

The two largest game animals in the Cueva Blanca area were the white-tailed deer (*Odocoileus virginianus*) and the collared peccary (*Pecari tajacu*). The most abundant small game consisted of three species of rabbits: the small Eastern cottontail (*Sylvilagus floridanus connectens*), the larger Mexican cottontail (*S. mexicanus*), and the still larger jackrabbit (*Lepus mexicanus*). There were, of course, many other small game species, but they were less frequently captured. Included were the coyote (*Canis latrans*), the gray fox (*Urocyon cinereoargenteus*), the raccoon (*Procyon lotor*), the opossum (*Didelphis marsupialis*), the cacomixtle (*Bassariscus astutus*), the coatimundi (*Nasua narica*), three genera of skunks (*Mephitis, Conepatus,* and *Spilogale*), and a large pocket gopher (*Orthogeomys grandis*) that has since disappeared from the region. The occupants of Cueva Blanca also ate the local mud turtle (*Kinosternon integrum*), which inhabits standing pools of water along the Río Mitla and its tributaries.

The most frequently eaten birds of the El Fuerte region were doves, pigeons, and quail. Included were the band-tailed pigeon (*Columba fasciata*), the mourning dove (*Zenaida macroura*), the white-winged dove (*Zenaida asiatica*), the white-fronted dove (*Leptotila verreauxi*), the ground dove (*Columbigallina passerina*), the bobwhite quail (*Colinus virginianus*), and the Montezuma quail (*Cyrtonyx montezumae*). Two birds of prey also turned up in Cueva Blanca. These were the barn owl (*Tyto alba*), which sometimes lived in the cave, and the red-tailed hawk (*Buteo jamaicensis*), which was almost certainly pursued for its feathers.

The Origins of Agriculture in Oaxaca

No plants were preserved in the Archaic strata at Cueva Blanca. All our information on early agriculture in the Mitla region therefore comes from nearby Guilá Naquitz Cave (Flannery 2009a). Fortunately, we now have 40 calibrated radiocarbon dates from the Archaic levels at Guilá Naquitz (Flannery 2009b: Table 1), making the plants from that cave one of the best-dated collections available.

Runner beans of the genus *Phaseolus* were well represented at Guilá Naquitz. Some 161 pod valves of runner beans were found in Stratigraphic Zone E, the oldest level. Ninety-nine of these valves were assigned by Lawrence Kaplan (2009) to a variety he called "Guilá Naquitz Type 1." Kaplan could not identify Type 1 beans to species because many of the diagnostic parts, including the flowers, were lacking. Pod valves of this bean type continued to show up in Zones D, C, and B1–B3. Only in higher stratigraphic levels such as Zone B2 + 3, however, did we recover the actual seeds of Type 1 beans, which were small and black. Fifteen seeds were found in Zone B1 alone (Kaplan 2009: Table 21.1 and Figure 21.3).

What is clear is that the occupants of Guilá Naquitz were eating runner beans throughout the Archaic. Calibrated dates from Zone E of the cave go back as far as 8995–8495 BC, and there is one calibrated date of 9005–8565 BC from Zone D. Kaplan had two of the Type 1 beans from Zone B1 directly dated, and the calibrated dates came out with two-sigma ranges of 6460–6260 BC and 6400–6220 BC (Kaplan and Lynch 1999).

Unfortunately, there is no conclusive evidence that Guilá Naquitz Type 1 beans were ever domesticated; their phenotype is that of a wild bean, with characteristically corkscrew twisted pods (Kaplan 2009: Figure 21.2). Kaplan was also unaware of any cultivar that had clearly descended from Type 1 beans.

Type 1 cannot be the wild ancestor of common beans (*Phaseolus vulgaris*), because it was hypogeal (that is, its cotyledons remained below the soil surface). Domestic runner beans (*P. coccineus*) are also hypogeal, but Kaplan (2009:283) found "insufficient evidence to evaluate [Type 1] as a possible ancestor of cultivars of this species." We therefore have the following two possibilities: either (1) the occupants of Guilá Naquitz were harvesting wild runner beans, or (2) they were growing a species of runner bean that never went on to produce a phenotypically domestic race.

Three species of wild beans (*Phaseolus anisotrichos, P. heterophyllus,* and *P. atropurpureus*) have been discovered growing in the Guilá Naquitz area today (Messer 1978, Kaplan 2009:283). None of these beans closely match Guilá Naquitz Type 1. This raises two possibilities: either (1) Type 1 beans were not native to the region—which would suggest that they had been introduced from elsewhere, and were being deliberately grown—or else (2) Type 1 was a wild species that, like the pinyon pines discussed earlier, grew in the Mitla area during the Early Archaic but has since disappeared.

As previously mentioned, Type 1 beans show no phenotypic signs of domestication. One hint that they might have been deliberately grown is their abundance at Guilá Naquitz, given the relatively low density of wild beans in the Mitla environment today. As I stated earlier,

> …on some living floors [at Guilá Naquitz], these black beans were so numerous as to imply a harvest area of 1–2 hectares—the same as for squash…
> I therefore suggested that the occupants of Guilá Naquitz may have encouraged or even planted these phenotypically wild beans, but gave up on them once superior varieties of beans had reached Oaxaca. (Flannery, 2009b:xx)

While the nature of our Archaic beans remains inconclusive, the domestic status of our gourds and squash is certain. Since no wild bottle gourds are native to Oaxaca, the very presence of gourds implies cultivation. Our earliest squash (*Cucurbita pepo*) already had seeds in the domestic size range, and the rinds of this squash displayed the orange color of a cultivar (B. D. Smith 1997).

Two rinds of bottle gourd (*Lagenaria siceraria*) from Zones C and B2 of Guilá Naquitz have been directly AMS dated, providing calibrated two-sigma ranges of 8030–7915 BC and

7020–6595 BC, respectively. Our oldest seed of *pepo* squash came from Zone C and had a calibrated two-sigma range of 8035–7920 BC (B. D. Smith 1997, Flannery 2009b: Table 1).

Despite this evidence that domestic plants were present in Oaxaca by 8000 BC, it is worth noting that the two oldest Archaic strata of Guilá Naquitz—Zones E and D—produced no cucurbit specimens. It would appear, therefore, that there was a period at the very start of the Archaic (perhaps 11,000–8000 BC) when the occupants of Guilá Naquitz possessed no phenotypically domestic plants. We presume that the Early Archaic occupants of Cueva Blanca were in a similar situation.

Finally, we come to maize (*Zea mays*), only a few specimens of which showed up in Archaic contexts at Guilá Naquitz.[1] We discovered five primitive two-rowed cobs or cob fragments in small lenses of ash (Figure 1.5). These lenses lay stratigraphically above Zone B1 (the youngest Archaic level) and below the scatters of Formative sherds that preceded the deposition of Zone A (Monte Albán IIIb–IV). Two of these maize specimens have been directly dated, producing calibrated two-sigma ranges of 4340–4220 BC and 4355–4065 BC (Piperno and Flannery 2001). These are, for the moment, our oldest dates on actual maize cobs (Benz 2001). It should be noted, however, that Schoenwetter and Smith (2009: Table 15.26) found pollen of maize or teosinte in Zone B2 (calibrated 7900–6500 BC).

The currently available DNA evidence suggests that the ancestor of maize was *Zea mays* ssp. *parviglumis*, a subspecies of annual teosinte native to the Balsas River drainage of Michoacán and Guerrero (Matsuoka et al. 2002). Piperno et al. (2009) have recently identified what they believe to be maize phytoliths and starch grains from a rockshelter near Iguala, Guerrero, in what is today the heart of *parviglumis* territory. Wood charcoal from the same level as the phytoliths and starch grains has produced a radiocarbon date with a calibrated two-

---

[1] The only Archaic maize cobs we recovered during our excavations at Guilá Naquitz were the five shown in Figure 1.5. All these cobs were turned over to the Departamento de Prehistoria, Instituto Nacional de Antropología e Historia, Mexico City. I mention this because it has recently come to my attention that the collections of the Riverside Metropolitan Museum (Riverside, California) contain two cobs purporting to come from the "Coxcatlán phase" at "Guilá Naquitz Cave." I can state categorically that (1) the Riverside cobs do not come from my excavations at Guilá Naquitz, and (2) I do not consider the term "Coxcatlán phase" appropriate for the Valley of Oaxaca sequence.

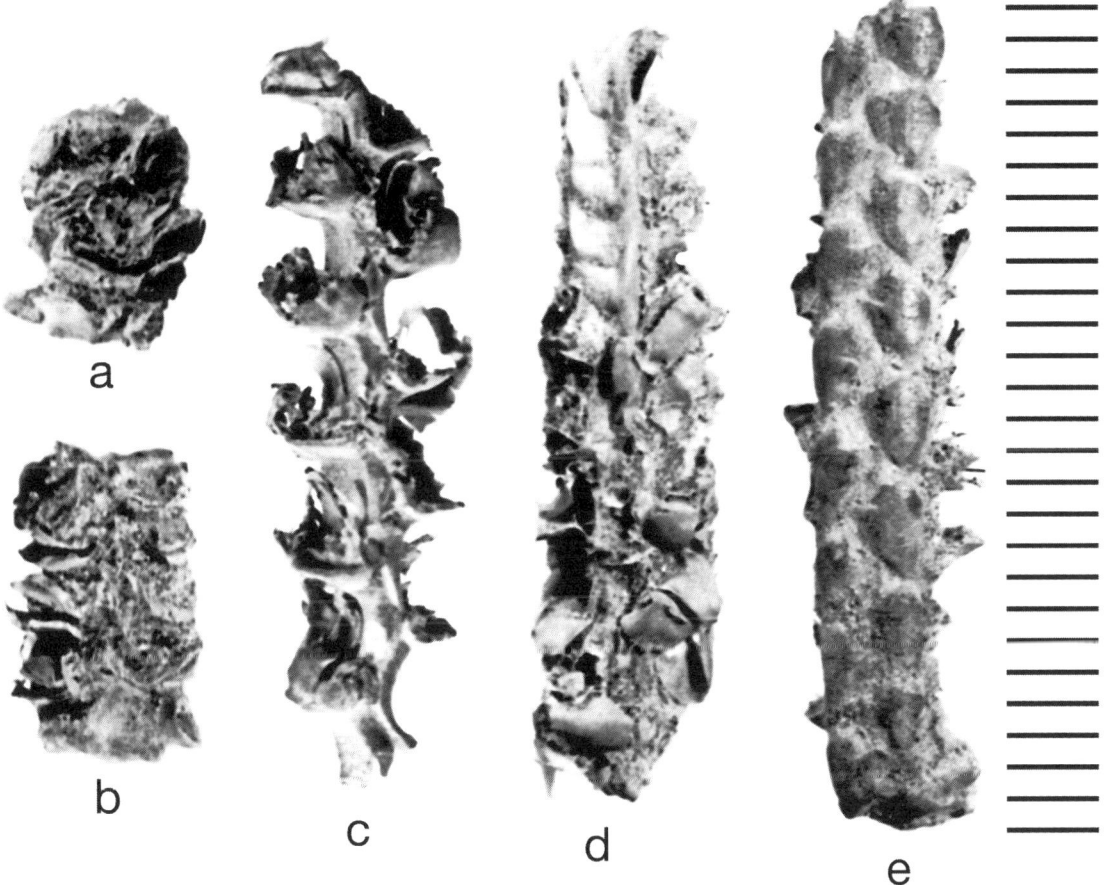

Figure 1.5. Five primitive maize cobs (or fragments thereof) found in ash lenses above Zone B1 at Guilá Naquitz. *a* and *b* are from Square C9; *c* is from Square D10; *d* and *e* are from Square D7. The scale at the right edge of the photograph is in millimeters. These cobs, shown here larger than life size, have been AMS dated to between 4355 and 4065 BC (calibrated).

sigma range of 7040–6660 BC. To be sure, it would be nice to have actual maize specimens to complement the microfossils.

Since maize was clearly present in the Mitla area before 4000 BC (calibrated), we presume that it was being grown by the Late Archaic occupants of Cueva Blanca. Unfortunately, plant preservation in the Late Archaic levels at Cueva Blanca was not good enough to confirm this.

Archaic Settlement Patterns in the Mitla Region

In the course of his work in the Tehuacán Valley, MacNeish (1964, 1972) distinguished two types of Archaic settlements. At times when resources were abundant at a specific locale, 15–25 individuals might come together to form a *macroband camp*. This relatively large group would remain together at that locale until so much food had been harvested that the point of diminishing returns had been reached.

During leaner seasons, macrobands might break up into a series of small family groups who then dispersed throughout the region and foraged on their own. MacNeish referred to the smaller encampments made by these groups of 2–5 individuals as *microband camps*. Such smaller camps could be occupied for anywhere from a day or two to most of a season. It should be acknowledged that MacNeish's microband-macroband model drew heavily on Julian Steward's ethnographic and ethnohistoric work with the Paiute and Shoshone of the Great Basin (Steward 1938, 1955).

If we apply the MacNeish-Steward scheme to the excavated sites of Tehuacán and Oaxaca, two sites stand out clearly as macroband camps. These are Gheo-Shih (OS-70), an open-air site near the Río Mitla, and Coxcatlán Cave (with its large terrace) in the southern Tehuacán Valley. Two examples of microband camps would be Guilá Naquitz Cave in the Mitla region and El Riego Cave in the northern Tehuacán Valley (Figure 1.6).

One of the goals of our research at Cueva Blanca was to determine how the Archaic levels of that cave fit into MacNeish's scheme. As later chapters of this volume will show, we believe that the region's inhabitants changed the way they used Cueva Blanca during the Archaic. To put such changes in context, let us consider Binford's (1980) proposal that most hunting-gathering societies occupy a position along a continuum from "foraging" to "collecting."

Foragers, in Binford's scheme, travel to where the food is, and their settlement pattern becomes dispersed (microbands) or aggregated (macrobands) according to the density and seasonality of resources. Collectors, on the other hand, tend to remain in one favored locality, sending logistically organized task groups out to bring back resources.

Our analysis suggests that the Early Archaic occupants of Cueva Blanca, like their counterparts at Guilá Naquitz, occupied the foraging end of the continuum and used the cave as a microband camp. As time went on, however, they began shifting toward the collecting side of the continuum. Zone C, the second of two Late Archaic living floors at Cueva Blanca, may have been created by an all-male task group who came from, and later returned to, a larger and more permanent camp elsewhere. Given the relatively late date of that living floor, we suspect that one of the factors involved in the shift from foraging to collecting was the increasing success of agriculture.

The Potential Contribution of Cueva Blanca

Cueva Blanca had abundant stone tools and animal bones, but no Archaic plant remains. In order to interpret its three Archaic living floors, we must therefore consider Cueva Blanca in the context of other sites, such as Guilá Naquitz and Gheo-Shih.

All the Archaic living floors at Guilá Naquitz and Cueva Blanca appear to have resulted from microbands. Gheo-Shih, on the other hand, was a macroband camp, featuring a whole range of activities not seen at microband camps. Among the latter were ornament manufacture and the construction of space for public ritual (Marcus and Flannery 1996:57–59).

It is significant that the calibrated radiocarbon dates for Gheo-Shih (7720–7560 BC) and for Zone B2 of Guilá Naquitz (7995–7325 BC) overlap. These dates suggest that during the eighth millennium BC, there were both macroband and microband camps within walking distance of each other.

Spatial analyses of the living floors at Guilá Naquitz (Spencer and Flannery 2009, Whallon 2009, Reynolds 2009) indicate that those floors were divided into men's work areas, women's work areas, hearths, pathways, and areas of discarded refuse. As later chapters of this volume will show, the same is true of Zones E and D at Cueva Blanca. Zone C of Cueva Blanca, on the other hand, however, lacks both a hearth and a plausible woman's work area. Zone C, therefore, may be an example of an all-male camp made by one of Binford's task groups, who came to Cueva Blanca from a more permanent macroband settlement to which they later returned.

Reconstructing the social organization of Archaic societies is difficult. There is no magic wand that we can wave, and today's modeling techniques will inevitably be superseded. All we can hope for is that future investigators will devote themselves to the same research questions and that a useful synthesis will arise from all our efforts. Whenever a variety of individuals—using a variety of approaches—come to roughly the same conclusions, we have reason to be hopeful.

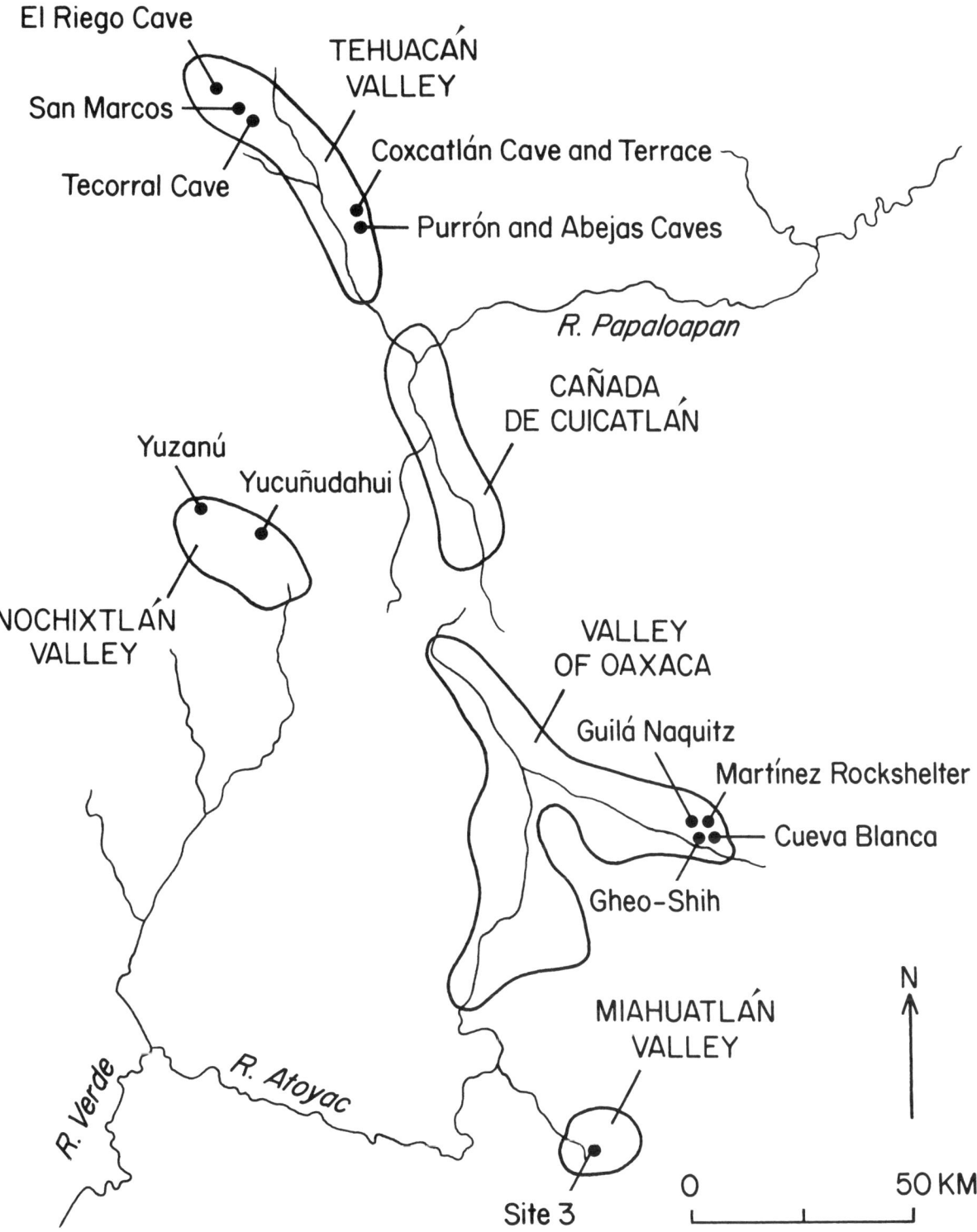

Figure 1.6. The valleys of Tehuacán, Cuicatlán, Nochixtlán, Oaxaca, and Miahuatlán, showing excavated Archaic sites and important Archaic surface finds.

2

The Discovery of Cueva Blanca

Kent V. Flannery

Cueva Blanca was a Christmas present. I found it December 24, 1964, while searching for caves in the mountains some 4 km northwest of Mitla (Figure 2.1). Cueva Blanca was the thirtieth—and by all appearances, the most promising—of all the caves and rockshelters I located that year.

Under a crust of modern cattle dung I found a stratum of Late Postclassic debris with ash, potsherds, desiccated maize cobs, agave quids, and squash peduncles. While there was no way to predict how ancient the deeper deposits would be, I did find Archaic atlatl points, crude blades, steep denticulate scrapers, and chert cores lying on the surface of the cave chamber, as well as on the talus slope outside (Figure 2.2).

Cueva Blanca (site OC-30) is located at latitude 16°57' north and longitude 96°22' west. Its altitude is 1813 m (5947 feet), which today places it in the *Quercus* facies of Thorn Forest A, one of Mitla's Holocene environmental zones (Figure 2.3). The mouth of the cave is a prominent opening in a north-south trending volcanic tuff cliff; the arroyo 14 m below it carries water toward the Río Mitla during the rainy season.

Cueva Blanca is actually the central cave of a group of three (Figure 2.4). Below and to the south was a smaller cave, OC-29; above and to the north was OC-31, which could be reached only by climbing the cliff. My crew's test excavations in OC-29 and OC-31 revealed Archaic deposits—apparently without preserved plants—below Postclassic debris. Neither cave was judged to be as promising as OC-30.

An interesting feature of the Cueva Blanca group was a series of five or six drylaid stone masonry terraces on the talus slope below the caves (Figure 2.5). These appeared to be agricultural terraces, but we had no idea whether they were precolumbian or recent. Eventually, after putting a stratigraphic test into the third terrace below the cave, we were able to conclude that the system was constructed during the period called Monte Albán V (calibrated date, AD 1383–1452).

We estimate the area of Cueva Blanca covered by the overhanging cliff to be 11 by 15 m, or roughly 165 m^2. Unfortunately, since the roof of the cave rises to a point 5 m high in front, the prevailing westerly winds tend to blow rain into the chamber. This meant that preservation of plants was not as great as in Guilá Naquitz Cave, which faces east (Flannery 2009a). As a result, only the Monte Albán V levels at Cueva Blanca had preserved plants.

I began the excavation of Cueva Blanca in February 1966 and, after having established its stratigraphy, suspended work there while excavating nearby Guilá Naquitz. In July, Frank Hole, who had come to Oaxaca to analyze our chipped stone tools, took over the excavation of Cueva Blanca. Both my work and Hole's utilized the same magnetic north-south grid

Figure 2.1. A view of Cueva Blanca from the northwest, showing its location relative to the Mitla Fortress, the town of Mitla, the Tlacolula subvalley, and Cerro Nueve Puntas, a prominent mountain range that delimits the valley.

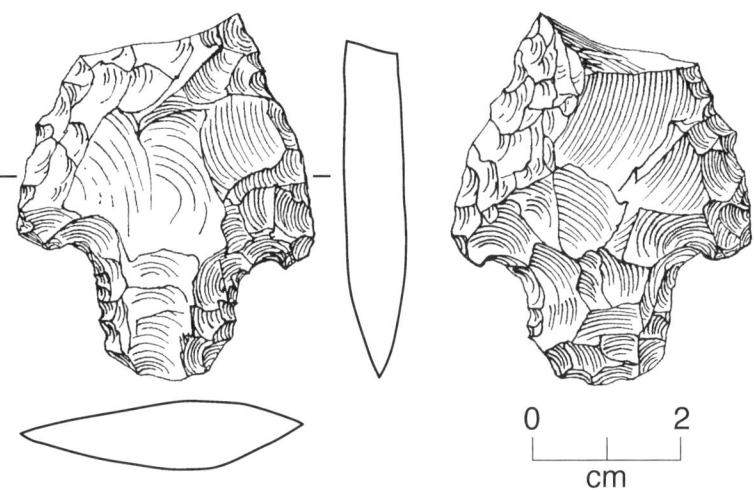

Figure 2.2. A broken atlatl point from the talus slope below Cueva Blanca.

of 1 x 1 m squares, laid out over the whole of the cave floor. In the end, however, Hole and I concentrated on 75 squares in the rear portion of the chamber, where the preservation was best and the stratigraphy clearest (Figure 2.6). Just as at Guilá Naquitz, once the stratigraphy had been revealed by the first test squares, the cave was excavated by its "natural" or "cultural" strata.

The soft upper strata at Cueva Blanca were excavated mainly with trowels, screwdrivers, ice picks, and paint brushes, while the indurated Pleistocene deposits at the bottom were so hard that they had to be excavated with barretas (miners' digging bars). All deposits were passed through 6 mm screen, and those with perishable remains were also passed through 2 mm screen. All retouched tools recognized in the field were plotted three-dimensionally, while the debitage was counted by 1 x 1 m square.

Back-plotting of the three-dimensionally recorded items revealed that the actual Archaic living floors were slightly basin-shaped, even though the "natural" strata encapsulating them appeared to be horizontal. This had happened because the bulk of the cave matrix consisted of fine particles of volcanic tuff, weathered from the walls and roof; these particles tended to accumulate in greater depth near the cave wall, causing the outer margins of each living floor to slope upward over sterile tuff deposits. Near the front of the cave—where rain had penetrated repeatedly—the stratigraphy was unreadable, and the deposits had a uniform gray color from top to bottom.

Stratigraphy

Before proceeding to our narrative of the excavation, let me discuss the six stratigraphic zones defined at Cueva Blanca. I will present these in order from oldest to youngest.

Zone F, the basal deposit, had the consistency of indurated sand. Its matrix consisted largely of volcanic tuff (ignimbrite) particles weathered from the walls and ceiling of the cave. Although tiny flecks of charcoal were found in this matrix, it produced no identifiable artifacts.

In Zone F, however, we did find lenses of animal bone whose closest similarities were with the Late Pleistocene fauna from Coxcatlán Cave in the Tehuacán Valley (Flannery 1967). For example, Zone F produced remains of the Texas gopher tortoise (*Gopherus berlandieri*), a species that can no longer be found in southern Mexico (Figure 2.7). The fact that this tortoise was available in Tehuacán and Oaxaca under Late Pleistocene conditions implies that today's thorn forest was not present. The gopher tortoise today is at home in a Chihuahuan environment, one featuring colder winters and lacking a monsoonal rainy season (Marcus and Flannery 1996:41–42).

Another similarity between the fauna of Zone F and the Pleistocene fauna of the Tehuacán Valley was the presence of

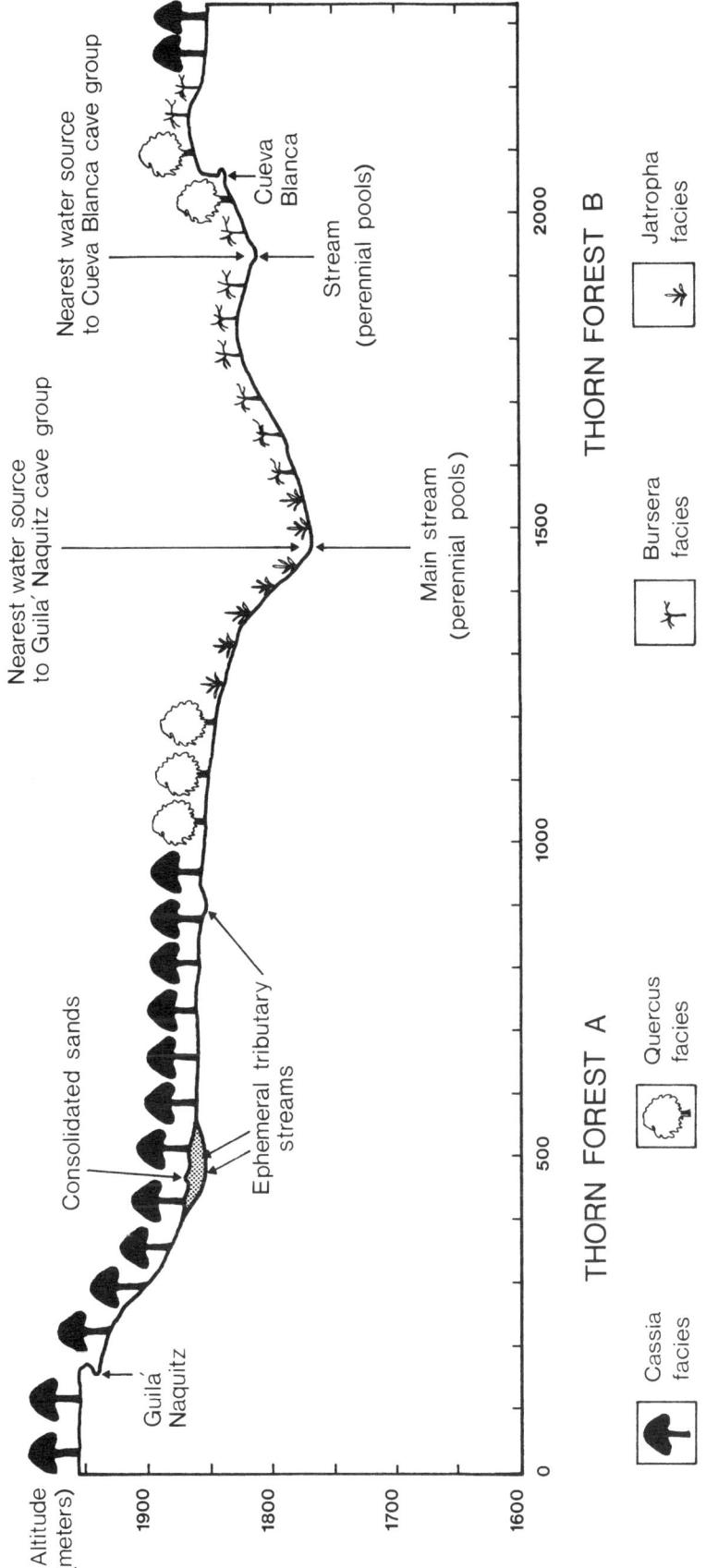

Figure 2.3. A cross section of the E. Fuerte caves region, from Guilá Naquitz Cave in the northwest to Cueva Blanca in the southeast. Most streams in this area carry water only in the rainy season, but pools of water can remain for months afterward.

Figure 2.4. The Cueva Blanca group (OC-29, OC-30, and OC-31) in its thorn forest setting.

an unidentified carnivore that calls to mind the red fox of North America. Neither Tehuacán nor Oaxaca is home to a red fox today.

Some faunal lenses in Zone F produced numbers of small rodents, almost certainly the product of disintegrating owl pellets. Like the Pleistocene rodent collections of the Tehuacán Valley (Flannery 1967), our Zone F rodent samples had relatively high numbers of wood rats (*Neotoma* spp.). This provides a contrast to our Holocene rodent samples, in which cotton rats (*Sigmodon* sp.) and spiny mice (*Liomys* sp.) were dominant.

Palynologists Schoenwetter and Smith (2009: Table 15.27) found that their pollen samples from Zone F of Cueva Blanca also reflected a Late Pleistocene climate cooler than today's. Pine pollen was notable in Zone F, accompanied by occasional pollen of spruce, fir, oak, and alder.

Given what we learned by excavating Guilá Naquitz Cave, my guess is that much of the Zone F pine pollen was from pinyon pine. Pinyon nuts were still readily available to foragers at Guilá Naquitz during the Early Archaic (C. E. Smith 2009), but dwindled in numbers over time and have long since disappeared from the Mitla environment.

The bones in Zone F did not look like the remains of animals dragged back to the lair of a predator, such as a mountain lion or a pack of coyotes. None of the bones were chewed. Many appeared fractured by human activity and a few had clearly been burned, which would account for the tiny flecks of charcoal found throughout Zone F.

In light of the circumstantial evidence for human activity, the lack of artifacts in this stratum is disappointing. We should remember, however, that the four Pleistocene strata in Coxcatlán Cave (Zones 25–28) contained only eleven artifacts—a strong contrast to the 1,200 identifiable animal bones in those same levels (MacNeish, Nelken-Terner, and Johnson 1967: Table 32). We thus have a precedent for low numbers of artifacts in Paleoindian living floors of the Puebla-Oaxaca region. To be sure, it is also possible that the main occupation of Zone F lay farther out near the mouth of the cave—or even on the talus—where we

The Discovery of Cueva Blanca

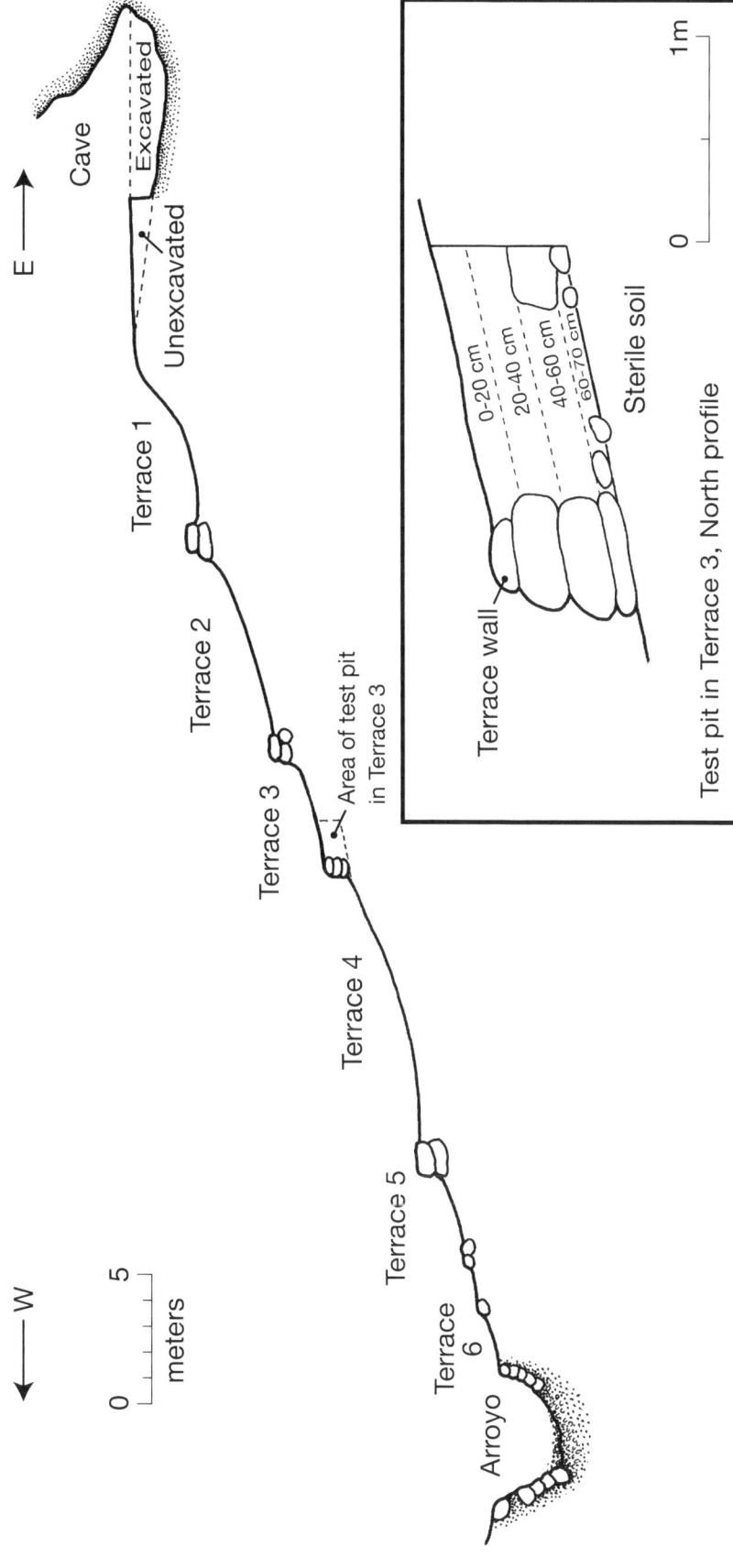

Figure 2.5. West-to-east cross section through Cueva Blanca and the agricultural terraces on the talus slope below it. The insert at lower right shows the north profile of the test pit into Terrace 3.

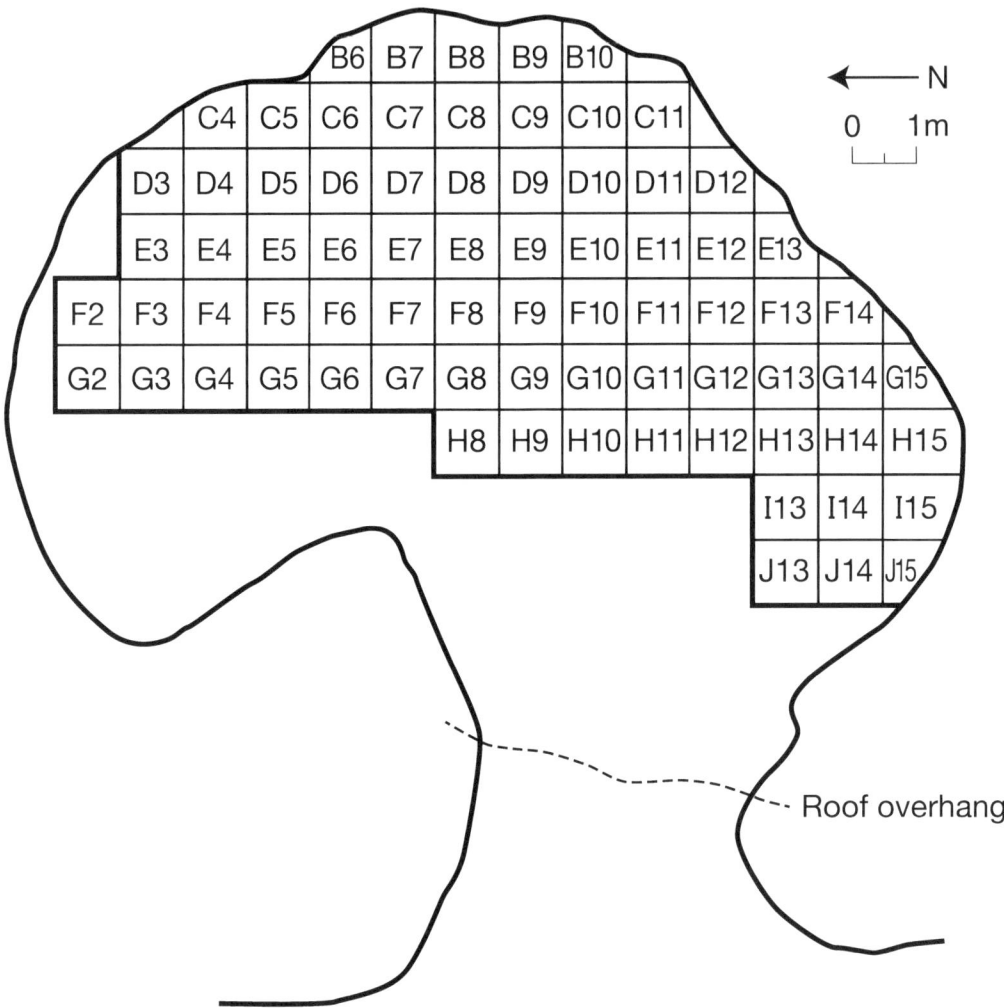

Figure 2.6. Plan view of Cueva Blanca, showing the 1 x 1 m squares that were excavated.

did not excavate, because preservation was poor and there was considerable Postclassic disturbance.

It is worth mentioning that there are two Paleoindian sites within 15 km of Cueva Blanca. The nearest is the Orlandini Site (OS-81), which lies less than a kilometer southwest of the cave. OS-81 produced the fluted point shown in Figure 2.8a. A second site, near San Juan Guelavía in the Tlacolula subvalley, produced the fluted point shown in Figure 2.8b. Visits to Cueva Blanca could easily have been made from either of these two sites.

We will deal with Zone F of Cueva Blanca in the future, when all the fauna from that level has been identified. For the purposes of this volume, all I can say is that it appears to be Late Pleistocene and that, despite the lack of artifacts, there is circumstantial evidence of human activity (setting fires, breaking and burning of bone).

Zone E was a layer characterized by gray ash with charcoal flecks; it averaged 15–20 cm thick and occupied only a portion of the total area we excavated. This living floor probably represented a short-term occupation made by a small group of Early Archaic hunter-gatherers. Charcoal from Zone E produced conventional ^{14}C dates between 8100 and 7430 BC; a hearth (Feature 15) extending below the living floor produced even earlier dates (9050–8780 BC). The number of chipped stone tools from Zone E was not large (Chapter 5); the animal bones, which included cottontail rabbits and deer, all appeared to be from species that live in Oaxaca today (Chapter 9).

Zone D was a stratum characterized by tan-gray to salmon-colored ash; this living floor had originally filled the entire area we excavated, and reached a thickness of 25–40 cm. We felt that this was the debris from a substantial camp made by at least 5–8 persons. White-tailed deer had been butchered in the northeast quadrant of the cave, and nine atlatl points and hundreds of chert flakes were found in this area. Among the atlatl points were the Palmillas, Tilapa, La Mina, and Trinidad types (Chapter 6).

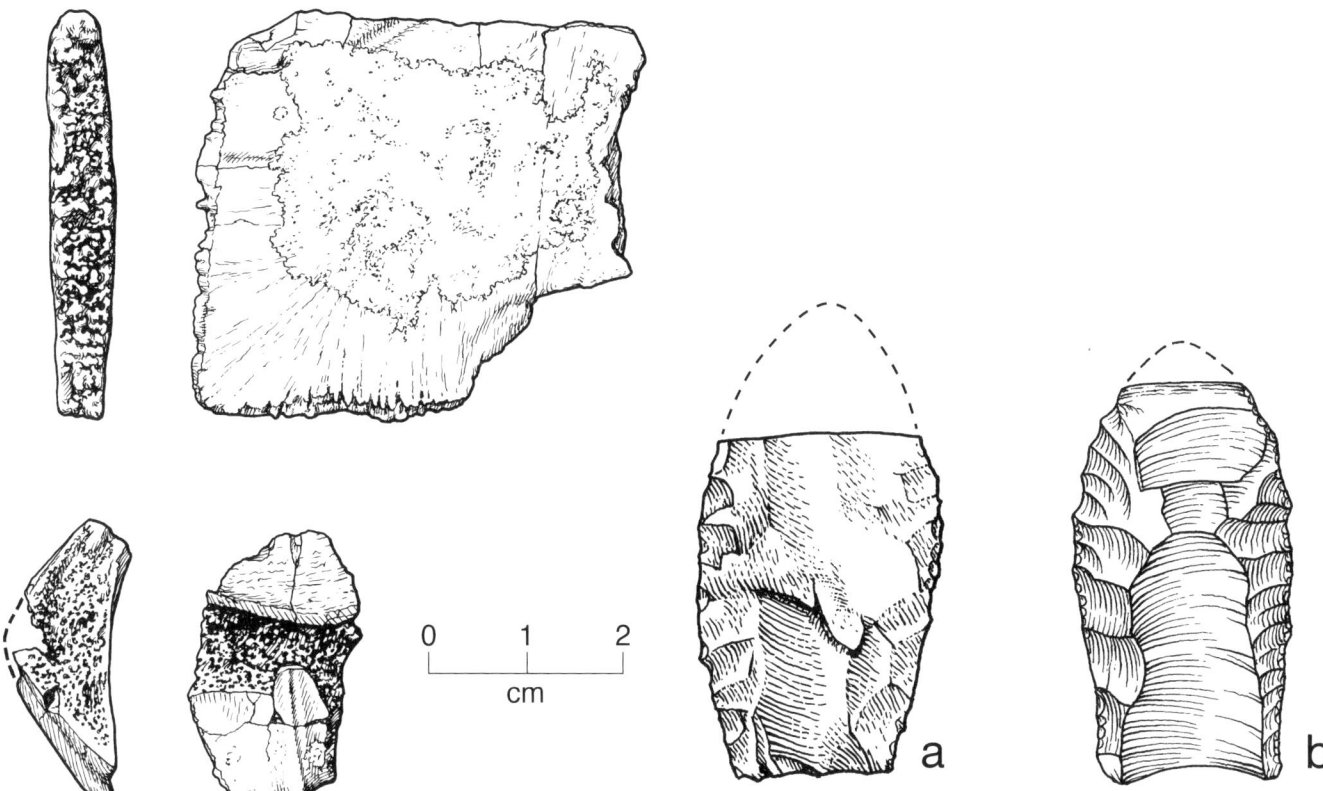

Figure 2.7. Fragments of Texas gopher tortoise from Zone F of Cueva Blanca. Above, plan view and cross section of a plastron fragment. Below, plan view and cross section of a carapace fragment.

Figure 2.8. Fluted points from sites within walking distance of Cueva Blanca. *a*, a broken point from the Orlandini Site (OS-81). *b*, a broken point from San Juan Guelavía (Finsten et al. 1989).

Zone D produced a hearth (Feature 18) with a conventional radiocarbon date of 3295 BC; charcoal from elsewhere on the living floor dated between 3060 and 2340 BC, placing Zone D in the Late Archaic.

Zone C contained a mixture of white ash and weathered volcanic tuff particles, varying from 20 cm to 40 cm in thickness and covering most of the area we excavated. Zone C is presumed to date to the Late Archaic; this occupation, however, seemed to have produced many fewer artifacts than that of Zone D. Especially around the edges of the living floor, the weathered ignimbrite particles vastly outweighed the ash.

The animal bones from Zone C included deer, cottontail, and mud turtle. The artifacts recovered included one-hand manos, chert scrapers, bifacial preforms, and atlatl points of the San Nicolás, La Mina, and Coxcatlán types.

It appears that after the deposition of Zone C, Cueva Blanca was not reoccupied by hunters and gatherers.

Zone B was an archaeologist's nightmare—essentially a layer of loosely consolidated firecracked rocks in whose interstices we found potsherds of several time periods. My reconstruction of this layer's formation is as follows.

Cueva Blanca lay abandoned for more than a millennium after the abandonment of Zone C. Then, during the Early Formative San José phase (1150–850 BC), brief visits were made to the cave. These visits continued into the Middle Formative, and some of the charcoal left behind gave us conventional dates of 795 BC and 440 BC. Reinforcing the younger of these two dates were potsherds in Monte Albán I style.

No actual living floors were created in the cave during the Formative period, but some of the visitors produced a bell-shaped cooking pit (Feature 4) in the rear of the cave and left behind Feature 16, which we have interpreted as an ash dump.

Cueva Blanca was not visited again on a serious basis until the Late Postclassic period (Monte Albán V). At that time, the

Figure 2.9. Our crew has finished the excavation of Zone A in Square D7, and Eligio Martínez is exposing the thick layer of firecracked rocks that comprised Zone B.

cave seems to have been used as an agave-roasting station. The Postclassic visitors created Feature 6 (an agave-roasting pit) in the earlier cave deposits and lined it with stones.

Typically, agave hearts are roasted or baked over heated stones in such pits. The creators of Feature 6 seem to have used not only unmodified stones from the talus slope of the cave, but also dozens of Archaic tools such as one-hand manos, steep denticulate scrapers, chert cores, and even atlatl points that had presumably been present on the surface of the cave when they arrived. After the roasting pit had cooled and the cooked agave had been removed, all these stones (by now firecracked and discolored) were thrown out on the surface of the cave chamber, and new stones were collected so that the pit could be reused.

What resulted was a layer of rocky rubble 20–40 cm thick, the product of multiple roasting-pit firings (Figure 2.9). This layer reached its greatest thickness near Feature 6 and was an archaeologically frustrating mixture of firecracked natural rocks, firecracked Archaic tools, and singed potsherds from both the Formative and Postclassic periods.

Obviously, Zone B of Cueva Blanca was a deposit too mixed to be analyzed the way we treated Zones E through C.

Figure 2.10. The talus slope below Cueva Blanca, with native vegetation partially removed to show the agricultural terraces added during Monte Albán V.

A number of the redeposited Archaic tools in Zone B, however, were sufficiently undamaged to be studied typologically and added to our sample.

Zone A—which represented the final prehispanic occupation of the cave—took the form of a layer of brown ash, with gray and black lenses here and there. This stratum was 20 cm thick on average, covering the entire area protected by the roof of the cave. It included a complex living floor, likely produced by an extended family that had lived in the cave for a year or more. It was clear from the debris in Zone A that Cueva Blanca had shifted from being an agave-roasting station to being a Monte Albán V farmstead.

There were tens of thousands of potsherds in Zone A, and their similarity to the sherds found in Terrace 3 on the talus below the cave left no doubt that they were contemporaneous. At that time, Cueva Blanca and its talus slope (Figure 2.10) would appear to have been part of a widespread series of Postclassic farmsteads and terraced hillsides, covering virtually the entire area between Cueva Blanca and the Mitla Fortress. Marcus and I have interpreted this area of terrace-farmed hillsides as part of the rural sustaining area for urban Mitla (Flannery and Marcus 2003:295–300).

Inside the cave, the occupants of Zone A had excavated a series of 12 medium-to-large storage pits (Features 1, 2, 3, 5, 7,

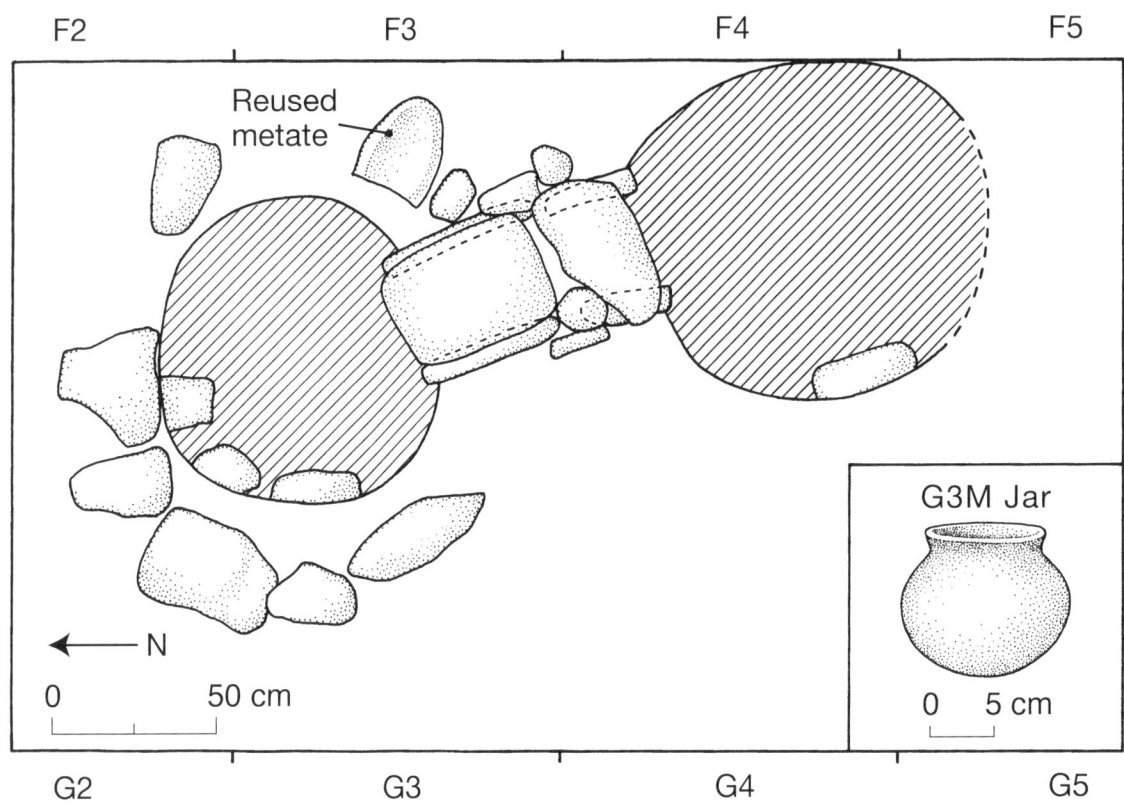

Figure 2.11. Plan view of Feature 8, a two-chambered pottery kiln found in Squares F2–F5 and G2–G5 of Zone A. Some of the stones used in construction were reused grinding stones. The kiln was used to make small Type G3M jars (see insert at lower right).

Figure 2.12. A blob of pottery clay from Zone A of Cueva Blanca, showing signs of squeezing and kneading. Some of the fingerprints in these clay blobs were clear enough to be used as evidence in a trial.

9, 10, 11, 12, 13, 14, and 17); some of these still contained plant remains. Among those plants were maize, squash, agave, prickly pear, acorns, black zapotes (*Diospyros* sp.), hackberries (*Celtis* sp.), *susí* nuts (*Jatropha* sp.), and tejocote fruits (*Crataegus* cf. *mexicana*). The maize and squash were probably grown on the terraces below the cave; the acorns, black zapotes, tejocotes, and *susí* nuts were presumably collected in the wild; and as for the agave and prickly pear remains, it was impossible to tell whether they were from wild or domestic stock. A conventional radiocarbon date places all this farming and plant-collecting activity at roughly AD 1430.

In addition to their agricultural tasks, the occupants of Zone A were engaged in pottery making. Judging by the abundant sherds and occasional kiln wasters, the most common vessel they made was a pattern-burnished jar of Type G3M, a gray ware of Monte Albán V times. Hole succeeded in finding the subterranean kiln in which this pottery was fired. Designated Feature 8, the kiln consisted of two stone masonry chambers—each a meter in diameter—connected by a stone-lined flue 70 cm long (Figure 2.11).

This kiln displays two features appropriate for the making of dark gray, highly uniform G3M ware. First, its subterranean placement would have ensured the reduced-firing atmosphere needed for making gray ware. Second, the fact that one of the kiln's chambers would have held the fuel and the other the vessels, with heated air moving through the flue between them, would have provided the even, indirect heat necessary to produce G3M pottery.

An unpublished study by Chris L. Moser (n.d.) suggests that Zone A may have contained 65,000 sherds of G3M jars—so many that it seems likely that the farmstead's production far exceeded the needs of its occupants. In other words, the family living in Cueva Blanca may have produced some of its G3M pottery for urban Mitla, which lay only 4 km away. The source of pottery clay was probably close at hand, since we found many squeezed and kneaded lumps of it in Zone A (Figure 2.12).

Zone A of Cueva Blanca will be discussed in detail in a future publication, devoted to rural Postclassic Mitla. For the purposes of this volume, we will concentrate exclusively on the three Archaic living floors.

3

The Excavation of Cueva Blanca

Kent V. Flannery and Frank Hole

The excavation of Cueva Blanca took seven months and can be divided into 10 stages. The first stage began with Flannery's initial stratigraphic test in February of 1966. The final stage took place in August of that year, when Hole completed his excavation of the last 1 x 1 m squares with readable stratigraphy.

Stage 1: The Initial Test, February 9–14, 1966

On February 9, 1966, Flannery established a permanent datum in Cueva Blanca by driving a metal spike into the rear wall of the cave at a point that became the northeast corner of Square B9 (see Figure 2.6). Beginning with that spike, he then laid out a series of five 1 x 1 m squares running east-to-west across the center of the cave's main chamber. Pending the results of the initial test, these squares were simply numbered 2–6. Once Flannery had determined that more extensive excavation was warranted, a full grid of squares was laid out over the cave, and test squares 2–6 became Squares C9, D9, E9, F9, and G9 of that grid.

Work at Cueva Blanca began with three supervisors (Flannery, Chris L. Moser, and Eligio Martínez) and a group of six Zapotec-speaking workmen from Mitla—don Juan Martínez, Félix Sosa, Alfredo Sosa, Pablo García, Carlos Pérez, and Genaro Luis. These six workmen were divided into two excavation teams, each consisting of one excavator, one screen operator, and a bucketman who carried the dirt from the square to the screen. The high ratio of supervisors to workmen was designed to ensure maximum control, and in fact, the supervisors routinely assisted in both excavation and screening.

The screens were of two sizes, 6-mm mesh and 2-mm mesh, and were set up on the cave talus where the sunlight was brightest. Dirt passing through the coarser screen went directly to the finer screen, and the bucketman assisted the screen operator in picking out artifacts, bones, and plant remains. Essentially, the methods of excavation used were identical to those described on pages 67–70 of the Guilá Naquitz site report (Flannery 2009a).

The first two squares excavated were E9 and G9, begun on February 9. In both units, the first 10 cm consisted of modern cattle dung, left by a herd from the nearby agencia of Unión Zapata. Immediately below this dung layer the crew encountered a complex series of interdigitated gray, brown, and white ash beds with abundant sherds of the Monte Albán V period. This layer became Zone A.

Below this layer, Squares E9 and G9 were somewhat different. Félix, working in Square E9, found the Monte Albán V deposits to consist of an upper gray ash member and a lower, very thick, brown ash member continuing down to 45 cm below the surface. At this point, he reached a layer of very loose stones that the crew thought at first might be rockfall from the roof. Closer examination, however, revealed that most of the stones were not even of the same composition as the cave roof; some were stream cobbles, many were firecracked rocks, and others were stone tools. This layer of loose rock, which varied in thickness from square to square, came to be called Zone B and was one of the most distinctive strata within Cueva Blanca. It was to remain enigmatic until July, when Hole finally discovered the feature from which the firecracked rocks had come.

Because the rocks in this layer were so loosely packed, they did not always seal off the layer below, except in those squares where the stones were thickest and densest. In E9, there were little pockets of sherds in the interstices among the stones, some of them Formative-looking and others clearly Postclassic. The crew also found chipped stone tools that were typologically Archaic, but had evidently been redeposited at the time the layer of rocks was created. Since this level was such a "mixed bag," Flannery felt somewhat relieved when he saw that Félix had removed the last of it at roughly 55 cm depth. The lowermost stones rested on a thin layer of white ash without sherds—possibly, Flannery hoped, an undisturbed Archaic layer. That white ash eventually came to be called Zone C.

Removing Zone C, Félix uncovered a layer with soft tan-gray ash, lots of chipped stone debitage, no sherds, and bones of cottontail rabbit. This relatively thick layer, running from 55 to 75 cm below the surface, resembled some of the Archaic levels in MacNeish's Tehuacán caves, except for the fact that it had no apparent preservation of plant remains. Now Flannery had growing confidence that he had reached Archaic levels. This stratum was eventually named Zone D.

At 75 cm depth, the deposits changed again. Félix had reached a layer somewhat harder in texture, composed partly of light gray ash with abundant charcoal flecks and partly of whitish sand, the latter recognizable as the weathering product of the volcanic tuff cliff. In this stratum, Félix recovered two Archaic sidescrapers/knives. Now Flannery was more confident than ever that this light gray ash layer, running from 75 to 95 cm below the surface, was Archaic. This layer became Zone E.

So far, all of Félix's excavation had been by trowel. At roughly 95 cm depth, however, the deposits became so hard that the point of his trowel would barely penetrate them. This was a layer of indurated white sand, clearly the weathering product of the cave itself, and hardened either by great antiquity or the weight of the overburden. At this point, excavation could only proceed by means of an iron barreta, or miner's digging bar, a tool with which our Mitla workmen were all familiar. Félix cut his way down through the indurated sand, eventually reaching a sterile layer of decomposing volcanic tuff at 115 cm depth. The layer of white sand produced nothing but a few small rodent bones, suggesting that it might have antedated human occupation of the cave. As will be clear later in this chapter, however, Hole's excavations would greatly modify our view of this layer, which was eventually labeled Zone F.

Don Juan, in the meantime, had been excavating Square G9. In the course of removing Zone A he discovered our first feature, a Monte Albán V pit filled with gray ash and sherds, which cut through the brown ash of the zone and was intrusive through all the Archaic layers. Labeled Feature 1, it would eventually prove to affect parts of Squares G7, G8, G9, H8, and H9. In the undisturbed parts of G9, don Juan reached Zone B, the same stratum of loose firecracked rock that Félix had found in E9. Here, however, that stratum was thinner than it had been in E9.

At 60 cm depth in the undisturbed parts of G9, don Juan reached an ashy layer 10 cm thick, containing chipped stone debitage and animal bones but lacking pottery. While somewhat thicker, this layer appeared to correspond to Zone C, the thin layer of white ash at 55 cm depth in Square E9; that eventually proved to be the case. Below it, at a depth of 70–80 cm, was a layer of soft gray ash with tan lenses, clearly related to Zone D, the ashy level Félix had found at a depth of 55–75 cm in E9. So similar were the two squares at this stage that Flannery now felt confident that Archaic living floors would span much of the cave's main chamber.

Flannery's confidence increased when, at a depth of 80 cm, don Juan found a layer of light gray ash with abundant charcoal flecks, identical to Zone E in Square E9. Now it seemed likely that removal of F9, the intervening square, would link up at least three Archaic levels over a stretch of three meters. Don Juan removed Zone E carefully and discovered below it Zone F, the same stratum of indurated white sand the crew had seen earlier in E9. Using a barreta, he picked through this zone to bedrock, finding only the bones of small rodents.

Now that letters had been assigned to all the stratigraphic levels, Flannery decided to excavate two more squares: F9 (which would link up E9 and G9) and D9 (which would extend his test to the east). F9, excavated by don Juan, proved to be relatively uncomplicated once the crew got below Zone A. The rocky layer called Zone B, running from 35–50 cm below the surface, essentially sealed off the Archaic levels below, and Zones C, D, and F appeared undisturbed.

Meanwhile, Félix was extending work to the east by excavating Square D9. Zone A in this square had a heavy deposit of brown ash, overlain by thin streaks of gray ash but not disturbed by pits of any kind. Monte Albán V sherds and prismatic obsidian blades were typical of the refuse. At a depth of 40 to 55 cm below the surface, Félix encountered the same layer of firecracked rock (Zone B) that all squares had contained so far.

All three Archaic living floors were intact in Square D9, and can be clearly seen in the photograph of the east wall of the square (Figure 3.1). Zone C was a layer of grayish-white ash, roughly 55–65 cm below the surface in the center of the square; Zone D was an even thicker layer of tan-gray ash, 65–80 cm below the surface. At a depth of 76 cm, 36 cm in from the south wall of the square and 84 cm in from the east wall, Félix found a

Figure 3.1. The east profile of Square D9, showing Zones A–F. This was one of the first squares excavated, and helped to establish the stratigraphy of the cave's central chamber.

complete Tilapa atlatl point *in situ* in Zone D. As in the adjacent squares, Zone E consisted of white sand and light gray ash with charcoal flecks, and Zone F was once again a layer of indurated sand above sterile, weathered volcanic tuff.

The crew had now excavated four squares, allowing Flannery and Moser to begin three profile drawings that could be extended by further excavation: the east profile of D9, the east profile of E9, and the north profile of D9–E9–F9–G9. Flannery then decided to remove one more square—C9—whose stratigraphy could already be seen in the east profile of D9, and whose excavation would allow him to extend the north profile of D9–G9 one meter farther east toward the back wall of the cave (Figure 3.2).

Chris Moser and Eligio Martínez dug Square C9 themselves, while the Mitla workmen carefully screened all the deposits. The crew was disappointed that no plant remains had so far appeared in the Archaic levels, and it was decided to double the screen crew temporarily, just to see if fine plant fragments were being missed. Eventually it became clear that while plants were preserved in Zone A, no plants had been preserved in the Archaic levels.

Stripping off the cattle dung, Moser and Martínez carefully removed the intercalated brown and gray ash beds of Zone A. They discovered that in Square C9, the loose rocks of Zone B covered only a small area, near the juncture with Square D9. These stones, with their mixture of Formative and Postclassic sherds, were removed and the level swept before excavation began on Zone C.

Both excavators commented on how hard Zone C was, compared to the softer ash of Zone A. Right at the top of the zone, 60 cm from the east wall of the square and 22 cm from the south, a complete atlatl point of San Nicolás type appeared *in situ*. Zone C also yielded two discoidal one-hand manos, one complete and one fragmentary. Now each of the three Archaic strata—C, D, and E—had produced artifacts that tied them to that period.

Zone D (tan-gray ash) and Zone E (white ash with charcoal flecks) yielded stone tools and debitage like those found in adjacent squares; once again, Zone F was an indurated sand layer with animal bones but no artifacts.

The Excavation of Cueva Blanca

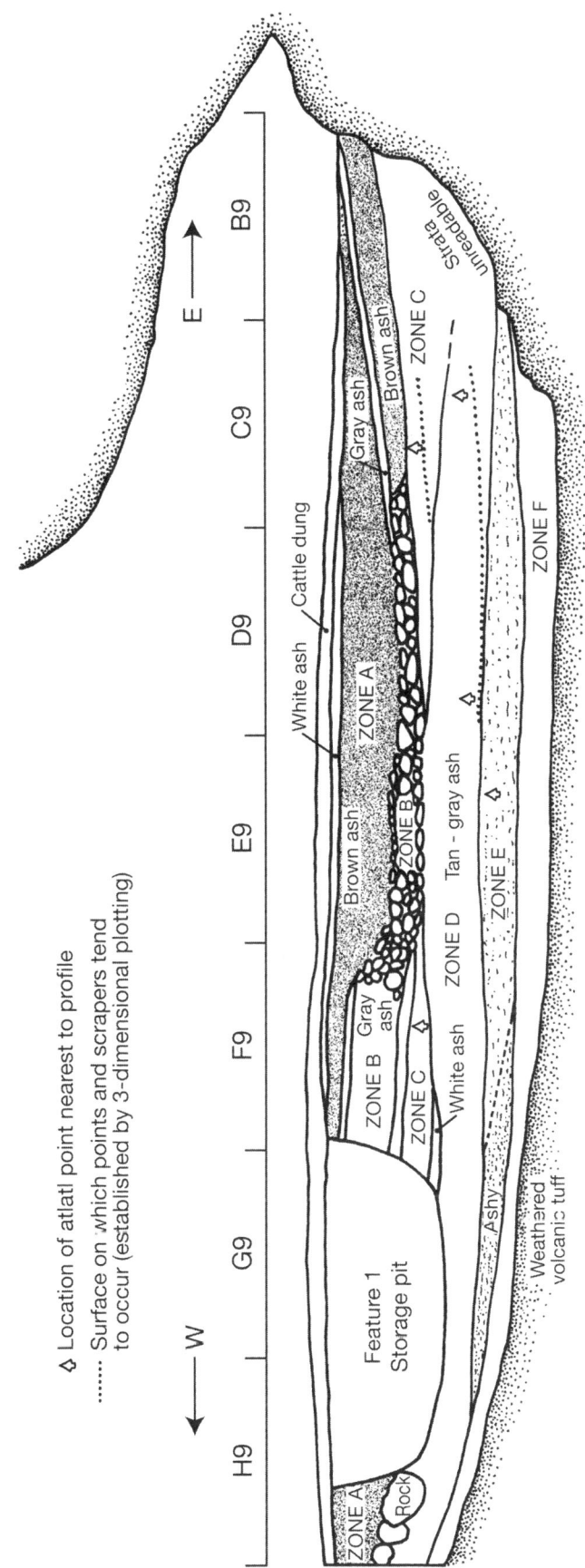

Figure 3.2. The north profile of Squares H9–B9.

During the second week of February Flannery briefly ended his excavation at Cueva Blanca, satisfied that the cave was worth excavating because of its stratified Archaic deposits and good faunal preservation. Several days were then spent testing other caves and rockshelters in the vicinity, none of which turned out to be as promising as Cueva Blanca.

Stage 2: Excavation of E5–E11, February 15–20, 1966

On February 15, Flannery returned to Cueva Blanca with the same crew of supervisors and workmen and laid out Squares E5–E11. Work began in E8 (taking advantage of the already exposed north profile of E9) and E6 (following R. S. MacNeish's strategy of digging alternate squares, so that the intervening square would have its stratigraphy exposed on two sides).

Don Juan Martínez, working in E8, peeled off the cattle dung and began to remove the dark brown ash of Zone A. Once Flannery saw that this square had no intrusive features, he took a pollen sample from the brown ash. At 25–30 cm below the surface, the loose rocks of Zone B appeared, along with the usual mixture of Formative and Postclassic sherds. In this square it was clear that Zone B included not only rubble and firecracked rock but also steep denticulate scrapers and cores of Archaic types, either collected from the surface and talus of the cave by later occupants or dug up from Archaic levels when they created features.

There was virtually no Zone C in Square E8, but Zone D was intact and up to 30 cm thick in places; as a result, we could distinguish an "upper D" and "lower D." A fragment of a basin-shaped metate appeared in this level, and Flannery took a pollen sample from Zone D in an area nicely sealed below Zone C. Zones E and F, below, looked very much as they had in Square E9.

Meanwhile, Félix was excavating Square E6. Zone A yielded a large charcoal sample in contact with Monte Albán V sherds. Zone B—thicker in the south half of the square than in the north—produced a few sherds that could be identified as Early and Middle Formative types. Unfortunately, there were Postclassic sherds present as well, so the level remained mixed. An atlatl point resembling MacNeish's Pelona type was found among the rocks, presumably redeposited from an Archaic level or collected from the talus when stones were needed for agave roasting pits. Fortunately, Zones C, D, E, and F were all intact and stratigraphically very clear in Square E6.

Once Squares E6 and E8 had been completed, Flannery decided to excavate E7 and E10. In the case of E10, his work would be guided by the stratigraphy exposed in the south profile of E9; in the case of Square E7, its stratigraphy had been exposed on both sides by the removal of E6 and E8.

The excavation of Square E7, undertaken by Félix, went very much as expected: each of the established stratigraphic zones could easily be traced from north to south, and all yielded the kinds of remains the crew was by now used to seeing. Square E10, excavated by don Juan, proved to be more complicated, since its southeastern quadrant had been disturbed by Feature 2, an intrusive pit that came down from Zone A and removed parts of the strata below it.

Zone A in Square E10 began as the usual deposit of dark brown ash with Monte Albán V sherds and obsidian. At the base of this deposit began Feature 2, about one-fourth of which lay in Square E10. This feature gradually expanded as it proceeded downward, disturbing a little bit more of each zone than the one above it. Don Juan carefully worked around it, isolating it from the intact parts of each Archaic living floor.

Zone B was very thick in Square E10, and where Feature 2 passed through it, the Postclassic creators of the pit had plastered its sides with mud to prevent the loose rocks of Zone B from sliding into it. (Additional features, discovered later in the excavation of Cueva Blanca, made it clear that mud and moss were regularly used by the Monte Albán V occupants to reinforce their constructions.) Among the rocks of Zone B the crew found a sherd from a tecomate or neckless jar with a specular hematite slip. Today this sherd would be considered a diagnostic element of the San José phase, but that Early Formative period had not yet been defined as of February 1966.

Outside the area disturbed by Feature 2, Zones D, E, and F looked very much as they had in Square E9 of Flannery's initial test. As in the case of Square E8, there was virtually no Zone C in Square E10.

Finally, the crew extended the row of "E" squares by excavating E5 and E11, taking advantage of the fact that both squares already had their stratigraphy exposed. Square E5, excavated by Félix, proved to be the least complicated, since it had no intrusive features (Figure 3.3). Beneath the thick rubble and firecracked rock of Zone B, all the Archaic living floors were intact. Zone C was particularly clear in this square, with an upper lens of whiter ash resting on a lower lens of yellower ash. In the whiter ash, 43 cm from the east wall of the square and 6 cm from the south, Félix found a complete San Nicolás atlatl point at a depth of 70 cm below the surface. Other discoveries in this layer included a discoidal one-hand mano and a series of animal bones. Flannery took a pollen sample from Zone F of this square.

In Square E11, don Juan's task was more difficult because he had to work around Feature 2, approximately one-fourth of which affected in this square. Zone C in Square E11 produced a complete La Mina atlatl point, some 30 cm from the south wall of the square and 32 cm in from the west. The undisturbed portion of Zone E yielded a nice ovoid scraper, and Zone F was once again a layer of indurated sand.

At this point, Flannery and Moser drew the east profile of Squares E5–E11 (Figure 3.4) and closed down Stage 2 of the Cueva Blanca excavation. Approximately one week was then devoted to washing, labeling, and examining the Archaic artifacts from this stage of field work so that the crew would be better informed during the third stage of excavation. Among other things, we needed to know how typical Cueva Blanca

The Excavation of Cueva Blanca

was among the Archaic sites of the Hacienda El Fuerte region. Consequently, during February 21–25, while one crew washed and labeled artifacts in the project's laboratory in Mitla, another crew tested Guilá Naquitz Cave (Flannery 2009a:65).

By the middle of March, 1966, we had a better sense of where Cueva Blanca fit within our overall sample of Archaic sites. We had reason to believe that it would have a larger sample of chipped stone tools and animal bones than Guilá Naquitz, but a smaller sample of plant remains. We also suspected, based on the limited sample of atlatl point types recovered so far, that the two caves were probably not occupied during the same periods. Obviously, we would learn a lot from excavating both.

Stage 3: March 18–30, 1966

On March 18, Flannery, Moser, and Martínez returned to Cueva Blanca with the same crew of workmen and laid out six more squares. Their goal was to extend the east-west column of "9" squares by digging B9 and H9, and the north-south row of "E" squares by digging E3, E4, E12, and E13 (Figures 3.5, 3.6). This would produce, in effect, two trenches that crossed each other at right angles, dividing the main chamber of the cave into four quadrants. Each of those quadrants would have its stratigraphy exposed on two adjacent sides, making it possible to excavate the rest of the chamber by working from a vertical face whose main strata were known in advance (Figure 3.7).

Flannery's crew began by digging Squares E4 and E12, extending the north-south trench. Félix, working in E4, found Zone A to have good preservation of maize, acorns, oak bark, and other plants. Zone B, the loose rock stratum, extended only into the southern half of the square; in the northern half, Zone A directly overlay Zone C. This fact made us skeptical about the tiny fragments of maize, prickly pear, and agave that turned up in the upper part of Zone C. Since no other part of Zone C displayed plant preservation, we suspected that these few specimens were intrusive, probably trampled down into Zone C by the occupants of Zone A.

An interesting aspect of Square E4 was that Zone C began at a depth of 30 cm in the north and 40 cm in the south. This was our first clue that some of the Archaic living floors might be basin shaped—a phenomenon that became clear when we started to compare the absolute depths of piece-plotted artifacts (see below). Piece-plotted tools in Zone C of Square E4 included a nice example of a chopper/knife at a depth of 43 cm, 20 cm from the north side of the square and 25 cm from the east.

The tan-gray ash of Zone D was very clear in this square, as was the gray ash layer with charcoal flecks that had been designated Zone E. In the latter zone, Félix was able to plot a possible unfinished Palmillas atlatl point and a nice sidescraper/knife made on red silicified tuff. Below this, Félix found the usual indurated white sand of Zone F.

Meanwhile, don Juan was excavating Square E12 and dealing with yet another Monte Albán V pit—Feature 3—that

Figure 3.3. Félix trowels his way through the Archaic levels in Square E5 (view from the south).

extended down from Zone A to a depth of 85 cm, and disturbed parts of the lower zones. Beyond the limits of this intrusive pit, however, the Archaic strata were very clear and could easily be traced through from Square E11. Perhaps the most interesting discoveries in Square E12 were made in Zone D. They included a fragment of slab metate and a bone pendant. The bone pendant—at that moment, our first hint of personal ornamentation in the Archaic—was found 5 cm from the north edge of the square and 30 cm from the east. One year later, of course, we discovered even earlier Archaic ornaments when Hole excavated Gheo-Shih.

The crew worked next on Squares B9 and H9, which completed the east-west arm of their cruciform trench system and allowed them to reach the back wall of the cave. Square B9, excavated by Pablo, had no Zone B or Zone E; evidently, neither of those deposits had extended to the east wall of the cave. Perhaps the most interesting stratum in this square was Zone C, where Pablo was able to piece-plot a steep denticulate scraper.

Square H9, excavated by don Juan, became the western terminus of the crew's east-west trench. In addition to the disturbance of the Archaic strata in this square by Feature 1—an intrusive Postclassic pit that the crew had encountered earlier in Square G9—Flannery could see that the crew would have further problems if they continued westward. For one thing, bedrock was

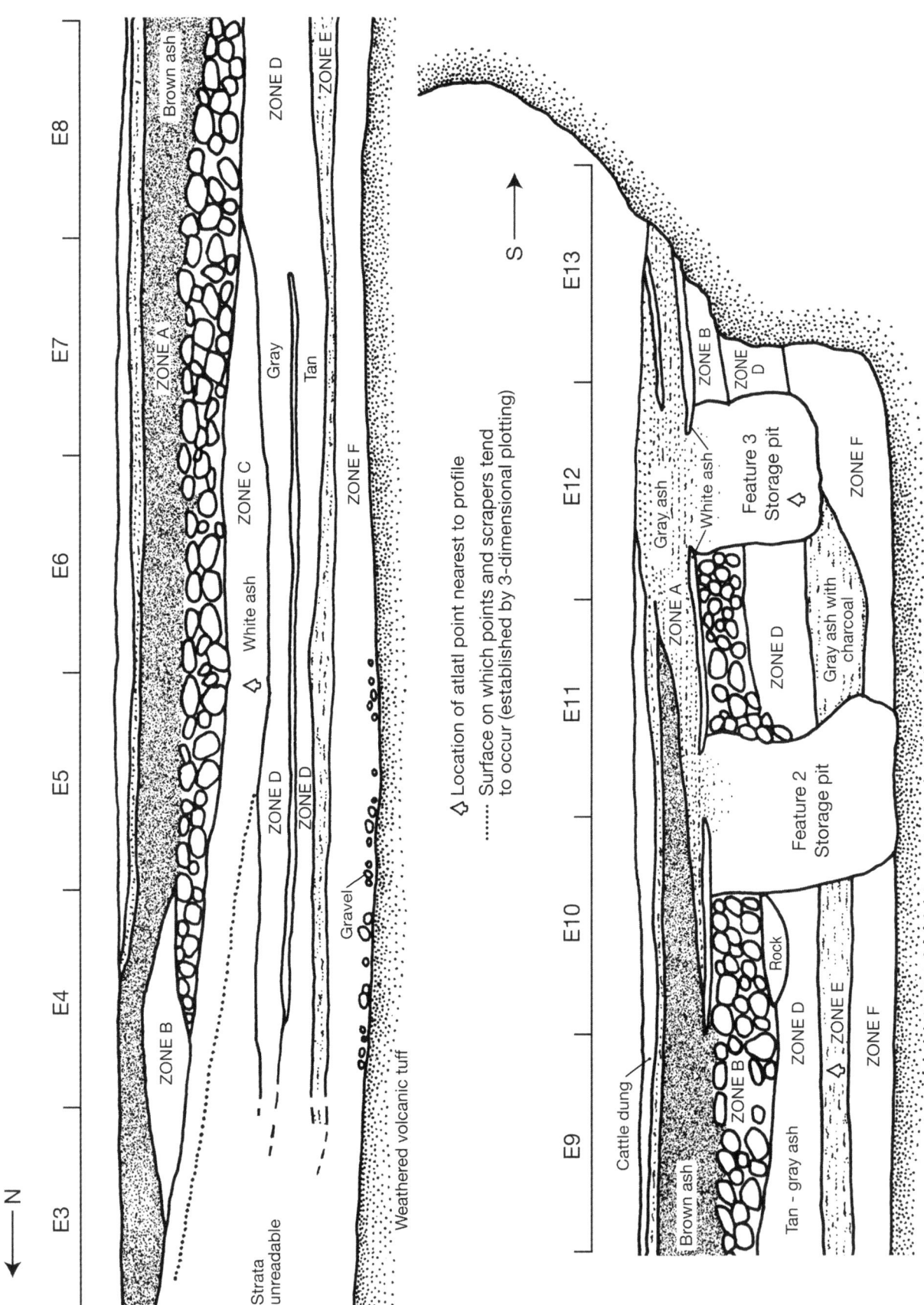

Figure 3.4. The east profile of Squares E3–E13.

Figure 3.5. The northern limits of the cave chamber. Eligio supervises Alfredo and Carlos as they begin Squares E3 and E4.

rising higher and higher as the crew moved toward the mouth of the cave, and one could see places to the west where it actually outcropped on the surface. For another thing, the closer the crew got to the limits of the cave overhang, the more it appeared that rain had entered over the centuries and obscured the color differences among strata. Zones B and E were missing at this point, and it was becoming increasingly difficult to detect the differences between Zones C and D. Upon completing Square H9, therefore, Flannery and Moser finished their drawing of the northern wall of Squares B9–H9 (see Figure 3.2). This 7-m-long profile then came to serve as the principal east-west section through the center of the cave chamber.

Now satisfied with their east-west transect of the cave, Flannery, Moser, and Martínez began work on Squares E3 and E13 to complete the north-south transect. Square E3, the northernmost, was excavated by Félix. Zone A in this area became shallower and less complex as it neared the cave wall, and there was no Zone B at all, the layer of loose rock having petered out in Square E4. The three Archaic strata were all intact below Zone A, but as they neared the cave wall, each gradually rose in elevation and faded in color. It was clear that by the time they reached the wall, each of the Archaic zones would consist mainly of the white, sand-like product of weathering from the walls and ceiling of the cave, with little color left from ash or decomposed organic debris. The strata were clearer in the west half of the square than along the east profile, where they could only be traced with difficulty.

Despite their faded color, the Archaic zones in Square E3 yielded interesting results. Fragments of charcoal from Zone C were later identified as oak, acacia, pine, and baldcypress, indicating that the occupants had collected firewood from a wide variety of trees.

One of the most unexpected objects found in Zone C was a marine shell, *Agaronia testacea*, that had been drilled in two places for suspension as an ornament (Figure 3.8). This olive shell is native to Pacific Coast sandy beaches and must therefore have

Figure 3.6. Work beginning on Zone A of Square E12, near the south wall of the cave chamber. This photo shows the intersection of the "E" row of squares (framed by two mason's chalk lines) and the "9" column of squares.

come from at least 140 km away. Its presence in Zone C suggests that already in Late Archaic times, small amounts of marine shell from the Pacific Coast were reaching the Valley of Oaxaca—a harbinger of the more extensive long-distance exchanges of shell that would one day characterize the Formative cultures in the area (Pires-Ferreira 1975).

Meanwhile, don Juan was excavating Square E13, at the southern limit of the north-south trench. Here, near the south wall of the cave, the Postclassic deposits of Zone A were well represented, and even seemed to include two mounds of Postclassic "backdirt" that may have resulted from the digging of Features 2 and 3. Zone B in this part of the cave was a layer of brown ash with Formative sherds, lacking the usual deposit of loose firecracked rock. All three of the Archaic strata showed signs of petering out as they neared the wall of the cave.

On completion of Squares E3 and E13, Flannery and Moser finished their drawing of the eastern wall of the entire row of "E" squares, giving them an 11-m profile that became their main north-south transect through the middle of the cave chamber (see Figure 3.4). Cueva Blanca was now divided into quadrants whose stratigraphy was visible on at least two sides.

Looking at the east profile of Squares E3–E13, one could practically hear Squares D3–D12 begging to be excavated. Nowhere was Zone D thicker and more distinctively colored; nowhere was Zone E richer in debitage or more distinctly flecked with charcoal. To be sure, Zone C had shrunk to a thin wisp of white ash in Squares E8–10, but we knew from our work in Squares E9–B9 that that zone would grow thicker as one moved to the north. The crew also knew that they would have to work around intrusive Postclassic pits like Features 2 and 3, but those

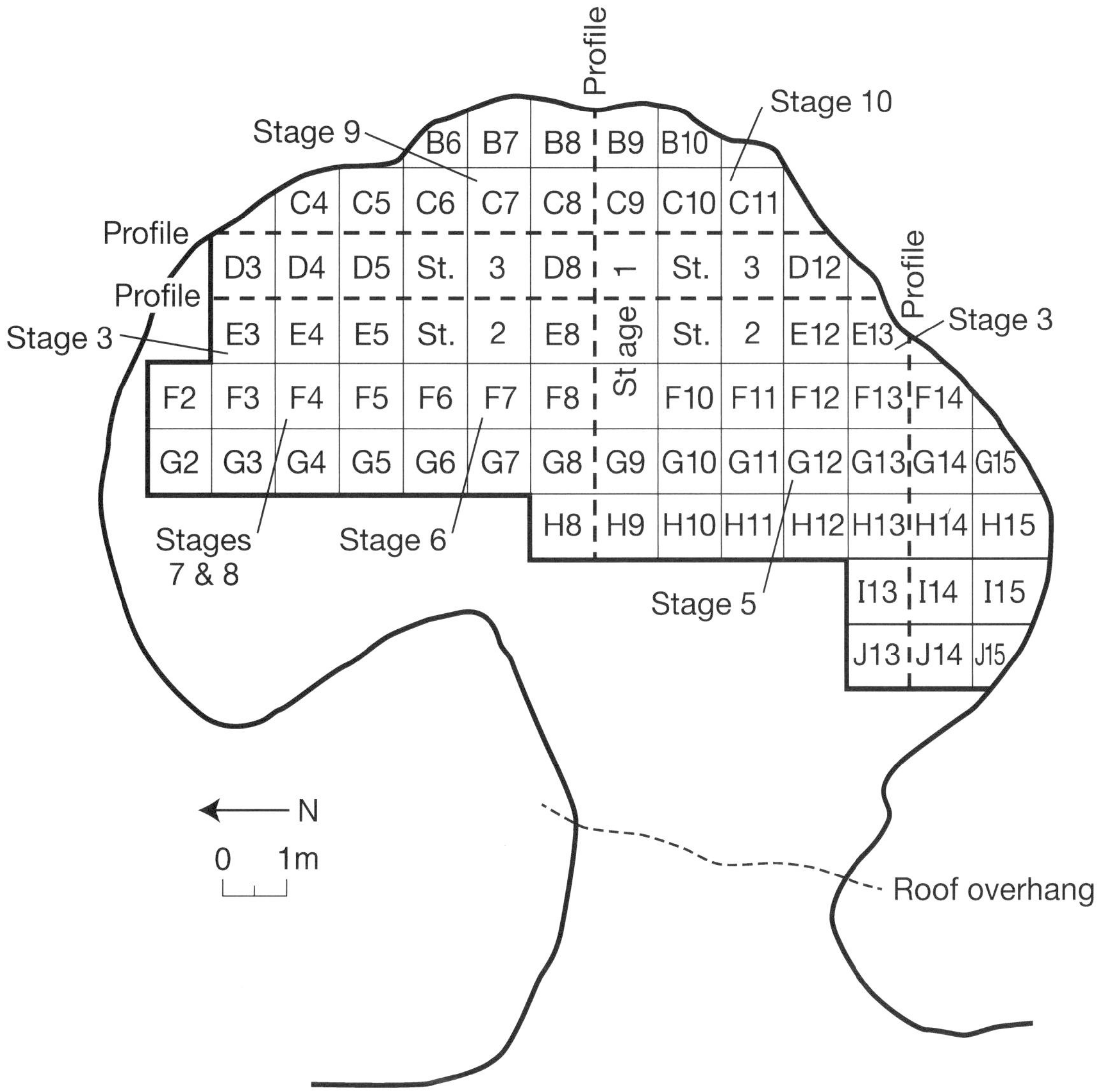

Figure 3.7. A plan view of Cueva Blanca, showing (1) the squares excavated during the ten stages of work and (2) the location of the four longest stratigraphic profiles included in this chapter.

pits were so clear that the workmen anticipated no problem in doing so.

Flannery decided to dig the "D" row by alternate squares, beginning with D5 and D7 (Figure 3.9). Félix began Square D5 by peeling off the brown ash of Zone A, recovering such characteristic Monte Albán V vessels as dark gray bowls with serpent-effigy legs. Zone B, the layer of loose rock, yielded some clear Formative sherds with "double-line-break" incising, as well as white-rimmed black ware. In Zone D, Félix piece-plotted a broken Trinidad atlatl point, 30 cm from the north edge of the square and 28 cm from the east.

In Square D7, meanwhile, Pablo had found an Hidalgo point redeposited among the loose rocks of Zone B. Below those rocks, Zone C was intact and extremely clear. Continuing downward into Zone D, Pablo encountered another Trinidad atlatl point as

Figure 3.8. An ornament made from olive shell (*Agaronia testacea*), discovered in Zone C of Square E3. This artifact provides our oldest evidence for the importation of marine shell into the Valley of Oaxaca.

Figure 3.9. The excavation of Squares D5 and D7 (view from the west). At this stage the "E" row of squares had been largely completed, providing a long north-south profile to guide our excavation of the "D" row by alternate squares.

well as an ovoid biface. Zone D was, in fact, particularly rich in chipped stone debris in this square. Proceeding downward, Pablo encountered Zones E and F intact and undisturbed. Because of the lack of intrusive features in Square D7, Flannery took a series of pollen samples from the Archaic strata in this square.

Don Juan, who dug Square D10, was not so lucky. In addition to having to work around the rest of Feature 2—a Monte Albán V pit—he encountered Feature 4, a bell-shaped pit that extended down from Zone B to a depth of 85 cm, disturbing portions of the lower strata (Figure 3.10). Fortunately Feature 4 was a relatively small pit, so substantial portions of the Archaic deposits in this square were left intact.

Once don Juan had completed Square D10, the crew saw that by excavating Squares D4, D6, and D8 they could provide another long north-south profile through the heart of the cave chamber (Figures 3.11, 3.12). The task of digging Square D6 fell to Félix. This proved to be a very productive square, especially in the case of Zone D, where Félix was able to piece-plot two atlatl points. He found a Palmillas point 35 cm from the north edge of the square and 15 cm from the east, and a Tilapa point 68 cm from the east edge and 85 cm from the north. By now it was clear that a number of our atlatl points belonged to types well known from the Tehuacán Valley (MacNeish, Nelken-Terner, and Johnson 1967).

Nowhere was that clearer than in Square D8, excavated by Pablo. First, a Trinidad point turned up in the brown ash of Zone A—presumably an artifact from an Archaic level, redeposited when the Postclassic occupants dug one of their storage pits.

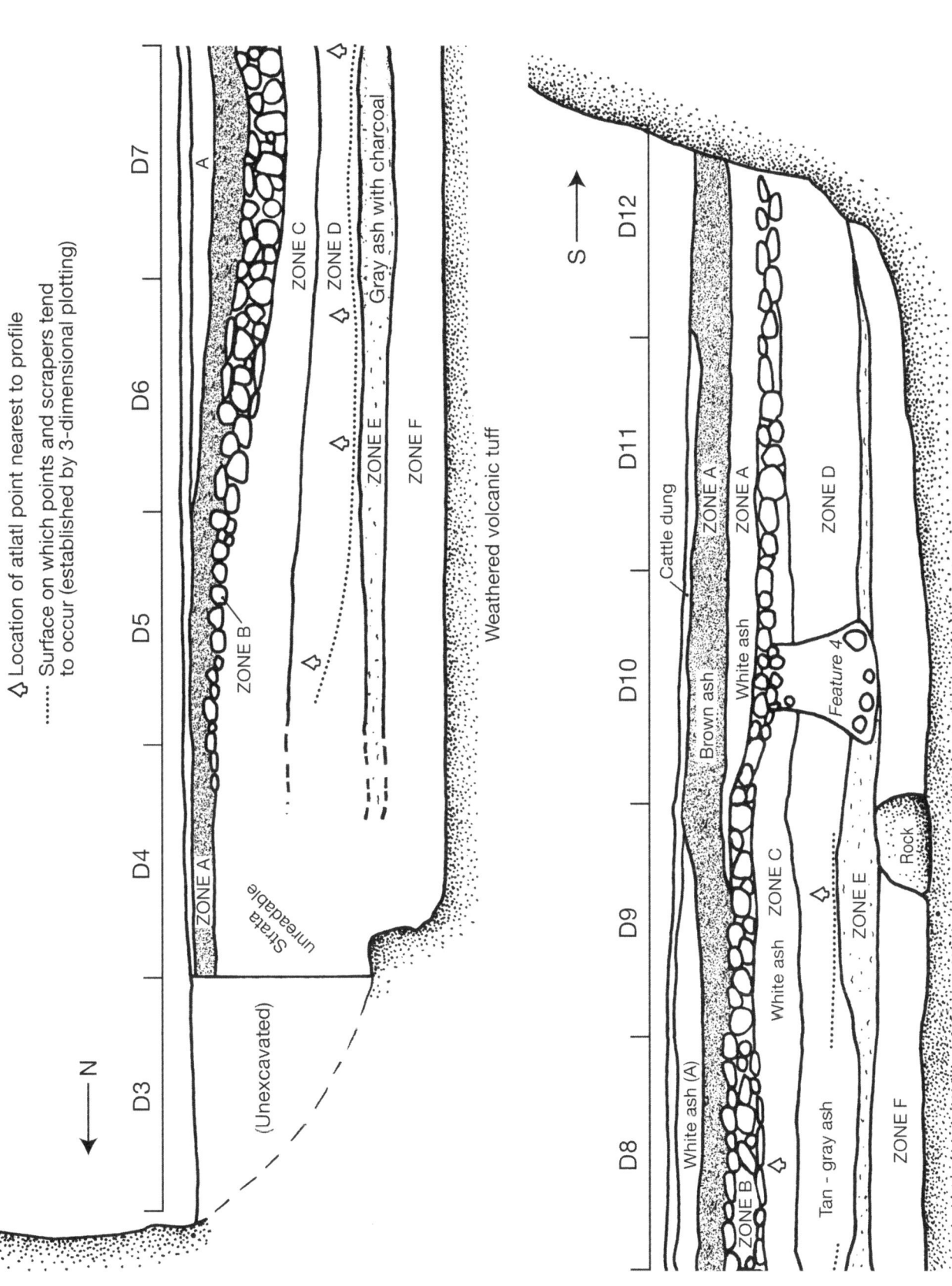

Figure 3.10. The east profile of Squares D3–D12.

Figure 3.11. The excavation of alternate Squares D4, D6, and D8 (view from the south).

Perhaps the most exciting discovery of the week, however, was made by Pablo in Zone C of Square D8, an undisturbed expanse of white ash with Archaic tools, rabbit bones, turtle carapace fragments, and other debris. At a depth of 44 cm in Zone C, 45 cm from the north edge of the square and 15 cm from the west, Pablo found an absolutely prototypic Coxcatlán point *in situ* (Figure 3.13). This point type—largely known from MacNeish's Tehuacán work—was most abundant during the Abejas phase in that region (MacNeish, Nelken-Terner, and Johnson 1967). Our Coxcatlán point even appeared to be made on nonlocal chert, raising the possibility that it was obtained in exchange.

Finally, Flannery's crew ended the third stage of excavation at Cueva Blanca by having don Juan complete Square D4. All three Archaic zones were beautifully intact in this square. Zone D, a deposit of tan gray ash rich in debitage and faunal remains, yielded a biface (Variety B), 10 cm from the east edge of the square and 95 cm from the north. Don Juan also piece-plotted a beautiful ovoid scraper, some 40 cm from the east and 80 cm from the north. Zones E and F, below, continued uninterrupted.

Excavations at Cueva Blanca paused for an intermission after the completion of Square D4. Flannery, Moser, and Martínez drew the east profile of Squares D4–D10, swept the floors of all excavated squares, and tried to leave everything as neat as they could in anticipation of Hole's arrival in July (Figure 3.14). During this intermission, Flannery and his crew returned to Guilá Naquitz for further excavation (Flannery 2009a).

Let us consider for a moment what Flannery's crew knew—or thought they knew—about Cueva Blanca at this point, about one-third of the way through the cave's excavation. To begin with, they knew that the cave had at least three stratigraphic levels that could be assigned to the Archaic period. Those levels—Zones E, D, and C—had produced no preserved plants, but they had good animal bone preservation and were much richer in artifacts than the Archaic levels at Guilá Naquitz.

The crew was also getting hints that the relationship between the Archaic *stratigraphic zones* (E–C) and the actual Archaic *living floors* encapsulated within them might be less straightforward at Cueva Blanca than at Guilá Naquitz. This eventually proved to be the case; the zones were horizontal, while the living floors were basin-shaped. Finally, Zone F appeared to be a layer of indurated sand with animal bones but as yet no artifacts. Hole was destined to make some surprising discoveries in that very ancient level.

Above Zone C was a very frustrating layer of firecracked rock that we had designated Zone B. We use the term "frustrating" here because there was no way Zone B could be interpreted as a living floor or assigned to a single time period. It had redeposited Archaic artifacts in it. It also, however, had Postclassic sherds in the spaces between the loose rocks. Perhaps just as frustrating, it contained a number of Formative sherds, suggesting that Cueva Blanca might once have had small Formative occupations that had later been completely disturbed and incorporated into Zone B.

Flannery's crew was frankly baffled by the loose rock layer, since they had found no evidence for the activity that produced it. As Michael Schiffer (1987) might say, we had a "site formation process" problem. Luckily, this problem would be solved by Hole.

Then there was Zone A, a deposit rich with sherds, artifacts, animal bones, and plant remains left during Monte Albán V. We were happy to have the Postclassic information it yielded, but we wished that the Monte Albán V people had not excavated so many intrusive features into the Archaic deposits. Not only had they reduced the extent of the intact Archaic remains and forced us to work carefully around their pits, they had also brought to the surface a number of Archaic projectile points that we would have preferred to have found *in situ* in Zones C, D, and E. We also wondered exactly what the Monte Albán V people had been doing in Cueva Blanca, just 4 km from the ancient Zapotec urban center of Mitla. Fortunately, Hole's work was destined to shed some light on this question as well.

Finally, we were happy with the care, patience, and intelligence our Mitla workmen were showing in their excavation, and with the outstanding supervision they were getting from Eligio Martínez. We were, however, still undecided as to whether they were better excavators or humorists. We had learned that the Zapotec loved performing labor in groups, considering it as much a chance for swapping jokes as for earning wages. Now

Figure 3.12. Looking north down the "D" and "E" rows of squares. At this stage almost the entire "E" row had been excavated, providing the stratigraphic profile shown in Figure 3.4. In the foreground, Pablo is beginning Zone E of Square D8.

Figure 3.13. Pablo points to a Coxcatlán point, found *in situ* in Zone C of Square D8. This point was indistinguishable from Tehuacán Valley specimens, and appeared to be made on nonlocal chert.

we were part of the audience. As Moser remarked, "There are probably only six Zapotec stand-up comedians, and we wound up with all six."

In July of 1966, Hole arrived in Oaxaca, and after spending some time visiting other sites in the El Fuerte region, he readied himself to excavate the remaining two-thirds of Cueva Blanca. In anticipation of this task, our team of Mitla workmen was expanded by adding Ambrosio Martínez, Ernesto Martínez, and Angel Sosa, giving Hole essentially the same group that had excavated Guilá Naquitz. After looking over the field notes and profile drawings, examining the artifacts already recovered, and discussing strategy with Flannery, Moser, and Martínez, Hole decided that he would deal with the F, G, and H rows of squares first, leaving the B, C, and D rows for later. One of the reasons for this was that the western part of the cave was a large, still unexplored area where the limits of Archaic occupation needed to be worked out. The eastern part was small by comparison, limited by the back wall of the cave, and already well defined by earlier work. Hole therefore chose to move westward into the unknown and potentially more challenging part of the cave.

Because Hole's larger crew would need more space to set up screens and accommodate backdirt, we decided at this time to clear some of the thorn forest off the talus slope below the cave. Not only would this allow us more room to operate, it would expose the stone masonry terraces we had first noticed when the cave was discovered. Given the goals of our project, we needed to know whether these probable agricultural terraces were contemporaneous with the Archaic occupation or more recent.

Using our larger crew, we cleared the thorn forest off the slope below the cave to reveal the terraces (see Figure 2.10). We took care not to cut down such valuable plants as mature columnar cacti, which we knew might take centuries to regrow.

Figure 3.14. Sweeping the completed "E" row of squares (left) and shaving the east profile of the "D" row with a sharpened, square-ended shovel (right).

Figure 3.15. Carlos begins work on a stratigraphic test in Terrace 3 of the agricultural terrace system below Cueva Blanca. In the background, Pablo and Angel screen material from the cave chamber.

We limited ourselves to clearing those species that we knew would re-establish themselves quickly (and in fact, by 1976 the slope below the cave appeared fully regrown). Our clearing of the brush revealed that the east bank of the small arroyo below the cave had been terraced as well, giving us a sixth terrace that we had not previously seen (see Figure 2.5).

Stage 4: The Excavation of Terrace 3

While Hole prepared for his excavation inside the cave, Flannery borrowed Pablo and Carlos and endeavored to date the terrace system on the slope below. The hillside descending from Cueva Blanca has a natural slope of 20°, and the east bank of the small arroyo lies 14 m below the mouth of the cave. By means of a series of low, drylaid stone masonry walls, less than a meter high and trending generally north-south, the slope had been divided in prehispanic times into a series of six terraces that varied between 3 and 10 m in width. None of these terraces were level; the smallest were concave in section, and the largest had a slope that approximated that of the natural hillside. Because of the many rocky spurs projecting out from the cliff behind Cueva Blanca, none of the terraces was very long, the maximum being about 15 m.

Flannery decided to place a 1 x 1 m pit just behind the wall of Terrace 3, the third terrace from the top (Figure 3.15). The earth was initially removed by arbitrary 10-cm levels, and since no detectable color or texture changes were found in the terrace fill, Flannery was forced to use metric stratigraphy throughout. The fill was all brown earth, penetrated to a depth of 60 cm by

Figure 3.16. The stratigraphic test in Terrace 3 has now been carried to sterile soil. The workman's trowel rests on a bedrock outcrop.

the rootlets of thorn forest vegetation, but essentially rootlet-free below that. At a depth of 70 cm, Flannery's crew reached the base of the terrace wall and sterile soil (Figure 3.16).

Monte Albán V sherds, usually small and badly broken, were found to a depth of 60 cm; between 60 and 70 cm depth there were only a few flint chips, none diagnostic. In the chinks between the stones of the terrace wall itself, we found Monte Albán V sherds to a depth of 70 cm. There was no evidence to suggest that the terrace was anything but a Postclassic feature.

One of the most interesting discoveries made during the Terrace 3 excavation was that, in spite of the fact that it had not rained for a week at the time of our work, the soil in the terrace was still moist to a depth of 40 cm. Our project geomorphologist, Michael Kirkby, suggested that this happened because Cueva Blanca was on the cooler and shadier side of the canyon, resulting in a lower evaporation rate. Thus, the very moisture that impeded the preservation of plants in the Archaic levels of the cave had made the slope below it more suitable for growing crops. We now suspected that the terraces had produced some of the agricultural plants found in Zone A of the cave.

Stage 5: The Southwest Quadrant

By the first week of July, Hole, Moser, and Martínez had begun work on the block of squares isolated on the north by Squares F9–H9 of our east-west trench and on the east by Squares E10–E13 of our north-south trench. Some squares, such as F10, had their stratigraphy exposed on two sides, making it easier to anticipate the nature and slope of the deposits as work proceeded.

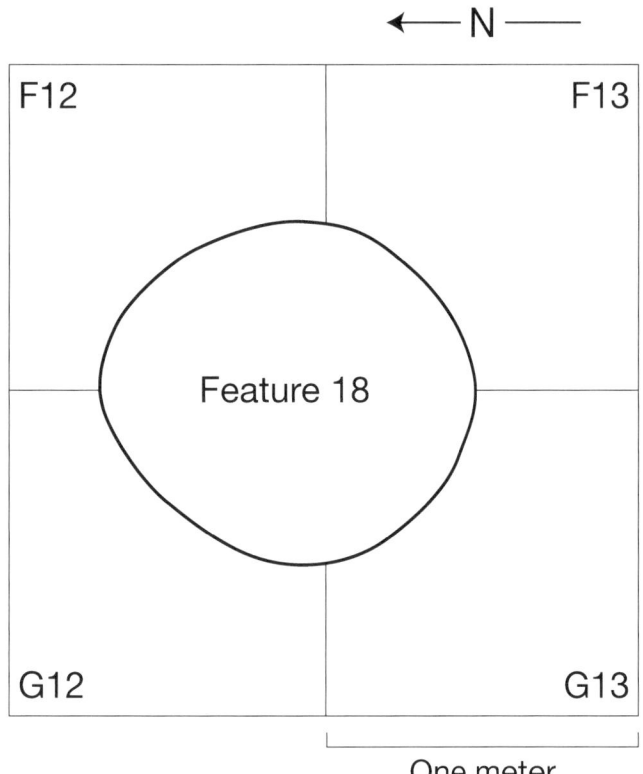

Figure 3.17. Plan view of Feature 18, a hearth originating in Zone D.

By digging F10 and F12 as alternate squares, one could leave F11 isolated on three sides to ensure maximum control of the stratigraphy.

That was the good news; the bad news was that it was often difficult to keep a straight profile in the firecracked rocks of Zone B. To make matters worse, the "F" row of squares contained a few giant boulders that had fallen from the roof in ancient times. Hole, Moser, and Martínez worked around these boulders and recovered more Monte Albán I sherds from Zone B.

Squares F11 and F12 were extremely productive of Archaic tools, but unfortunately, most of these artifacts had been redeposited in the rocky rubble of Zone B. A second Coxcatlán point—made on nonlocal chert, like the one found earlier in Zone C—had been redeposited in Zone B of Square F11. From the same level in Square F12, Félix recovered an ovoid biface, a fragmentary atlatl point, and an Archaic sidescraper/knife. In Squares F11–F12 it seemed clear that Zone C had been disturbed by the people responsible for the firecracked rock layer; thus it is possible that some of the Archaic tools found in Zone B of these squares might originally have been lying on the surface of Zone C.

It was in Square F2 that, for the first time, our views of Zone F began to change. At a depth of 100 cm, Félix reached the top of that layer of indurated sand, a layer so hard that it had to be loosened by a digging bar before it could be troweled. Suddenly Félix came upon some scutes from the carapace of a turtle larger than the ones we were used to seeing—larger, that is, than the scutes of mud turtle (*Kinosternon* sp.) found in the Archaic levels.

The large scutes from Square F2 turned out to be from *Gopherus berlandieri*, the Texas gopher tortoise, a species also found in the Late Pleistocene levels of Coxcatlán Cave in the Tehuacán Valley (Flannery 1967). This large tortoise—absent in southern Mexico since the end of the Pleistocene, but still present in Coahuila and Texas—had been eaten by Paleoindian foragers in Tehuacán. Now we knew that Zone F might, in fact, be as old as the Early Ajuereado phase of the Tehuacán Valley, and that we should be alert to the possibility of finding Paleoindian remains.

As Hole and his crew moved south into Square F13, the rocky rubble of Zone B began to thin out. A highly visible rodent burrow in the southwest corner of the square—ending in a small nest full of chaff—had to be isolated and cleaned out. Below this burrow was an intact and undisturbed Zone C, 10–15 cm thick near the south edge of the square but thinner near the north. This situation duplicated the one found earlier in Square D4—that is, several of the Archaic strata seemed to get thicker as they neared the wall of the cave. In addition, as they approached the wall their artifact content dwindled and the few tools present seemed to occur higher up in the stratum, as if resting on a talus of sterile debris.

Eventually, Félix reached the south wall of the cave chamber by excavating Square F14. There were very few artifacts in the Archaic strata at this point, but a fragment of unfinished atlatl point or biface had been redeposited in Zone B.

Hole next assigned don Juan to Square D10 and Pablo and Félix to G12—a square so complicated that it required a two-man team with the patience of brain surgeons. The biggest problem in G12 was Feature 6, an agave roasting pit so extensive that it had affected Squares G10, G11, G12, H10, H11, and H12. Feature 6 was associated with Zone B, and while a giant agave roasting pit was the last thing Hole had wanted to find, it suddenly clarified the nature of Zone B.

Large roasting pits or "earth ovens" were used by the prehispanic Zapotec to cook the heart of the *dobh-gih* (*Agave potatorum*). Feature 7 of Guilá Naquitz Cave was just such a roasting pit (Flannery 2009a:91), and many others have been found in the rockshelters of the Mitla region. What the Zapotec did was to dig up the agave and trim off its leaves with a flint flake, leaving intact the heart of the plant, which resembles a large pineapple. (Repeated use of the same flint flake on the tough, fibrous, and sometimes dirty leaf bases produced a kind of sheen on the flake, which will be discussed in Chapter 5.)

The Zapotec then excavated a basin-shaped pit, lining it with stones and fueling it with slow-burning wood such as oak (*Quercus* sp.) or manzanita (*Arctostaphylos* sp.). Once the stones had become very hot, one or more agave hearts were placed in the oven, covered with agave leaves to keep them clean, and sealed below a layer of dirt (see Thoms et al. 2018: Figure 1a for similar earth ovens). After 24–72 hours, depending on the size and number of agaves, the roasting was complete and the oven could be opened. With the removal of the cooked agave, the resulting firecracked rock was also thrown out. The process could then be repeated by bringing in new rocks, new fuel, and new agave hearts.

When roasting continued for any length of time, it produced massive scatters of firecracked rock. In Texas, such accumulations are called "burnt rock middens" and were often associated with the prehistoric roasting of *Agave lechuguilla* (Shafer 1986). In Cueva Blanca, thousands of firecracked rocks thrown out of Feature 6 had formed a kind of "burnt rock layer"—Zone B, our previously enigmatic stratum of loose rock and ash, which was thicker in the vicinity of Feature 6 than anywhere else. The redeposition of Archaic flint tools in Zone B evidently resulted from the fact that the agave roasters considered every Archaic tool they could find on the surface to be just as suitable for lining a roasting pit as a chunk of roof fall.

It appeared to Hole that the use of Feature 6 had continued right up until the start of the occupation in Zone A. At that point a different occupation began in the cave, the use of Feature 6 came to an end, and the brown ash layer we called Zone A formed above the roasting pit.

There was one other discouraging sign in Square G10: moss was growing in the upper 10 cm of the square. Evidently G10, in spite of the fact that it lay 5 m east of the dripline or cliff overhang, was close enough to the cave mouth so that it had been reached by wind-driven rain. In all probability, this meant that the soil color changes we had relied on to distinguish strata in the back of the cave would start to fade as Hole moved west into the "H" and "I" rows of squares. This gradual loss of color, combined with the increasingly dense growth of moss and rootlets, contributed to setting the western limits of our excavation, although there were other factors (see below).

Just beyond the limits of the agave roasting pit, however, the Archaic levels were intact and produced a number of interesting discoveries. For example, in Squares F12–F13 and G12–G13, Hole uncovered a basin-shaped hearth, Feature 18, excavated down from Zone D into Zone E (Figure 3.17). The hearth was roughly a meter in diameter and contained chunks of carbonized wood with a conventional radiocarbon date of 3295 BC ± 105 years. The floor of the basin, which in places rested on the indurated sand of Zone F, showed signs of burning.

Félix and Pablo next excavated Square G11, which had been isolated when G10 and G12 were removed. This square's stratigraphy was exposed on three sides, making it easy to isolate the portion of Feature 6 that passed through it. Two Monte Albán V sherds were found in the roasting pit, confirming its date.

In Zone F of Square G11—a level we now suspected of dating to the Late Pleistocene—Hole recovered the complete metapodial of a white-tailed deer (Figure 3.18). The metapodial showed no signs of chewing or gnawing by predators, raising the possibility that this deer had been brought to the cave by Paleoindian hunters.

Hole completed the "F" row of squares with the removal of F13 and F14. The Archaic strata were reasonably clear in these

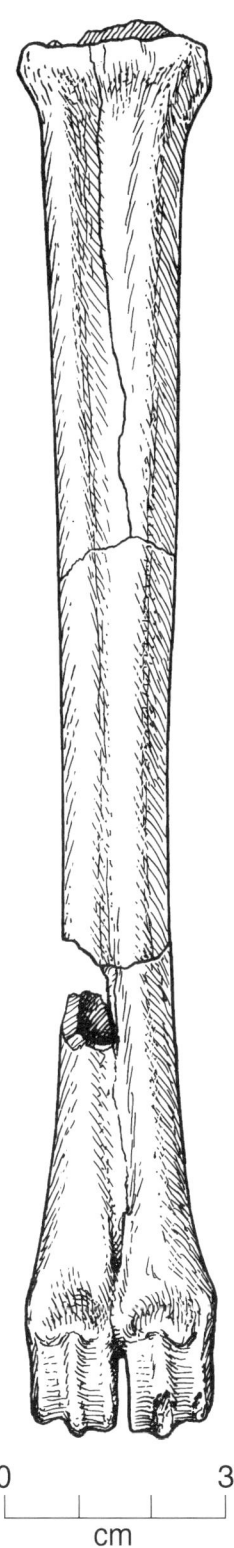

Figure 3.18. This left metatarsal of *Odocoileus* was recovered from Zone F, a stratigraphic level believed to date to the Late Pleistocene.

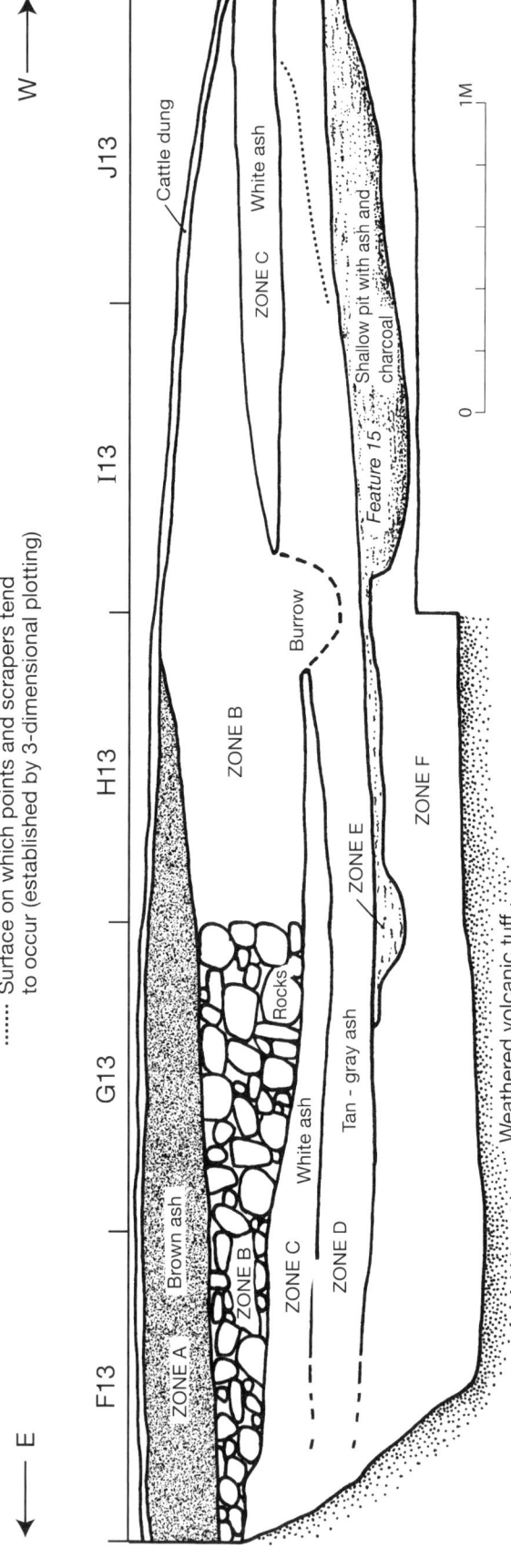

Figure 3.19. The south profile of Squares F13–J13.

squares, but their artifact content grew increasingly meager as our crew approached the south wall of the cave. Hole isolated a rodent nest, filled with fine chaff, in the southwest corner of Squares F13; fortunately, it had only disturbed Zone B, which by then was hardly our favorite stratum anyway.

One of the major tasks carried out during July was the completion of another east-west profile drawing—the south wall of Squares F13, G13, H13, I13, and J13 (Figure 3.19). To facilitate this drawing, Hole had his crew move west from F13, digging alternate squares until the complete profile was exposed.

Square G13, excavated by Pablo, produced two complete Archaic atlatl points; unfortunately, both were redeposited among the firecracked rocks of Zone B. In this square, there were actual remains of *Agave* sp. in among the Zone B rocks, strengthening our conclusion that this stratum was a byproduct of agave roasting.

Another interesting discovery made in Square G13 was a mass of small rodent remains in Zone F. These remains appeared to have resulted from the disintegration of owl pellets, giving us a useful sample of local wild rodents from what we now believed was a Late Pleistocene stratum.

As Félix excavated Square H13, we came upon our first major change in the nature of Stratigraphic Zone B. Near the boundary between Squares G13 and H13, the firecracked rocks of Zone B ended abruptly, giving way to a dump of ash (see Figure 3.19). It seemed likely that this layer of soft, floury, nearly sterile ash (more than 20 cm thick in places) had come from the same agave roasting pit as the firecracked rocks. Hole noted that many stones along the interface between the ash dump and the rock layer were so badly burned that they fell into small pieces when touched.

Except for an animal burrow that had disturbed Zone C (near the border between Squares H13 and I13), all three Archaic layers were relatively clear, intact, and easily followed along the F13–J13 profile. In Square I13, Hole found a feature connected to the base of Zone E. This was a large but relatively shallow ash-filled pit, Feature 15, which included enough charcoal to provide us with three internally consistent radiocarbon dates (Figure 3.20). Measuring 1.2 m in diameter, this apparent hearth pit was spread over the intersection of Squares I13, I14, J13, and J14; however, it had been excavated only 20 cm into the indurated sand layer below (see Figure 3.19). Our three radiocarbon samples from Feature 15 provided conventional dates of 8780 BC ± 220, 8960 BC ± 80, and 9050 BC ± 400. We are intrigued by the fact that these dates fall virtually at the transition from Paleoindian to Archaic (Chapter 4).

A few artifacts in this southwest quadrant of the cave chamber are worthy of special mention. In Square J14, Pablo discovered a broken Palmillas point in Zone D, 20 cm from the west side of the square and 8 cm from the north. He also recovered a large bone needle or punch in Zone C of Square I15.

Two discoveries convinced Hole not to continue his excavation west of Squares H8–H12 or J13–J15. One was the fact that the Archaic strata were beginning to rise toward the surface, suggesting that bedrock would eventually emerge as

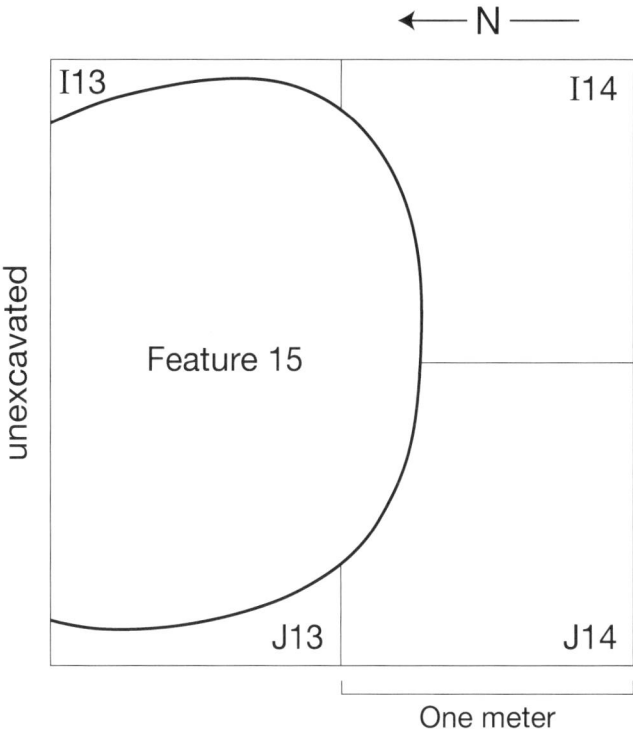

Figure 3.20. Plan view of Feature 15, a large but shallow hearth apparently originating in Zone E.

an outcrop near the limits of the roof overhang. In addition, as the Archaic strata neared the cave mouth their artifact content became increasingly meager.

Hole's second discovery was that intrusive Postclassic features seemed to be increasing in number as he moved west, further reducing the area of intact Archaic deposits. In addition to the large agave roasting pit (Feature 6), Hole found five more Postclassic features in the southwest quadrant of the cave. These were Feature 9 (a shallow hearth in Square J13), Feature 11 (a bell-shaped pit in Squares G14–G15 and H14–H15), and Features 13, 14, and 17 (small pits in Squares I14–I15 and J14–J15). As a result of these discoveries, it seemed that the point of diminishing returns for Archaic materials had been reached in this part of the cave.

Stage 6: The Northwest Quadrant

Hole next turned his attention to the block of squares isolated on the east by Squares E3–E8 of the north-south trench, and on the south by Squares F9–H9 of Flannery's initial test. Hole began F8, a square whose stratigraphy was exposed on two sides, on July 19; Genaro began Square F6 so that when he and Pablo were finished, Square F7 would have its stratigraphy exposed on three sides.

Figure 3.21. Squares F2–F4 and G2–G4, showing Feature 8, a Monte Albán V pottery kiln (see Figure 2.11). The rectangular opening of the flue connecting the kiln's two chambers can be seen.

Zones A and B in Square F8 looked much as they had in E8. Zone C, the uppermost Archaic living floor, was well preserved here but seemed to be thinning as it ran west. Near the east margin of F8, this stratum was 15–20 cm thick, but it gradually sloped upward and was reduced to 10 cm in thickness near its border with G8. Hole piece-plotted a very large spear point some 18 cm from the north edge of the square and 35 cm from the east.

Zones D and E of Square F8 yielded significant amounts of chert debitage. Hole continued down into Zone F, the indurated layer we now believed to be Late Pleistocene in age, finding abundant small rodent remains. We suspected that this microfauna had come from owl pellets and might be useful for reconstructing the Late Pleistocene environment.

Zone A in Square F6 proved to be complicated. In addition to the usual Postclassic debris, it produced a redeposited Hidalgo point that could be assigned to the Late Archaic on typological grounds. It also had a few redeposited sherds that we could assign to Monte Albán I. Genaro carefully isolated a large animal burrow, filled with bones, chaff, and sticks, which Hole designated Feature 7. This burrow reached only as deep as Zone B, since the animal had been unable to dig past the rocky rubble comprising this stratum. Additional Formative sherds were found among the loose rocks, suggesting that Zone B might be the ultimate source of the Monte Albán I pottery redeposited in Zone A.

Zone C in Square F6 produced an unclassifiable atlatl point fragment, some 45 cm from the north edge of the square and 12 cm from the west. Zones D and E were present in this square but produced little material; F was virtually sterile.

On July 20 Genaro excavated F7, the intervening square. Because F7 had been exposed on three sides and its stratigraphy was very clear, the excavation was almost problem-free. Only Zone B was more complex than usual, since it consisted of two facies: the usual firecracked rocks rested on a layer of gray ash that might have been shoveled out of the Feature 6 agave roasting pit.

Hole next turned his attention to Squares F3, F4, and F5, using Félix and Pablo as his trowelmen. Here he encountered the most interesting and complex feature of the entire excavation: a complete two-chambered pottery kiln of the Monte Albán V period, whose outer edge had already been revealed (and designated Feature 8) during the excavation of the adjacent Stage 6 squares.

Stage 7: Cleaning Up Feature 8

The Feature 8 kiln—cleaned and left in place by Hole over a three-day period—had disturbed Squares F2–F4 and G2–G4 so thoroughly that it was impossible to glean any information from the Archaic levels in that part of the cave.

This Monte Albán V kiln consisted of a pair of circular stone masonry chambers, each a meter in diameter, connected by a stone-lined flue some 70 cm long (see Figures 2.11, 3.21). While some of the stones used in construction were cobbles or boulders from the arroyo below the cave, others were reused metates and manos. The inside of each chamber had been plastered with a mixture of grass and clay, and all the chinks between the stones had been filled with adobe fragments, clay, and grass. There were enough fragments of adobe brick to suggest that the domed roof of each chamber might have been made of such material.

According to ceramicist William O. Payne (personal communication, 1968), this is the kind of indirect-firing kiln that could have maintained the even firing temperatures and reducing atmosphere necessary to produce the thin, well-made Monte Albán V gray ware known as G3M (Caso, Bernal, and Acosta 1967). The fuel would have been placed in one chamber and the pottery in another, with heated air moving from fuel to pottery through the flue. Once each batch of pottery had been fired, the adobe roof could be broken open and the vessels removed.

It would appear that Feature 8 was used almost exclusively to fire thin gray G3M globular jars (*ollas*) with pattern-burnished designs. A study of the Monte Albán V ceramics from Zone A of Cueva Blanca revealed more than 65,000 sherds of such jars, far exceeding the needs of the extended family who would have lived in the cave at that time (Moser n.d.). It is therefore likely that the people who occupied Zone A of Cueva Blanca were producing G3M ollas for the nearby town of Mitla.

Stage 8: Finishing the Northwest Quadrant

Having cleaned and pedestaled Feature 8, Hole began the delicate task of working around it on the west. This meant excavating all those parts of Squares G2–G8 that had not been affected by the kiln.

As it turned out, the entire northwest alcove of the cave had very little depth of deposit. Bedrock in Squares G2 and G3 was only 20 cm below the surface. In G4 and G5, despite sloping downward toward the center of the chamber, bedrock was still only 30–35 cm below the surface. The result was that the only stratum present in Squares G2–G3 was Zone A, while G4–G5 had only Zones A and B. Feature 10, an oval pit some 83 x 96 cm in diameter, spanned parts of Squares G4 and G5. Originating in Zone A, it had been dug to bedrock some 35 cm below the surface.

South of Square G5, bedrock dropped off steeply; it lay 95 cm below the surface in G6. In the latter square Genaro found the usual Zone B firecracked rocks, accompanied by 50 cm of ash. Zones C, D, and E were present in G6, but neither was particularly rich in chipped stone.

In Squares G7 and G8, Hole found the northern half of Feature 1, the large Postclassic storage pit whose south half had been exposed by Flannery's initial test squares. Hole excavated one final square—H8—in order to complete the exposure of this feature, which was 1.65 m in diameter. Because of the area disturbed by Feature 1, Zones C, D, and E were only intact in parts of Squares G7, G8, and H8. An atlatl point of the San Nicolás type had been redeposited in Zone B of Square G7, just outside Feature 1.

Work on this part of the cave was completed on July 23.

Stage 9: The Northeast Quadrant

During the last week of July, Hole began to excavate the block of six squares remaining in the northeast quadrant of the cave: B6–B8 and C4–C8. He began with C8 and moved northward, so that each square would have its stratigraphy exposed on two sides before it was excavated.

Genaro was the trowel man for Square C8. One of his first discoveries was a broken Archaic ovoid biface, redeposited in Zone A. It was clear that we were near the limits of Zone B in this part of the cave, since that layer consisted mainly of ashy gray fill with only a few firecracked rocks.

The Archaic levels were also thinning out in Square C8. Zone C in that square consisted almost exclusively of sterile white sand, the weathering product of the volcanic tuff cave wall. Zone D was still recognizable as a thick layer of tan ashy soil, yielding a complete atlatl point that did not conform to any of the Tehuacán types. This point was piece-plotted *in situ* some 13 cm from the north edge of the square and 35 cm from the east. Zone E was an ash-flecked layer only 10 cm in thickness, ending 1 m below the surface. Both Zones E and F were so indurated in this area that they had to be excavated with miners' digging bars.

Genaro moved next to Square C7. Here three Archaic atlatl points (La Mina, Gary, and Abasolo types) had been redeposited in the rocky rubble of Zone B. Zone C, while 25 cm thick in this square, consisted mostly of weathered material from the cave wall. Zone D, although still nicely sealed beneath C, also seemed to be reaching its eastern limits. On the west side of the square it was still soft and ashy, but as it ran east it began to turn into compact, white, disintegrated tuff. Hole piece-plotted a reworked La Mina point 50 cm from the south edge of the square and 7 cm from the east. Zone E, found between 85 and 105 cm below the surface, showed a mixture of ash, charcoal flecks, and volcanic tuff sand.

Once Genaro had begun C6, it was clear that it might be the last square in its row to produce much of a sample. As Hole's crew neared the north wall of the cave, all stratigraphic zones became poorer in artifacts, and the matrix became harder and more compact. Nevertheless, all three Archaic levels were still

Figure 3.22. In the foreground, Hole supervises don Juan (right) and Félix (left) while they excavate Square C11. At this stage, our excavation of the cave chamber was nearing completion.

present. In Zone D, Hole plotted a Variety A biface, some 55 cm from the north edge of the square and 70 cm from the east. Four scrapers of various types were found in association with the biface, raising the possibility that Hole had come upon a "drop zone" or activity area of some kind (see Chapter 14).

Squares C4 and C5, excavated by Félix, yielded little Archaic material, even though all three Archaic strata were present in those squares. Perhaps the best preserved stratum was Zone D, composed of tan ash that gradually sloped upward as it neared the cave wall. In Square C5, Félix piece-plotted a broken Palmillas point and a Variety C biface and collected some charcoal for radiocarbon dating.

The last three squares in this block—B6, B7, and B8—were all partially truncated by the back wall of the cave. Although all three Archaic strata were present, they yielded few items. Two Hidalgo points, however, had been redeposited in the Postclassic levels of those squares. One was found among the firecracked rocks of Zone B in Square B7; the other was found at the bottom of Zone A in Square B8. Zone B also produced Feature 16, an apparent ash dump, which occupied parts of Squares B7 and B8.

Once all the squares in this northeast quadrant had been dug, several aspects of the depositional history of the cave became clear. First, all the Archaic living floors reached their greatest depth near the center of the cave chamber and were shallower near the margins, where each living floor had to pass over a talus of white sand weathered from the cave walls. Second, given the low cave ceiling in the northeast quadrant, it would have been impossible to stand upright in most of the B6–B9 squares once Zone D had been deposited.

Stage 10: Finishing the Last Squares

By July 30, only a few squares with readable Archaic stratigraphy were left in Cueva Blanca. Squares B10 and B11 took Hole to the back wall of the cave; the deposits were so shallow that only Zone A was present.

Hole then continued along the south wall of the cave chamber until Squares C11, D12, F14, and G15 had been completed (Figure 3.22). While all three Archaic strata tended to be present in those squares, they merged with the talus of indurated white sand sloping down from the cave wall and were relatively poor in artifacts. It also turned out that the original bedrock cave floor was basin-shaped and sloped upward to meet the south wall, greatly reducing the volume of deposit there. In Square F14, Hole found no Zone E at all.

Finally, convinced that there was no point in continuing the excavation westward toward the dripline of the cave mouth, Hole closed down the operation with 75 complete squares and a few partial squares excavated. While Zone A appeared to continue out onto the talus of the cave, the Archaic strata were fading at that point. Also, the area west of Squares H8–H12 appeared to be full of intrusive Postclassic features and was much wetter than the center of the chamber. Hole therefore packed up his equipment and went back to the Frissell Museum in Mitla to wash and analyze the chipped stone tools.

4

The Radiocarbon Dates from Cueva Blanca

Kent V. Flannery

Eighteen radiocarbon dates are currently available from Cueva Blanca. All are based on wood charcoal collected during the excavation of the cave in 1966. It should be remembered that in that year, neither AMS dating nor modern calibration was available. In those days, radiocarbon laboratories wanted us to provide them with 8–10 grams of charcoal for each date, and that is the size of the samples we submitted. This requirement made it difficult to come up with samples from Zones F and C at Cueva Blanca; those strata did have charcoal flecks, but most of them were the size of a period in 12-point type. In 1966, few of us imagined that it would ever be possible to date such a tiny speck of charcoal.

The first dates run on Cueva Blanca charcoal were done by radiocarbon labs at the Smithsonian Institution (SI) and the University of Michigan (M). These were conventional dates in years before the present, and we determined the BC date by subtracting 1950 from the BP date. Neither of these laboratories exists today.

We later had Geochron Labs (Gx) run two additional samples, once again settling for conventional dates. Neither date was calibrated.

In 1995, as part of Bruce Smith's research into the chronology of early plant domestication in the Valley of Oaxaca (B. D. Smith 1997, 2001), he and I had Beta Analytic (Beta) run eight additional dates on charcoal collected at Cueva Blanca in 1966. I am grateful to Smith for his help in refining the Archaic sequence in Oaxaca.

Finally, in 2017, Darden Hood of Beta Analytic generously agreed to calibrate all 18 dates from Cueva Blanca, including the old Smithsonian, Michigan, and Geochron dates. He did this using the latest program available, IntCal13 (Reimer et al. 2013). We are very appreciative of Hood's contribution to our Archaic chronology.

Problems with the Cueva Blanca Samples

We are aware of at least two problems inherent in our Cueva Blanca charcoal samples. The first has to do with what European archaeologists refer to as "the old wood problem." Suzanne Harris of the University of Michigan's Laboratory of Ethnobotany analyzed a number of charcoal fragments from Cueva Blanca. She found evidence of pine, oak, acacia, and baldcypress, and additional taxa that could not be identified owing to a lack of comparative material. Our first problem is that different trees live to different ages. The branch of a young pine tree may be only 10 years old; oaks can live 100 years or more; baldcypress can live beyond 1000 years. Such differences in longevity can produce substantial variation in dates from the same stratum.

A second problem is the redeposition of older charcoal in younger levels. The occupants of Cueva Blanca created hearths, storage pits, an agave roasting pit, and a large kiln. Every time they excavated one of these features into an earlier stratum, they ran the risk of digging up earlier charcoal or artifacts and redepositing them in a later stratum. We know from the number of Archaic atlatl points redeposited in Zones A and B that this actually happened.

We note that our deepest Archaic level (Zone E) and deepest Archaic feature (Feature 15) show no evidence of redeposited charcoal. The farther up the stratigraphic column one goes, however, the greater the likelihood of redeposition. Two of the six radiocarbon samples from Zone D/Feature 18 appear to be redeposited. In Zone A, half the radiocarbon dates (one of two) appear to be on redeposited charcoal.

Because of these problems, we have chosen not to average the dates from any stratigraphic level (see Bronk Ramsey 2009). It makes no sense to us to average dates on trees of different ages, or to average redeposited charcoal with *in situ* charcoal.

Zone F

Zone F, the Pleistocene stratum at the base of the stratigraphic column, contained only tiny specks of charcoal, none of which were large enough to date according to 1966 requirements. We eventually submitted the distal humerus of a deer from Zone F to see whether it could be dated (Figure 4.1). Unfortunately, we learned that so little organic material remained in the bone that it could not be dated. This may mean that the bones in Zone F were semifossilized.

Feature 15

Feature 15, a broad but shallow cooking pit, appeared to have been dug down from Zone E. Its charcoal fragments produced three very consistent radiocarbon dates.

SI-511, a Smithsonian date, came out 10,910 ± 80 BP. Subtracting 1950 produces a conventional date of 8960 BC ± 80. When this date is calibrated, there is a 95.4% probability that the true date falls between 11,037 and 10,745 cal. BC.

SI-511 R was a date run on additional charcoal left over from the running of Sample SI-511. It came out 10,730 ± 220 BP, and subtracting 1950 gives us a conventional date of 8780 BC ± 220. When this date is calibrated, there is a 95.4% probability that the true date falls between 11,132 and 10,090 cal. BC.

M-2094, a Michigan date, came out 11,000 ± 400 BP. Subtracting 1950 produces a conventional date of 9050 BC ± 400. When this date is calibrated, there is a 95.4% probability that the true date falls between 11,810 and 9870 cal. BC.

Not only are these three dates internally consistent, they are unexpectedly early. Calibrated dates falling in the millennium

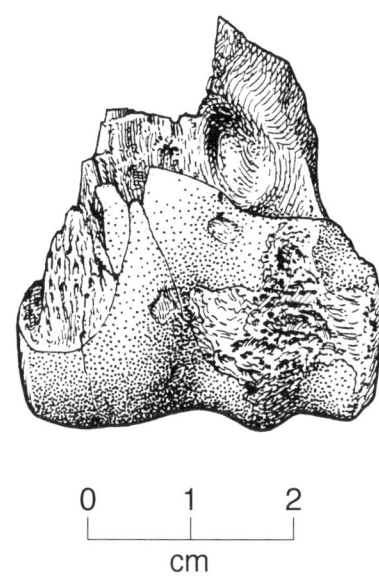

Figure 4.1. The left distal humerus of a white-tailed deer from Zone F of Cueva Blanca (Square G11). There was insufficient organic material left in this bone to provide a radiocarbon date.

between 11,000 and 10,000 BC could be considered Terminal Pleistocene, or dating to the Pleistocene-Holocene transition. They make us wonder how old Zone F might be.

Zone E

All four radiocarbon samples from Zone E provided us with conventional dates in the 8100–7430 BC range. This grouping of four dates places Zone E in the Early Archaic.

Beta-82191, from Square I13, came out 9380 ± 130 BP. Subtracting 1950 produces a conventional date of 7430 BC ± 130. When this date is calibrated, there is an 83.1% probability that the true date falls between 8941 and 8304 cal. BC.

Beta-82189, from Square E3, came out 9830 ± 100 BP. Subtracting 1950 produces a conventional date of 7880 BC ± 100. When this date is calibrated, there is a 90% probability that the true date falls between 9696 and 9121 cal. BC.

Beta-82190, from Square I13, came out 9840 ± 90 BP. Subtracting 1950 produces a conventional date of 7890 BC ± 90. When this date is calibrated, there is a 93.8% probability that the true date falls between 9675 and 9136 cal. BC.

M-2093, from Square D8, came out 10,050 ± 350 BP. Subtracting 1950 produces a conventional date of 8100 BC ± 350. When this date is calibrated, there is a 95.4% probability that the true date falls between 10,718 and 8761 cal. BC.

Given the possibility that the charcoal used for our Zone E dates came from trees of different ages, we are pleased with the consistency of the results. We note, however, that both the conventional and calibrated dates for Feature 15 are slightly older than the dates for Zone E. We did not expect this to happen, given the fact that there was no visible disconformity between the two proveniences; Feature 15 appears to have been created by the occupants of Zone E. Since there are a number of plausible explanations for the different dates, we will not put too fine a point on it. We have acknowledged the fact that trees live to different ages. We also know that any stratum in a cave can, in fact, result from multiple visits whose remains coalesce over time, owing to the weight of overburden (see discussion of Zone B of Guilá Naquitz Cave in Flannery 2009a:87–89).

Zone D

Six radiocarbon dates are available for Zone D; two of them appear to reflect charcoal redeposited from Zone E. Let us begin with the four we believe to date Zone D.

Beta-82186, from Square E13, came out 4290 ± 50 BP. Subtracting 1950 produces a conventional date of 2340 BC ± 50. When this date is calibrated, there is an 86% probability that the true date falls between 3028 and 2861 cal. BC.

M-2092, from Square E13, came out 4750 ± 190 BP. Subtracting 1950 produces a conventional date of 2800 BC ± 190. When this date is calibrated, there is a 95.4% probability that the true date falls between 3961 and 3013 cal. BC.

Beta-82187, from Square E6, came out 5010 ± 60 BP. Subtracting 1950 produces a conventional date of 3060 BC ± 60. When this date is calibrated, there is a 93.2% probability that the true date falls between 3953 and 3694 cal. BC.

Gx-0782 was run on charcoal from **Feature 18**, a hearth that appears to have been created by the occupants of Zone D. This date came out 5245 ± 105 BP. Subtracting 1950 produces a conventional date of 3295 BC ± 105. When this date is calibrated, there is an 89.1% probability that the true date falls between 4330 and 3915 cal. BC.

We note that our three conventional dates from Zone D are grouped into a 700-year span, and their calibrated ranges are no more widely separated. Just as we saw with Feature 15 and Zone E, Feature 18 came out a bit older than Zone D, though its calibrated range overlaps with those of two of the Zone D dates.

What these four dates make clear is that Zone D dates to the Late Archaic. Stated differently, there seems to have been a hiatus of at least 4000 conventional radiocarbon years between Zone E and Zone D.

Now let us examine the two dates we believe were run on redeposited charcoal.

Beta-82188, from Square C7, came out 9230 ± 150 BP. Subtracting 1950 produces a conventional date of 7280 BC ± 150. When this date is calibrated, there is a 91.2% probability that the true date falls between 8862 and 8187 cal. BC.

SI-512, from Square C5, came out 9470 ± 190 BP. Subtracting 1950 produces a conventional date of 7520 BC ± 190. When this date is calibrated, there is a 95.4% probability that the true date falls between 9265 and 8316 cal. BC.

Both of these dates fall comfortably within the span of our four Zone E radiocarbon determinations. We believe them to be based on charcoal from Zone E, redeposited when the occupants of Zone D created intrusive pits (such as Feature 18).

Zone C

Zone C, despite its sample of Archaic atlatl points and one-hand manos, simply did not produce much in the way of radiocarbon samples. Scattered throughout the stratum were tiny flecks of charcoal, almost none of them large enough to satisfy the requirements of dating in 1966. In the 1990s, when it had become possible to date smaller samples, we submitted a small piece of charcoal from Zone C to Beta Analytic. The results suggest that it was redeposited.

Beta-82185, from Square B6, came out 7610 ± 80 BP. Subtracting 1950 produces a conventional date of 5660 BC ± 80. When this date is calibrated, there is a 91.9% probability that the true date falls between 6636 and 6352 cal. BC.

Since Zone C is stratigraphically above Zone D, this date cannot be accurate. Based on the types of atlatl points we found, we believe that both Zones D and C are contemporaneous with the Abejas phase of the Tehuacán Valley. Conventional radiocarbon assays date this phase to 3400–2300 BC. Based on the tree ring data available in the late 1960s, Johnson and MacNeish (1972:5) proposed a date (adjusted to "sidereal time") of 4150–2850 BC for Abejas.

Both the conventional and "sidereal" dates for the Abejas phase correlate well with our dates from Zone D and Feature 18. Date Beta-82185, therefore, likely represents redeposited charcoal.

Zone B

We knew from the beginning that dating the firecracked rock layer known as Zone B would be problematic. What we did, therefore, was to take our charcoal samples from the interface of Zones C and B, hoping that by so doing we might indirectly date Zone C. Unfortunately, both samples from the C–B interface appear to have come from Zone B.

Beta-82184, from Square E6, came out 2390 ± 60 BP. Subtracting 1950 produces a conventional date of 440 BC ± 60. When this date is calibrated, there is a 79% probability that the true date falls between 671 and 382 cal. BC. This is a Monte Albán I date, which makes sense to us, since Monte Albán I sherds were found in Zone B.

Gx-0874, from Square E6, came out 2745 ± 90 BP. Subtracting 1950 produces a conventional date of 795 BC ± 90.

When this date is calibrated, there is a 94.3% probability that the true date falls between 1130 and 778 cal. BC. This is a late Early Formative or early Middle Formative date, which seems reasonable, since sherds of that age were also found in Zone B.

Zone A

Owing to the thousands of Monte Albán V sherds in Zone A, we had few doubts about the date of that stratum. Of the two Zone A charcoal samples we submitted, however, one yielded an acceptable Postclassic date and one appears to have been on redeposited charcoal.

SI-510, from Square E6, came out 520 ± 50 BP. Subtracting this from 1950 produces a conventional date of AD 1430 ± 50. When this date is calibrated, there is a 65.7% probability that the true date falls between 1383 and 1452 cal. AD, and a 29.7% probability that the true date falls between 1304 and 1365 cal. AD. Regardless which calibration you choose, this is an acceptable Monte Albán V date.

M-2091, from Square E9, came out 1330 ± 130 BP. Subtracting this from 1950 produces a conventional date of AD 620 ± 130. When this date is calibrated, there is a 90% probability that the true date falls between 526 and 980 cal. AD.

This date falls in Monte Albán IIIb–IV, a period from which no sherds were found during our excavation of Zone A. While the charcoal used for M-2091 appears to have been redeposited, we are unsure of its original place of origin. It is possible that the cave was visited briefly during Monte Albán IIIb–IV, only to have the remains from that visit disturbed, scattered, and redeposited when the layer of firecracked rock was created.

Part II

The Artifacts

5

The Chipped Stone Tools

Frank Hole

We recovered more than 400 chipped stone tools and 2700 pieces of debitage from Zones E, D, and C of Cueva Blanca. Included among the tools were atlatl points, bifaces of three varieties, end scrapers, sidescrapers/knives, choppers/knives, steep denticulate scrapers, utilized flakes, notched flakes, flakes with sheen, burins, and drills. While varied, the chipped stone industry of Archaic Oaxaca can probably best be described as "expedient," with a great many flakes used "as is" or with minimal modification. Since lengthier descriptions of all these Archaic tool types can be found in Hole (2009), I present shorter versions here.

In addition to the hundreds of tools recovered from the three Archaic strata, scores of additional Archaic tools were found redeposited among the loose rocks in Zone B. These tools could easily be recognized as Archaic because they contrasted with the artifacts typical of the Postclassic period. When appropriate, we drew and photographed these redeposited tools to increase our sample of Archaic artifacts.

We see at least two reasons why so many Archaic tools were redeposited in Zone B. One reason is that the Postclassic occupants of the cave dug pits into the earlier strata, inevitably recovering Archaic artifacts. Perhaps an even more compelling reason is that the creators of Zone B appear to have collected hundreds of stones with which to line a large agave roasting pit (Feature 6). The stones they gathered for this purpose evidently included scores of Archaic tools from the surface and talus of the cave. Especially useful for lining Feature 6 were larger tools such as steep denticulate scrapers and choppers/knives. Many of these Archaic tools showed the effects of the heat they endured while lining the agave roasting pit.

Archaic tools were also redeposited in Zone A, whose occupants dug numbers of storage pits. Nowhere, however, were redeposited artifacts as numerous as among the loose stones of Zone B.

Sources of Raw Material

The raw material used for the chipped stone tools at Cueva Blanca included chert, flint, chalcedony, secondarily silicified volcanic tuffs (ignimbrites and rhyolites), and a secondarily silicified sedimentary rock tentatively identified as siltstone. Virtually all of this raw material would have been available within a two- or three-day round trip from the cave.

Cueva Blanca lies in a region of volcanic tuff foothills and mesas to the north of the Río Mitla. There are veins of silicified tuff throughout this area. Many watercourses near the cave display cobbles of silicified raw material, which survives in stream beds because it is more durable than ordinary tuff. The so-called Mitla

Fortress, a rocky mesa one kilometer east of the cave, was a known prehistoric quarry for silicified tuff (Holmes 1897, Williams and Heizer 1965).

Five to seven kilometers southwest of Cueva Blanca, in the foothills on the opposite side of the Río Mitla, is an area of sandstones and marls (Whalen 2009: Figure 7.1). There are veins of silicified sedimentary rock here that could also be used as raw material.

Silicified tuffs and sedimentary rocks were suitable for many of the tools used at Cueva Blanca. When Archaic knappers wanted to make atlatl points, however, they often turned to higher quality cherts and chalcedonies. These raw materials came from father away, but still within the valley.

A useful summary of the valley's chert and chalcedony sources can be found in Whalen (2009). Flints and cherts of average quality occur in the limestone formations of Rojas de Cuauhtémoc, some 25 kilometers northwest of the Mitla caves. By far the highest quality raw material, however, was available 45–55 kilometers away, in the Etla subvalley. The best of these sources is a limestone cliff known as the Peña de Matadamas, located almost directly across the Atoyac River from the Formative site of San José Mogote. Running through this limestone are veins of waxy chalcedony, varying in color from white to bluish-white, grayish-white, or brownish-white (Whalen 2009:143).

Foragers from Cueva Blanca could have reached the Matadamas quarries by walking for a day and a half. They could then have camped there, preparing dozens of bifacial roughouts for later conversion into points, and returned to Cueva Blanca in another day and a half. Some of the finest atlatl points we recovered were made of Matadamas chalcedony.

It is worth noting that we did not find a single piece of obsidian in the Archaic strata. This stands in strong contrast to the Postclassic levels at Cueva Blanca, where obsidian was common.

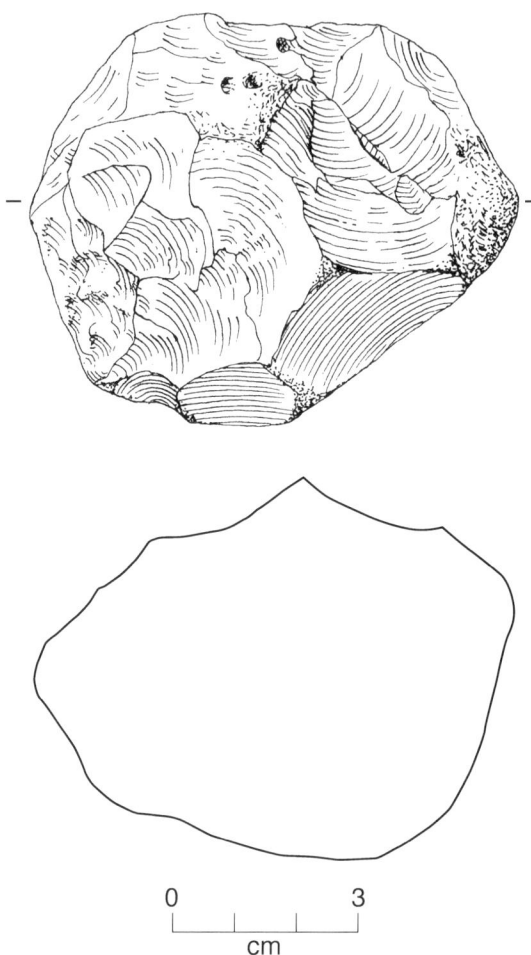

Figure 5.1. A hammerstone from Zone D (Square H9).

Tools for Basic Flake Production

Hammerstones

Hammerstones (Figures 5.1, 5.2) are chunks of silicified volcanic tuff or chert, battered while being used as a hammer. While some of our hammerstones may have been used for pounding plant foods or breaking marrow bones, the battering on others suggests that they were used for percussion flaking, including the striking of primary flakes from cores.

Typical flake cores

Flake cores (Figures 5.3, 5.4) are chunks of silicified volcanic tuff or chert that have one or more platforms from which flakes of a usable size have been struck. Flake cores can usually be distinguished from steep denticulate scrapers by the fact that the

Figure 5.2. A typical Archaic hammerstone.

latter do not show flake scars large enough to have produced the kinds of flakes used as tools during the Oaxaca Archaic.

Discoidal cores

Discoidal cores (Figure 5.5) have been roughly chipped around their edges, usually bifacially, resulting in a sinuous edge that recalls the manner in which Paleolithic hand-axes were flaked.

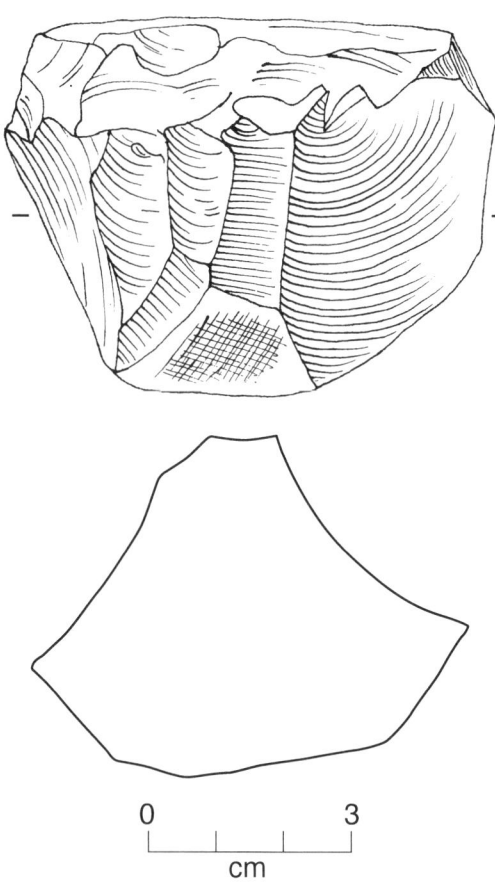

Figure 5.4. A typical Archaic flake core, redeposited in Zone B.

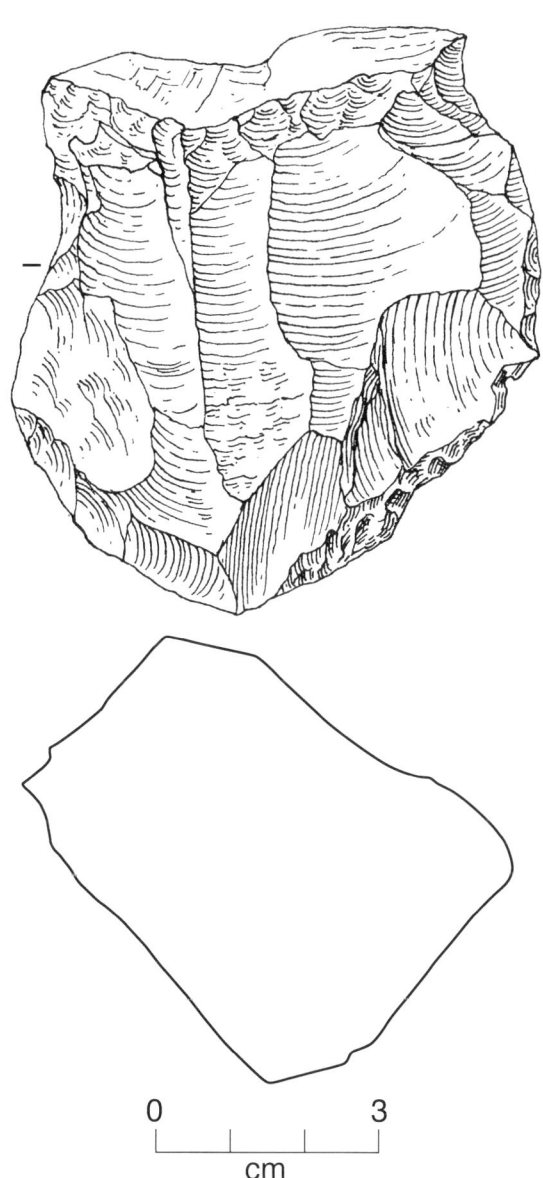

Figure 5.3 (above). A typical Archaic flake core from Zone C (Square D11).

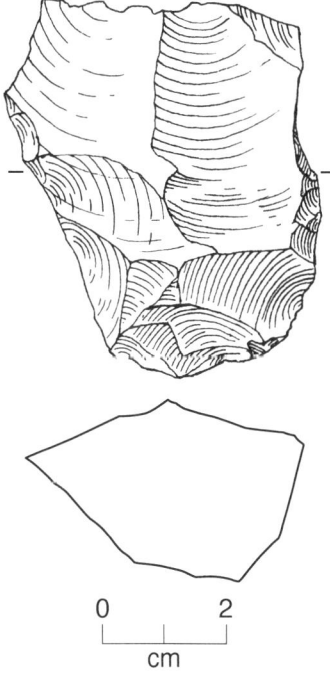

Figure 5.5. A discoidal core from Zone D (Square D6).

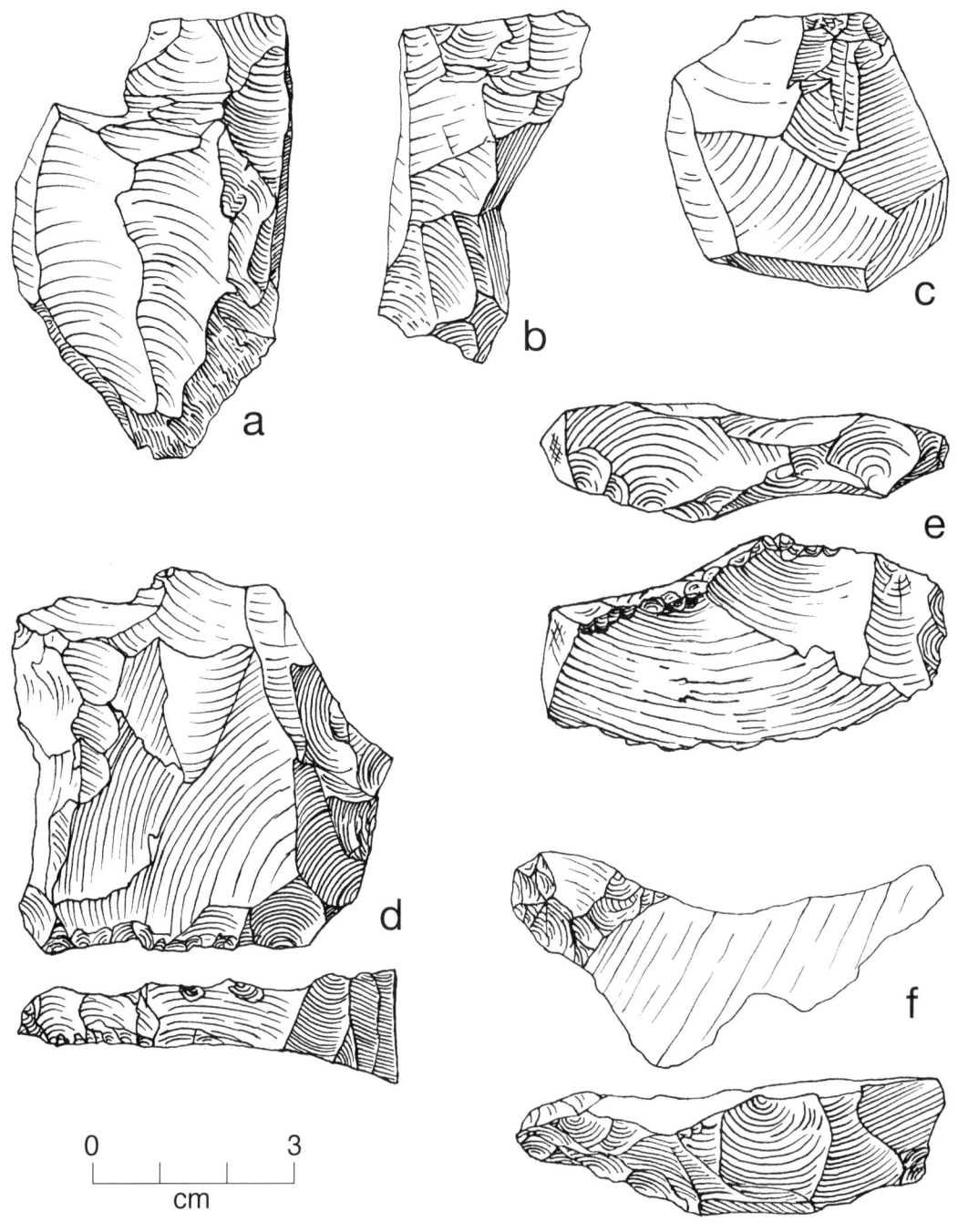

Figure 5.6. Fragments of Archaic cores, redeposited in Zone B. *a–c*, core faces. *d*, core tablet. *e*, *f*, core platform edges.

Figure 5.7 (opposite page). A large utilized flake.

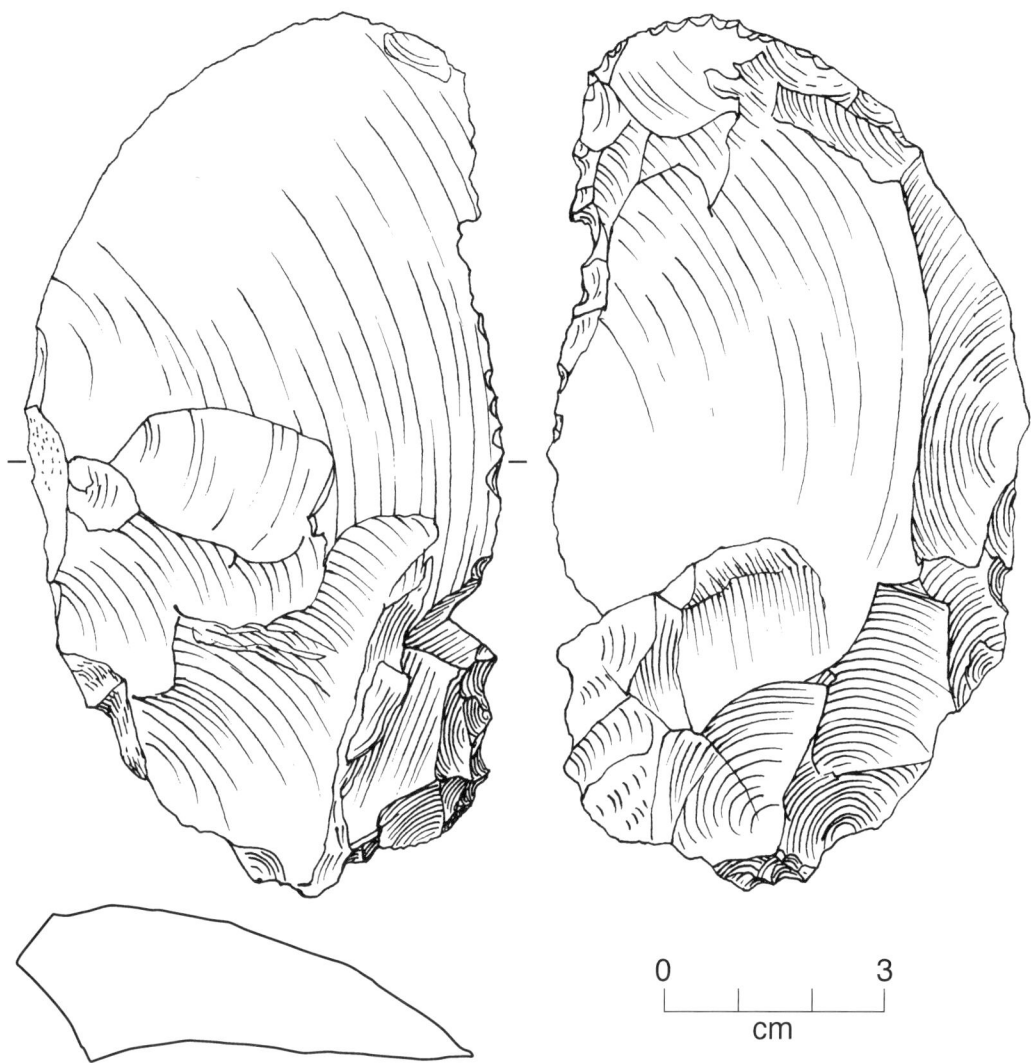

Core faces

Core faces (Figure 5.6 *a–c*) are fragments from the sides of flake cores, removed by a blow directed down from the platform. The blow occurred far enough back from the edge of the platform to remove the whole face of the core rather than just one flake.

Core edges

A core edge (Figure 5.6 *e, f*) is defined as the edge of a striking platform, removed (in almost all cases) by a blow directed from the side of the core rather than from above.

Core tablets

A core tablet (Figure 5.6 *d*) is defined as the upper portion of a flake core that has been removed by a blow parallel to the plane of the striking platform. While no core tablets were found *in situ* in Zones E–C, several had been redeposited in Zone B.

Debitage

This category includes all these fragments of chipped stone that do not show any signs of retouch (whether caused deliberately or by use) and that cannot be identified as being a specific part of a core. I hesitate to refer to these as "waste flakes," since some fragments are naturally sharp enough to have been used for light cutting tasks.

Flake tools

Many of the chipped stone tools at Cueva Blanca were flakes that had been modified minimally or by use alone. The six main categories are listed below.

Utilized flakes

Utilized flakes (Figures 5.7, 5.8) are flakes or chunks of silicified tuff, sedimentary rock, or chert that have light, shallow chipping

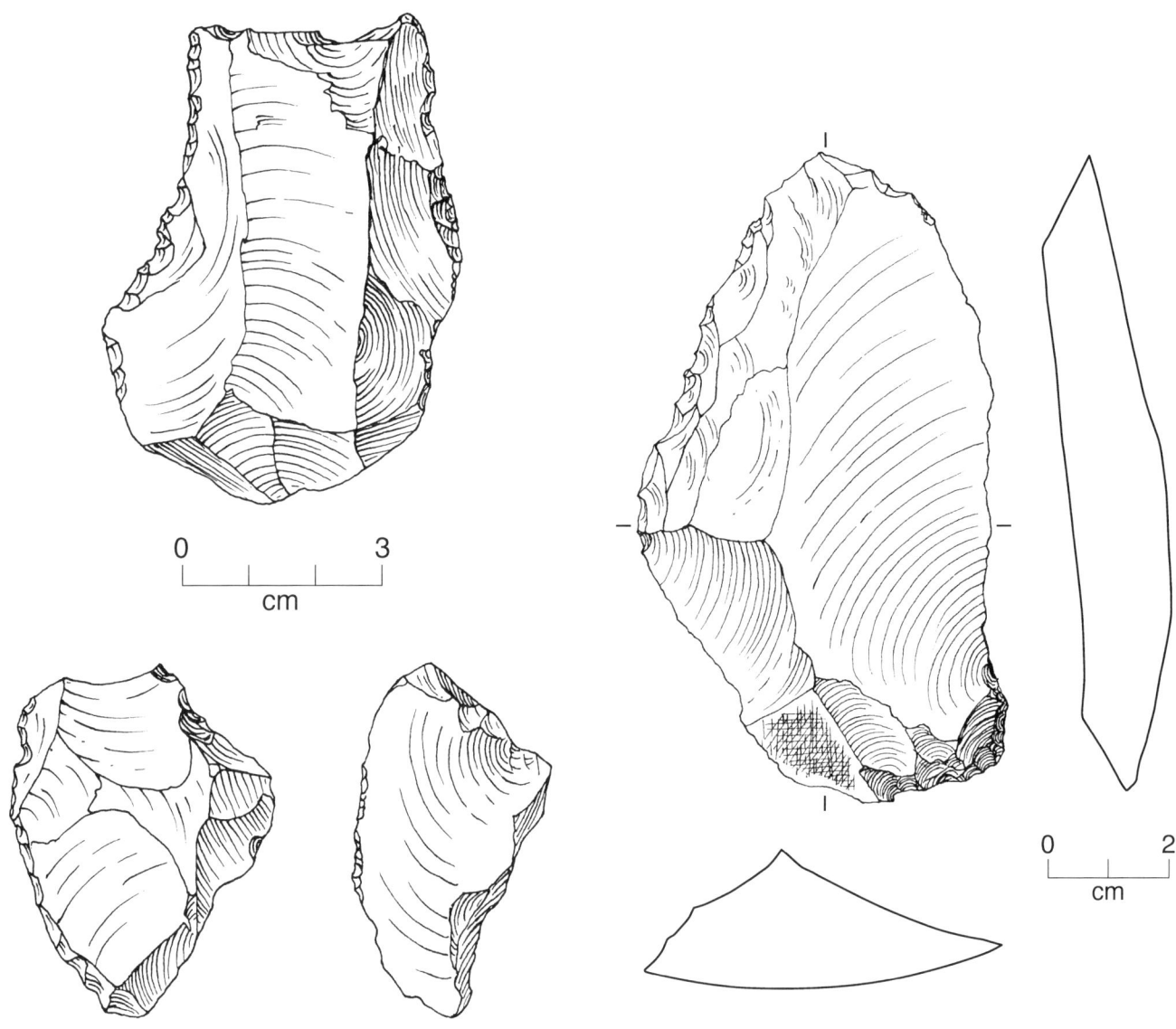

Figure 5.8. Small to medium-sized utilized flakes.

Figure 5.9. A large notched flake, discovered *in situ* in Zone D (Square D5).

limited to part of an edge. In view of the irregular occurrence of the chipping, it appears to have resulted from light use. Just as at Guilá Naquitz (Hole 2009), it appears that the Archaic occupants of Cueva Blanca simply picked up whatever conveniently shaped flake they found when cutting was required.

Notched flakes

These flakes (Figures 5.9–5.12) may be of any size or shape and have one or more notches chipped into an edge. The chipping that produced the notch may have been either deliberate or caused by use on a hard material. Some flakes, in fact, show both purposeful notches and those caused by use. Some of the most deliberately notched flakes may have been spokeshaves.

Crude blades, plain

In the course of removing flakes from their cores, Archaic knappers occasionally struck off flakes that were at least twice as long as they were wide, and had relatively parallel sides (Figures

Figure 5.11 (right). Small to medium-sized notched flakes. *a* was discovered *in situ* in Zone D (Square C8). *b* and *c* were redeposited in Zone B.

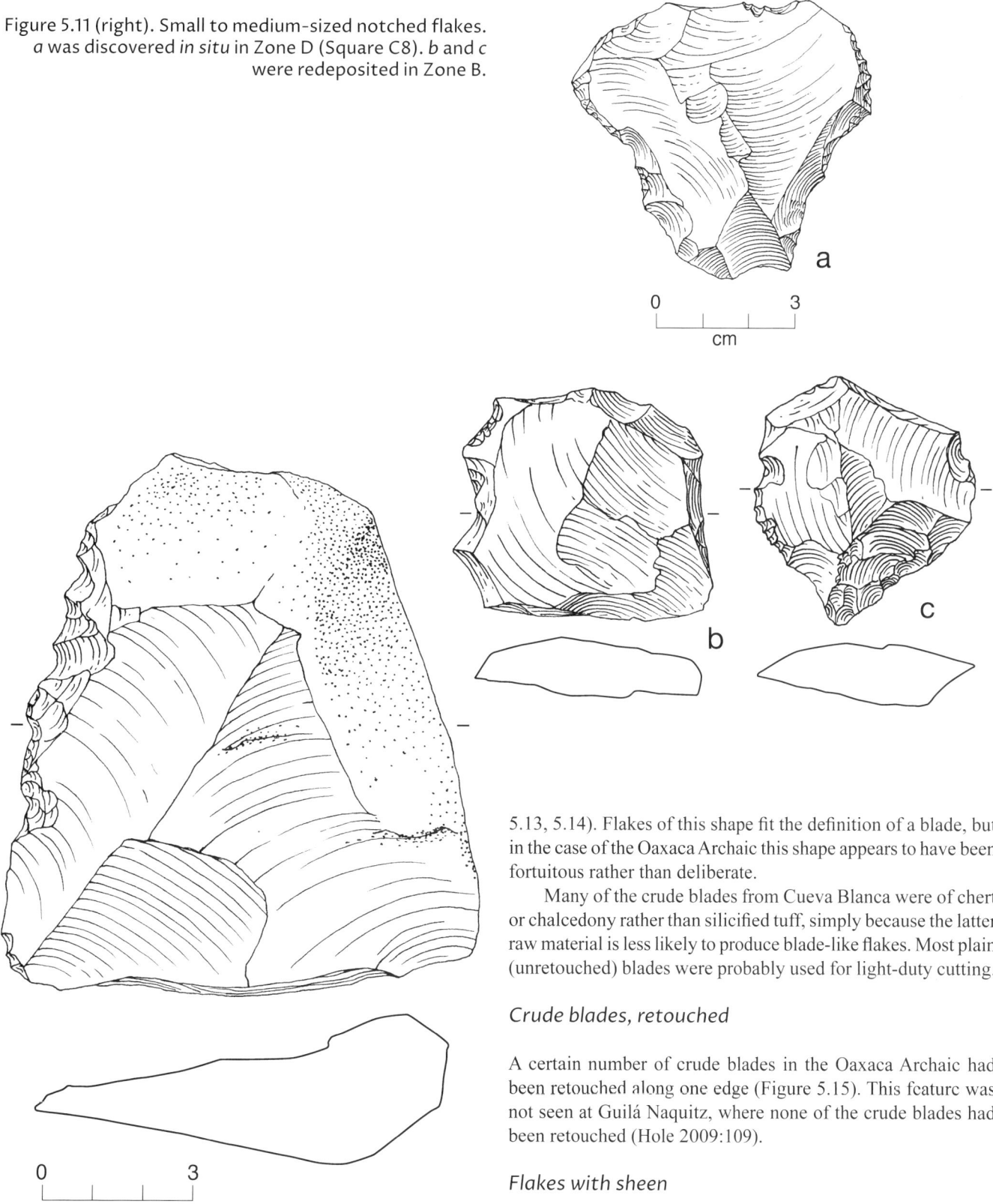

5.13, 5.14). Flakes of this shape fit the definition of a blade, but in the case of the Oaxaca Archaic this shape appears to have been fortuitous rather than deliberate.

Many of the crude blades from Cueva Blanca were of chert or chalcedony rather than silicified tuff, simply because the latter raw material is less likely to produce blade-like flakes. Most plain (unretouched) blades were probably used for light-duty cutting.

Crude blades, retouched

A certain number of crude blades in the Oaxaca Archaic had been retouched along one edge (Figure 5.15). This feature was not seen at Guilá Naquitz, where none of the crude blades had been retouched (Hole 2009:109).

Flakes with sheen

This category consists of flakes with a glossy sheen on one or more edges (Figures 5.16–5.18). As at Guilá Naquitz, one possible cause of this sheen was the prolonged and repetitive

Figure 5.10. A large notched flake, redeposited in Zone B.

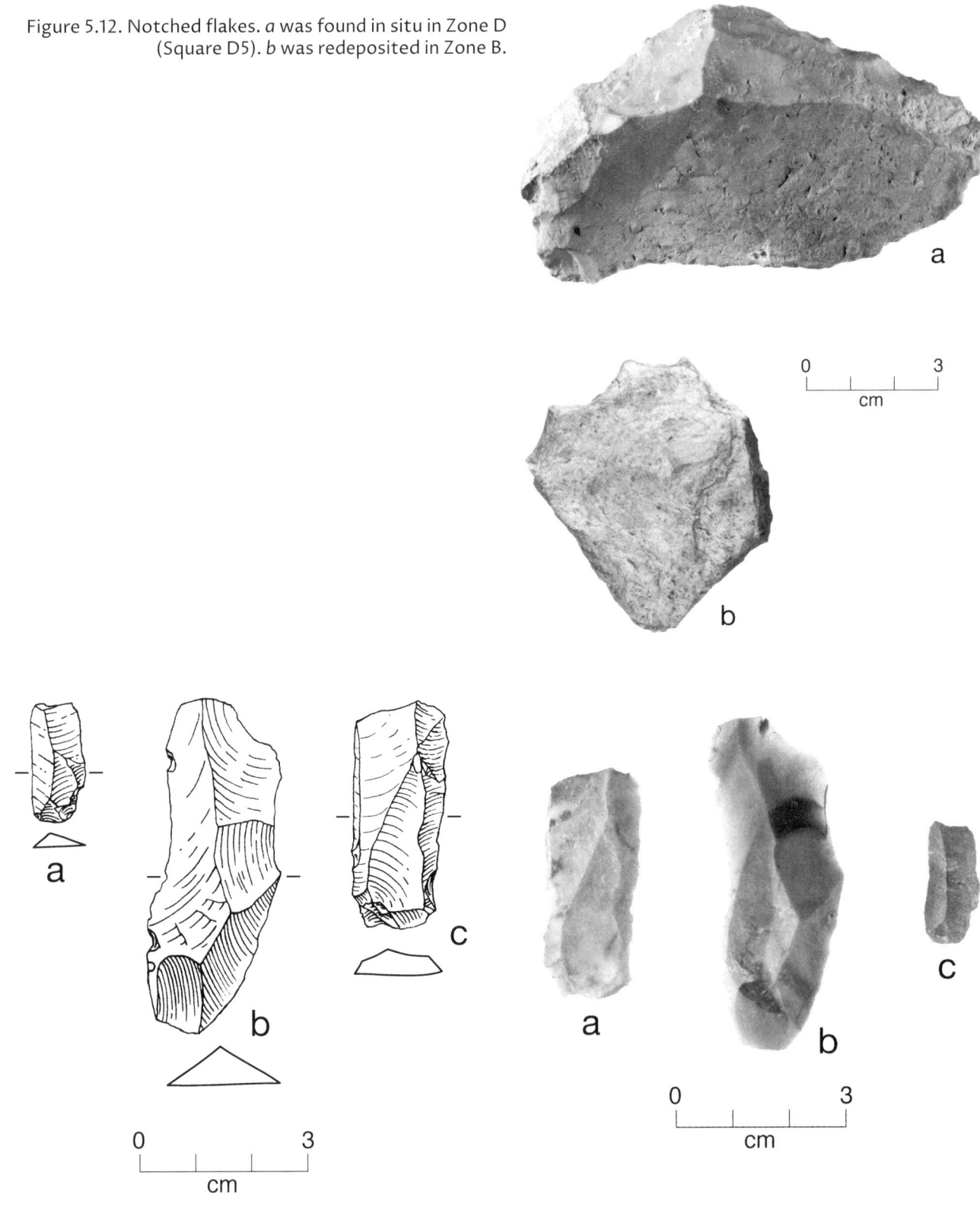

Figure 5.12. Notched flakes. *a* was found in situ in Zone D (Square D5). *b* was redeposited in Zone B.

Figure 5.13. Crude blades, plain, discovered *in situ* in Zones E, D, and C. *a*, Zone E (Square E6). *b*, Zone D (Square E8). *c*, Zone C (Square H13).

Figure 5.14. Crude blades from Archaic strata. *a* is from Zone C (Square H13). *b* is from Zone D (Square E8). *c* is from Zone E (Square E6).

The Chipped Stone Tools 67

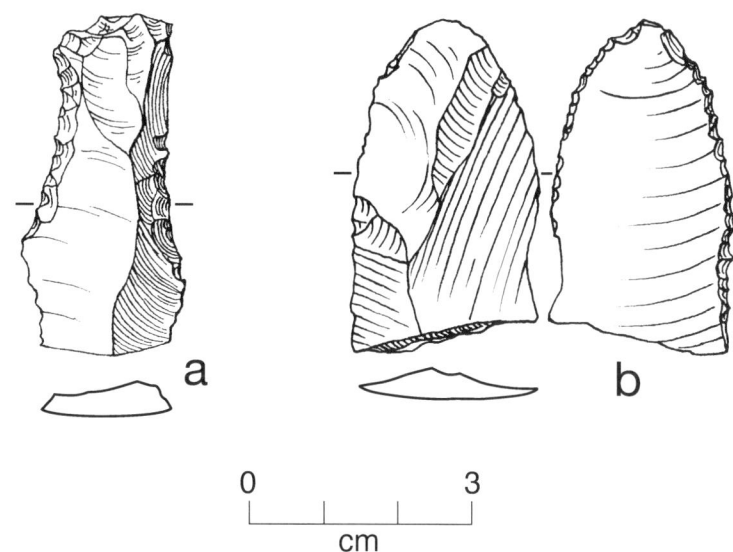

Figure 5.15. Crude blades, retouched. *a* was found *in situ* in Zone E (Square E10). *b* was redeposited in Zone B.

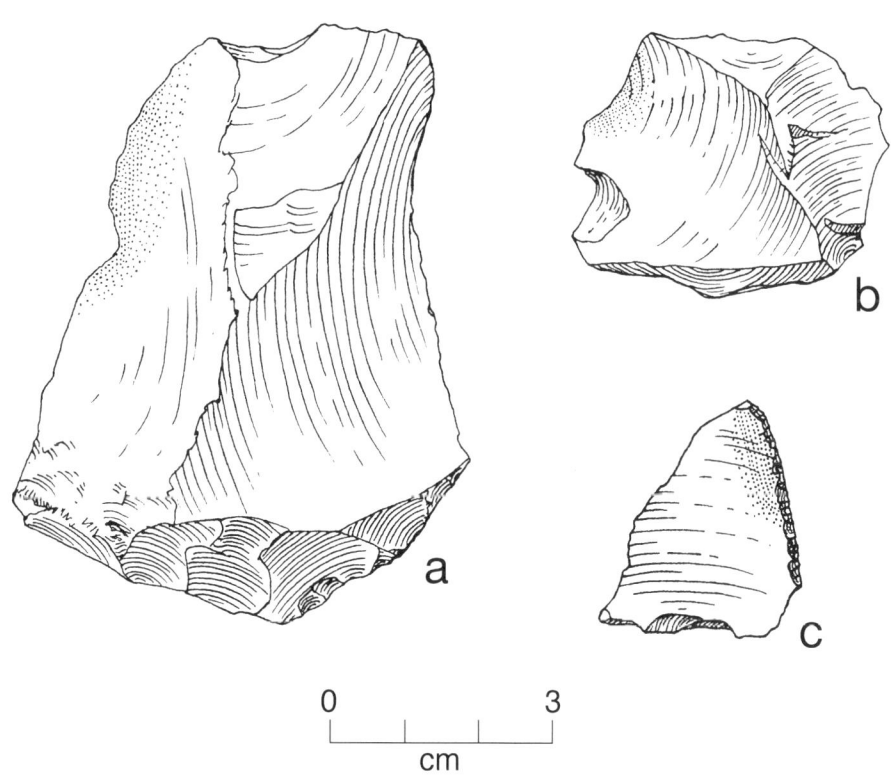

Figure 5.16. Flakes with sheen, discovered *in situ* in Zones E, D, and F. The area of sheen is indicated by stipple. *a*, Zone C (Square C7). *b*, Zone D (Square E13). *c*, Zone E (Square G12).

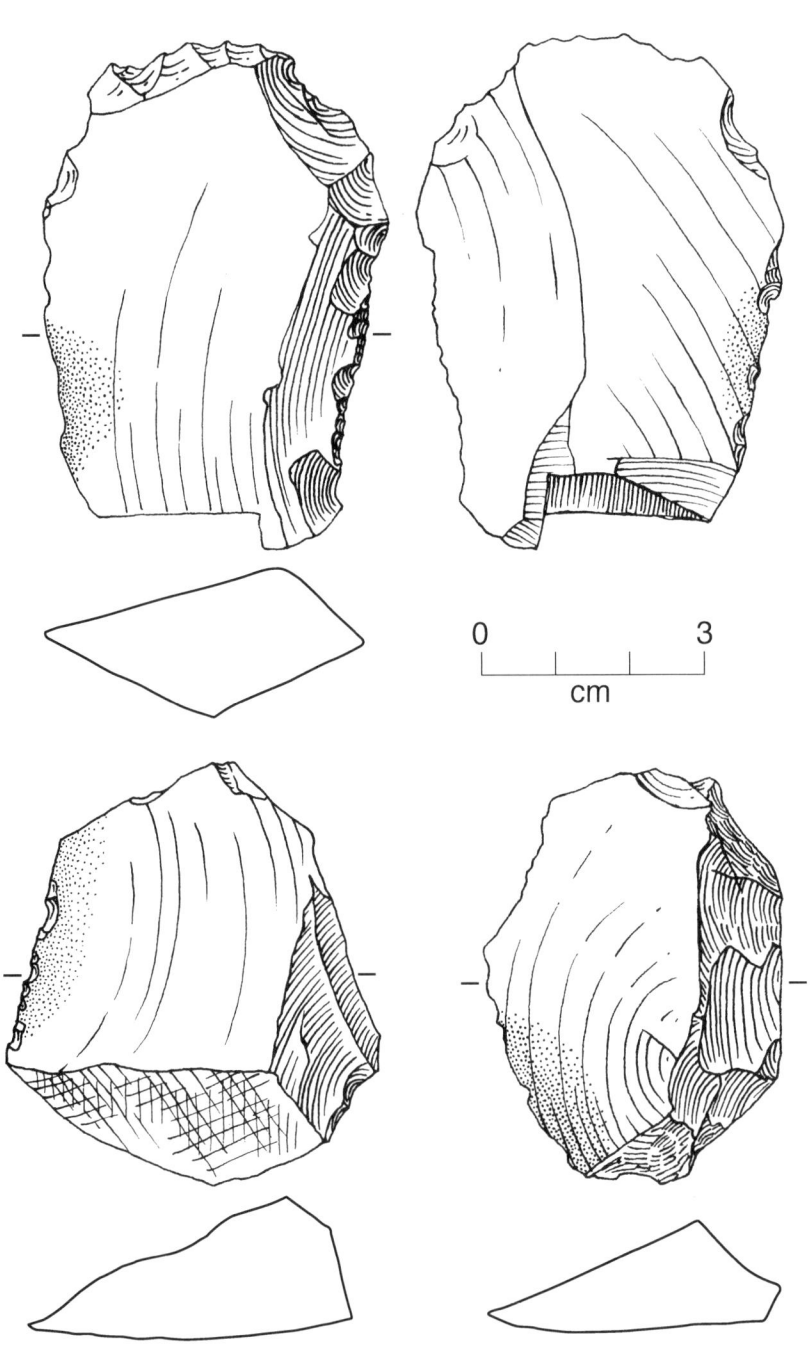

Figure 5.17. Typical Archaic flakes with sheen, redeposited in Zone B. The area of sheen is indicated by stipple.

Figure 5.18. A flake with sheen, found *in situ* in Zone C (Square C7). An area of sheen can be observed on the left edge of the flake.

trimming of the leaves from an agave heart prior to roasting. In the process of sawing through the tough, fibrous leaves, any flake would be subject to a great deal of abrasion. In addition, since the heart of an agave must be dug from the ground, its leaf bases tend to be covered with sandy earth that increases the likelihood of abrasion (Hole 2009:111–112).

Polished flakes

These flakes were used for cutting or scraping long enough to have developed a perceptible beveling or smoothing of an edge. These could be considered a variety of utilized flake. No polished flakes were found *in situ* at Cueva Blanca; they were, however, recovered at other Archaic sites.

Choppers/Knives

These artifacts (Figures 5.19–5.24) are large, heavy flakes, chunks, or nodules of silicified tuff or chert that have been chipped to give a sharp cutting edge or edges. The retouch is usually coarse, giving the edge a sinuous appearance.

These tools may have been used for both cutting and chopping; some, for example, may have been multipurpose tools for the butchering of deer. A number of specimens show signs of battering on one or more edges.

Scrapers

The scrapers from Cueva Blanca fell into four general types: end scrapers, sidescrapers/knives, ovoid scrapers, and steep denticulate scrapers. The diversity of scrapers at Cueva Blanca was greater than that at Guilá Naquitz (Hole 2009).

End scrapers

These tools are flakes with one end blunted by steep retouch (Figures 5.25, 5.26). The retouched edge is generally convex in outline. Traditionally, end scrapers have been considered tools for working hides. While end scrapers were not particularly common at Guilá Naquitz and Cueva Blanca, they were so common in the Archaic caves of the Tehuacán Valley that MacNeish, Nelken-Terner, and Johnson (1967:30–43) devoted an entire chapter to them.

Sidescrapers/knives

These tools are flakes with one edge largely covered with shallow, steep, or scaling retouch (Figures 5.27–5.29). The retouched edge is smooth rather than denticulate and may be either straight or curved in outline. Like the sidescrapers/knives found at Guilá Naquitz (Hole 2009:106), these tools were likely used for the skinning of animals and/or the working of hides. At Cueva Blanca, sidescrapers were more common than end scrapers.

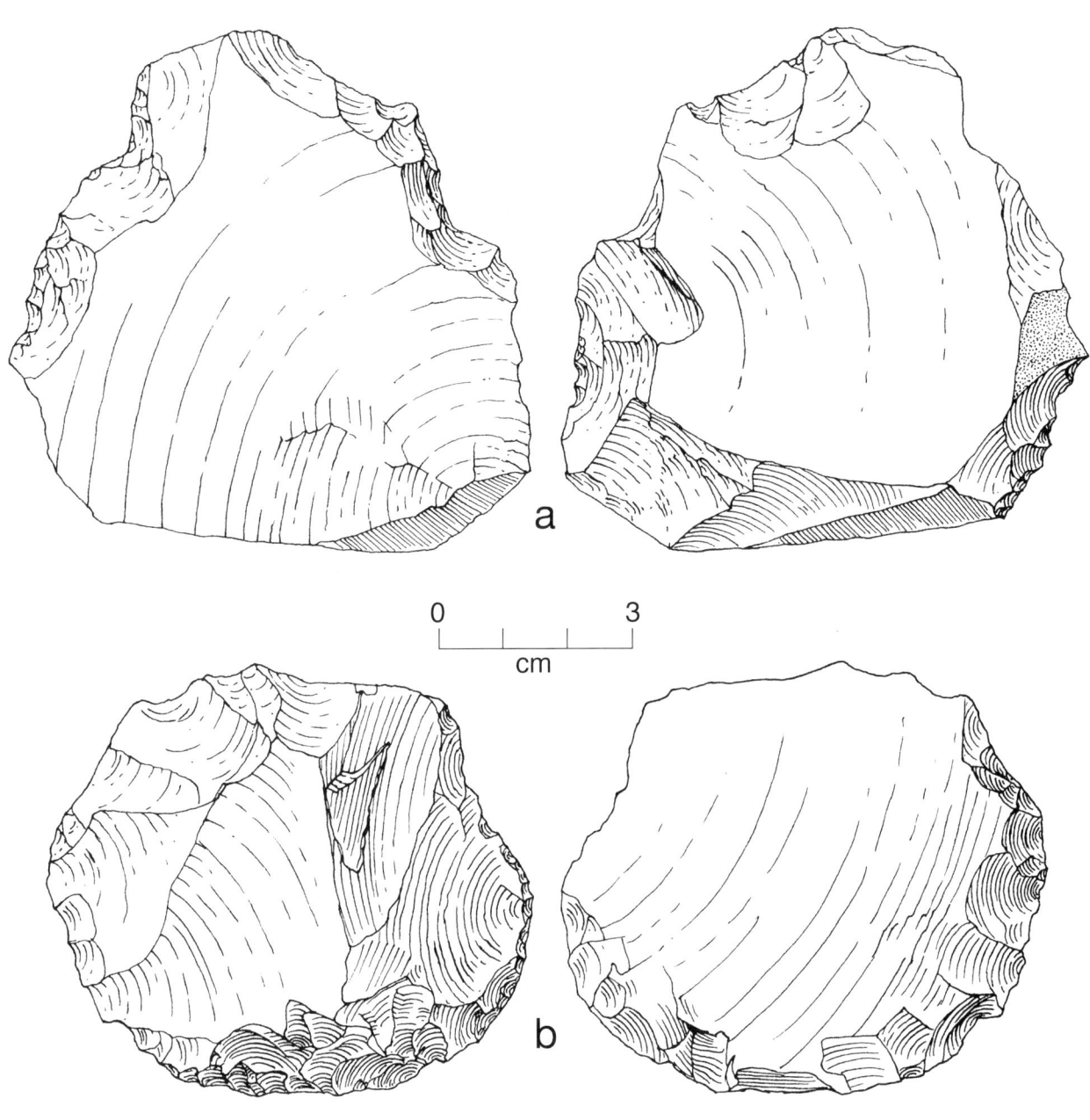

Figure 5.19. Choppers/knives, found *in situ* in Archaic strata. *a* was discovered in Zone C (Square E4). *b* was discovered in Zone E (Square E11).

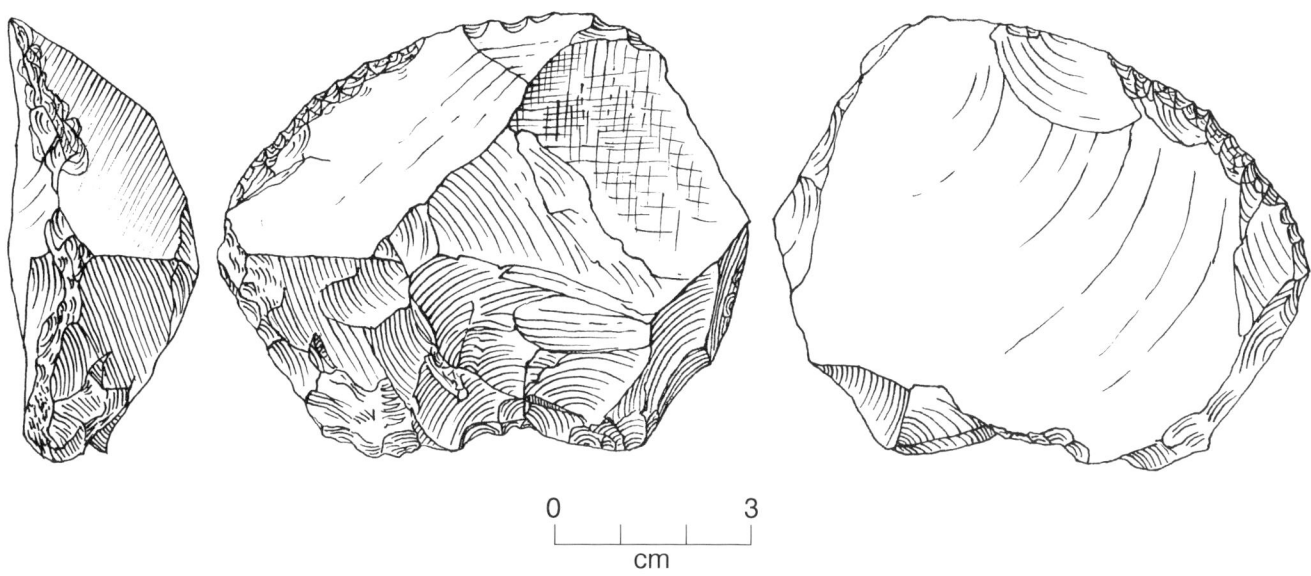

Figure 5.20. Bifacial Archaic scraper/knife, redeposited in Zone B.

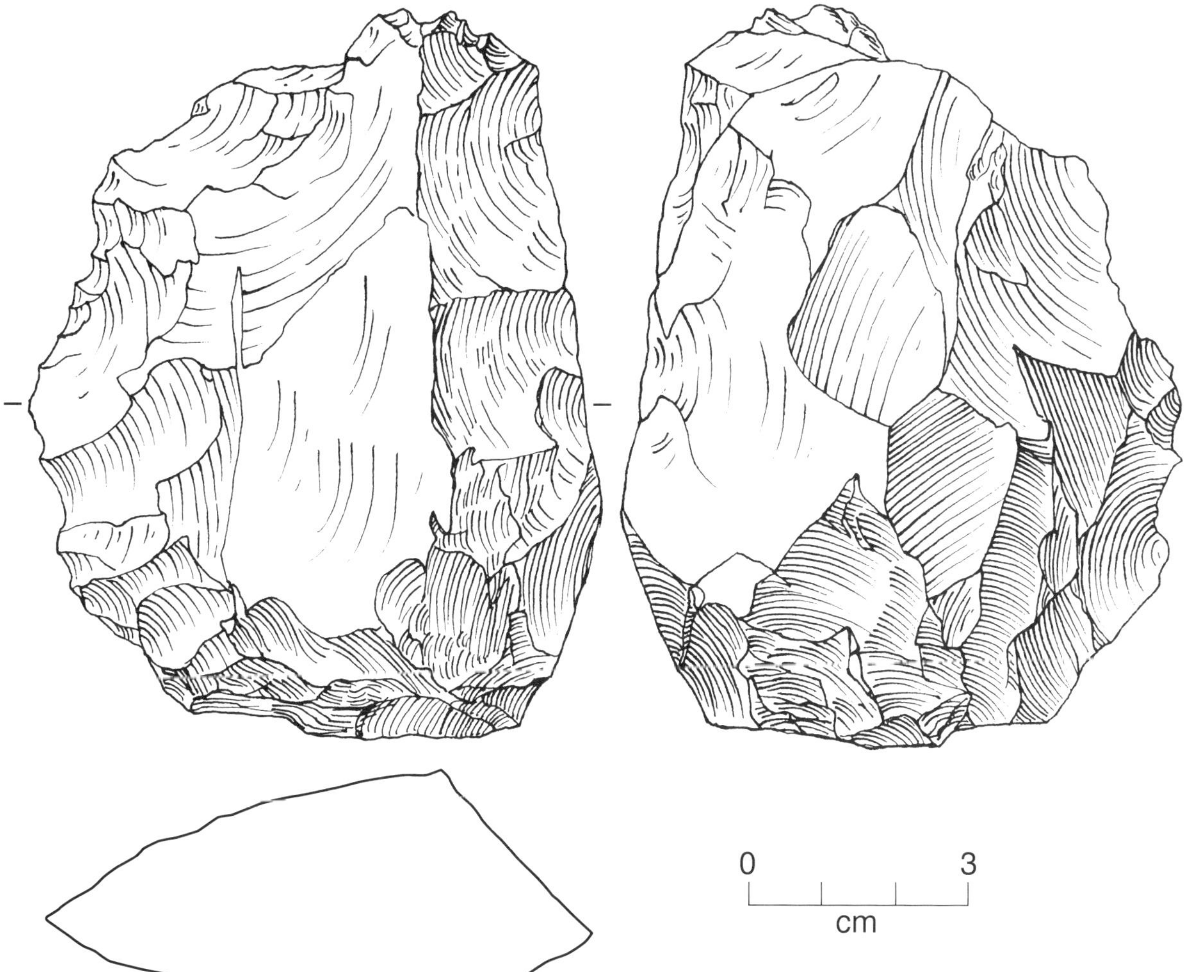

Figure 5.21. Bifacial Archaic chopper/knife, redeposited in Zone B.

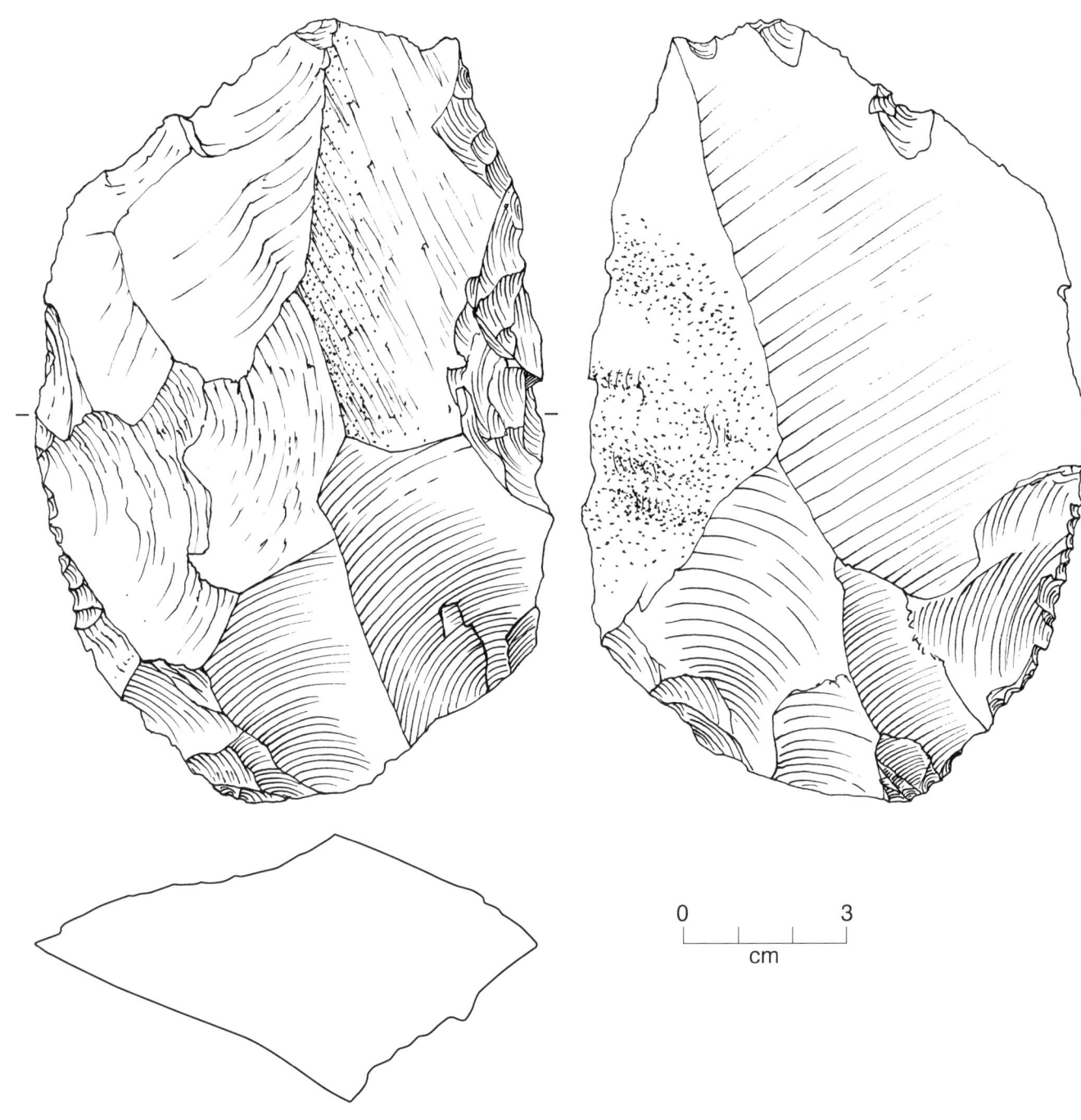

Figure 5.22. Large bifacial Archaic chopper/knife, redeposited in Zone B.

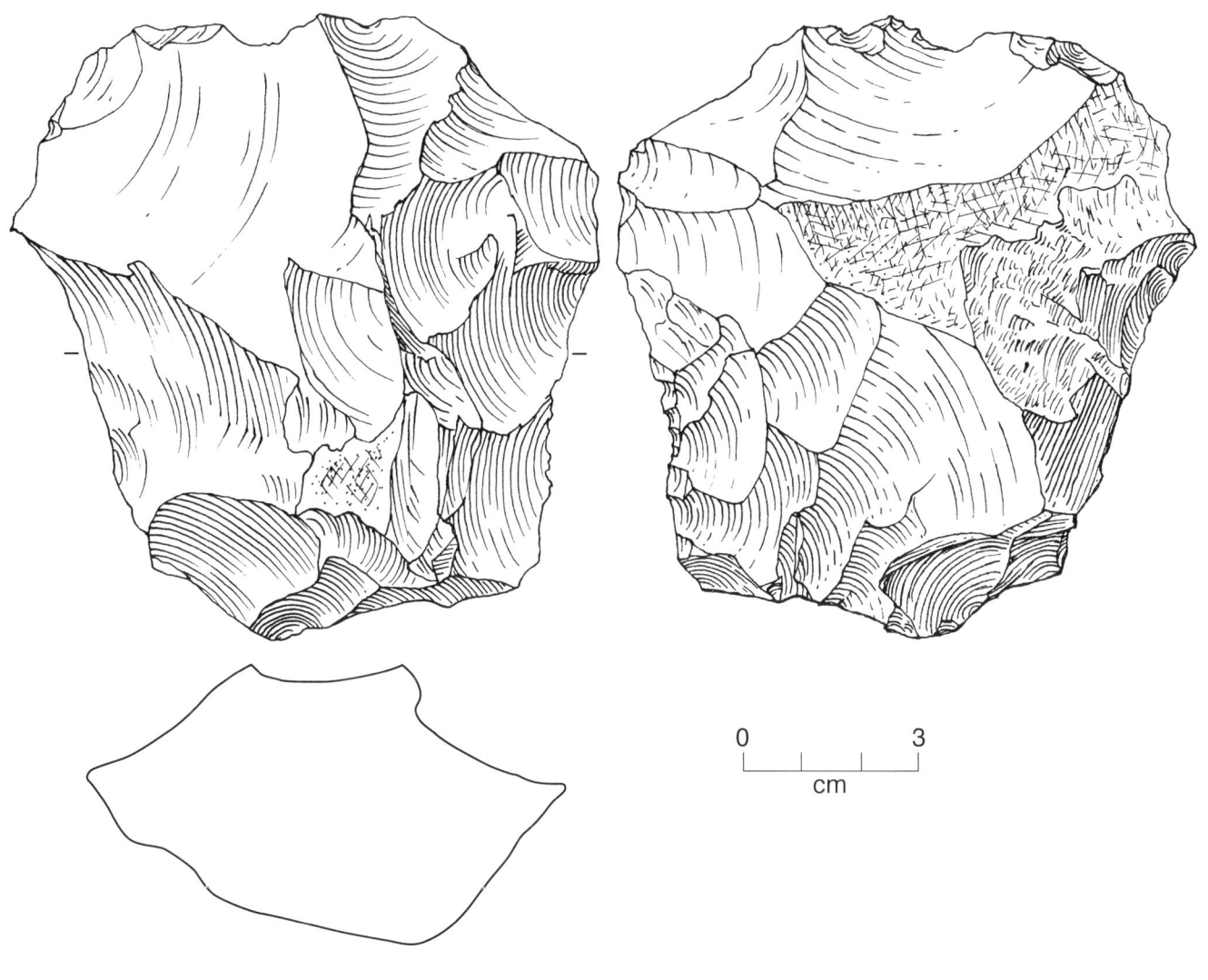

Figure 5.23. Large bifacial Archaic chopper/knife, redeposited in Zone B.

Figure 5.24. Large Archaic chopper/knife, redeposited in Zone B. This tool bore evidence of battering on several of its edges.

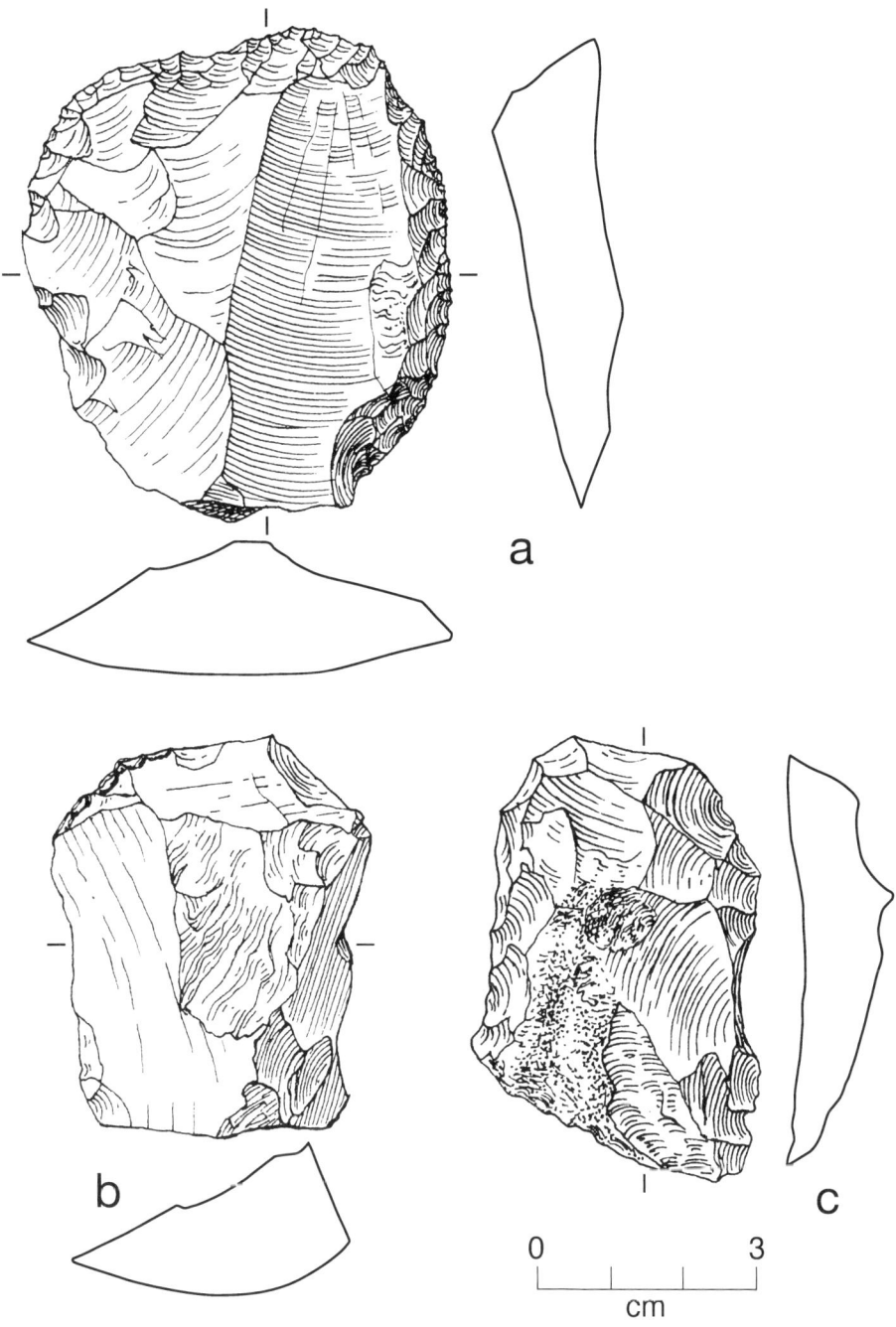

Figure 5.25. End scrapers, found *in situ* in Archaic strata. *a* was found in Zone D (Square D7). *b* was found in Zone C (Square E5). *c* was found in Zone D (Square E6).

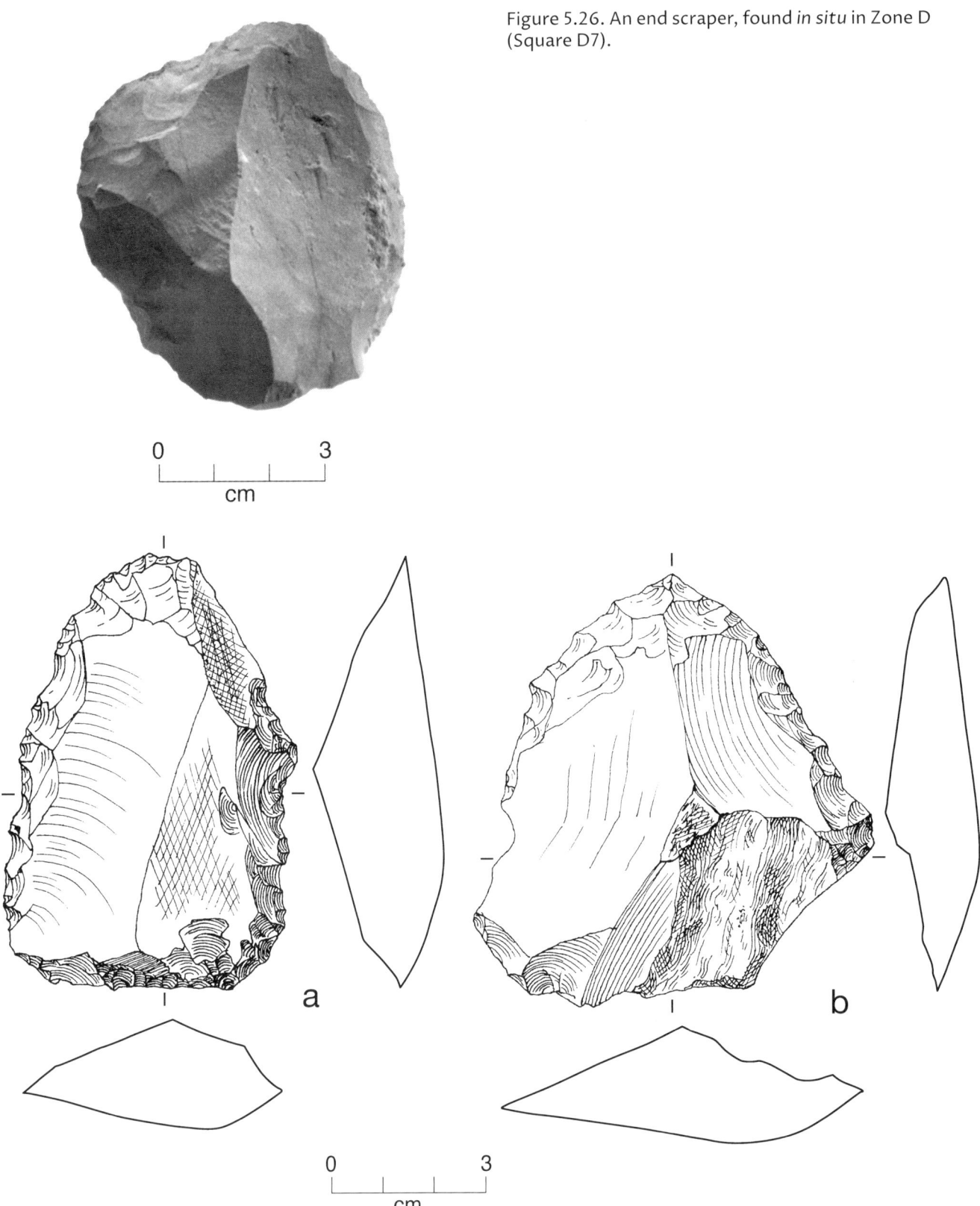

Figure 5.26. An end scraper, found *in situ* in Zone D (Square D7).

Figure 5.27. Sidescrapers/knives, found *in situ* in Archaic strata. *a* was found in Zone E (Square E4). *b* was found in Zone C (Square H9).

The Chipped Stone Tools

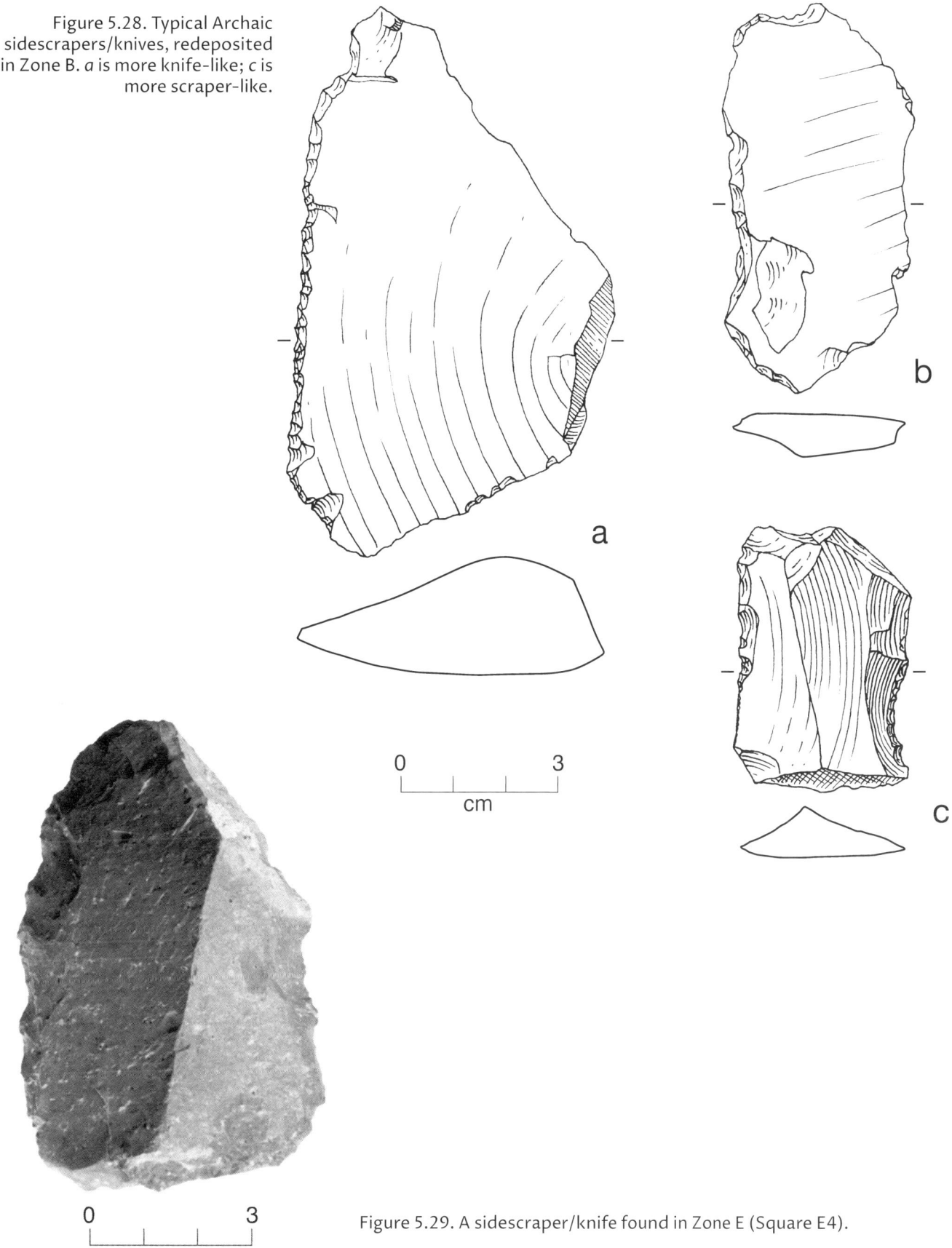

Figure 5.28. Typical Archaic sidescrapers/knives, redeposited in Zone B. *a* is more knife-like; *c* is more scraper-like.

Figure 5.29. A sidescraper/knife found in Zone E (Square E4).

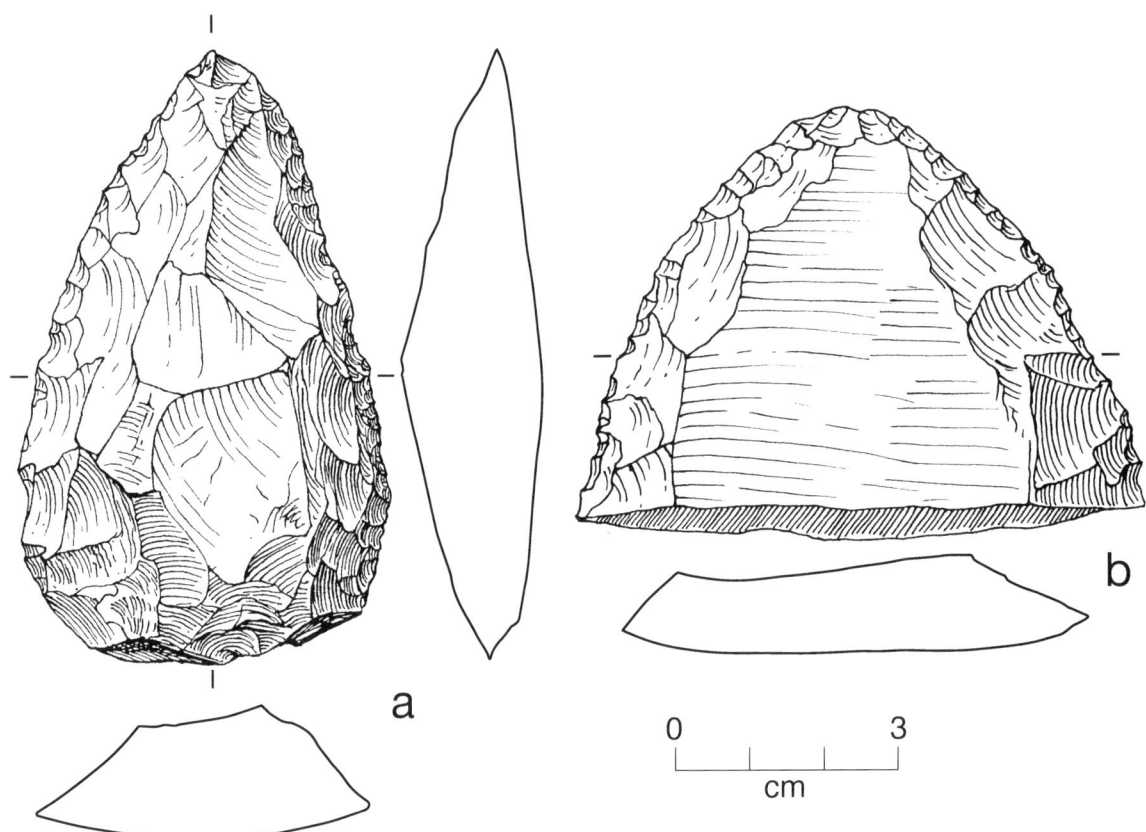

Figure 5.30. Ovoid scrapers, found *in situ* in Archaic strata. *a* was found in Zone D (Square D4). *b* was found in Zone E (Square E11).

Ovoid scrapers

These tools were made on flakes that had an oval outline to begin with, and had been retouched along one part of the periphery (Figures 5.30–5.32). Some may have been used much as sidescrapers were used, but differ in morphology from the latter.

Steep denticulate scrapers

These are heavy flakes or chunks of silicified tuff or chert with one or more edges chipped by coarse percussion retouch that is relatively steep to the plane of the chipping surface (Figures 5.33–5.39). The retouched edges have been denticulated or notched (rather than smoothed) by the chipping.

The larger examples of this type most closely resemble the "scraper planes" of the Tehuacán caves (MacNeish, Nelken-Terner, and Johnson 1967:36–39). It is generally believed that such tools were used in the processing of coarse plant material, including the shredding or pulping of fibrous plants such as agaves or prickly pear. Some steep denticulate scrapers from Cueva Blanca, however, are probably too small to have been employed conveniently as planes.

Tools for Slotting and Perforating

Archaic tools for slotting and perforating included burins and drills. While a number of these artifacts showed up at the site of Gheo-Shih—a large "macroband" camp—they were less common at Cueva Blanca.

Burins

The burins from Cueva Blanca (Figures 5.40–5.42) all have an acute angle formed by the removal of flakes roughly perpendicular to one another or from the intersection of a transverse break and

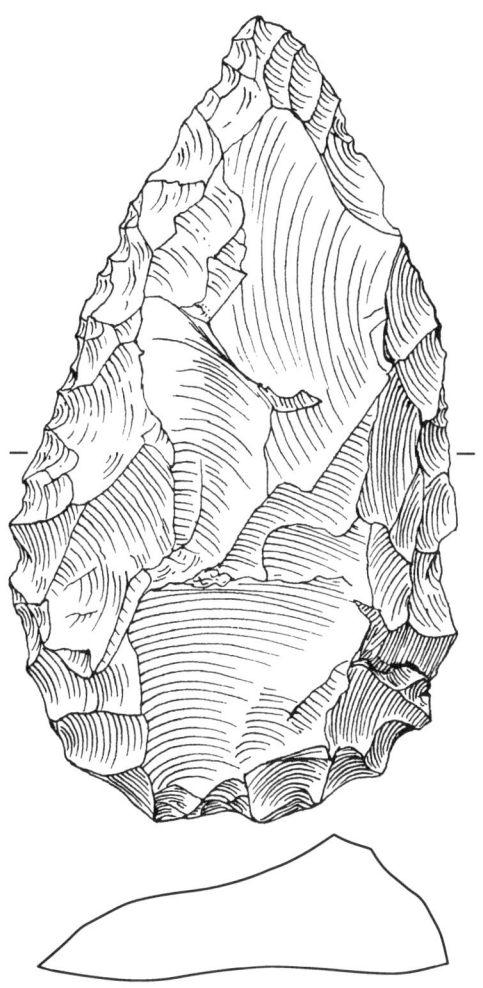
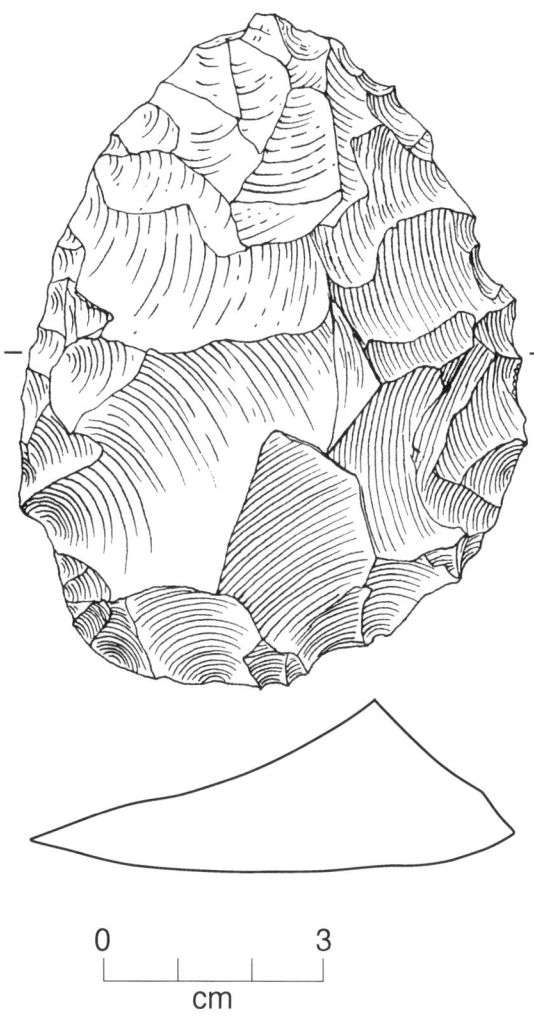

Figure 5.31. Typical Archaic ovoid scrapers, redeposited in Zone B.

Figure 5.32. Typical Archaic ovoid scraper, redeposited in Zone B.

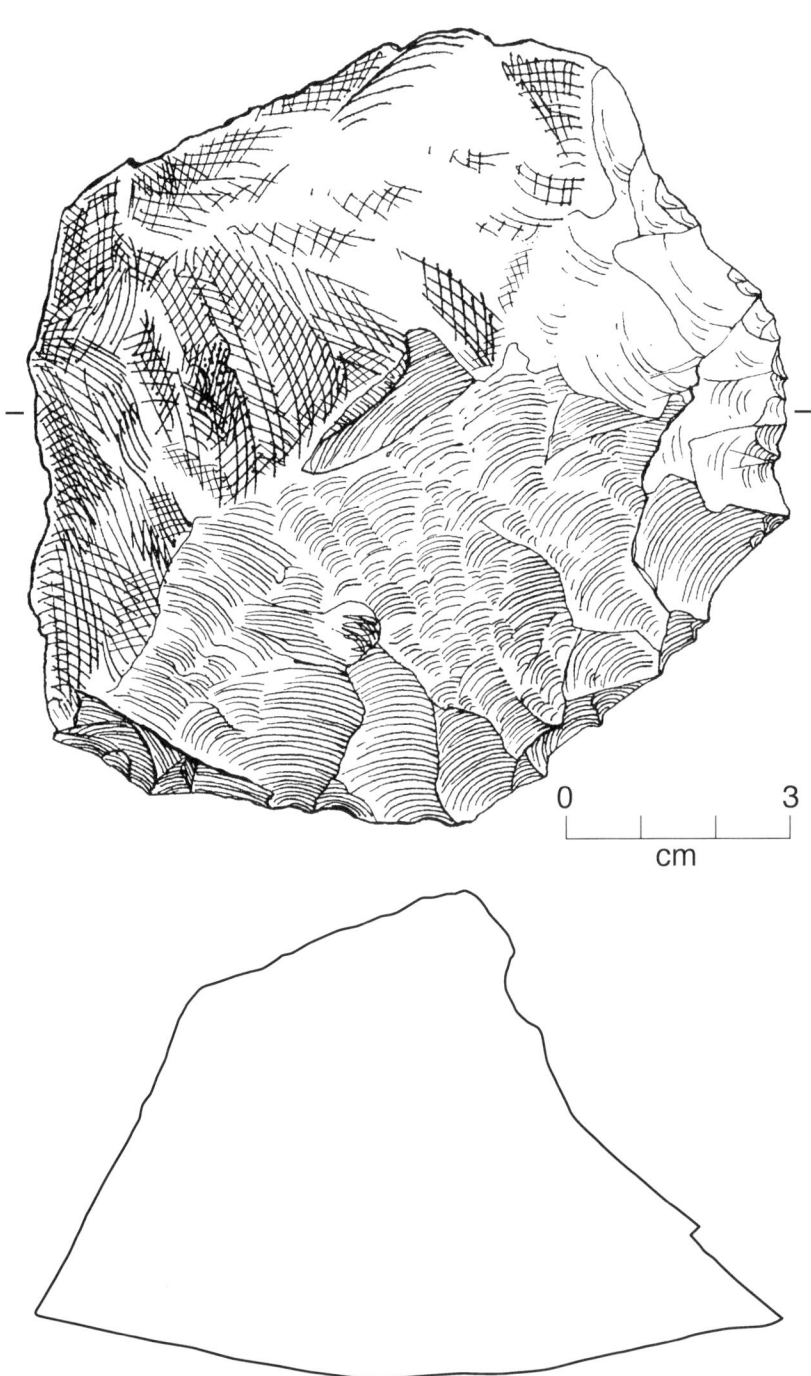

Figure 5.33. A steep denticulate scraper, found *in situ* in Zone D (Square E8).

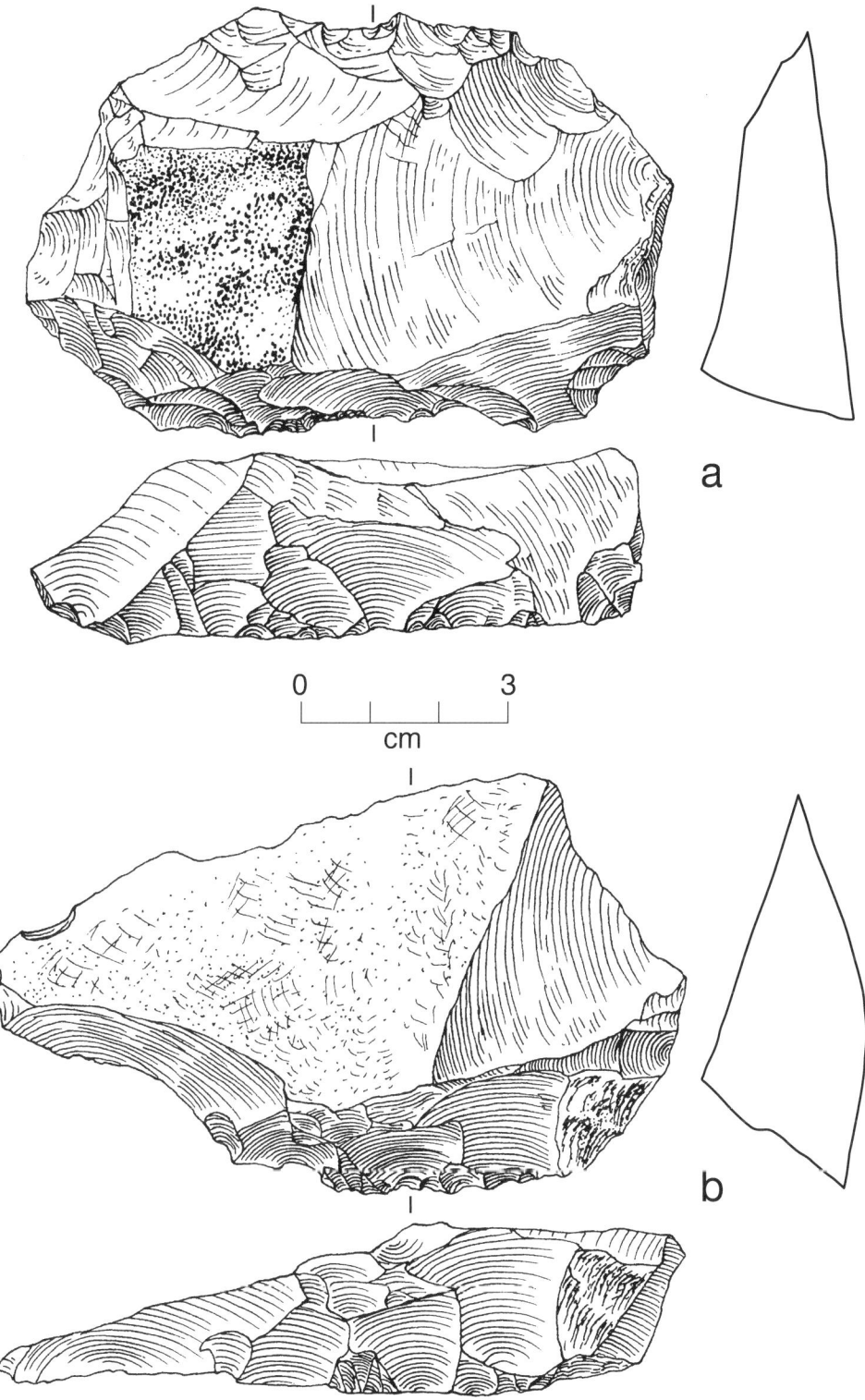

Figure 5.34. Steep denticulate scrapers, found *in situ* in Archaic strata. *a* was found in Zone D (Square E5). *b* was found in Zone E (Square G6).

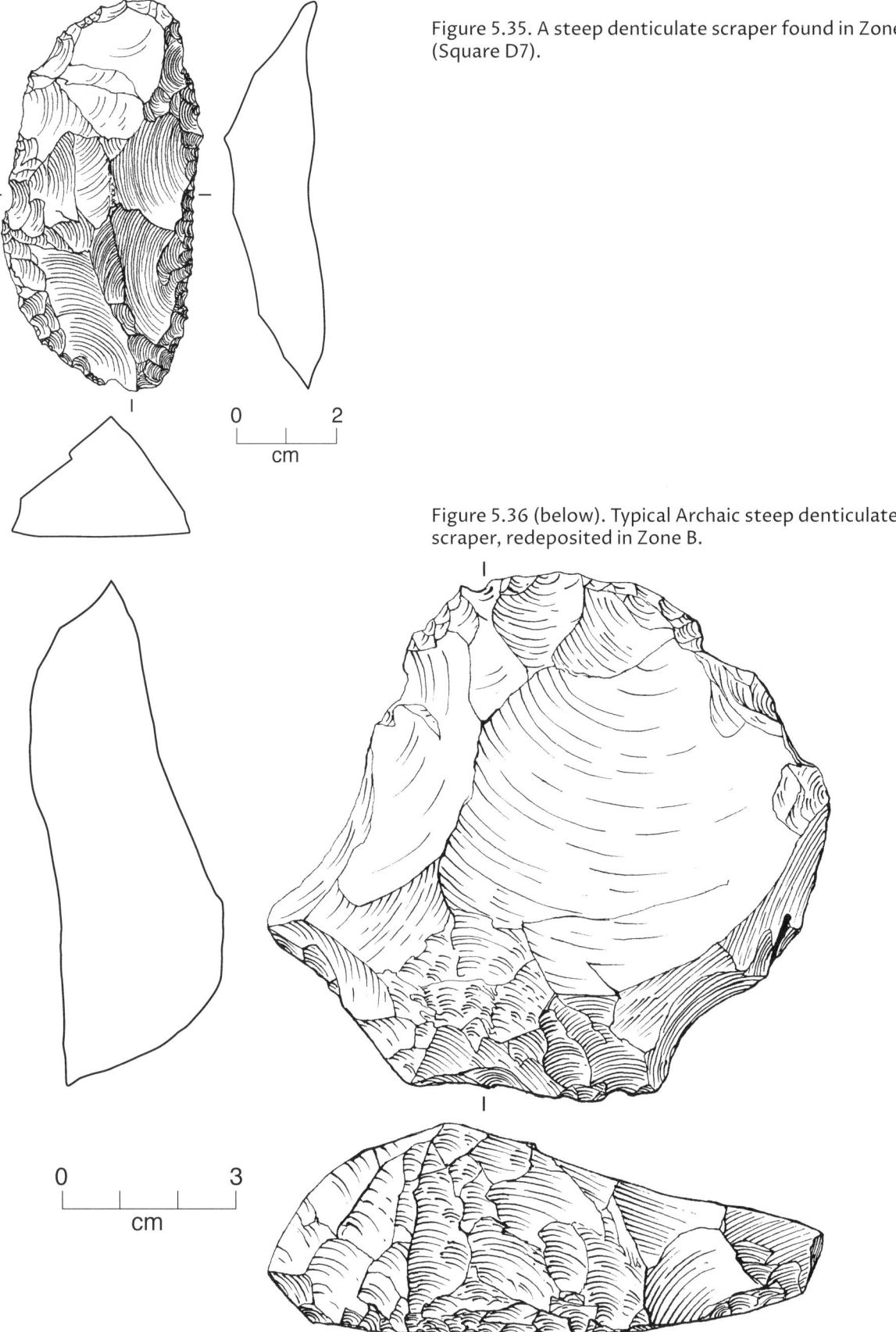

Figure 5.35. A steep denticulate scraper found in Zone D (Square D7).

Figure 5.36 (below). Typical Archaic steep denticulate scraper, redeposited in Zone B.

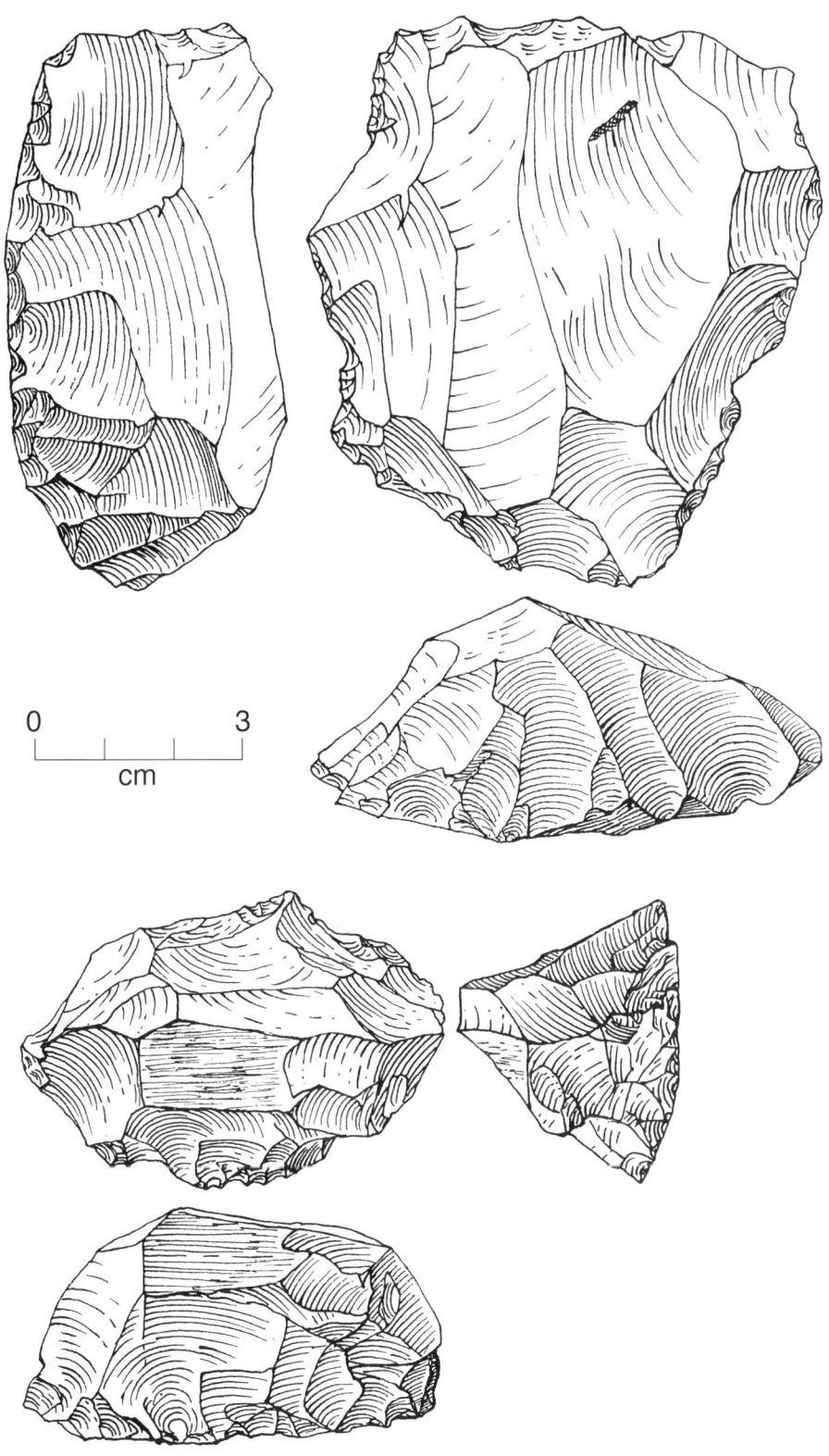

Figure 5.37. Two typical Archaic steep denticulate scrapers, redeposited in Zone B.

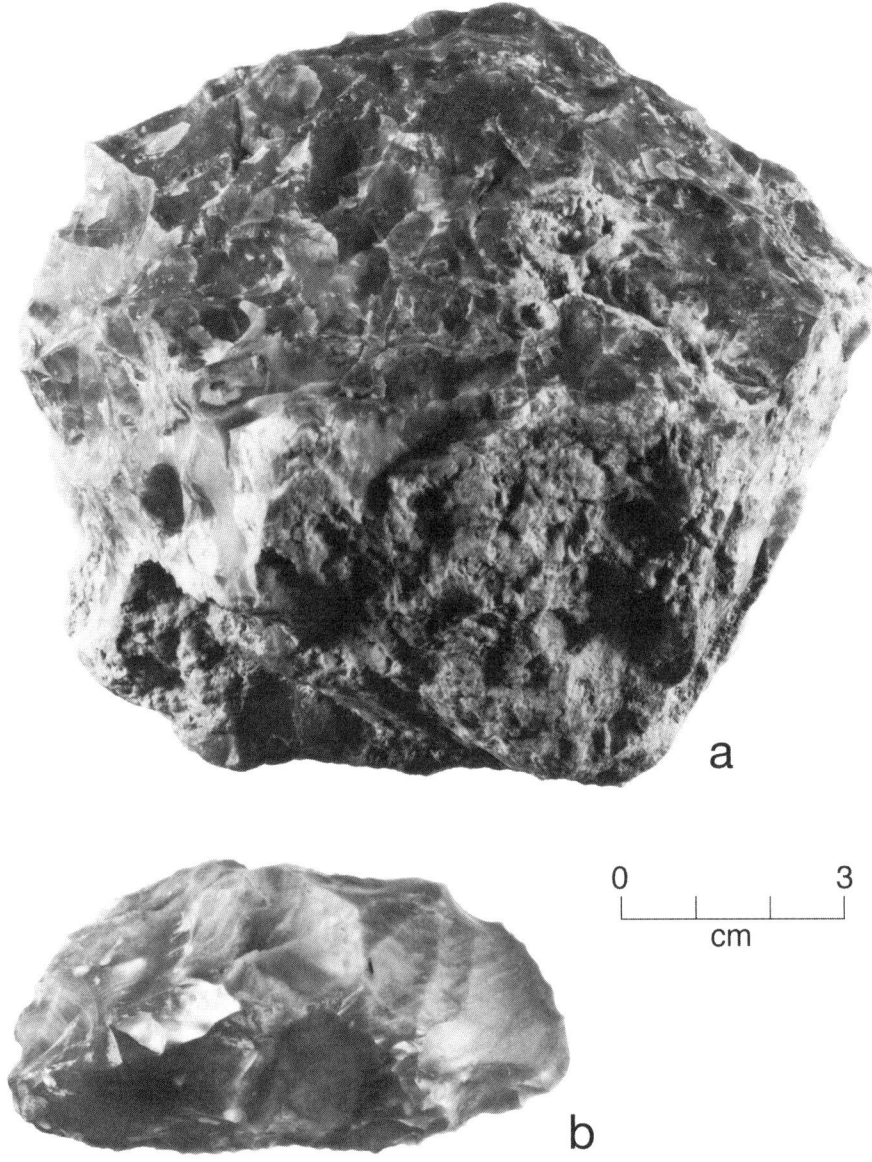

Figure 5.38. Two steep denticulate scrapers found *in situ* in Zone D, showing the range of variation in size. *a* is from Square E8, *b* from Square D7.

The Chipped Stone Tools

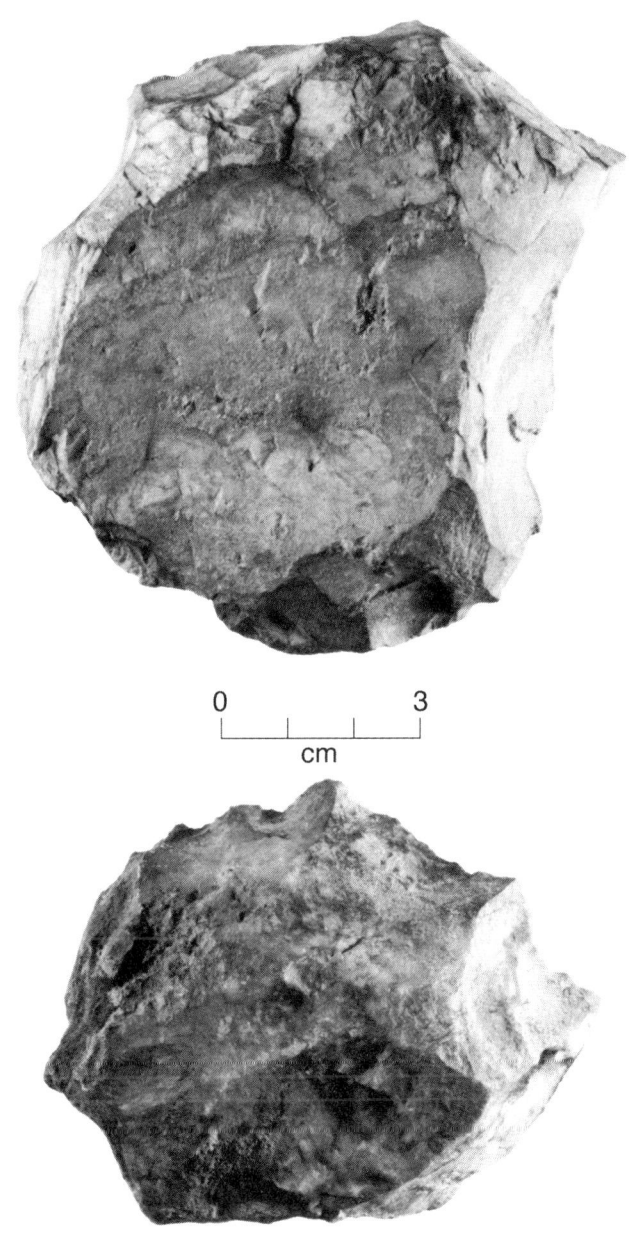

Figure 5.39. Two typical Archaic steep denticulate scrapers, redeposited in Zone B.

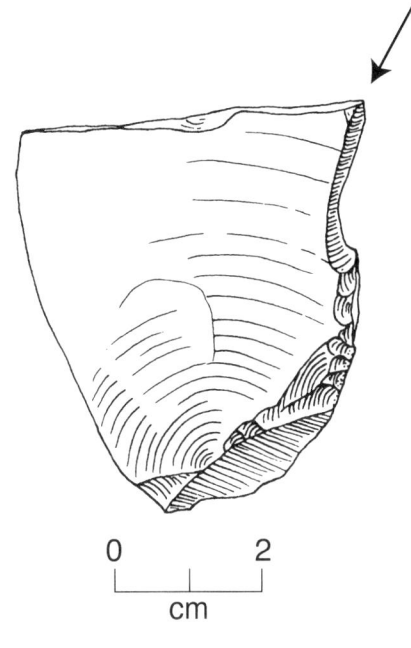

Figure 5.40. A burin, discovered *in situ* in Zone D (Square D11).

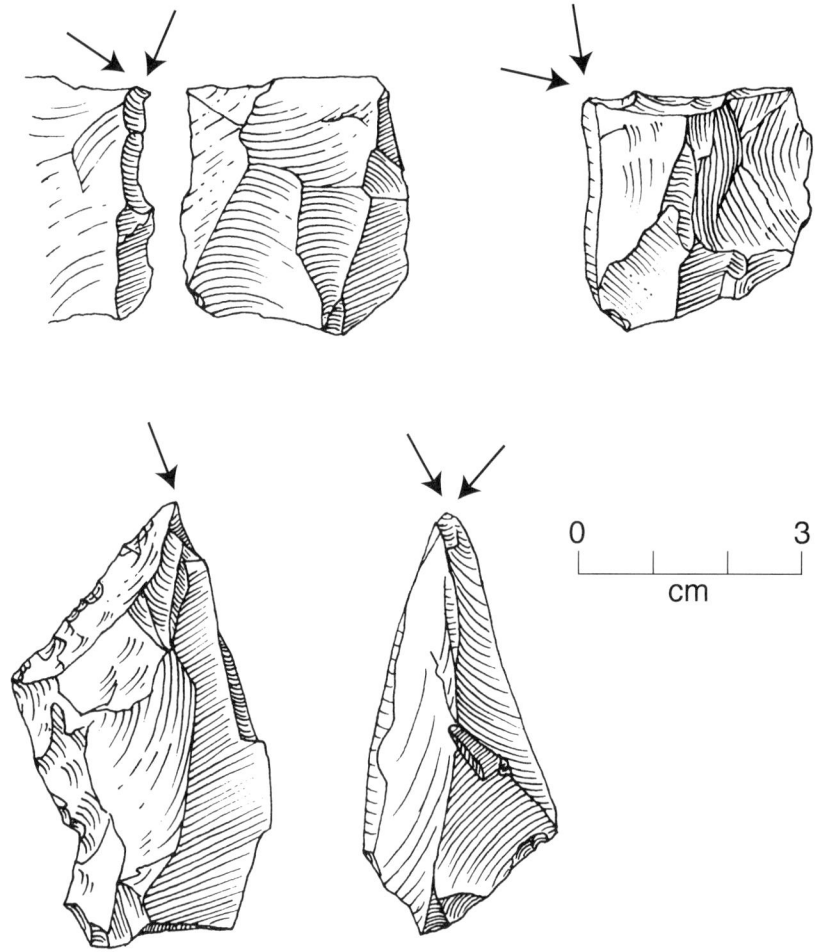

Figure 5.41. Typical Archaic burins, redeposited in Zone B.

Figure 5.42. A burin found in Zone D (Square D11).

The Chipped Stone Tools 87

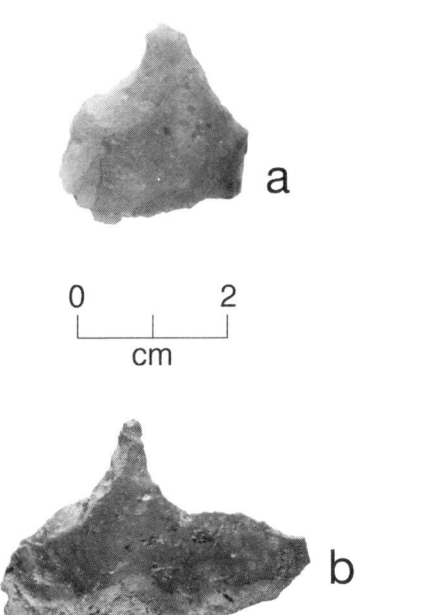

Figure 5.43. Archaic drills. *a* was discovered *in situ* in Zone D (Square G14). *b* was redeposited in Zone A.

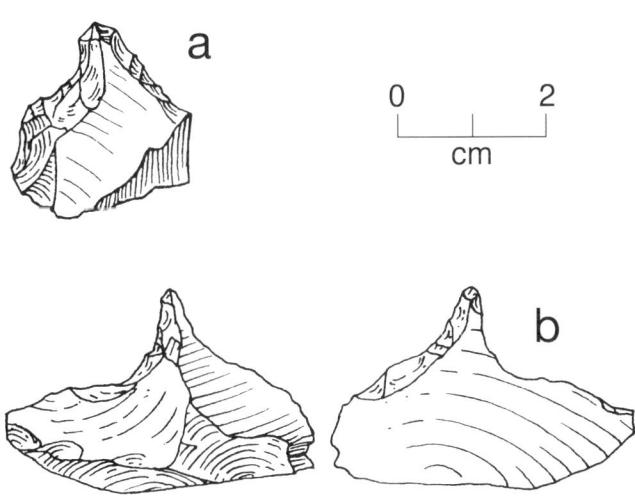

Figure 5.44. Archaic drills. *a* was found *in situ* in Zone D (Square G14). *b* was redeposited in Zone A.

a perpendicular flake. This artifact type was so infrequent in our collections that we did not deem it worthwhile to distinguish between simple and polyhedric burins. At Cueva Blanca, we suspect that burins were used for slotting, gouging, and cutting wood or bone.

Drills

Drills (Figures 5.43, 5.44) were not common in the Oaxaca Archaic. At Gheo-Shih, some Archaic drills showed wear suggesting that they had been used to perforate sandstone discs for use as beads or pendants, but no such discs were found at Cueva Blanca.

A typical Archaic drill is an elongated flake with retouch on one end, producing a point. The retouch can occur on both edges of the tip and is directed from both the dorsal face and the bulbar face. At Cueva Blanca, drills may have been used to produce the sockets in wooden fire drill hearths (see Flannery 2009a: Figure 10.3).

Bifaces

This category includes bifacial preforms or roughouts for projectile points, bifaces that could be used as knives, and the points for spears or atlatl darts. Almost every type of biface came in multiple varieties.

Bifaces, Variety A

This variety of biface (Figures 5.45–5.47) consists of our best-made examples—formed on flakes thinned with careful bifacial retouch on the planar surfaces—and sometimes referred to as "Martínez bifaces." The edges are smooth and straight. While many Variety A bifaces are probably preforms or blanks for projectile points, some could have been used as bifacial knives in their own right. Bifaces comparable to our Variety A were also recovered at Cueva del Texcal, Puebla (García Moll 1977: Lám. 11).

Bifaces, Variety B

This variety (Figures 5.48, 5.49, 5.51*a*, 5.52*a*) consists of flakes with good bifacial chipping, mostly confined to the edges, leaving the flake relatively thick (unless it happened to be thin already when it was struck from the core). The bases are usually unfinished when present and show either a clean break or a platform. There is a tendency toward an ogival silhouette, with the ends sometimes blunt. I have previously illustrated two Variety B bifaces from Guilá Naquitz (Hole 2009: Figures 6.32, 6.33).

Bifaces, Variety C

This variety (Figures 5.50, 5.51*b*, 5.52*b*) consists of the crudest of our bifaces in terms of manufacture; most of these items were

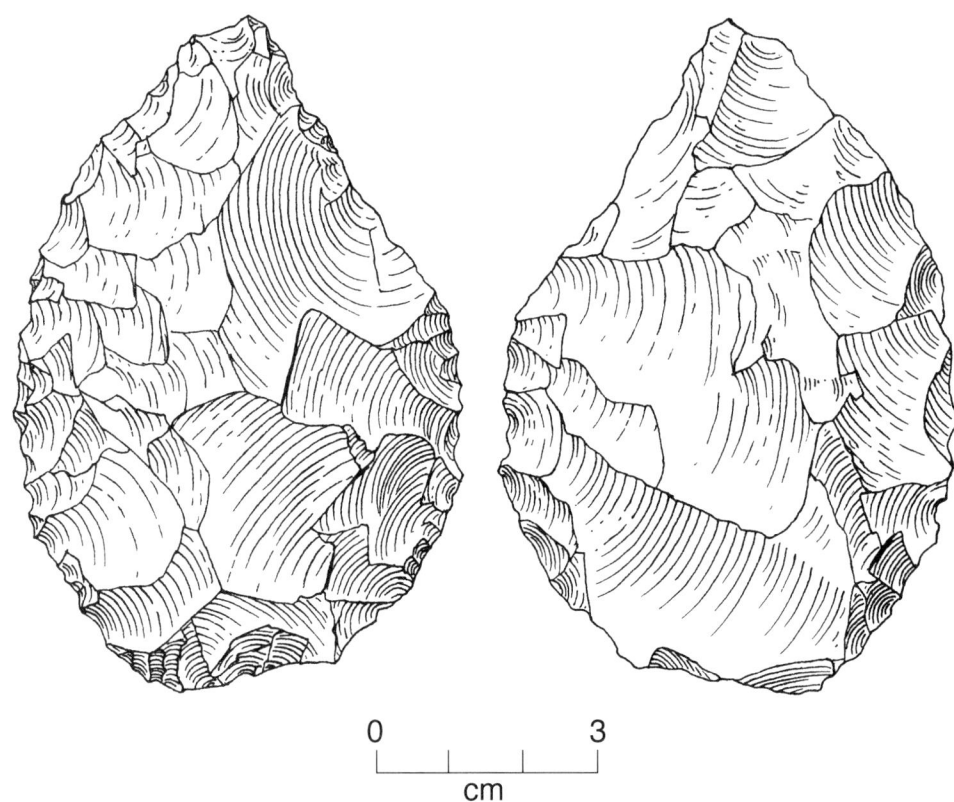

Figure 5.45. A Variety A biface, found *in situ* in Zone D (Square C6). These well-made artifacts, known as Martínez bifaces, could be used as tools in their own right or as the "blanks" or "preforms" from which atlatl points were made.

Figure 5.46. A Variety A ("Martínez") biface from Zone D (Square C6).

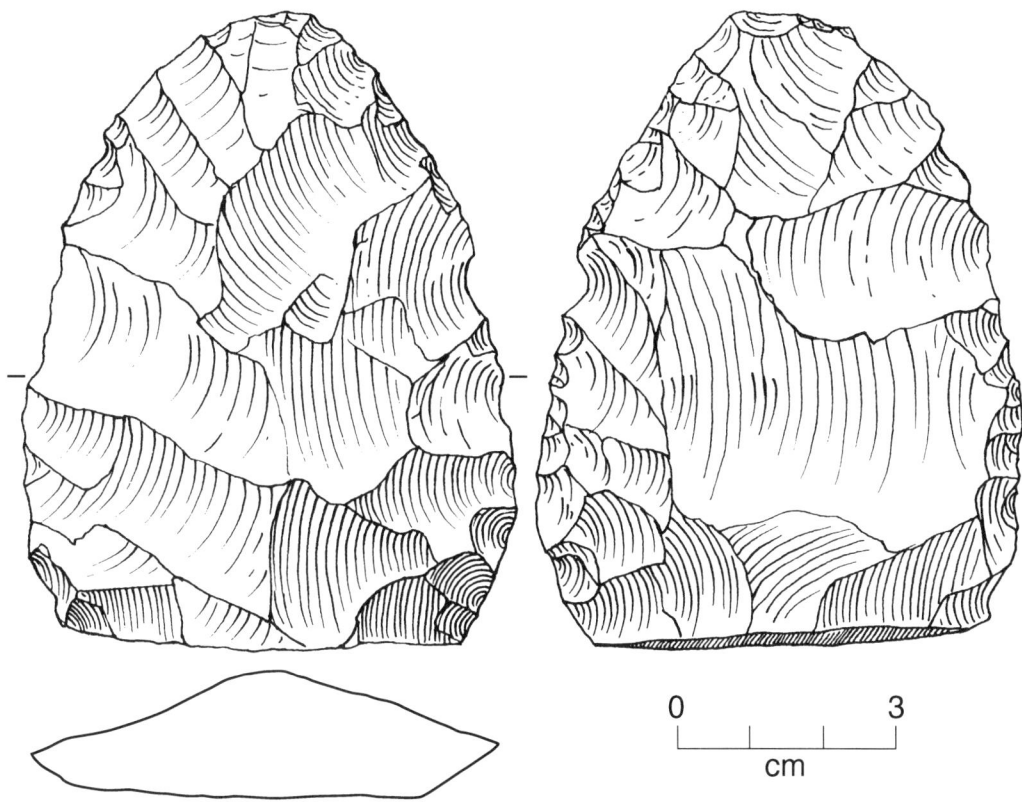

Figure 5.47. A broken Variety A biface, redeposited in Zone B.

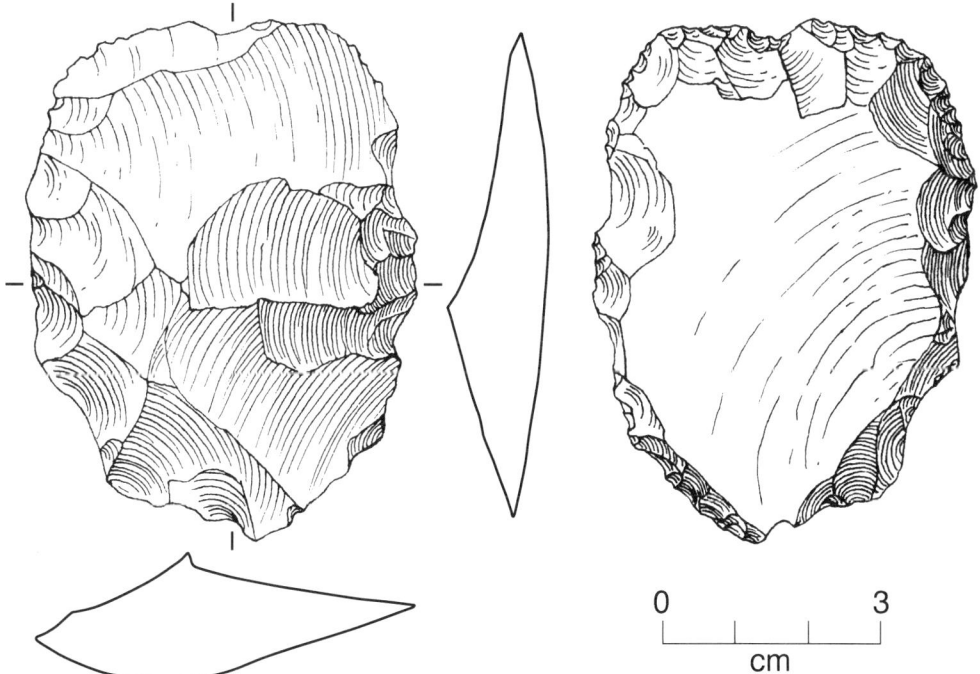

Figure 5.48. A Variety B biface, discovered *in situ* in Zone D (Square D7).

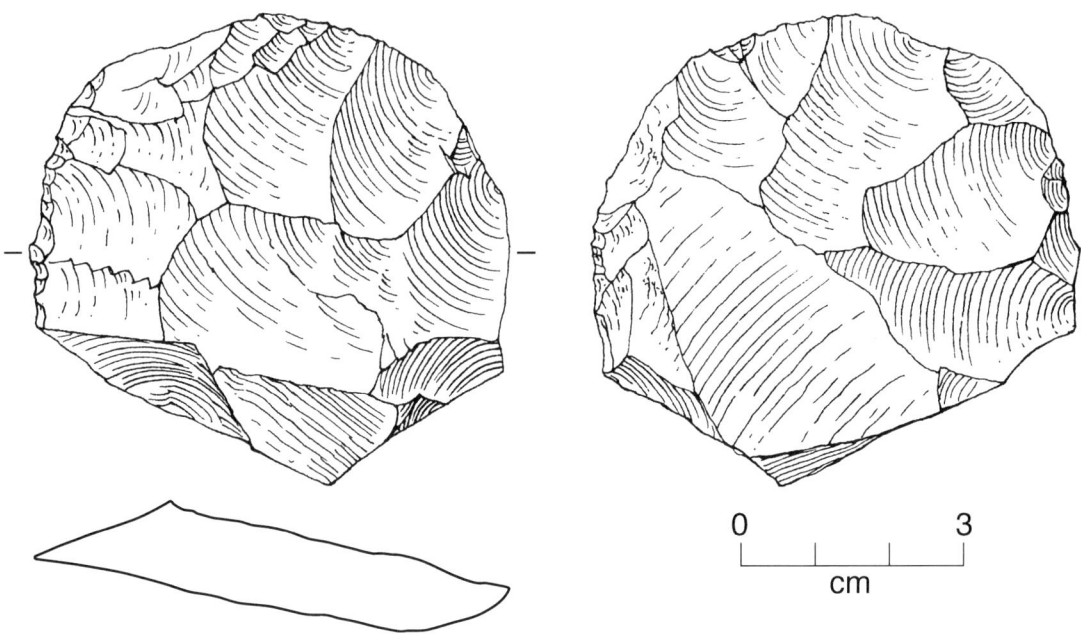

Figure 5.49. A broken Variety B biface, redeposited in Zone B.

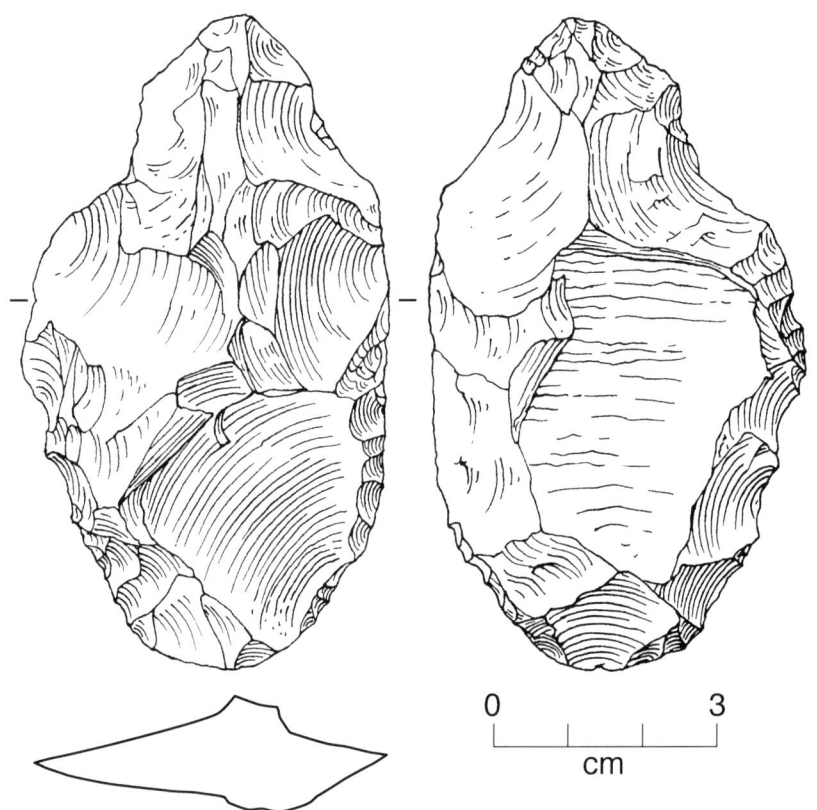

Figure 5.50. A Variety C biface, redeposited in Zone B.

The Chipped Stone Tools 91

likely tools in their own right, rather than preforms for atlatl points. They are generally thick flakes with one or more edges chipped by coarse bifacial retouch. The bodies of the flakes are not thinned. These bifaces are generally round or oval in outline, but there is a considerable range of variation. I have previously illustrated several Variety C bifaces from Guilá Naquitz (Hole 2009: Figures 6.34–6.36).

Projectile points

Cueva Blanca provided us with a larger sample of projectile points than Guilá Naquitz. All were bifacially worked, relatively large points, likely intended for use as atlatl darts; to be sure, one or two could have been appropriate for a thrusting spear. At Cueva Blanca, projectile points could be made of chert, chalcedony, silicified volcanic tuff, or silicified sedimentary rock.

No other Archaic tool type provided us with as much stylistic information as the projectile point. Because of this fact—and because of a series of issues related to the reworking of damaged points—Flannery and I have devoted Chapter 6 to these artifacts.

Unique Tools

In addition to the types described above, we found a number of unique chipped stone tools at Cueva Blanca. Three of these tools are shown in Figures 5.53 and 5.54.

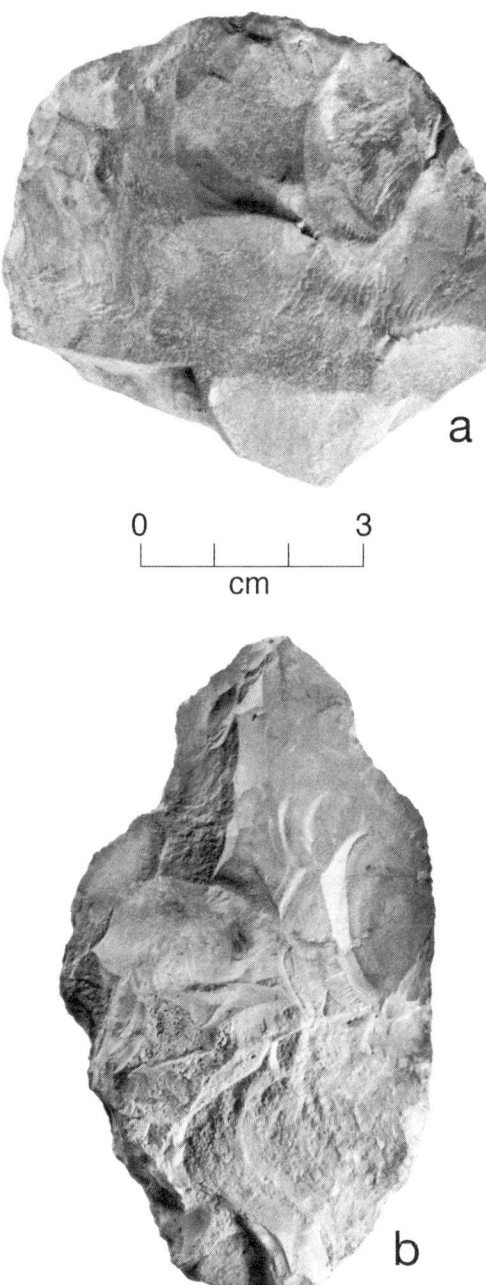

Figure 5.51. Typical Archaic bifaces, redeposited in Zone B. *a* belongs to Variety B. *b* belongs to Variety C.

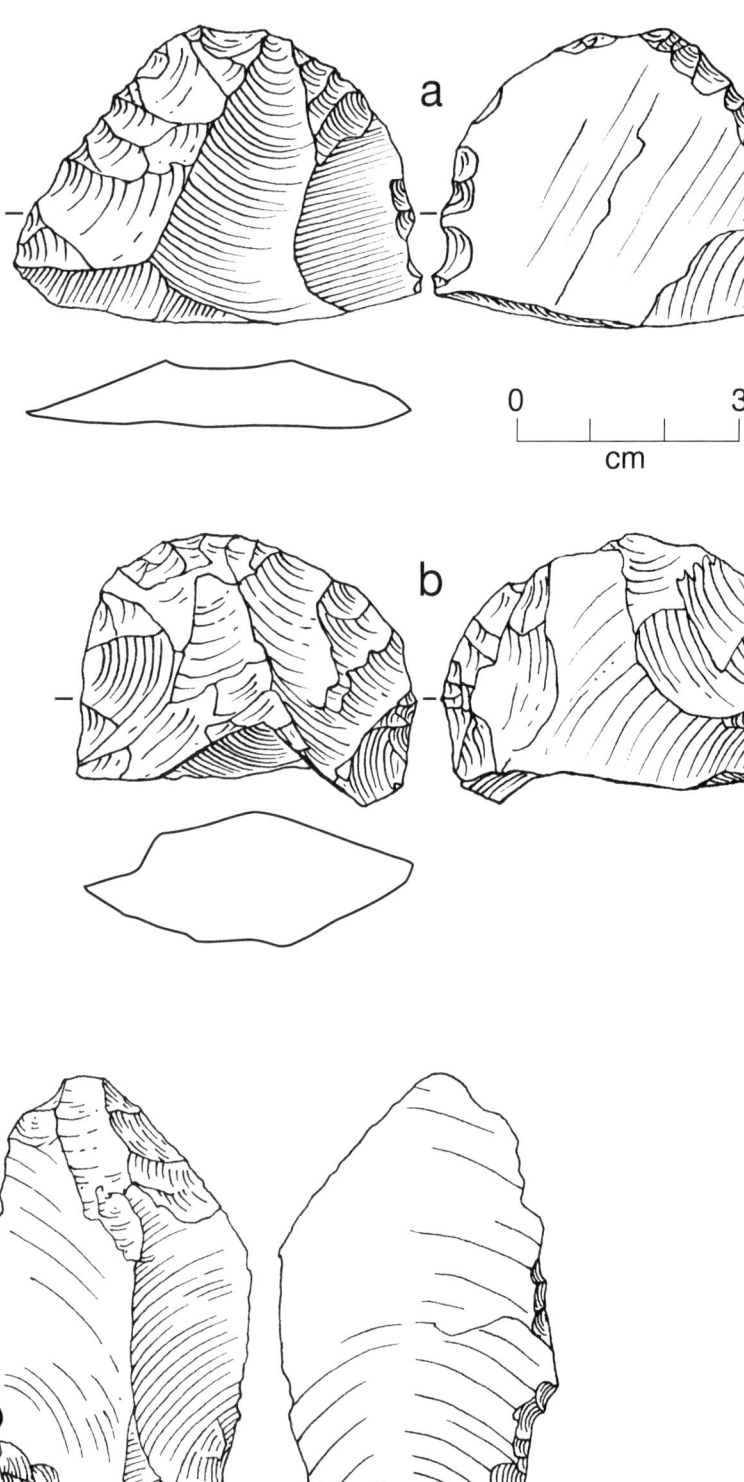

Figure 5.52. Biface fragments, redeposited in Zone B. While their fragmentary nature makes diagnosis difficult, *a* appears to belong to Variety B and *b* appears to belong to Variety C.

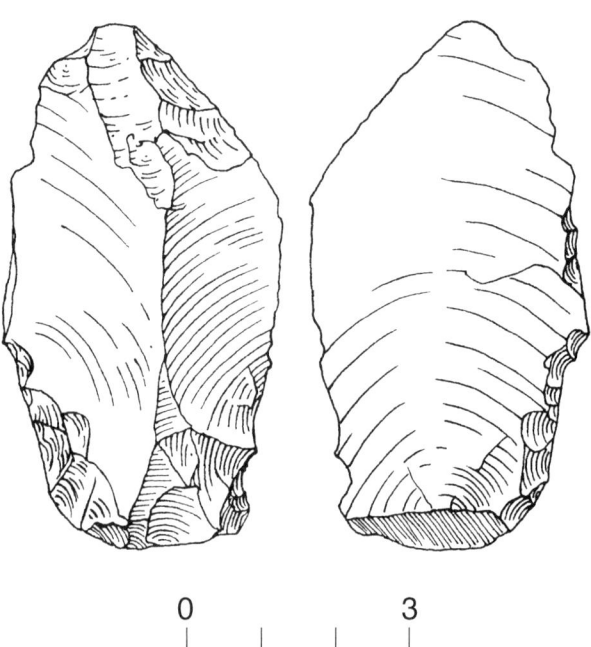

Figure 5.53. This flake with a chipped base was a unique tool at Cueva Blanca. It was discovered *in situ* in Zone C (Square E7) and therefore dates to the Late Archaic.

The Chipped Stone Tools 93

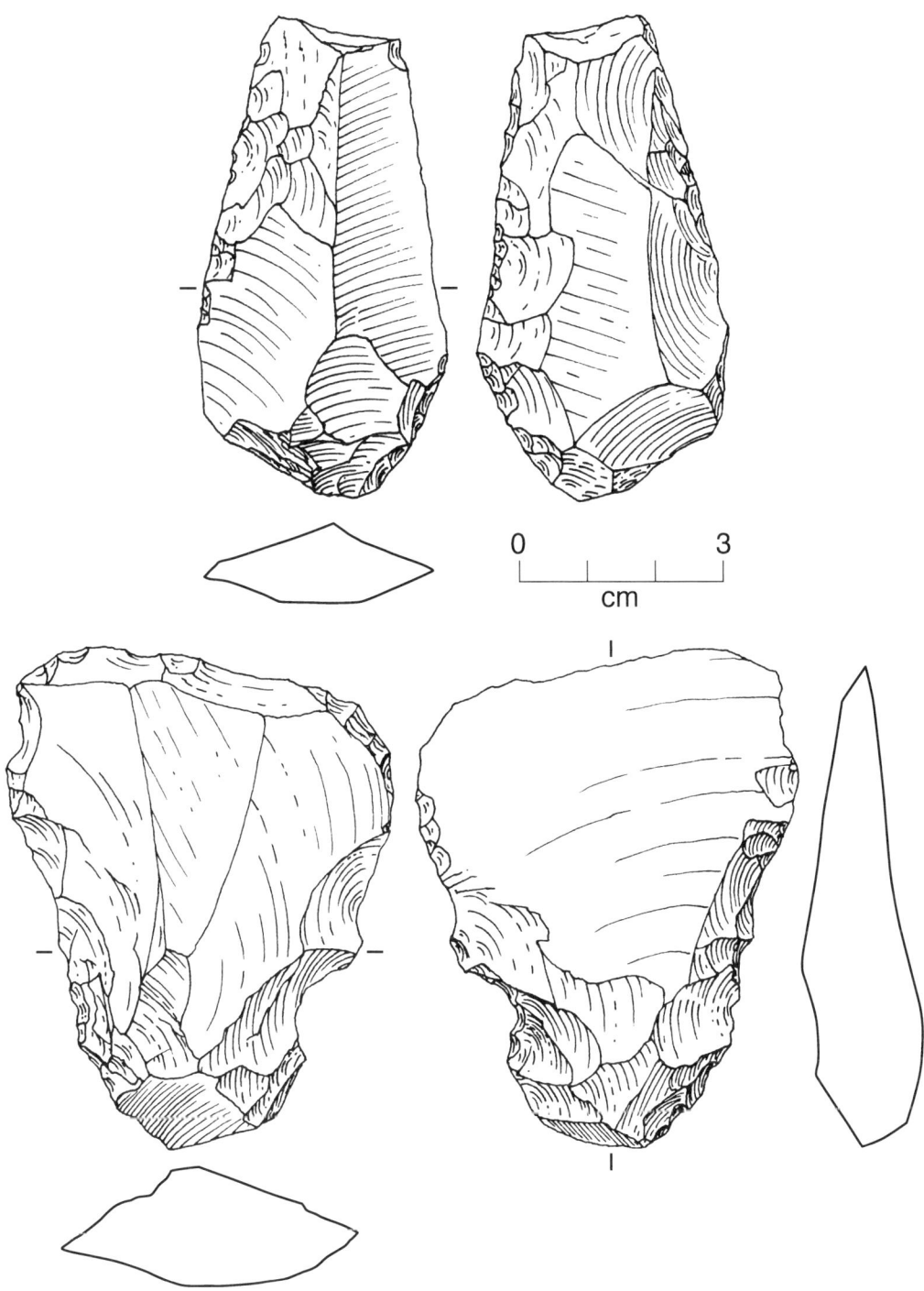

Figure 5.54. These two chipped stone artifacts, found in Zone A, were unique at Cueva Blanca. Neither would be typical of Postclassic Oaxaca. We suspect that both are redeposited Archaic tools, but since each is unique we cannot be sure.

Table 5.1. Distribution of tool categories by 1 × 1 m square, Stratigraphic Zone E (Part 1).

	B6	C4	C5	C6	C7	C8	D3	D4	D5	D6	D7	D8	D9	D10	D11	D12	E3	E4	E5	E6	E7	E8	E9	E10	E11	E12
Hammerstones																		1								
Typical flake cores						1																				
Discoidal cores																										
Core faces				1									1						1						1	
Core edges																							1			
Core tablets																										
Debitage		2	2	6	3	7	1	6	2	7	12	9	10	11	3	3	6	2		12	1	1	18	2	24	3
Utilized flakes	1			1	1				1	1				1	1											
Notched flakes	1					1	1			1		1	2	1				1		1		1	1	1	1	1
Crude blades, plain																				1				1		
Crude blades, retouched																								1		
Flakes with sheen																				1						
Polished flakes																										
Choppers/knives																									1	
End scrapers				1																						
Sidescrapers/knives				1									1					1		2			2			1
Ovoid scrapers																									1	
Steep denticulate scrapers		1									1												1			
Bifaces, Variety A																		1								
Bifaces, Variety B																		1								
Bifaces, Variety C																										
Projectile points													1					1								
Totals	2	3	2	10	4	9	2	6	3	9	13	10	15	13	4	3	6	8	1	17	1	2	23	5	28	5

Table 5.1. Distribution of tool categories by 1 x 1 m square, Stratigraphic Zone E (Part 2).

	F6	F7	F8	F11	F12	G6	G7	G9	G10	G11	G12	G13	H12	H13	I13	I14	I15	J13	J14	J15
Hammerstones																				
Typical flake cores		2		1	1															
Discoidal cores																				
Core faces			1				1													
Core edges															1					
Core tablets																				
Debitage	6	14	26		16	8	11	8	3	3	35	27	17	2	4	5	18	6	2	13
Utilized flakes																			1	2
Notched flakes	1	1	3	1	1	2				1	3	2	1							
Crude blades, plain			1	1																
Crude blades, retouched																				
Flakes with sheen			1								1									
Polished flakes																				
Choppers/knives																				
End scrapers																				
Sidescrapers/knives					1			1												
Ovoid scrapers																				
Steep denticulate scrapers	1					1														
Bifaces, Variety A																				
Bifaces, Variety B																				
Bifaces, Variety C			1																	
Projectile points																				
Totals	8	17	33	4	19	11	12	9	3	4	39	29	18	2	5	5	18	6	3	15

Table 5.2. Distribution of tool categories by 1 × 1 m square, Stratigraphic Zone D (Part 1).

	B6	B7	B8	C4	C5	C6	C7	C8	C9	C10	D3	D4	D5	D6	D7	D8	D9	D10	D11	D12	E3	E4	E5	E6	E7	E8	E9	E12	E13
Hammerstones																			2										
Typical flake cores	1					1	1						1		1					1	1	1	1				2		
Discoidal cores														1															
Core faces	1									1						1					1				1	1			
Core edges																2							1						
Core tablets																										1			
Debitage	3	10	7	3	5	17	43	29	19	9	6	21	27	26	72	97	29	14	9	22	23	27	34	17	19	55	51	30	21
Utilized flakes							1				1	2	2		3	3	1	1		2	1	1	1		2	1	1		
Notched flakes			1			1	2	1	1	1			3		2	2			1	1	1		3	1		1		1	
Crude blades, plain									1						1				1					1					
Crude blades, retouched																										1			
Flakes with sheen																									2				1
Polished flakes																													
Choppers/knives						1																							
End scrapers							1								2									1			1		
Sidescrapers/knives						1		1				1		1	1									1				1	
Ovoid scrapers						1						1																	
Steep denticulate scrapers						2	2	3					2	2	1	3					1			3	1	2		2	
Burins																			1										
Drills																													
Bifaces, Variety A						1																							
Bifaces, Variety B																					1								
Bifaces, Variety C					1			1	1						1	1													
Projectile points							1	1				1	1	2			1												
Totals	5	10	8	3	7	25	51	36	21	11	7	27	36	32	85	109	31	15	15	26	29	29	41	24	25	63	55	35	22

Table 5.2. Distribution of tool categories by 1 × 1 m square, Stratigraphic Zone D (Part 2).

	F6	F7	F8	F9	F10	F11	F12	F13	F14	G6	G7	G8	G9	G10	G11	G12	G13	G14	H9	H12	H13	H14	H15	I13	I14	I15	J13	J14	J15
Hammerstones																			1	1									
Typical flake cores			1	1		1										1				1				1	1			2	
Discoidal cores																													
Core faces			1			1						1							1	2									
Core edges																													
Core tablets																													12
Debitage	25	25	31	32	6	23	16	24	4	9	28	12	1	14	41	27	24	17	17	27	6	14	31	13	82	49	8	55	
Utilized flakes																		2		1	1		3		2	1	1		1
Notched flakes	1	1		1			2	1				1	1		1			1	1	6		2	6		1		1	1	1
Crude blades, plain							1																						
Crude blades, retouched																													
Flakes with sheen												1												1		1			
Polished flakes																													
Choppers/knives																													
End scrapers													1																
Sidescrapers/knives	2						2				1									1			1				2		
Ovoid scrapers																													
Steep denticulate scrapers			1				1							1									1						1
Burins																													
Drills																		1											
Bifaces, Variety A																													
Bifaces, Variety B																													
Bifaces, Variety C																													
Projectile points																												1	
Totals	28	26	34	35	6	26	22	25	4	9	29	15	3	15	42	28	24	21	21	39	7	16	42	15	86	51	12	59	15

98 Chapter 5

Table 5.3. Distribution of tool categories by 1 x 1 m square, Stratigraphic Zone C (Part 1).

	B6	B8	B9	C4	C5	C6	C7	C8	C9	C10	D3	D4	D5	D6	D7	D8	D10	D11	E3	E4	E5	E6	E7	E9
Hammerstones				1		1								1						1	1			
Typical flake cores					1	1	2	1			1			1				1			1		2	
Discoidal cores																							1	
Core faces					1				2					1						1				
Core edges									1				1											1
Core tablets																								
Debitage	24	6	12	8	32	27	20	9	39	17	12	19	14	8	8	40	6	4	24	19	18	16	18	12
Utilized flakes			2		1		1				2	1		1	1	1				1		2	2	
Notched flakes	2				3	1			1		1	1						1		1	2	2		
Crude blades, plain								1		1														
Crude blades, retouched				1			1																	
Flakes with sheen									1															
Polished flakes																								
Choppers/knives												1								1			1	
End scrapers												1									1			
Sidescrapers/knives								1		1														
Ovoid scrapers															1	1					2		1	
Steep denticulate scrapers			1																					
Bifaces, Variety A																								
Bifaces, Variety B					1					1									2					
Bifaces, Variety C																								
Projectile points									1							1				1	1			
Totals	26	6	15	10	39	30	24	12	45	19	16	23	15	12	10	43	6	6	26	25	26	20	25	13

The Chipped Stone Tools

Table 5.3. Distribution of tool categories by 1 x 1 m square, Stratigraphic Zone C (Part 2).

	E11	E12	E13	F6	F7	F8	F9	F13	F14	G6	G7	G12	G14	H9	H12	H13	H14	H15	I13	I14	I15	J13	J14	J15
Hammerstones																		1	1					1
Typical flake cores			1													1								
Discoidal cores																								
Core faces	1						1						1											
Core edges						1																		
Core tablets																								
Debitage	64	36		5	36	55	17	8	8	5	14	13	5	18	61	57	1	19	29	4	13	31	44	12
Utilized flakes	5	1				3		3	2						1	2		2						
Notched flakes	1					1	2	4	2		1			1	2			2	4			1		
Crude blades, plain	2								1						1	1	1							
Crude blades, retouched							1																	
Flakes with sheen	1																							
Polished flakes																								
Choppers/knives																								
End scrapers														1										
Sidescrapers/knives		1																						
Ovoid scrapers		2																						
Steep denticulate scrapers						1		1																
Bifaces, Variety A																						1		
Bifaces, Variety B													1											
Bifaces, Variety C														1										
Projectile points	1			1																				
Totals	75	40	1	10	36	61	21	16	13	5	15	13	7	21	65	61	1	24	34	4	13	32	44	13

Table 5.4. Tool category totals for Zones E, D, and C.

	E	D	C
Hammerstones	1	7	11
Typical flake cores	5	18	9
Discoidal cores	--	2	1
Core faces	6	11	8
Core edges	2	4	4
Core tablets	--	--	--
Debitage	377	1418	971
Utilized flakes	10	35	35
Notched flakes	31	50	36
Crude blades, plain	4	6	5
Crude blades, retouched	1	--	--
Flakes with sheen	3	7	6
Polished flakes	--	--	--
Choppers/knives	1	1	3
End scrapers	--	6	2
Sidescrapers/knives	9	17	4
Ovoid scrapers	1	2	--
Steep denticulate scrapers	8	34	9
Bifaces, Variety A	1	1	--
Bifaces, Variety B	1	3	5
Bifaces, Variety C	1	4	1
Projectile points	2	10	7
Totals	464	1636	1117

6

The Archaic Projectile Points

Kent V. Flannery and Frank Hole

We recovered 43 whole or fragmentary projectile points from Cueva Blanca. Nineteen of these points were found *in situ* in Zones E, D, and C. An additional 24 Archaic points or fragments thereof were recovered from Zone B, Zone A, or the features in those zones. Many of these additional points were probably redeposited when the occupants of Zones A and B created storage pits, pottery kilns, or agave roasting pits that intruded into the Archaic strata. Other Archaic points may have been picked up from the surface or talus of Cueva Blanca when its Postclassic occupants were collecting stones with which to line agave roasting pits.

We should add, parenthetically, that chipped stone atlatl points were "rare to absent" in the Valley of Oaxaca during the Formative era (Flannery and Marcus 2005:55). Atlatl points remained uncommon during the Classic and gave way during the Postclassic to small arrow points, usually of the Harrell type (MacNeish, Nelken-Terner, and Johnson 1967:77). These characteristics of Oaxaca's later time periods made it easy to identify the 24 points in Zones A and B as redeposited Archaic artifacts.

The Relevance of the Tehuácan Sequence for Archaic Oaxaca

During the 1960s, MacNeish, Nelken-Terner, and Johnson (1967) analyzed more than 3000 points from excavated sites or surface collections in the Tehuacán Valley. The Archaic chronology they produced has served as a reference point for all subsequent research in the Puebla-Oaxaca highlands, including ours. In Early Archaic levels at Guilá Naquitz Cave we recovered an unfinished Lerma point, an Almagre point, and fragments of two possible Trinidad points (Hole 2009: Figures 6.26–6.28). All three of these types were also found in the Early Archaic of the Tehuacán Valley. In Late Archaic levels at Cueva Blanca, we found Trinidad, La Mina, San Nicolás, Tilapa, and Coxcatlán points (this volume). All five of those types were also found in the Late Archaic of the Tehuacán Valley.

To be sure, there were also differences between the two valleys. We found Palmillas corner-notched points in Archaic levels at Cueva Blanca (this volume), and a fragment of corner-notched point also came to light at Guilá Naquitz (Hole 2009: Figure 6.28*b*). Given the number of Palmillas points we recovered at Cueva Blanca, we now suspect that the corner-notched point from Guilá Naquitz belonged to that type as well. This contrasts with the situation in Tehuacán, where there is little or no evidence for Palmillas points during the Archaic. We can say, therefore, that the two Archaic sequences were similar in their broad outlines but different in their details.

Projectile points are relevant to the longstanding debate over whether archaeologists "discover" types or "create them" for analytical purposes. Were we to confine ourselves to a concrete attribute such as stem shape, for example, we could probably claim to have "discovered" four discrete types. That is, Archaic hunters could choose to make (1) laurel-leaf-shaped or teardrop-shaped points with no stem at all; (2) corner-notched points with expanding stems; (3) points with straight-sided stems; or (4) points with contracting stems.

The moment one moves to types based on overall point morphology, however, it becomes harder to claim that the archaeologist is "discovering" rather than "creating" types. Virtually every morphological type has a range of variability, presumably caused by some combination of differential motor skills, individual style preferences, and differences in raw material. Often the outliers in one type's range of variability overlap with the outliers of another type.

To see this phenomenon at work, turn to Figure 43 in MacNeish, Nelken-Terner, and Johnson (1967), the range-of-variation photograph of Trinidad points. Examine the point at the upper right corner of the photo and note its similarity to the Tilapa points in Figure 48. Then turn to their Figure 52, the range-of-variation photograph of Shumla points. Examine the point that lies second from the left in the lower row and note its similarity to the Coxcatlán points in Figure 49. It is easy to distinguish those Trinidad, Tilapa, Shumla, and Coxcatlán points that fit the archaeologist's ideal prototype. Throw in the outliers in the range of variation, however, and not every archaeologist would create the same boundaries between types.

Whether one relies on discrete stem types or the more subjective overall morphological types, the Tehuacán sequence provides a useful starting point for the Archaic of the southern Mexican highlands. During the half century since the excavation of the Tehuacán caves, however, a series of ethnographic and ethnoarchaeological studies have given us new insight into the reasons why Archaic Mexico may have had so many morphological point types and ranges of variation. In the sections that follow, we consider two studies that were not available when the Tehuacán points were studied.

Deliberate Stylistic Variation in Projectiles: An Ethnographic Case

Many hunting-gathering societies had well-established rules that determined how the carcass of a slain animal would be divided among the members of a hunting party. Among the !Kung of Botswana, for example, the carcass would traditionally be divided into 11 portions, and the man credited with the kill was allowed to decide how those portions would be allocated. Hunters therefore needed a way to determine whose arrow had actually killed the animal.

In the 1950s and 1960s, the !Kung used arrows with a metal point, set in a poison-coated foreshaft (Thomas 1959:94–98). On the most general stylistic level, all these projectiles would have been recognized as typical !Kung arrows. At the individual level, however, each hunter decorated his arrows in such a way that it would be recognized as his in the event that it caused a kill (Lee 1979:247).

Deliberate stylistic variation such as this might help explain why certain prehistoric societies—including the Archaic of the Tehuacán Valley—displayed such a variety of projectile point types, rather than conforming to one standardized type. It also raises the following question: If we were to discover a well-preserved Archaic living floor, might we find a distinctive type of atlatl point associated with each hunter's work area?

The answer, provided by additional data gathered from the !Kung, is "not necessarily." Wiessner (1977) reports that the !Kung reduced economic risk through a system of reciprocal gift-giving called *hxaro*. Partners established through *hxaro* exchanges could be counted on to aid each other in lean times.

Arrows were included among the gifts exchanged, and they played an interesting role in maintaining egalitarian relationships. Were it not for *hxaro*, the most skilled !Kung hunters would soon have emerged as a meritocracy, because their arrows would regularly be found to have killed an animal. By exchanging arrows, the !Kung provided every hunter with the opportunity to have one of his arrows credited with a kill.

Lee (1979:248) once examined the quivers of four !Kung men who were hunting together. All but one had arrows made by four to six different men, and two of the men were carrying literally no arrows they themselves had made. In an Archaic society with such a tradition of reciprocal exchange, any given hunter's work area on a living floor might yield atlatl points of several different types. This fact should be borne in mind when considering the diversity of points in Zones D and C of Cueva Blanca.

Rejuvenation as a Source of Morphological Variation in Projectiles: An Ethnoarchaeological Case

There is yet another way in which archaeologists' ideas have evolved during the half century since the Tehuacán Project. It has become increasingly clear to chipped stone analysts that whenever possible, damaged projectile points were reworked rather than being replaced (Frison et al. 1976). In the course of being reworked, many points were so altered that they could be considered a different morphological type.

The concept of reworking, or "point rejuvenation," allows us to look at the Tehuacán and Cueva Blanca collections with fresh eyes. Not only does reworking help to explain some of the variation we see, it even raises the possibility that certain morphological types—Hidalgo points, for example—might consist mainly of reworked specimens.

One of the most useful studies of atlatl point rejuvenation is Flenniken and Raymond's (1986) experiment with Elko corner-notched points. The Elko point was a common Great Basin type, considered a "time-sensitive" artifact. In their undamaged state Elko points had corner notches, resulting in an expanding stem that one might compare to a turkey's tail.

What Flenniken and Raymond did was to make 30 prototypic Elko points from obsidian. These points were then hafted into willow foreshafts, attached to main shafts, and thrown at a target using an atlatl. In the course of this ethnoarchaeological experiment, many of the points were damaged. All but the most severely damaged points were then rejuvenated by Flenniken and Raymond, who reworked them into useful projectiles.

In the process, Flenniken and Raymond discovered one reason why damaged points might have been rejuvenated rather than replaced. It took them 40 minutes, on average, to manufacture an Elko point, while a broken point could be reworked into a functional projectile in an average of only three minutes. In perhaps one of three cases, however, the rejuvenation produced a point that would have been considered a different morphological type, such as a Gatecliff point or a Rosegate point. Some rejuvenated points, for example, went from corner-notched to contracting-stemmed; others, while retaining their original stem, were of necessity given a shorter body (Figure 6.1).

What the experiments by Flenniken and Raymond did was to throw a monkey wrench into the practice of confidently assigning every atlatl point to a named morphological type. We now have to look critically at each point, assessing whether its shape is the product of design or rejuvenation. To be sure, Archaic points did come in many distinctive shapes. Because of widespread rejuvenation, however, there may not have been as many morphological types as archaeologists believed in the 1960s.

Point Types Shared by the Tehuacán Caves and Cueva Blanca

Having considered some of the causes of morphological variation in atlatl points, let us now examine the morphological types present at Cueva Blanca. They were—in approximately the chronological order in which they appeared—Palmillas, La Mina, Trinidad, Tilapa, San Nicolás, Coxcatlán, Hidalgo, Abasolo, Pelona, and Gary. Because all these types have been previously defined in the Tehuacán Valley, we will draw on the original descriptions written by MacNeish, Nelken-Terner, and Johnson (1967).

Palmillas Points

Perhaps the most distinctive feature of the Palmillas point (Figure 6.2) is that it is corner-notched, giving it an expanding stem with a convex base. Points with this type of stem seem to have been favored earlier in Oaxaca than in Tehuacán, since we found corner-notched points in Early Archaic levels at both Cueva Blanca and Guilá Naquitz (Hole 2009: Figure 6.28b and this volume).

La Mina Points

La Mina points (Figures 6.3, 6.4) have "short, straight-sided stems with straight to slightly concave bases" (MacNeish, Nelken-Terner, and Johnson 1967:62). The stem is usually more than half the width of the base of the body and "is separated from it by a sharp shoulder at right angles to the main axis." The time span of La Mina points in Tehuacán and Oaxaca appears to be similar; they were well represented in the Late Archaic.

Trinidad Points

The distinctive feature of the Trinidad point (Figure 6.5) is a relatively wide, slightly contracting stem with a rounded or convex base. The shoulders "are usually marked with fairly prominent short barbs" (MacNeish, Nelken-Terner, and Johnson 1967:62). Trinidad points were popular during most of the Archaic in the Tehuacán Valley.

Tilapa Points

Tilapa was one of the most common point types of the Coxcatlán phase in the Tehuacán Valley, and two examples showed up in Zone D of Cueva Blanca (Figure 6.6). The bodies of these large points were "often wider than they are long" (MacNeish, Nelken-Terner, and Johnson 1967:64) and their most distinctive features were the huge barbs at the junction of body and stem. The stem itself was large, with a convex base.

San Nicolás Points

These were long, narrow projectile points with short, wide contracting stems and convex to almost pointed bases (Figure 6.7). "The shoulder where the stem joins the body is not well marked; at most, there is a short step roughly at right angles to the main axis" (MacNeish, Nelken-Terner, and Johnson 1967:63). In the Tehuacán Valley, San Nicolás points were most common in the Abejas phase, and we found two in Zone C of Cueva Blanca.

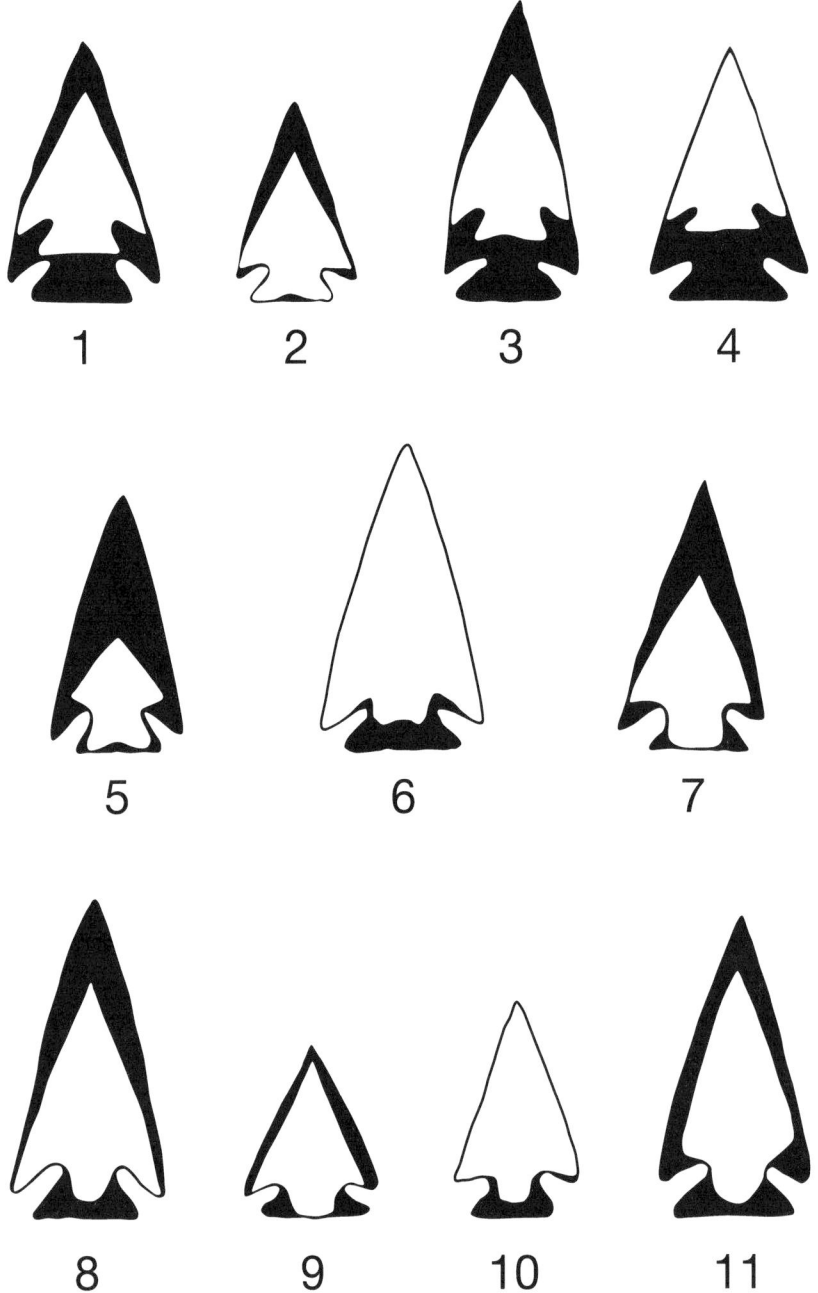

Figure 6.1. The effect of rejuvenation on damaged Elko points. The black silhouettes show the original shape of the point; the white figures show the same point after reworking. While Specimens 1–4 at least retained their expanding stems/corner notching, Specimens 5–11 became so modified as to constitute new point types. (Redrawn, with modification, from Flenniken and Raymond 1986: Figures 4 and 5).

Coxcatlán Points

These very distinctive points (Figure 6.8) are almost wafer thin "and have been made with careful, delicate precision" (MacNeish, Nelken-Terner, and Johnson 1967:65). Their most distinctive features are the extremely pronounced shoulder barbs, which can make the point wider than it is long. These barbs, extending back at a 45° angle, almost reach to the base of the tapering stem.

In the Tehuacán Valley, Coxcatlán points were most common in the Abejas phase, contemporary with Zone C of Cueva Blanca. The two Coxcatlán points we recovered do not appear to be made on local raw material and may well have been obtained through reciprocal gift-giving with another group.

Hidalgo Points

MacNeish, Nelken-Terner, and Johnson (1967:61) describe Hidalgo points (Figure 6.9) as having "contracting stems that are as long as or longer than their bodies." Our suspicion is that these unusual proportions are the result of point rejuvenation, and those suspicions are only strengthened by examining Figure 42 of MacNeish, Nelken-Terner, and Johnson (1967). The points shown at upper right and lower left in that photograph clearly appear to be reworked specimens of other point types.

Since we have not seen with our own eyes every point MacNeish called "Hidalgo," we cannot guarantee that their morphology was always the result of reworking. We see a real possibility, however, that many of the points classified as "Hidalgo" are rejuvenated specimens of other types.

Abasolo Points

Abasolo points had no stem (Figure 6.10a). They bore "the outline of a tear drop, with rounded bases, slightly convex sides, and tapering tips" (MacNeish, Nelken-Terner, and Johnson 1967:57). This point type was rare in the Archaic of Oaxaca and were it not for its small size, it could be mistaken for an ovoid biface.

Pelona Points

The Pelona (Figure 6.10b) was another stemless teardrop-shaped point, one that could be confused with an ovoid biface. Its distinguishing feature was that "the edges from the midpoint to the tip are serrated and contrast with the smooth edges of the basal half" (MacNeish, Nelken-Terner, and Johnson 1967:70). In the Tehuacán Valley these points were most common in the Abejas phase.

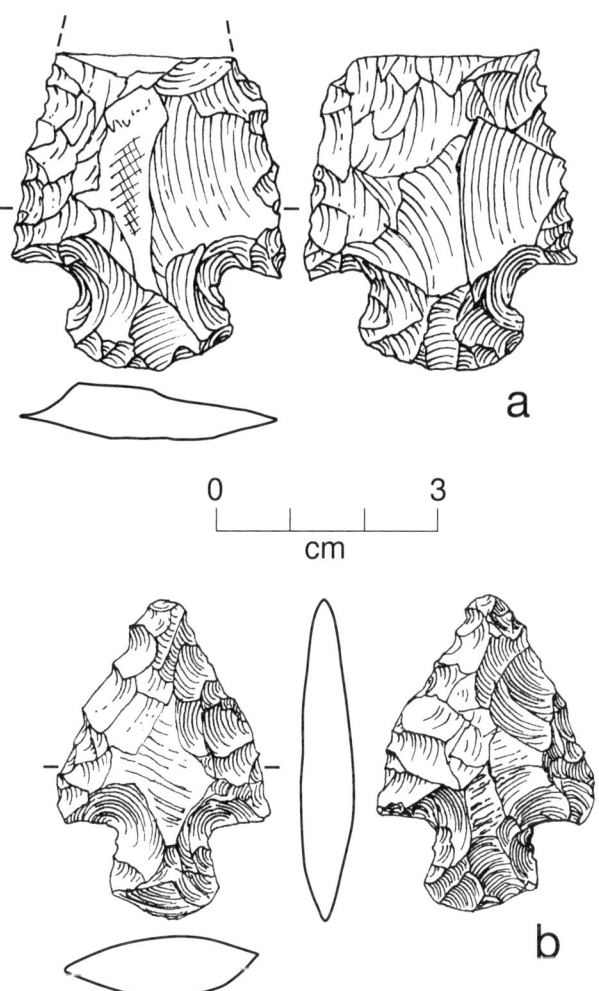

Figure 6.2. Two Palmillas points recovered from Zone D of Cueva Blanca. *a*, discarded in Square J14, was evidently considered too damaged to rejuvenate. *b* was found in Square D6.

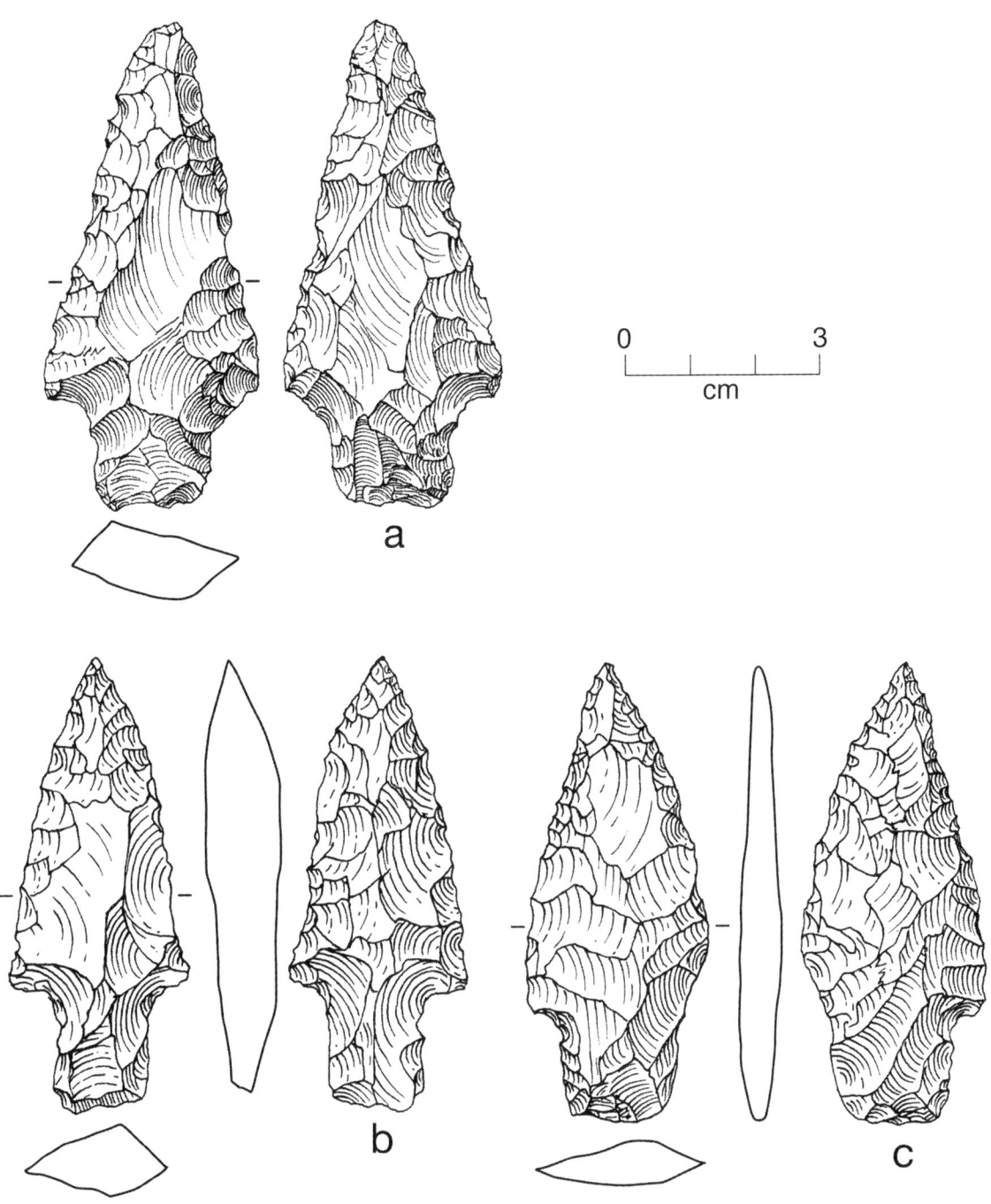

Figure 6.3. La Mina points from Cueva Blanca. *a* was found *in situ* in Zone C (Square E 11). *b* and *c* were both redeposited in Zone B. Although *c* appears to have a damaged shoulder barb, all three of these points are prototypically La Mina.

The Archaic Projectile Points

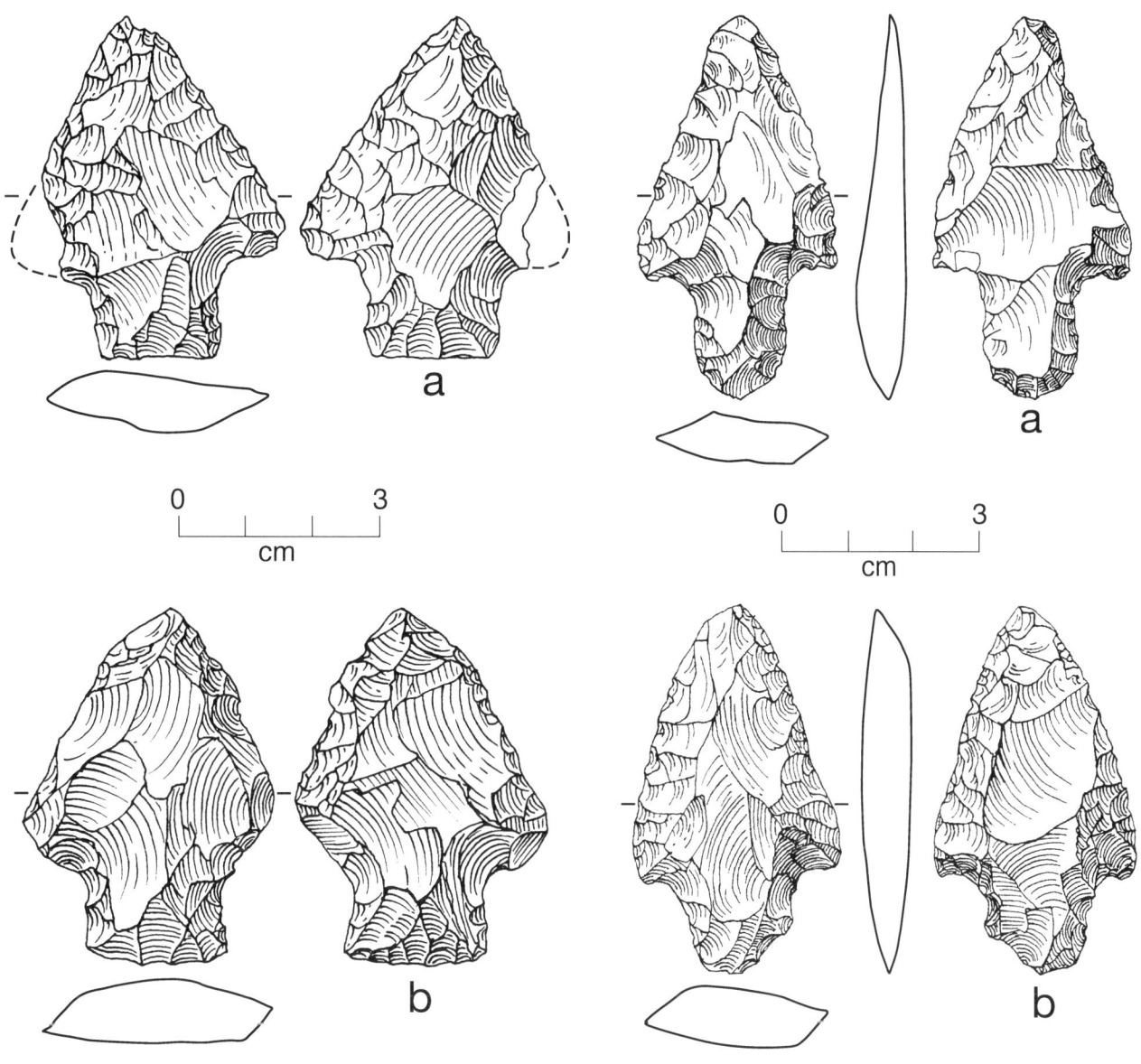

Figure 6.4. When La Mina points were damaged and rejuvenated, the stem often remained the same while the body became shorter. *a* was found *in situ* in Zone D (Square C7). *b* was redeposited in Zone A.

Figure 6.5. Trinidad points from Cueva Blanca. *a* was discovered in Zone D (Square D7). *b* was redeposited in Zone A.

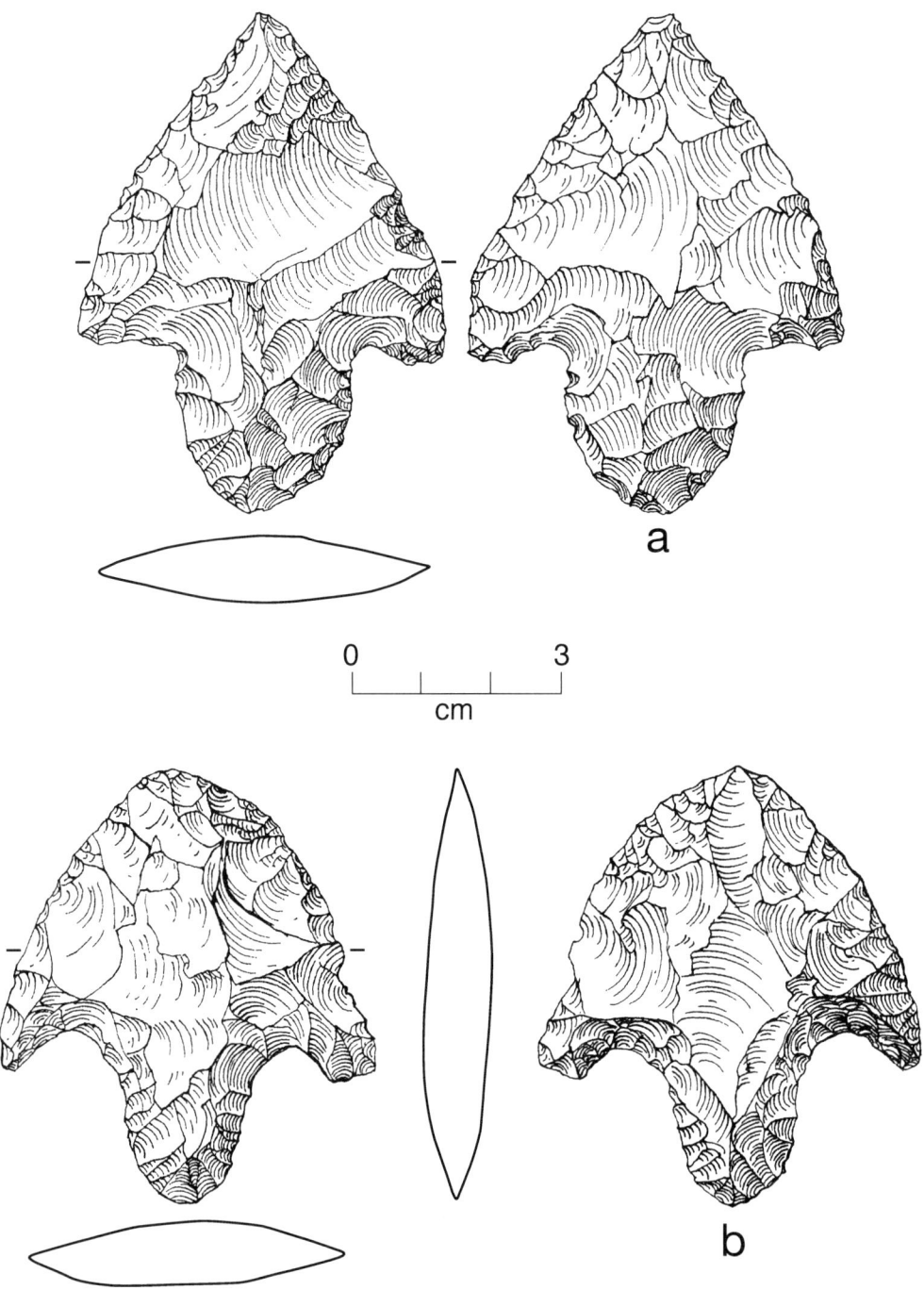

Figure 6.6. These two Tilapa points, both recovered in Zone D, exemplify the morphological change that rejuvenation can bring about. *a*, found in Square D9, is relatively undamaged. *b*, found in Square D6, has clearly undergone reworking following damage.

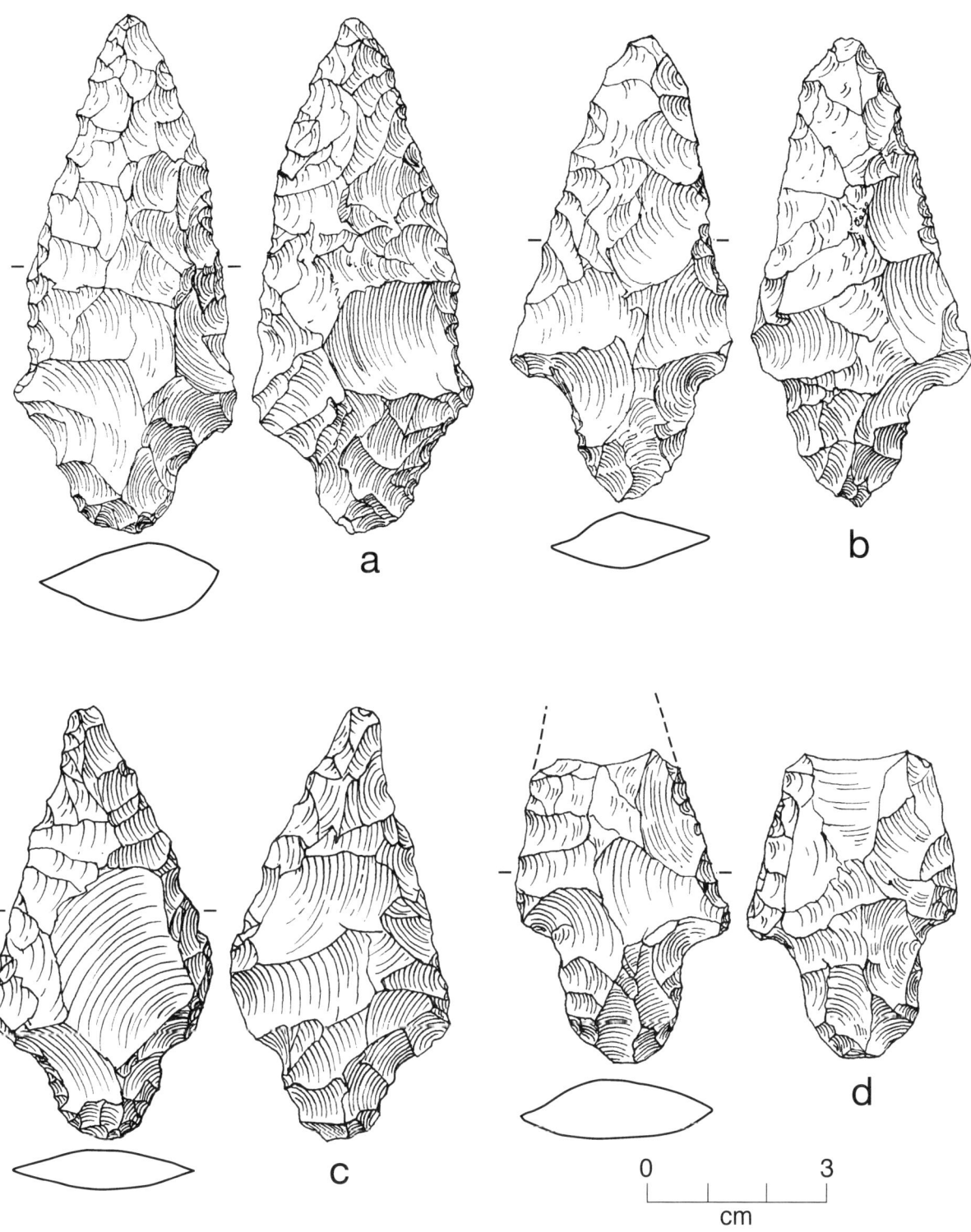

Figure 6.7. San Nicolás points. *a* and *b* were found in Zone C of Cueva Blanca (in Squares C9 and E5 respectively). *c* was redeposited in Zone B of Cueva Blanca. *d* was found on the talus of Cave OC-27, 150 m to the south of Cueva Blanca.

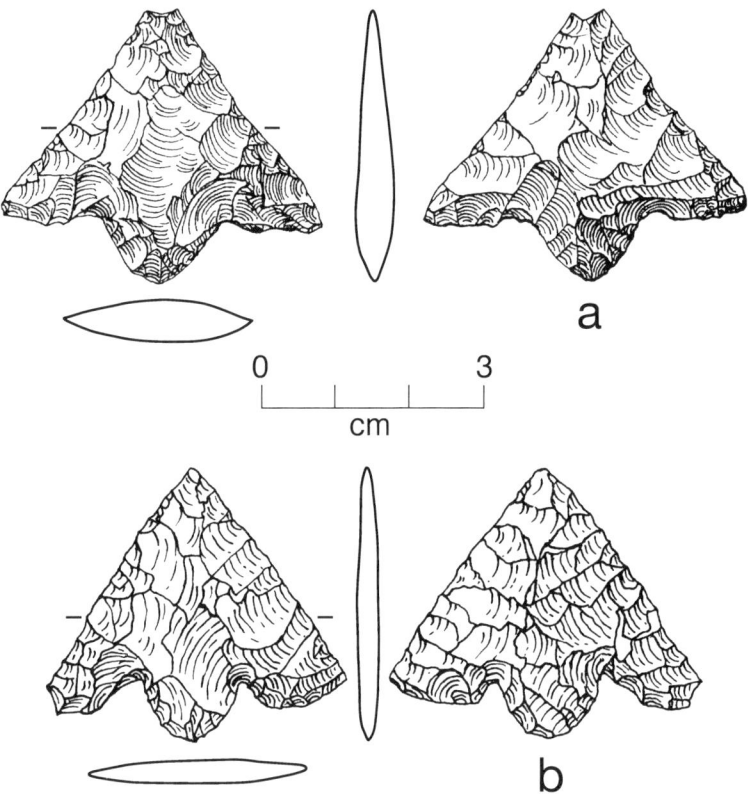

Figure 6.8. Coxcatlán points from Cueva Blanca. *a* was found *in situ* in Zone C (Square D8). *b* was redeposited in Zone B.

Gary Points

Gary points (Figure 6.11) were rare in Oaxaca, and even in the Tehuacán Valley they were represented only by a diminutive version that MacNeish, Nelken-Terner, and Johnson (1967:66–67) named "Garyito." Gary points were characterized by a broad triangular body, short shoulder barbs, and a strongly tapering stem. This type could most easily be confused with a Trinidad point.

Points that do not Fit any Known Tehuacán Type

In addition to the point types mentioned above, we found isolated specimens that could not be fitted conveniently into any of MacNeish, Nelken-Terner, and Johnson's types. Since these points were each represented by only one specimen, it made no sense to create new type names for them.

Figure 6.12 illustrates a unique point from Zone D. The stem of this large point is not unlike a La Mina stem, but the body of the point is larger and more spade-shaped than that of a typical La Mina point.

Figure 6.13 illustrates an unusually large point with a missing stem. We could more easily see this artifact as a spear point than an atlatl dart point. We cannot assign it to any Tehuacán type, especially because we do not know the shape of its stem.

Figure 6.14 illustrates two points that, owing to their fragmentary condition, cannot be assigned to any of MacNeish, Nelken-Terner, and Johnson's types.

The Points from Zone E

Let us now consider the stratigraphic context of Cueva Blanca's *in situ* projectile points, beginning with Zone E. Unfortunately, this modest Early Archaic occupation produced only two points (Figures 6.15, 6.16). In Square E4 we found what appeared to be an unfinished Palmillas point made of dark silicified siltstone. Some five meters away, in Square E9, we recovered a point too badly damaged to be classified. All we know for sure is that this point had a contracting stem and prominent barbs and appears to have been made of black-and-gray chert with white speckles.

The Points from Zone D

Our largest sample of *in situ* Late Archaic points—10—was recovered from Zone D (Figures 6.17, 6.18). Eight of these points

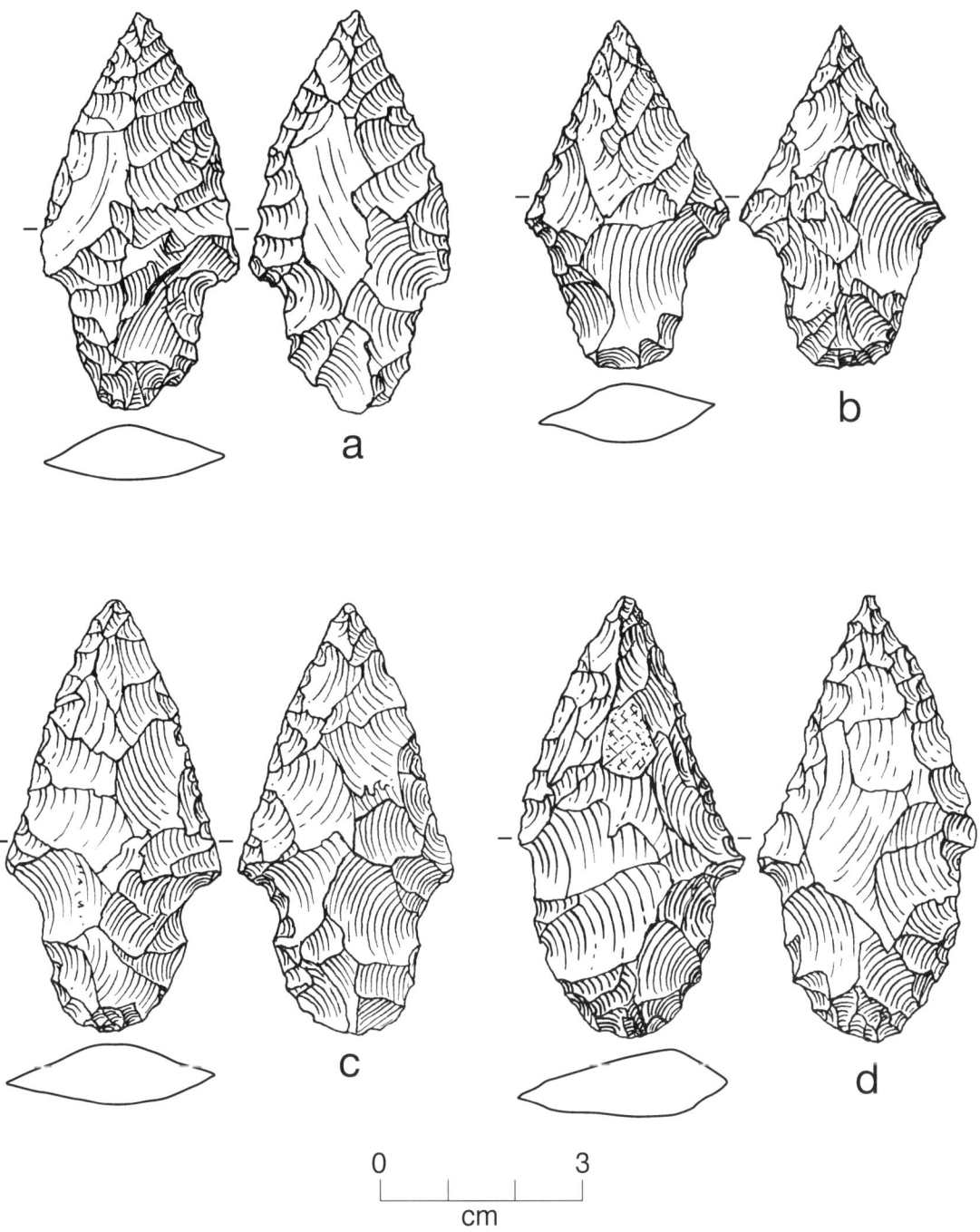

Figure 6.9. Many points assigned to the type "Hidalgo" appear to have been rejuvenated, and would probably have been assigned to other types before they were damaged. In the case of the points shown here, *b* and *d* show signs of damage to the body and *a* shows damage to the stem. (*a* and *b* were redeposited in Zone B; *c* and *d* were redeposited in Zone A.)

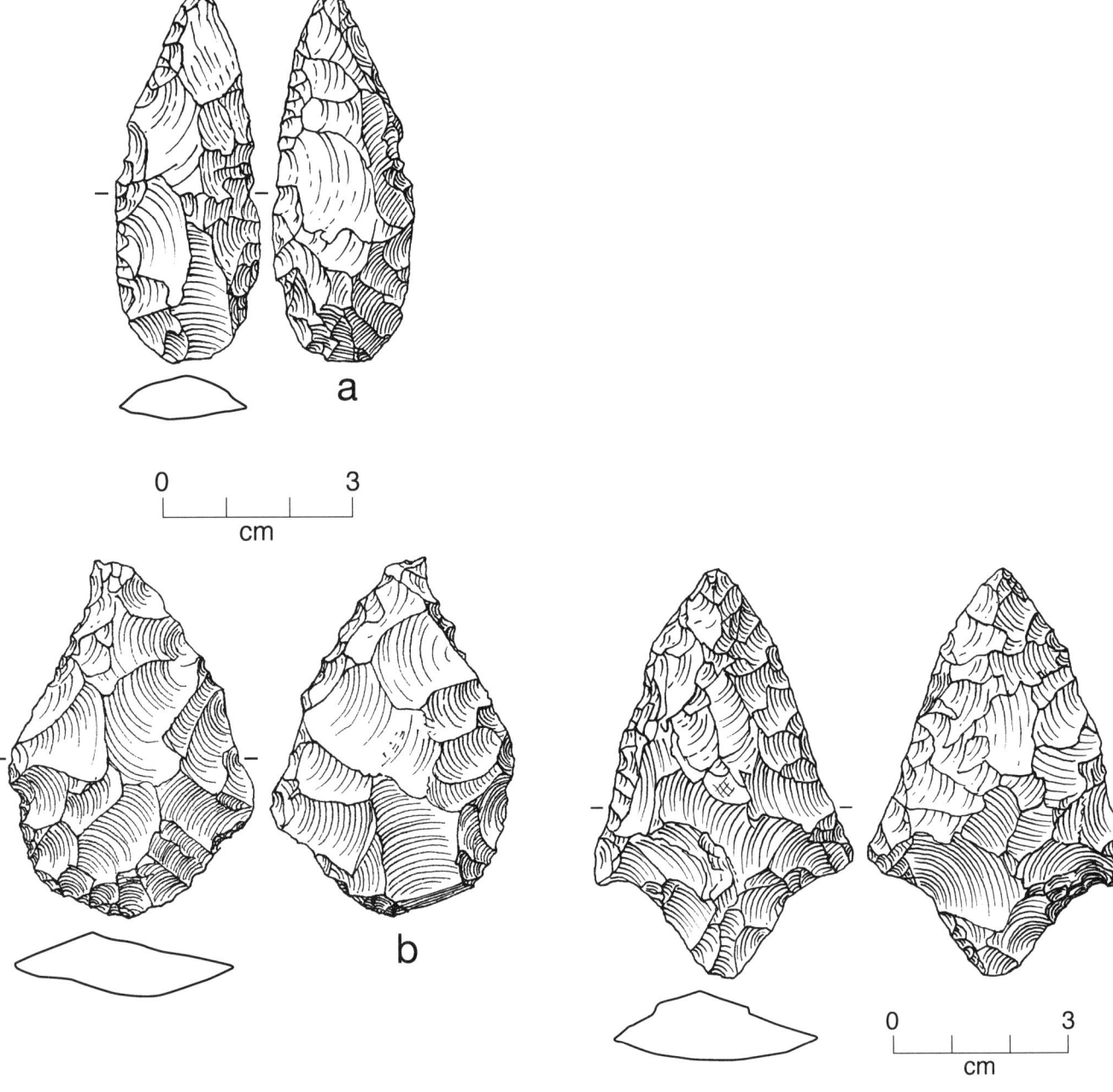

Figure 6.10. Stemless Archaic points redeposited in later levels at Cueva Blanca. *a* is an Abasolo point from Zone A. *b*, which was recovered from Zone B, appears to be a damaged Pelona point.

Figure 6.11. A Gary point redeposited in Zone B.

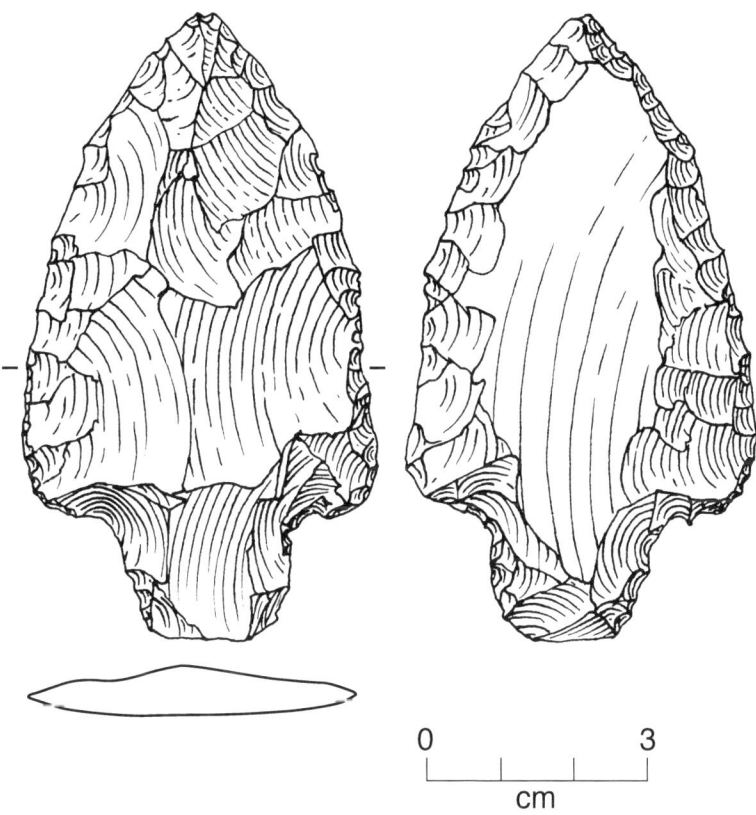

Figure 6.12. This point, discovered *in situ* in Zone D (Square C8), does not readily conform to any of the Tehuacán Valley types.

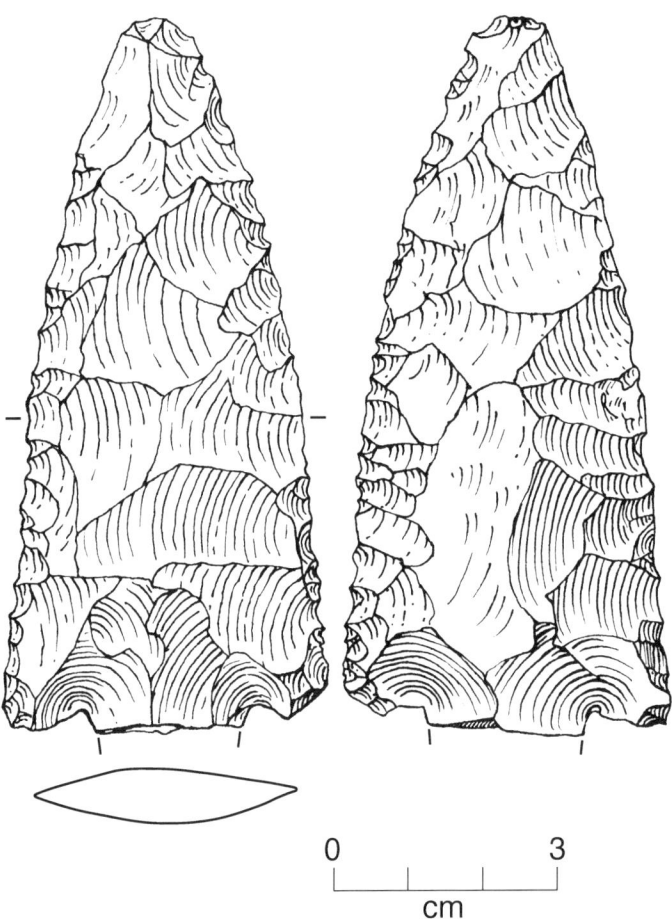

Figure 6.13. An unusually large point recovered from Zone C (Square F8). This point cannot be classified, owing to the fact that we cannot see the shape of its stem. It is large enough to have been a spear point, rather than an atlatl point.

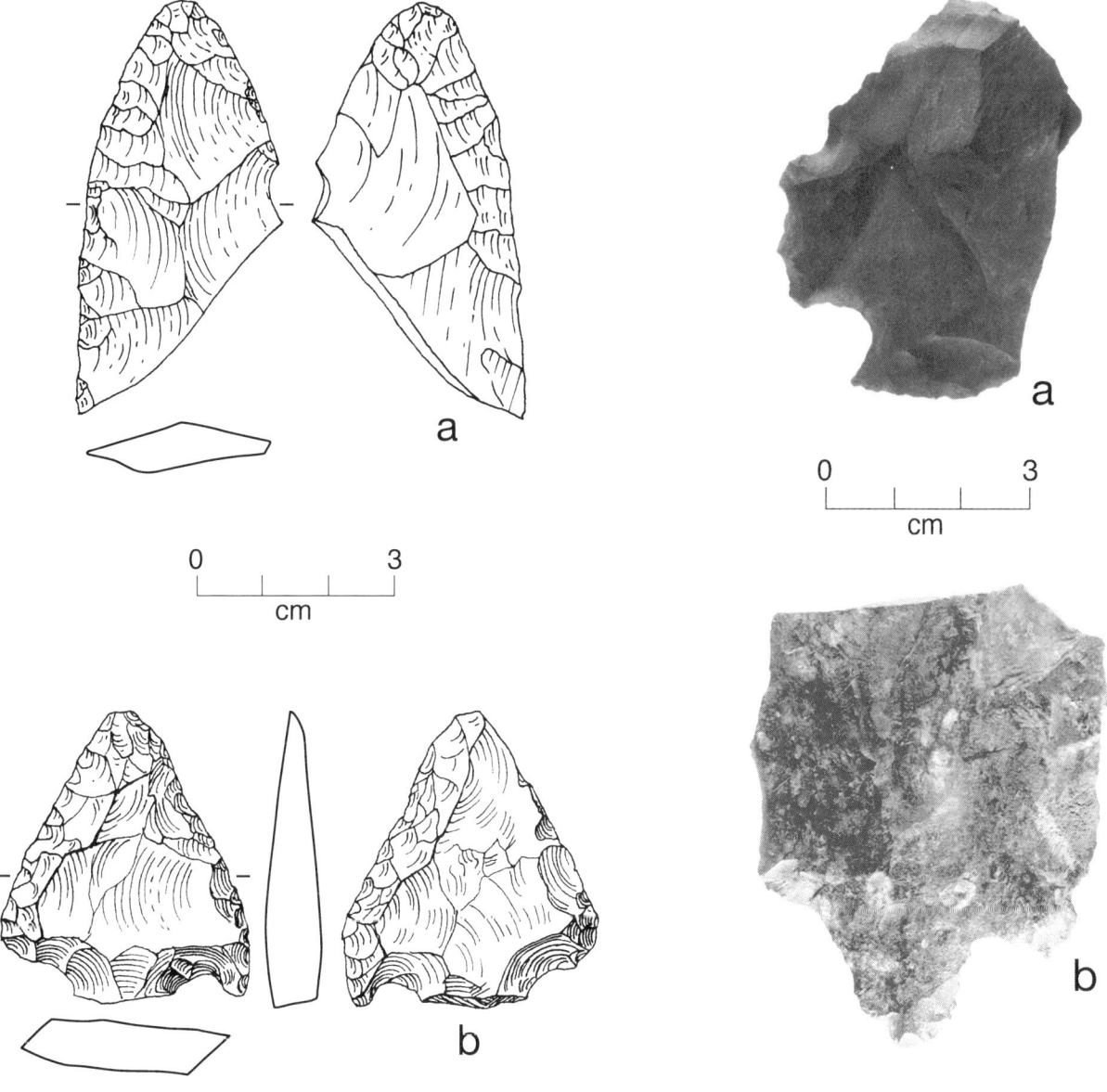

Figure 6.14. Unclassified point fragments redeposited in Zone A features. *a* was found in Feature 1. *b* was found in Feature 3.

Figure 6.15. Two atlatl points from Zone E. *a*, unfinished Palmillas point of dark gray siliceous siltstone (Square E4). *b*, contracting-stem point of mottled black, white and gray chert, too damaged to classify (Square D9).

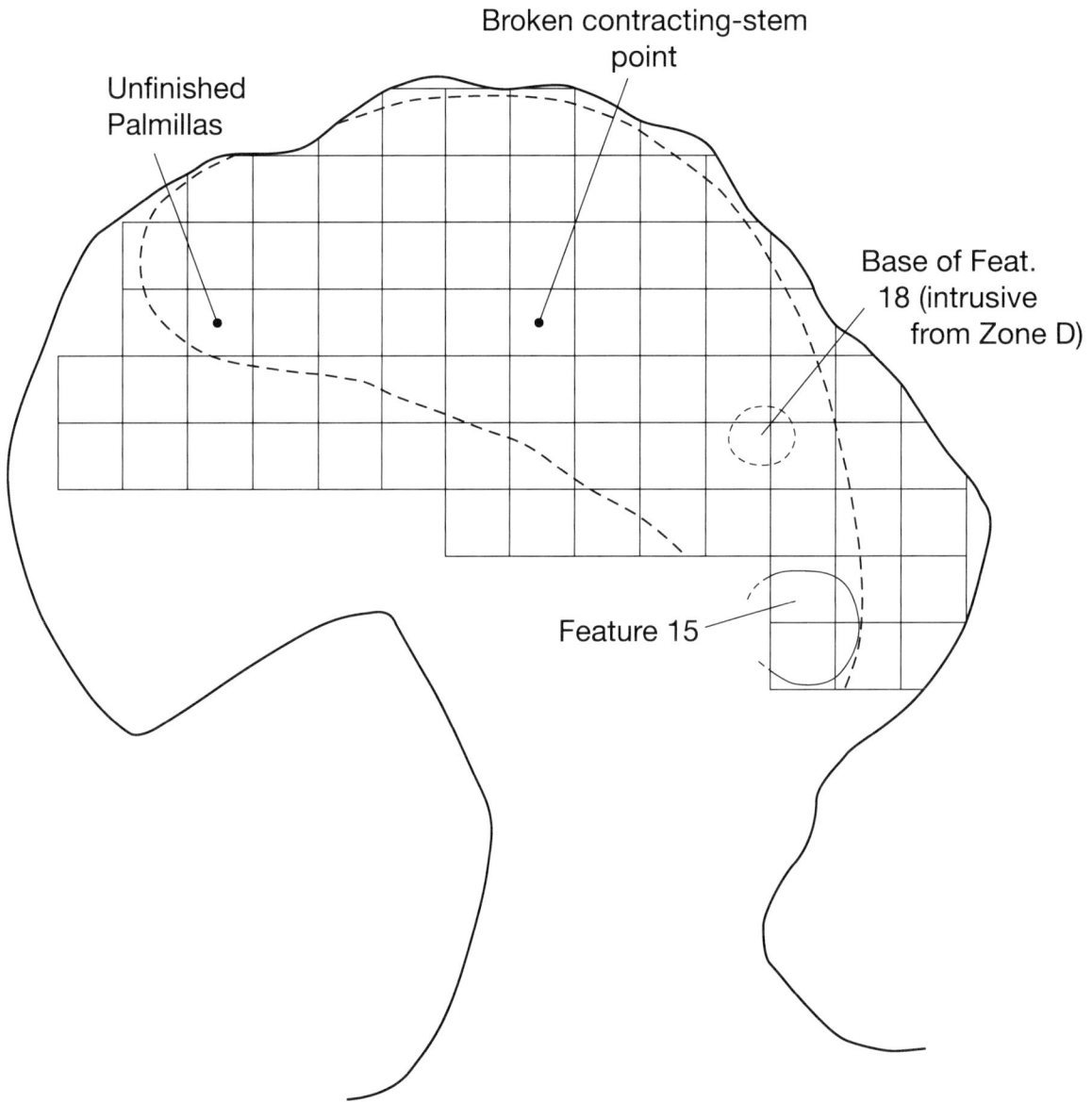

Figure 6.16. The distribution of projectile points in Zone E. The suspected limits of the Zone E living floor are indicated by a dashed line.

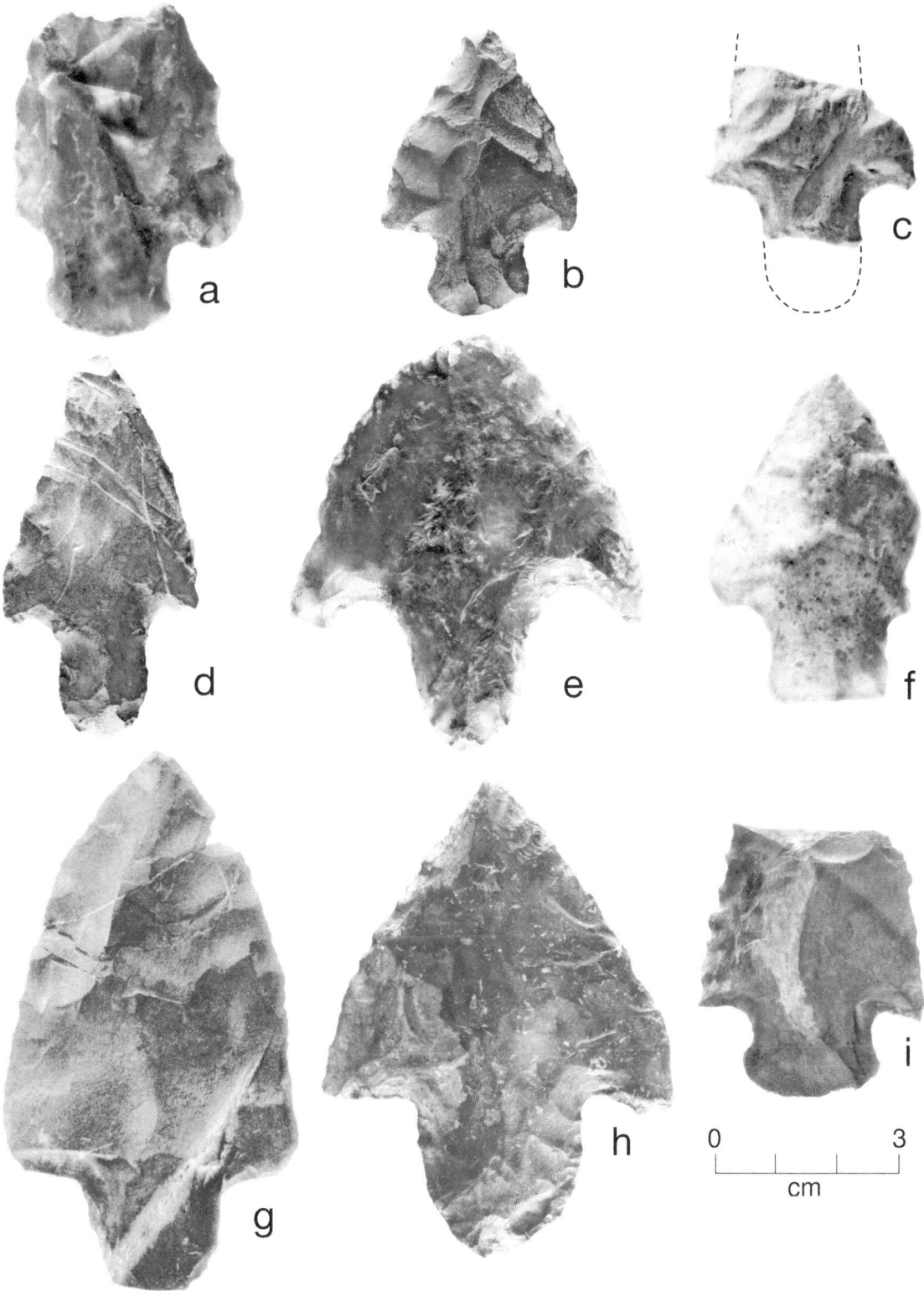

Figure 6.17. Atlatl points from Zone D. *a*, Palmillas point from Square C5. *b*, Palmillas point from Square D6. *c*, broken Trinidad point from Square D5. *d*, Trinidad point from Square D7. *e*, rejuvenated Tilapa point from Square D6. *f*, La Mina point from Square C7. *g*, unclassified point from Square C8. *h*, Tilapa point from Square D9. *i*, Palmillas point from Square J14.

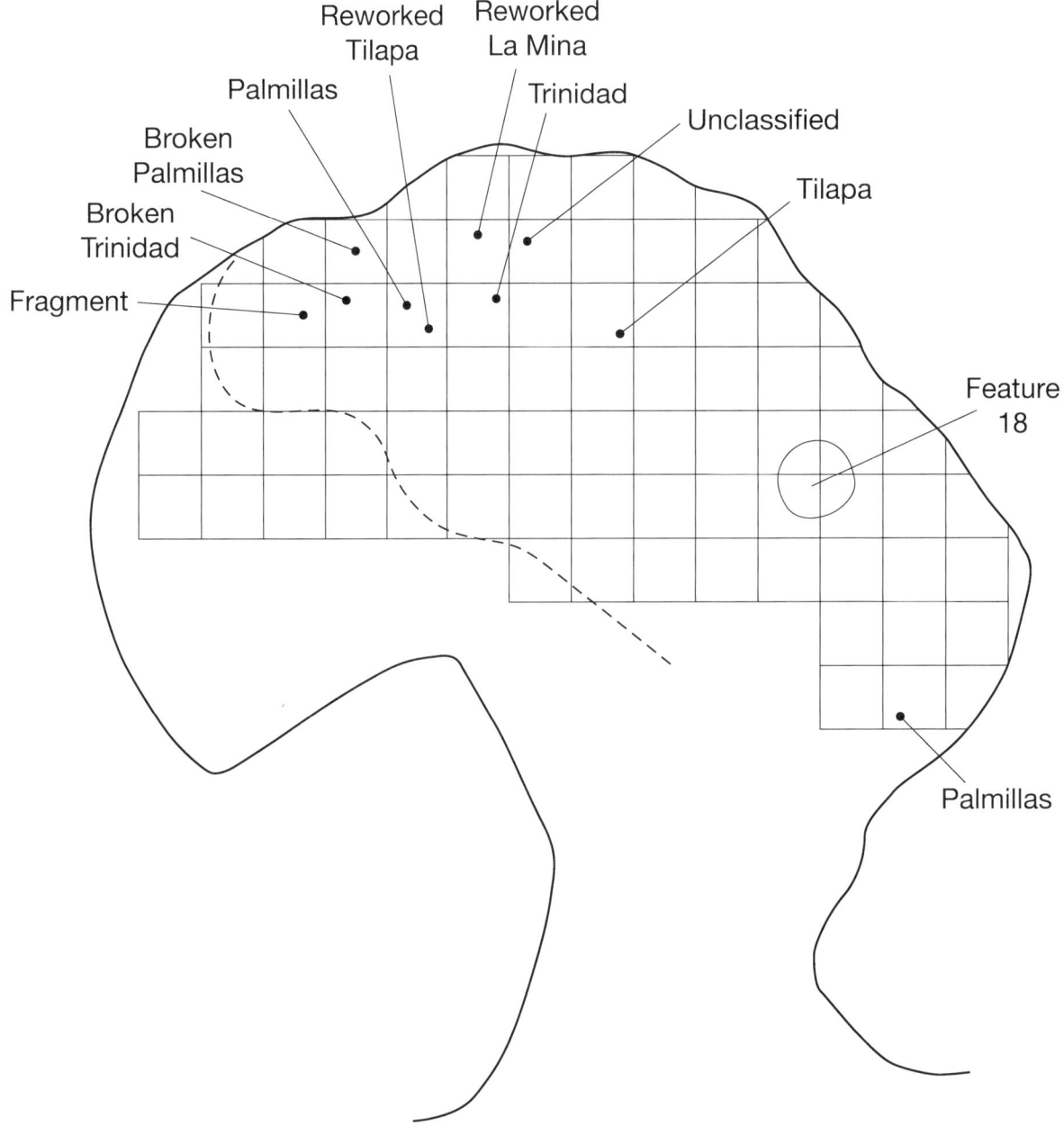

Figure 6.18. The distribution of projectile points in Zone D. The suspected limits of the Zone D living floor are indicated by a dashed line.

occurred in a 10 m² area in the northeast quadrant of the cave; a ninth lay not far from this cluster. The tenth point from Zone D lay far to the southwest in Square J14. Almost all the points in Zone D could be assigned to one of four morphological types: Palmillas, Trinidad, Tilapa, or La Mina.

Let us look first at the cluster of eight points in the northeast quadrant. We found two Palmillas points in C5 and D6, two squares that shared a corner. Two Trinidad points were plotted in Squares D5 and D7. A rejuvenated Tilapa point was found in Square D6, and what appeared to be a reworked La Mina point in Square C7. A large point found in Square C8 did not fit conveniently into any of the Tehuacán types. Finally, an unclassifiable point fragment was recovered in Square D4.

A second Tilapa point, discovered in Square D9, may have been an outlier from the cluster just described. The tenth atlatl point from this stratum, however, was found in Square J14, too many meters from the cluster to be related. This tenth specimen was the third Palmillas point we recovered from Zone D.

When one examines the raw material from which the Zone D points were made, an interesting pattern emerges. Two of the Palmillas points (those from Squares D6 and J14) were made on the same dark gray silicified siltstone. Both Trinidad points, on the other hand, were made of chert. In the case of the Square D5 specimen, this chert was whitish, while in the case of the Square D7 specimen, it was gray with thin white bands.

Both Tilapa points were made on similar waxy gray chert or chalcedony. In the case of the Square D6 specimen this material had reddish veins, while in the case of the Square D9 specimen it had light speckles. One could argue that the products of at least three different hunters were represented in Zone D, each hunter having chosen his own raw material and preferred point morphology. At the same time, we must consider the possibility that these hunters practiced gift exchanges of points (Lee 1979:248).

As for the remaining Zone D points, the unclassified specimen from Square C8 (Figure 6.17g) was made on the same dark gray silicified siltstone as two of the Palmillas points. The Palmillas point from Square C5, on the other hand, was made of waxy chert with white, black, and brown bands, distinct from the siltstone used for the other two Palmillas points. The La Mina point was made on whitish chert with specks of gray, not unlike the Trinidad point from Square D5.

The Points from Zone C

We recovered seven projectile points from Stratigraphic Zone C. These points were not as clustered as those in Zone D had been; instead, they were scattered over a 4 x 8 m area (Figures 6.19, 6.20). The recognizable morphological types were San Nicolás, La Mina, and Coxcatlán. Two San Nicolás points occurred in Squares C9 and E5; one La Mina point was found in Square E11. The unusual point found in Square F8 did not fit into any of the usual Tehuacán types, and was large enough to have belonged to a spear rather than an atlatl dart. Squares E4 and F6 produced unclassifiable point fragments, one of which was in the spear-sized category like the point in Square F8.

One of the most exciting discoveries made in Zone C was the prototypic Coxcatlán point found in Square D8. This artifact was strikingly similar to Coxcatlán points found in the Tehuacán Valley and was made on a waxy gray chert with red and white speckles that does not match other raw material from Zone C. It would not surprise us, therefore, to learn that this point had been obtained in exchange from a hunter in a neighboring band.

As for the other points in this stratum, the two large enough to be spear points (Squares F6 and F8) were both made on gray chert. The two San Nicolás points were made on different raw material; the specimen from Square C9 was made on light brown to pink chert with white bands, while the specimen from Square E5 was made from silicified volcanic tuff with glassy inclusions. The La Mina point from Square E11 was made on waxy chert with pink and gray bands. Both the diversity of raw material used in Zone C, and the strongly nonlocal appearance of the Coxcatlán point, leave us open to the suggestion that we are dealing with men who hunted together and occasionally exchanged gifts of atlatl darts.

Points Redeposited in Zone B

Zone B of Cueva Blanca, as previously mentioned, featured thousands of loose firecracked rocks and a frustrating mixture of artifacts from the Archaic, the Formative, and the Postclassic. Included were 13 Archaic atlatl points or fragments thereof, all redeposited and out of their original context (Figure 6.21).

Five of the points in Zone B belonged to types known from Zones D and C. Included were two La Mina points, one Trinidad point, one San Nicolás, and one Coxcatlán. Five additional Archaic points from Zone B could be classified in the Tehuacán system, but belonged to types not represented in Zones D and C. Two would have been classified by MacNeish, Nelken-Terner, and Johnson (1967) as Hidalgo; one appeared to be a broken Abasolo point; one appeared to be a damaged Pelona point; and two others would have been classified as Gary points. Finally, Zone B produced three Archaic points that were too fragmentary to classify.

In terms of raw material, the two La Mina points were different. One had been made of dark silicified siltstone; the other was made of waxy light brown chert or chalcedony with specks of white, brown, red, and black. The Trinidad point was of dark silicified siltstone; so, too, was the San Nicolás point.

The Coxcatlán point redeposited in Zone B, just like the one discovered *in situ* in Zone C, had been made on nonlocal waxy gray chert with red and white speckles. While we cannot be sure that it was redeposited from Zone C, it is similar enough to the Zone C specimen to have been made by the same person.

The raw materials used for the two Hidalgo points in Zone B were not dissimilar. One point was made of dark gray chert; the other had been made of gray chert with brown and purple bands.

Figure 6.19. Projectile points from Zone C. *a*, San Nicolás point from Square C9. *b*, San Nicolás point from Square E5. *c*, La Mina point from Square E11. *d*, Coxcatlán point from Square D8. *e*, large unclassified point from Square F8. *f*, fragment of unclassified point from Square F6.

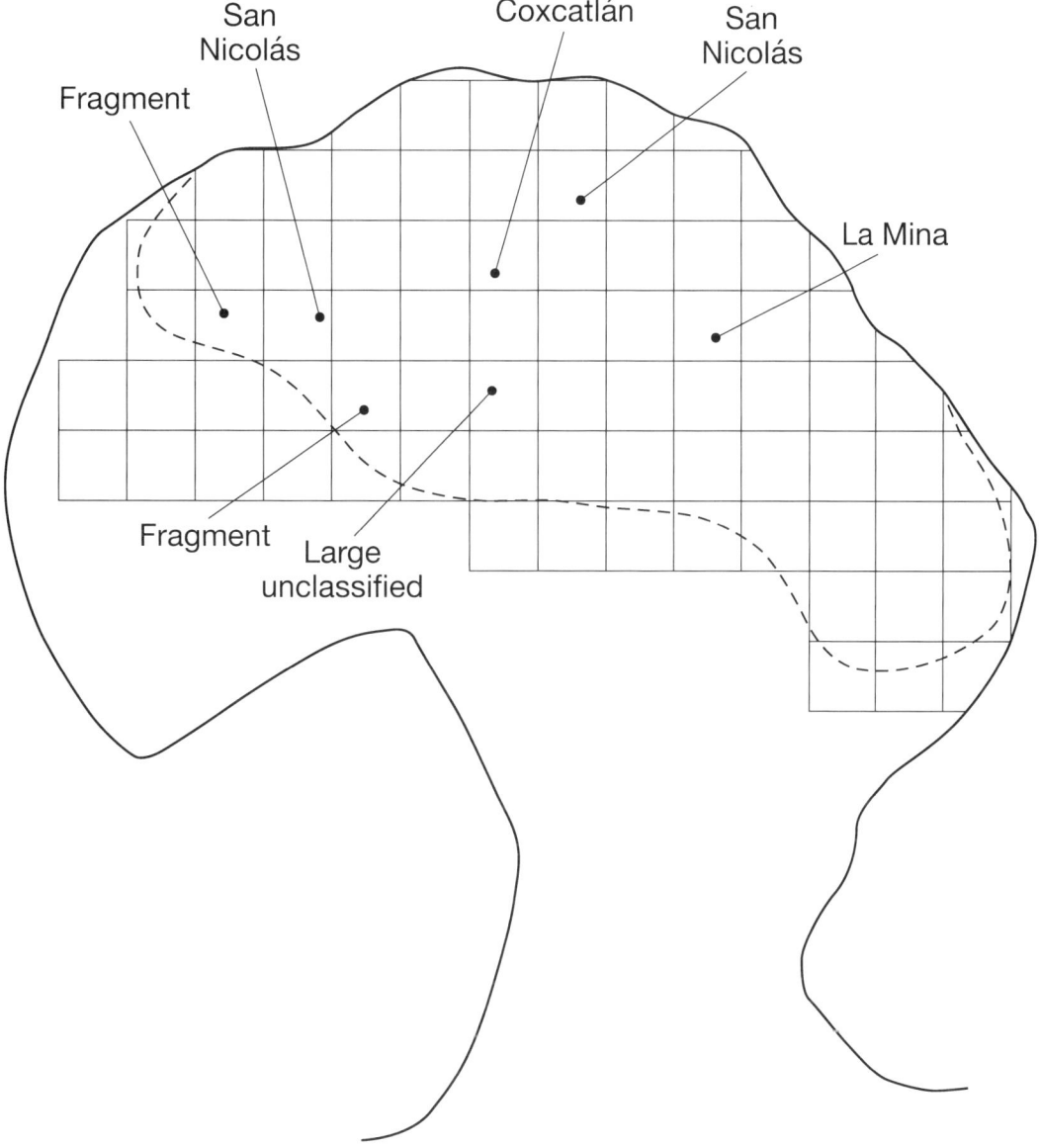

Figure 6.20. Distribution of projectile points in Zone C. The suspected limits of the Zone C living floor are indicated by a dashed line.

Figure 6.21. Representative Archaic points redeposited in Zone B. *a*, *b*, La Mina points. *c*, San Nicolás point. *d*, Coxcatlán point. *e*, Hidalgo point. *f*, broken Abasolo point. *g*, Pelona point. *h*, Gary point. *i*, reworked Gary point.

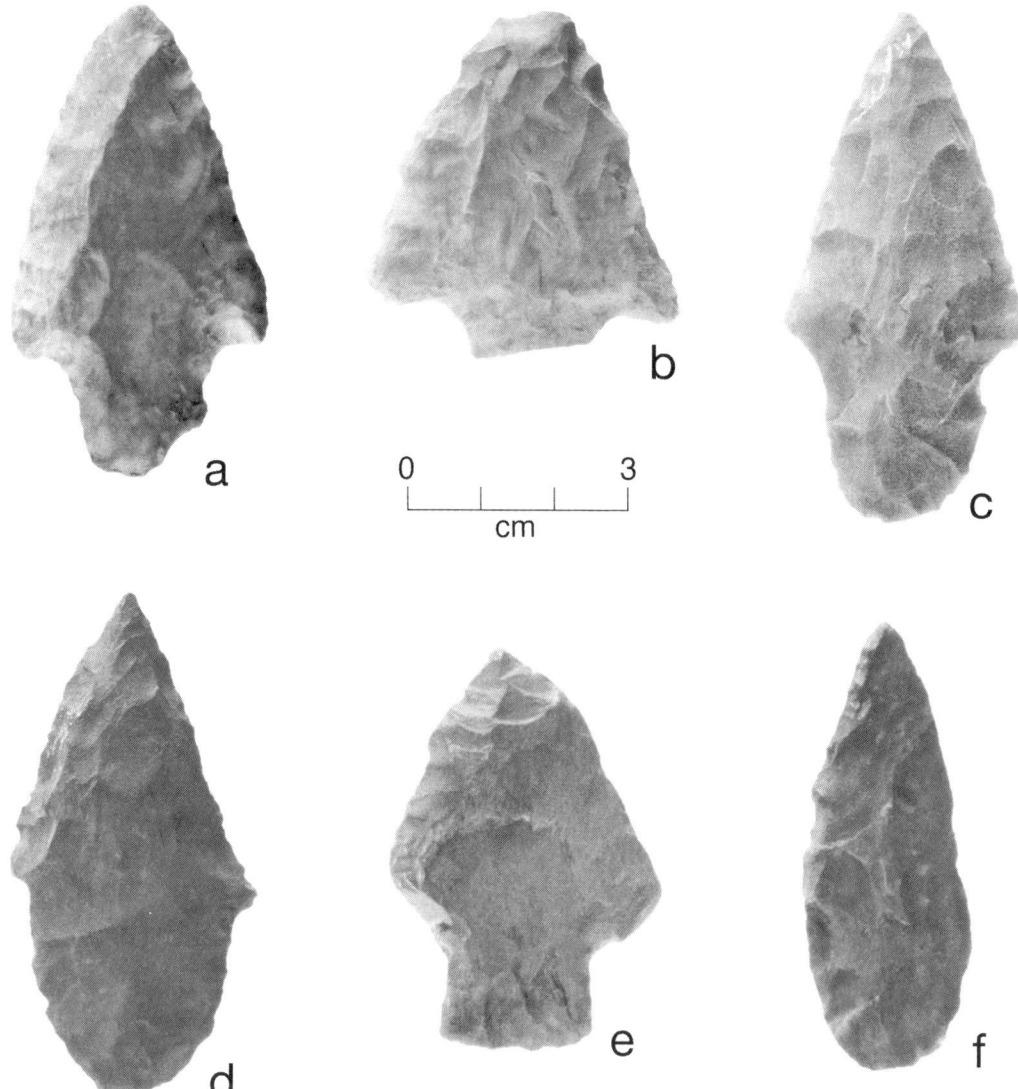

Figure 6.22. Representative Archaic points redeposited in Zone A. *a*, Trinidad point. *b*, broken Trinidad point. *c*, Hidalgo point. *d*, Hidalgo point that appears to be a reworked version of another point type (perhaps Tilapa). *e*, reworked La Mina point. *f*, Abasolo point.

The two Gary points were both made from chert. One, however, had been made from white chert, while the other was made from waxy gray chert. The damaged Pelona point was made of whitish-brown chert with red specks.

We suspect that many of the Archaic points from Zone B were redeposited when the creators of that stratum dug intrusive pits or collected stones for roasting pits. The fact that we recovered no Hidalgo, Abasolo, Pelona, or Gary points in any of our three Archaic strata, however, raises another possibility. That possibility is that there had once been an additional Late Archaic living floor stratigraphically above Zone C—a stratum whose artifacts were later disturbed and incorporated into the mixed deposit we called Zone B. Unfortunately, there is no way to test this possibility.

Points Redeposited in Zone A

Zone A, a Postclassic stratum with multiple storage pits and a subterranean kiln, produced seven more redeposited Archaic atlatl points (Figure 6.22). Included were two Trinidad points, two Hidalgo points, one reworked La Mina, and one Abasolo. All of these points belonged to types found in lower levels of the cave. The sixth point was a fragment too small to classify.

Three of the Archaic projectiles from Zone A—the La Mina point and both Hidalgos—were made of dark silicified siltstone. The Abasolo point was made of dark purplish silicified volcanic tuff. One Trinidad point was made of light brown chert; the other had been made of waxy gray chert or chalcedony. The unclassified point fragment was made from waxy, whitish-gold chert or chalcedony.

Points Redeposited in Zone A Features

We recovered four additional Archaic point fragments from Features 1, 3, 8, and 17 of Zone A (Figure 6.14). All of these features were storage pits, intrusive into the underlying strata. The point fragment from Feature 3 appears to have been corner-notched but was too incomplete to classify. Its raw material was waxy white chert or chalcedony, possibly from the Peña de Matadamas quarries in the Etla subvalley.

Conclusions

With a few exceptions, the Archaic projectile points from Cueva Blanca coincide with morphological types defined by MacNeish, Nelken-Terner, and Johnson for the Tehuacán Valley. For example, the Late Archaic points from Cueva Blanca include types known from the Coxcatlán and Abejas phases, such as La Mina, Trinidad, Tilapa, San Nicolás, Coxcatlán, Hidalgo, Abasolo, and Pelona. Perhaps the biggest difference between the two areas is the fact that Palmillas corner-notched points appeared earlier, and in greater numbers, in Oaxaca.

We find it significant that we did not find a single Pedernales point associated with the Late Archaic occupation at Cueva Blanca. This point type was well represented at the nearby site of Gheo-Shih, and two additional Pedernales points were found during our work at Guilá Naquitz (Hole 2009). When one combines this fact with the available radiocarbon dates it suggests that Pedernales points were largely confined to the Middle stages of the Archaic, at least in the Valley of Oaxaca.

We acknowledge the utility of the Archaic sequence from Tehuacán and will continue to use it in our research. Given the mounting evidence for atlatl point rejuvenation, however, we remain alert to the possibility that archaeologists have tended to recognize more morphological types than the ancient hunters did. Consider Figure 6.23, a hypothetical series of stages through which an Archaic point could pass. First, a Type A biface "preform" is made into a Tilapa point. Damaged by use, the Tilapa point is reworked as an Hidalgo point. Damaged by further use, the Hidalgo point is finally reworked into an Abasolo point. We don't know if it ever happened; the point is that it could have.

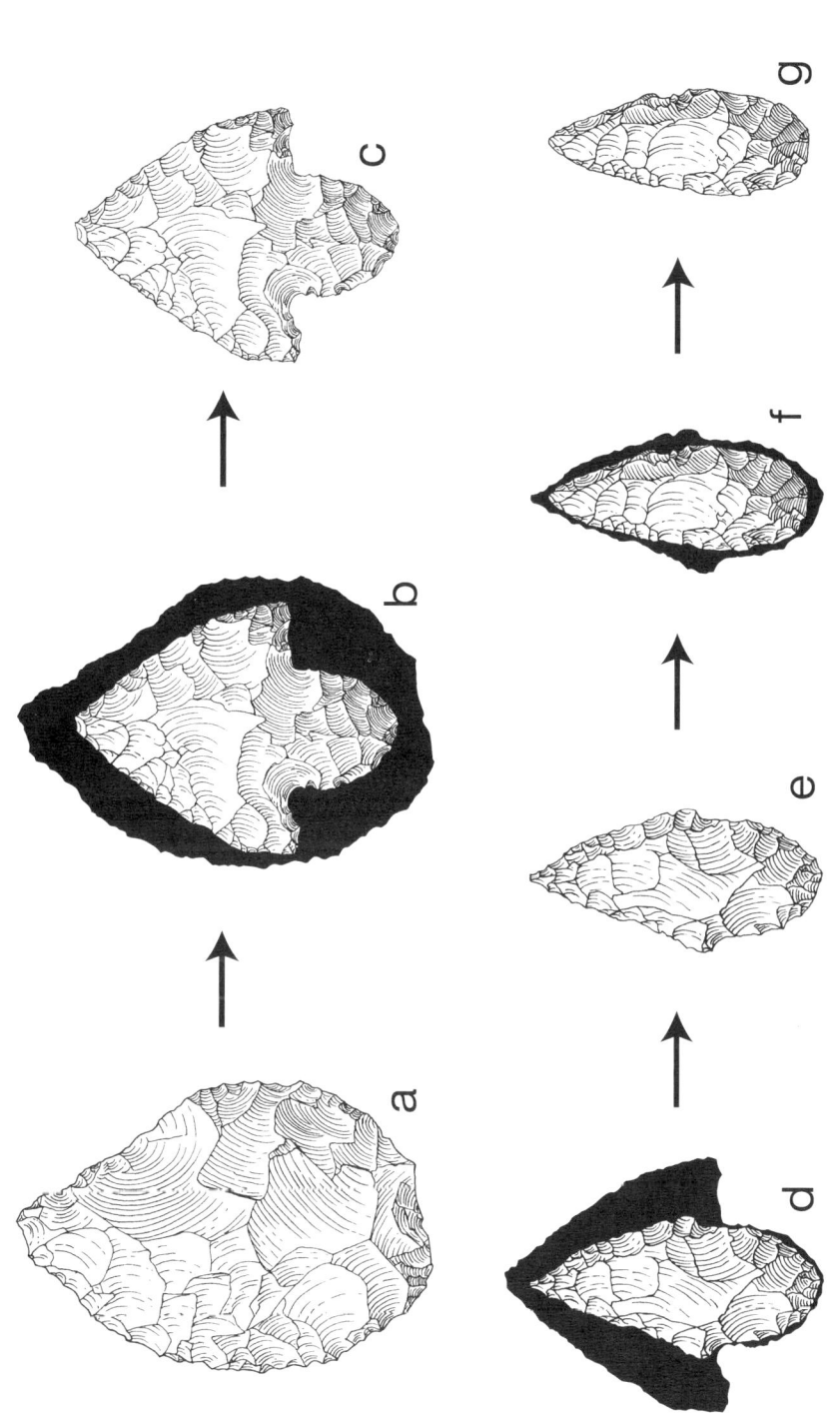

Figure 6.23. Hypothetical series of modifications during which a Type A biface (*a*) serves as the blank for a Tilapa point (*b*, *c*); after the barbs of the Tilapa point are damaged, it is rejuvenated as an Hidalgo point (*d*, *e*); and after the Hidalgo point is damaged, it is rejuvenated as an Abasolo point (*f*, *g*).

7

The Ground Stone Tools

Kent V. Flannery

Only six ground stone tools were recovered from the Archaic levels at Cueva Blanca. All belonged to types known either from Guilá Naquitz or from the Archaic sites of the Tehuacán Valley.

One-Hand Manos

At both Guilá Naquitz and Cueva Blanca, one-hand manos were the most common grinding implements. These were rough-and-ready tools, made from volcanic tuff cobbles taken from a stream bed and shaped almost as much by stream action and use as by design. None were complete when found, but all would originally have been about 9–10 cm in diameter.

While we found four varieties of one-hand mano at Guilá Naquitz, the only variety recovered at Cueva Blanca was the discoidal one-hand mano with two convex grinding surfaces (Flannery 2009a:148 and Figure 8.1c). Most manos of this variety appear to have been used with a rotary grinding motion, although in a few cases a back-and-forth motion cannot be ruled out.

One-hand manos could have been used either by men or by women. They fit comfortably in the hand and could have been used not only for grinding but also for direct pounding. It may, in fact, have been pounding of the latter type that damaged the mano shown in Figure 7.1a.

Slab Metate

At Guilá Naquitz, we used the term "slab metate" to refer to barely modified slabs of volcanic tuff rockfall or scree with one flat or slightly concave grinding surface (Flannery 2009a:151). Only one fragment of such a metate was found at Cueva Blanca.

Basin-Shaped Metate

At Guilá Naquitz, we defined this type of metate as having "a concave upper surface that is smoothed from use in grinding. The undersurface has been pecked to provide a more even and regular base" (Flannery 2009a:151). Such metates had presumably been used longer, or for more vigorous grinding, than the slab variety, and may have been predominantly women's tools. Only one fragment of such a metate was found at Cueva Blanca.

Zone E

No ground stone tools were found in Stratigraphic Zone E, our earliest Archaic occupation. This is perhaps not too surprising,

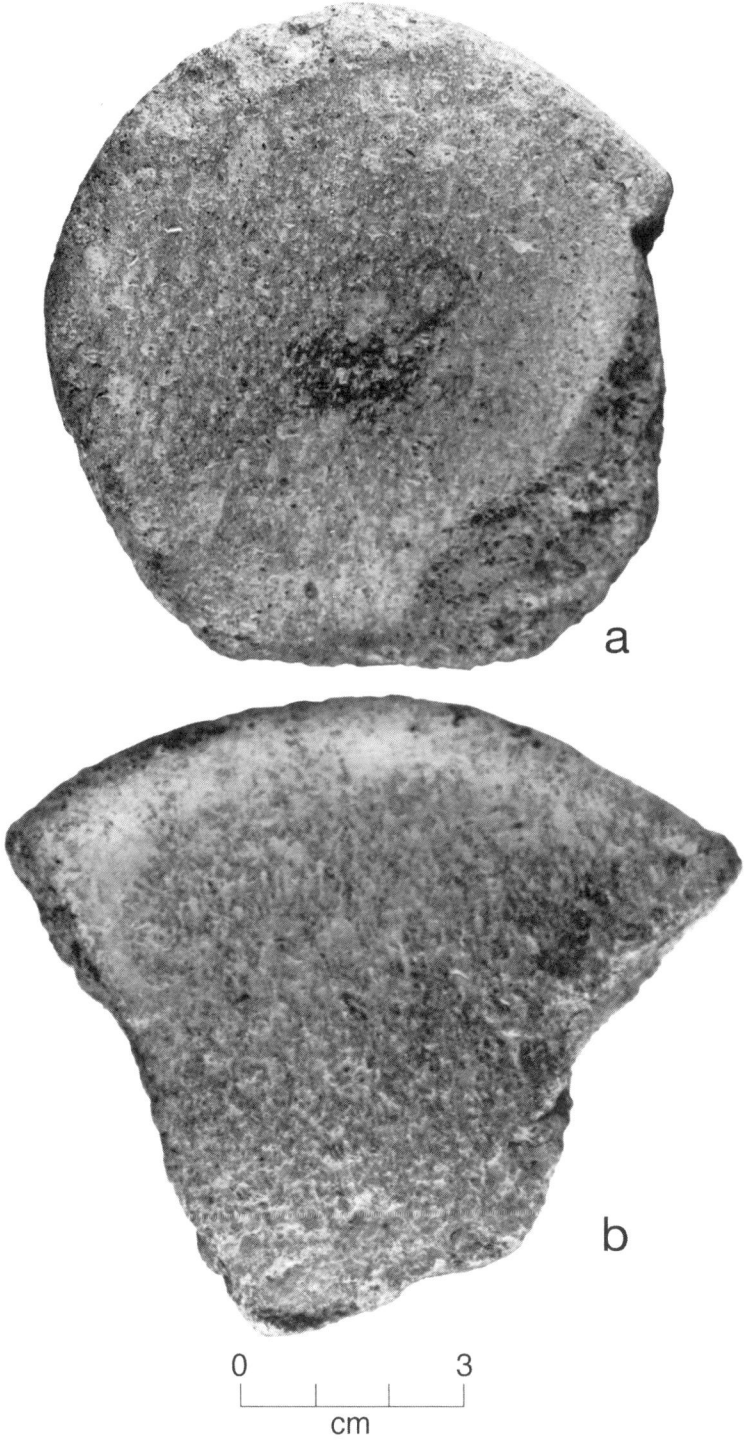

Figure 7.1. Examples of Archaic ground stone tools from Cueva Blanca. *a* is a discoidal one-hand mano, damaged, from Zone C (Square E5). *b* is a fragment of basin-shaped metate from Zone D (Square E8).

since only one fragment of a slab metate was found in Zone E of Guilá Naquitz, the earliest level at that cave (Flannery 2009a: Table 8.2).

Zone D

Zone D, a Late Archaic level, produced two metate fragments. We recovered a piece of slab metate in Square E12 and a piece of basin-shaped metate in Square E8 (Figure 7.1*b*). The discovery of these two metates is circumstantial evidence that women were present in Zone D. Neither, however, was complete when found. Since each was only a fragment, its location cannot be used as a guide to where women in Zone D tended to do their work.

Zone C

All four of our discoidal one-hand manos were found in Zone C, a Late Archaic level. One fairly complete mano and the fragment of a second one came to light in Square C9. Two additional manos were found in Squares C10 and E5.

No metates were found in Zone C. The fact that one-hand manos were the only grinding tools found on that living floor reinforces our suspicion that this stratum may represent an all-male camp (see Chapter 12).

8

Artifacts of Bone and Shell

Kent V. Flannery

The Late Archaic levels at Cueva Blanca produced a small number of bone and shell artifacts. One of the most significant was an olive shell ornament from Square E3 of Zone C, which has already been described and illustrated (Figure 3.8). This constitutes our oldest evidence for the importation of Pacific coast marine shells into the Valley of Oaxaca.

Bone Pendant

In Square E12 of Zone D we recovered a slightly damaged bone pendant, 38 mm long and 16 mm wide (Figure 8.1a). Presumably cut from a flat section of deer bone, the pendant had been drilled at its narrowest end for suspension.

Bone Toggle

Zone D also produced the unusual bone toggle shown in Figure 8.1b. This carefully polished artifact, measuring 44 mm in length, came to light in Square J15. While we cannot be sure of its function, our Zapotec workmen suggested that it might be the trigger from a trap of some kind. It is interesting that this possible evidence for small mammal trapping was found in the southwest quadrant of the chamber, an area with abundant small mammal bones.

Large Needle or Punch

Square I15 of Zone C produced the 71-mm fragment of needle shown in Figure 8.1c. This artifact, undoubtedly ground and polished from a deer bone splinter, is too large to be a sewing needle. Because of its damaged condition, we do not know whether it had an eye (like a basketry needle) or was eyeless (like a leather punch).

Pressure Flakers?

In the course of excavating the Archaic levels at Cueva Blanca, we came across numerous examples of antler tines that had been

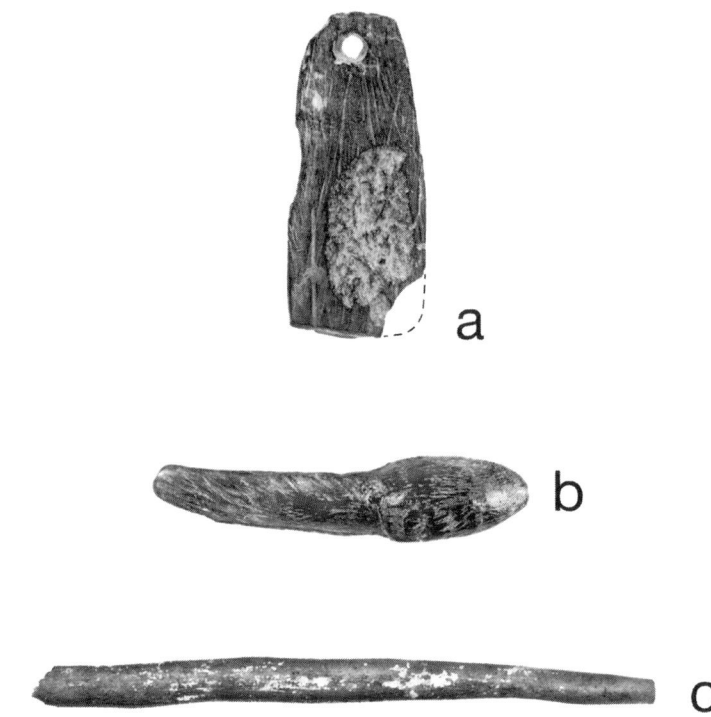

Figure 8.1. Archaic artifacts carved from deer bone. *a*, bone pendant from Zone D. *b*, bone toggle from Zone D. *c*, needle or punch from Zone C.

deliberately burned. One likely explanation is that these tines had been heat-treated so that they could be used to pressure-flake chert or chalcedony tools.

Possible pressure flakers were found at Guilá Naquitz (Flannery 2009a: Figure 12.1) and in the Archaic levels of the Tehuacán caves (MacNeish, Nelken-Terner, and Johnson 1967:142 and Figure 119). Heat-treated antler tines with the type of damage characteristic of pressure flakers appeared in Zones A and B of Cueva Blanca; unfortunately, none of the burned tines from the Archaic levels showed such damage.

In Square E11 of Zone C, we did find two likely pressure flakers made from deer bone splinters. One was made on a rib, the other on a splinter of metapodial.

Metapodial Awl

In Square G11 of Zone E, we found a bone awl made from the metatarsal of a deer.

Part III

Environment and Subsistence

9

Animal Bones from the Archaic Living Floors

Kent V. Flannery and Jane C. Wheeler

Cueva Blanca lies less than two kilometers east of Guilá Naquitz. It is therefore no surprise that the lists of species taken by Archaic hunters at both sites are similar. Cueva Blanca, the larger of the two caves, produced a slightly larger faunal sample. Even if we exclude all the rodents and songbirds that appear to have come from owl pellets, Cueva Blanca yielded more than 389 identifiable bones to Guilá Naquitz's 360 (Flannery and Wheeler 2009b). The list is as follows:

Large mammals
    White-tailed deer (*Odocoileus virginianus*)
Small mammals
    Jackrabbit (*Lepus* cf. *mexicanus*)
    Mexican cottontail rabbit (*Sylvilagus cunicularius*)
    Eastern cottontail rabbit (*Sylvilagus floridanus connectens*)
    Pocket gopher (*Orthogeomys grandis*)
    Coyote (*Canis latrans*)
    Gray fox (*Urocyon cinereoargenteus*)
    Cacomixtle (*Bassariscus astutus*)
    Raccoon (*Procyon lotor*)
Reptiles
    Mud turtle (*Kinosternon integrum*)
    Traces of unidentified small lizards
Birds
    Red-tailed (?) hawk (*Buteo* cf. *jamaicensis*)
    Barn owl (*Tyto alba*)

For the Cueva Blanca fauna, we calculated both NISP (number of identified specimens) and MNI (minimum number of individuals). Neither statistic is ideal. Previous researchers (e.g., Payne 1985, Reitz and Wing 1999) have pointed out that NISP exaggerates the importance of species whose elements are easy to identify.

For its part, MNI may exaggerate the importance of rare animals, since a single element is taken to represent one individual. For example, at both Cueva Blanca and Guilá Naquitz, the raccoon was represented by only one identified element. In both caves we suspect that most bone fragments were discarded outside the area covered by the overhang.

Our calculations of NISP at Cueva Blanca suggest that, just as at Guilá Naquitz, the three categories of animal most frequently eaten were deer, cottontail rabbits, and mud turtles. Other game animals were rare. Collared peccary was eaten at Guilá Naquitz, but its bones did not show up at Cueva Blanca. Coyote, gray fox, cacomixtle, and pocket gopher were occasionally eaten at Cueva Blanca, but did not show up at Guilá Naquitz. Raccoons were present, but rare, at both sites.

At both Guilá Naquitz and Cueva Blanca we recovered the remains of a barn owl and a possible red-tailed hawk. Barn owls had clearly lived in both caves from time to time and seem to have been responsible for introducing hundreds of rodents and songbirds in their regurgitated pellets. (The rodents they introduced are given in Chapter 10; the birds they introduced belonged mainly to the families Tyrannidae, Icteridae,

Table 9.1. The distribution of animal bones by square in Zone E, Cueva Blanca.

Square	Deer	Rabbit	Mud turtle	Coyote	Fox	Cacomixtle	Gopher	Mice	Birds
C6			1						
D6			1						
D7		3		1					
D8	1	1							
D9		2						7	
D10	3	3	1					7	2
E9	1							15	
E10	1	4						4	2
E11	2	1				1		1	1
E12			1						
F6	1	2						79	5
F7	3							256	8
F8		1							
G6	1							6	
G7	1	4						85	
G9		2						29	1
G10								17	2
G11	1	1					1	1	
G12		1		1				9	
G13	2							1	
H12	3	8						46	7
I14	1								
J15		1	1					1	
Totals	21	33	6	1	1	1	1	564	28

Note: Mice are mostly unidentified postcranial elements from owl pellets. Bird bones include the coracoid and scapula of a red-tailed hawk (in D10); the remaining bones are mostly unidentified postcranial elements from songbirds in owl pellents.

Thraupidae, Emberizidae, and Fringillidae.) Missing from Cueva Blanca were the quail, doves, and pigeons occasionally found at Guilá Naquitz (Flannery and Wheeler 2009b: Table 22.9). As for the hawk, we suspect that it was more likely hunted for its flight feathers than for food.

In addition to the ubiquitous mud turtle, Cueva Blanca also yielded some unidentified remains of small lizards, possibly racerunners. We found no conclusive evidence that these lizards had been eaten.

Zone E

Only 65 identifiable animal bones (exclusive of the rodents and songbirds introduced by owls) were recovered from Zone E of Cueva Blanca. That number is small enough to suggest that most bones were discarded outside the cave; many of those remaining inside appeared to be small scraps resulting from meals. This impression is reinforced by the fact that 14 identifiable bones—roughly a fifth of the total—occurred in Squares H12, I14, and J15 in the extreme southwest corner of the excavation, in what we believe was a cooking and eating area near the Feature 15 hearth.

Concentrations of both identifiable and unidentifiable bones were found in Squares D10–E10 (16 fragments) and F6–F7 (19 fragments). All in all, the bones in Zone E seem to be associated with areas where people occasionally ate as they worked, rather than with butchering areas.

Only 21 fragments could be assigned to white-tailed deer (Table 9.1, Figure 9.1). In addition, in Square G11 we found an awl made from the left distal metatarsal of a deer. Four deer elements—three long bone splinters and a piece of rib—were burned, but no cut marks were noticed on any of the Zone E deer bones. Obviously, most of the bulky deer bones had not been left in the cave.

As for the minimum number of deer and the seasons in which they were killed, it depends on whether or not the metapodial awl

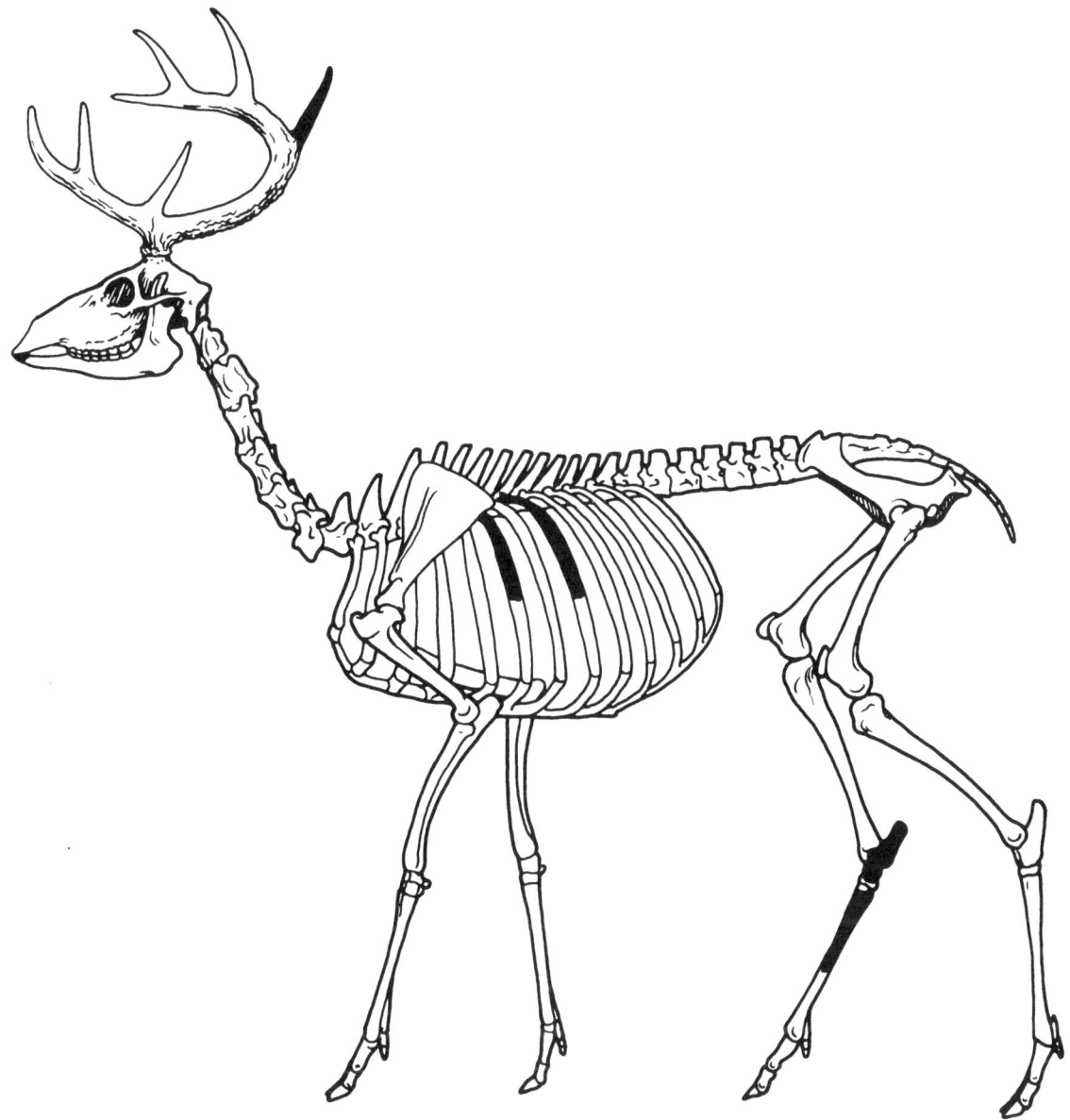

Figure 9.1. The skeleton of a white-tailed deer, with the skeletal elements present in Zone E colored black.

is included in the total. The awl was made from the metatarsal of a young animal and had a barely fused articular end. This awl could, of course, be from a young deer killed some time prior to the Zone E occupation.

The fully hardened antler tine found in Square 114, on the other hand, was from a buck whose metapodials would long since have fused. Since antler tines were often saved to be made into artifacts, however, we cannot rule out the possibility that this tine (like the metapodial awl) had been kept around for some time.

Zone E produced 33 fragments of cottontail rabbit bone. Evidently cottontails were brought back to the cave intact, since virtually all long bones were represented. The fact that carpals, tarsals, and toes were underrepresented may simply mean that the feet were either discarded outside the cave, or remained with the hide when the animal was skinned.

The majority of the Zone E bones were from the Eastern cottontail (*Sylvilagus floridanus connectens*). Only three bones were large enough to be from the Mexican cottontail (*S. cunicularius*), and all were found in Squares E10–E11. Based on the presence of three left maxillae, a minimum of three Eastern cottontails were scattered through Zone E. The *S. cunicularius* fragments would represent a fourth cottontail, and there must also have been a fifth *Sylvilagus* that was juvenile.

As in the case of the deer bone, one scatter of cottontail debris (8–11 fragments) lay in the southwest corner of the excavation in what may have been a cooking and eating area.

Another scatter (14 fragments) lay in Squares D7–D10 and E10–E11, areas of high-density debris where people may have engaged in both working and eating.

Remains of other small mammals were meager. A shattered scapula in Square G7 may have belonged to the local jackrabbit (*Lepus mexicanus*). Square G11 produced one humerus of the pocket gopher (*Orthogeomys grandis*), a rodent common in Formative sites in the Valley of Oaxaca but no longer present in the valley today (Flannery and Marcus 2005:58). One possible tooth of gray fox (*Urocyon cinereoargenteus*) was found in Square G12, and an innominate of coyote (*Canis latrans*) appeared in D7. The ulna of a cacomixtle (*Bassariscus astutus*) occurred in Square E11. Such small game was probably taken opportunistically. Only two small mammal bones from Zone E were unidentifiable, and both were in the size range of rabbit.

While reptile remains were not particularly common in Zone F, there are hints that at least one mud turtle (*Kinosternon integrum*) might have been turned upside down and roasted over hot coals at Cueva Blanca. This was the way that turtles were cooked at Guilá Naquitz (Flannery and Wheeler 2009b:287). At least four carapace scutes and two limb bones were scattered through the cave.

Zone E also produced two wing bones of *Buteo* cf. *jamaicensis*, a hawk whose flight feathers might have been put to a variety of uses.

Zone D

Zone D was the richest in fauna of the Archaic strata; not counting rodents and songbirds, it produced 187 identifiable bone fragments. As in the case of Zone E, one of the largest scatters of animal bone occurred in the southwest corner of the excavation—34 identifiable fragments in Squares H12–H15, I13–I15, and J14–J15 (Table 9.2). We suspect this location was a woman's work area, close to the Feature 18 hearth. Another large scatter occurred in the center of the cave chamber—63 identifiable fragments in Squares D7–D9, E7–E9, and F6–F9. Those squares also contained high-density debris from presumed men's activities (Chapters 12 and 14). The bone fragments there may have been discarded by individuals who sometimes ate while sitting in their activity areas.

An interesting difference between the two scatters is that deer bone seems particularly well represented in the center of the chamber, while rabbit bone was particularly well represented just southwest of the hearth. This could reflect differences in the relative amounts of deer and rabbit consumed by men and women, but we need to see more cases to be convinced.

We identified some 76 fragments as belonging to white-tailed deer; a minimum of four individual deer were represented. Included were an adult buck with large antlers, another deer roughly 1.5 years old, a fawn less than four months old, and a pregnant doe whose foetus we did not count as a fifth individual. Square E8 contained the vertebra and calcaneum of an adult, along with the unfused metapodial and first phalanx of a young animal.

Squares F6–F7 produced a maxilla whose tooth eruption and wear suggested a deer 1.5 years old, as well as a mandible whose tooth eruption and wear indicated an older animal. Square G8 yielded a fragment of ischium from a baby deer; an unfused innominate from what may have been a foetal deer was found in Square I15. Unerupted milk teeth from very young deer occurred in Squares H15 and I14. As was so often the case, we suspect that the actual number of deer killed may have been significantly greater than the MNI.

Figure 9.2 shows the parts of the deer skeleton represented in Zone D. Although more elements were present in D than in any other Archaic stratum, we still believe that most bones were discarded outside the cave. Of the 11 noticeably burned fragments, 10 were antler tines from Squares F14, I14, and J14 in the southwest quadrant of the excavation. Since antlers are inedible, we suspect that the occupants of Zone D were fire-hardening them for use as artifacts.

Bones with signs of butchering were found in Squares D8–D9, E8, and G9. Four long bone fragments from D8 and D9 showed cut marks at right angles to the long axis of the bone, perhaps made with a chopper/knife or sidescraper/knife. An astragalus in Square E8 had been struck with a chopper of some kind. A calcaneum and phalanx in Square G9 had also been struck repeatedly with a chopper, suggesting that this was the way lower limbs were sometimes divided into manageable sections.

These were several clues to the seasons during which the cave was occupied. The doe pregnant with a late-term foetus might have been killed between May and July. There are also hints of a fawn less than four months old, suggesting a kill in the July–September period. On the other hand, the buck with fully hardened antlers was probably killed in the autumn (September–November). What this means is that Zone D might have been visited over the period from May to November. This period—the rainy season plus the early dry season—is when plant resources in the area are at their peak. It also coincides with the time when afternoon sunlight would have been optimal for Squares C7–E7 and C8–E8 (Chapter 12).

Some 93 bones from Zone D belonged to cottontail rabbits. Of these, 50 were in the size range of the Eastern cottontail, while 6 were in the size range of the Mexican cottontail; the remaining 37 could be identified only as *Sylvilagus* sp. The densest concentrations of cottontail bone occurred (1) in the southwest corner of the excavation near the Feature 18 hearth, and (2) in the center of the cave chamber.

The 50 bones of Eastern cottontail came from a minimum of 11 individuals; 11 left and 10 right mandibular rami were scattered through Zone D, with 4 rami found in Square D11 alone. The 6 bones of Mexican cottontail include 3 right mandibular rami (hence an MNI of 3), with two-thirds of the bones found to the south and west of the hearth. The 21 bones identifiable only as *Sylvilagus* sp. were from a minimum of

Table 9.2. The distribution of animal bones by square in Zone D, Cueva Blanca.

Square	Deer	Rabbit	Mud turtle	Coyote	Fox	Mice	Birds
B9		2					
C4				1		1	
C5		1				1	
C6	2	4				6	
C7	10	1				1	
C8	1	1			3	10	
C11		2					
D4		2		1		2	
D7	1	2				6	
D8	5	5	1				2
D9	6	3				9	
D10		1				1	
D11		4				13	1
D12	3	3	1				
E4	2	3				2	
E5	1	1					
E6	1	2	2			1	
E7	1	3			1		
E8	10	4	2	2		91	6
E9	2	3				13	1
E13			1	1		3	1
F5			1	1			
F6	1	4				36	3
F7	2	4			3	81	4
F8	1					1	
F9	1	1				72	3
F11	3	1					
F12	1						
F13	1	2			1		
F14	1					1	
G6	3					16	1
G7	1	1				10	2
G8	1	2				53	5
G9	3	1				91	4
G10		2				19	
G12	1	1				4	
G14		2				1	
H9	1					3	1
H12	2	2				10	2
H13	1	1				1	
H14		4				7	
H15	1	3				14	
I 13		1					
I 14	3	2				3	
I 15	1	3				1	
J14	1	9				3	1
J15	1						
Totals	76	93	8	6	8	587	37

Note: Mice are mostly unidentified postcranial elements from owl pellets. Bird bones are mostly unidentified postcranial elements from songbirds in owl pellets.

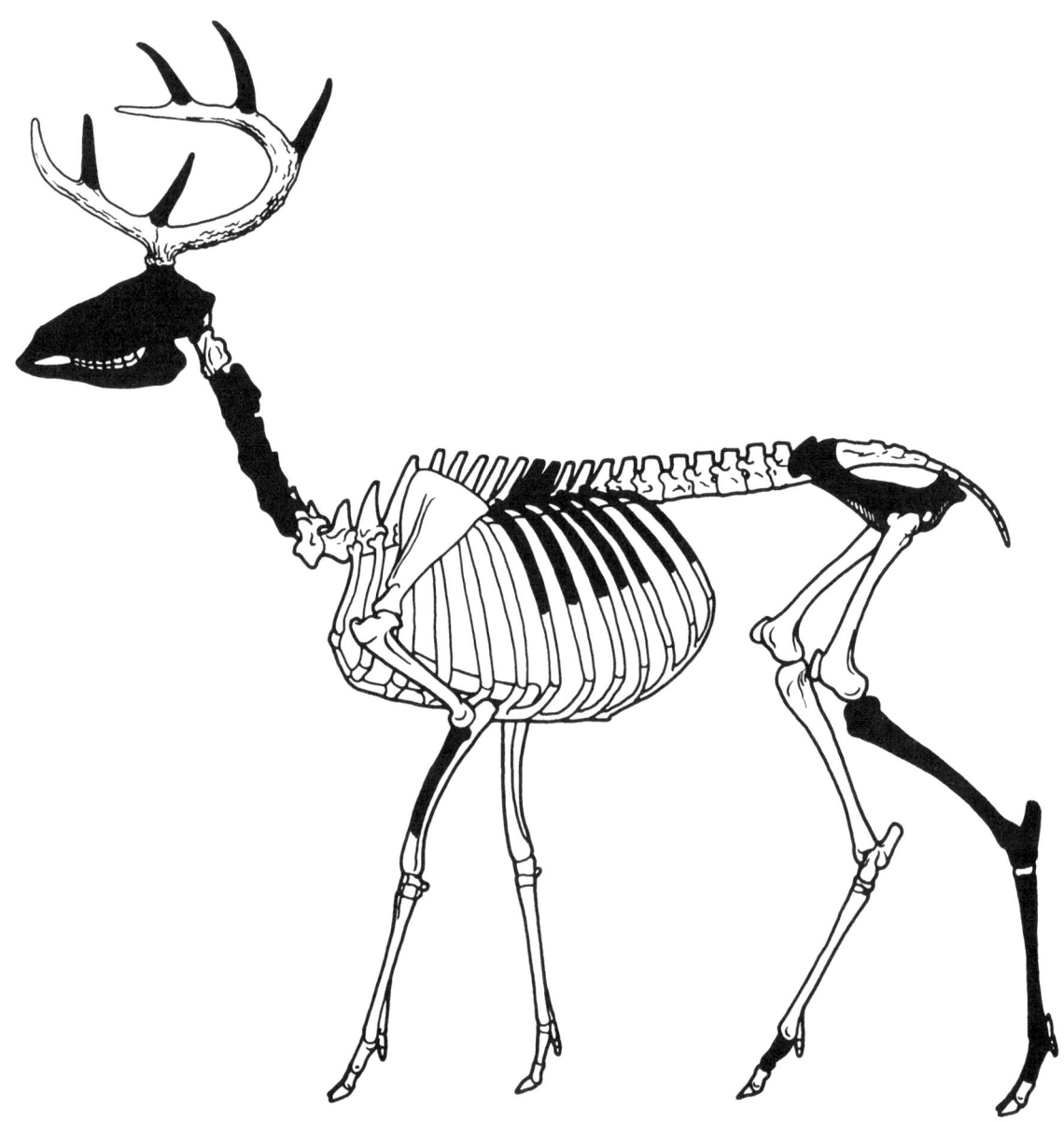

Figure 9.2. The skeleton of a white-tailed deer, with the skeletal elements present in Zone D colored black.

3 juveniles. Thus at least 17 cottontails were killed during the occupation of Zone D, and the actual number may have been much higher.

Not one bone from this stratum could be confidently assigned to jackrabbit. That fact suggests that the occupants trapped cottontails in the nearby thorn forest, but did not hunt jackrabbits in the more open areas of the valley floor.

Eight fragments from two different gray foxes were recovered from activity areas in the center of the cave chamber, mainly Squares C8 and F7. There were also two scraps of coyote bone. While it is reasonable to suspect that these canids were eaten, they may have been even more valued for their hides. Some 24 small mammal bones from Zone D were unidentifiable. Most were in the size range of rabbits.

Eight plastron scutes or limb bones of mud turtle were scattered throughout Zone D. Squares D8 and E6 contained identical marginal scutes from two different turtles. The fact that a minimum of two individuals were represented by only eight fragments suggests that most turtle remains were tossed or swept out of the cave.

Zone C

Zone C produced 137 identifiable animal bones, exclusive of rodents and songbirds from owl pellets. This was fewer than Zone D, but more than twice as many as Zone E. Two-thirds of the identifiable bones were concentrated in three areas: (1) near the north wall of the chamber, in Squares D3, E3, and E4 (28 fragments); (2) near the center of the chamber, in Squares F7–F9 and G7 (24 fragments); and (3) near the southwest corner of the excavation, in Squares H12–H15 and J13–J14 (35 fragments). Although many of the bones were burnt, no formal hearth was found within the excavated area. While some cooking must have been done during the Zone C occupation—perhaps outside the cave—it is significant that the southwest quadrant of the excavation did not seem to have been dedicated to cooking activities, as was the case in Zones E and D.

Fifty bone fragments were assigned to white-tailed deer (Table 9.3). At least two minimum individuals were represented, one adult and one young. Skull fragments were present but no antler tines, raising the possibility that we might be dealing with a doe and a fawn (to be sure, the true number of deer killed might well be greater). As for the season in which the deer were taken, we can offer only a rough approximation: the fawn might have been 3–6 months old, which would suggest a kill in the period from September to November. This is precisely the time when afternoon sunlight would have been optimal for the cave chamber (Chapter 12).

Some deer bones are curiously underrepresented—no femora, no phalanges, very few vertebrae (Figure 9.3). As discussed elsewhere, the tool kits (Chapter 13), the density contours (Chapter 12), and the lack of a hearth in the southwest quadrant all lead us to suspect that Zone C represented an all-male hunting camp, so it may be that significant portions of each deer killed were transported to a base camp elsewhere.

Some 15 bone fragments, nearly a third of the total, were burned. Most of them were splinters of long bones or vertebrae, and they were found in all three of the major concentrations of bone.

While no antler tines or antler artifacts occurred in Zone C, other parts of the deer skeleton had been made into artifacts. In Square E11, one splinter of distal metapodial had been chipped in such a way as to suggest a pressure flaker, and a fragment of rib had been modified in a similar way. Once again, we cannot rule out the possibility that these artifacts were made on bones acquired during earlier hunts.

Some 50 bones could be linked to cottontail rabbits. We assigned 30 fragments, five of them burned, to the Eastern cottontail. These 30 fragments included four left mandibular rami and four left innominates, giving us an MNI of four. Another five fragments, none of them burned, were assigned to the Mexican cottontail; Square H15 produced two right mandibular rami, giving us two minimum individuals. The remaining 15 cottontail bones—one of them burned—were from juvenile individuals and could not be identified to species. Included were two unfused left femora, giving us a minimum of two juvenile *Sylvilagus* sp.

We believe, therefore, that we recovered a minimum of eight individual cottontails, two of them not fully grown. Most of the skeleton was present, although the feet, ribs, and vertebrae were underrepresented. We suspect that the true number of cottontails killed was higher than eight. No jackrabbit bones were recovered from Zone C, once again suggesting that most rabbit trapping was done in the nearby thorn forest.

Other small mammals were represented only by occasional scraps. Two bones from the center of the cave chamber (Squares F8–F9) appeared to have come from the local gray fox, present in all Archaic levels but never common. An ulna of raccoon (*Procyon lotor*) appeared near the south wall of the cave (Square E12). The fact that only one bone from this animal had remained in the cave reinforces our impression that most elements were discarded outside, and did nothing to increase our confidence in the accuracy of MNI. Some 52 small mammal bones from Zone C were unidentifiable. Most were in the size range of rabbits.

More remains of mud turtle were found in Zone C than in any other Archaic stratum. By far the densest scatter was found near the north wall of the cave in Squares E3 and E4. Here we recovered a total of 17 scutes from the carapace and plastron of the same turtle, most of them carbonized in such a way as to suggest that the animal had been turned upside down and roasted over hot coals. Three more burnt scutes lay in the center of the cave in Square D8. Seven scutes from a second turtle appeared in Square F8, not nearly so burnt. Three more scutes, possibly from the second turtle, turned up near the south wall of the cave in Squares E12 and F13.

Zone C produced the remains of a barn owl (*Tyto alba*), the species responsible for introducing virtually all the small rodents and songbirds we found in Cueva Blanca. Zone C also

Table 9.3. The distribution of animal bones by square in Zone C, Cueva Blanca.

Square	Deer	Rabbit	Mud turtle	Raccoon	Fox	Mice	Birds
B6	1						
B8		1					
B9	1						
C5	1						1
C8		1					
C9	2	1					
C10		1					
D3	2	3				4	
D7	1						
D8		1	3				
E3	1	1	10			8	1
E4	3	1	7				2
E5	4						
E6		1	1			1	
E11	3	1					
E12	3		2	1		4	
F6		2				4	
F7		9				23	
F8	1	1	7		1	9	
F9		4			1	54	5
F13	3	2	1				
F14	1					2	
G7	6					30	
G14	1						
H12	6	2				16	
H13	3	2				14	
H14		2				2	
H15	2	7				15	1
I 13		1					
J13	5	2					
J14		4				14	
J15						4	
Totals	50	50	31	1	2	204	10

Note: Mice are mostly unidentified postcranial elements from owl pellets. Birds include one coracoid of red-tailed (?) hawk (in E4) and two bones of barn owl (in C5 and E4); remaining bird bones are mostly unidentified postcranial elements of songbirds from owl pellets.

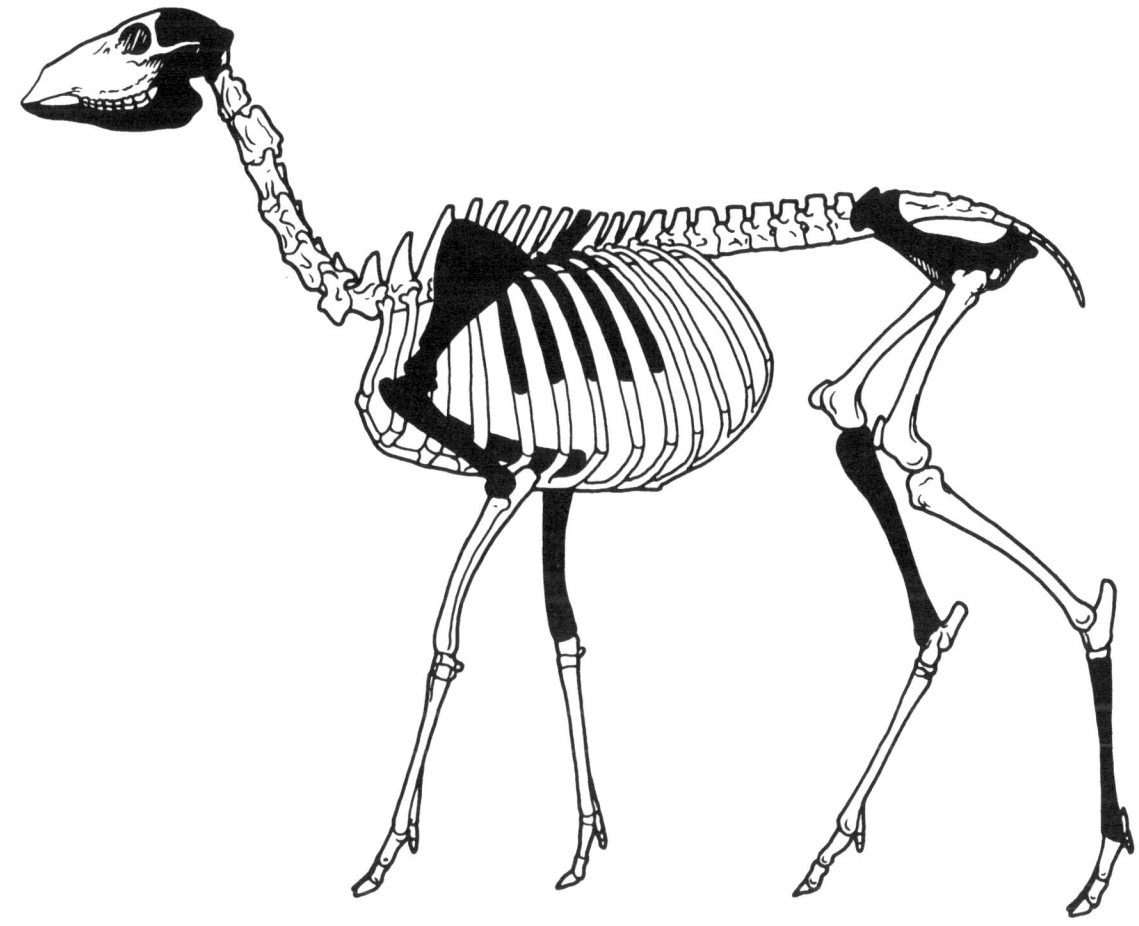

Figure 9.3. The skeleton of a white-tailed deer, with the skeletal elements present in Zone C colored black.

gave us a coracoid of *Buteo* cf. *jamaicensis*, the same hawk found in Zone E.

Conclusions

Foragers made at least three different visits to Cueva Blanca, once in the Early Archaic (Zone E) and twice in the Late Archaic (Zones D and C). As nearly as can be determined from the deer remains, these visits were made sometime between May and November. Both Zones E and D had evidence for men's and women's work areas. Zone C, on the other hand, lacked much of the evidence for women's activities seen in Zones E and D. We suspect that this zone may represent an all-male hunting camp. We know that the occupants of Zone C hunted and butchered deer, trapped rabbits, and roasted a mud turtle. They ate some venison themselves, but may have transported portions of the deer carcasses back to the macroband camp from which they had come.

10

The Microfauna from Cueva Blanca

Kent V. Flannery and Jane C. Wheeler

Cueva Blanca, like most of the caves in the El Fuerte region, had been occupied from time to time by barn owls (*Tyto alba*). At dusk such owls fly over an area roughly 2–3 kilometers in diameter, hunting both rodents and small birds. Swallowing its prey whole, the owl returns to the cave and roosts while digestion takes place. A capsule of hair forms around the complete but disarticulated skeleton of each rodent or bird. This pellet of bones and fur is then regurgitated onto the floor of the cave. Over time, a sample of the locally available wild rodent population accumulates. This sample serves as a guide to the local environment.

Many of the El Fuerte caves contained samples of owl pellets from both prehispanic times and the twentieth century. For example, the surface of Cueva de los Afligidos (a cave only a few hundred meters from Guilá Naquitz) was covered with nearly 500 recent owl pellets when Flannery discovered it in 1966. We were able to compare the rodents from those pellets to the rodents on the Archaic living floors at Guilá Naquitz (Flannery and Wheeler 2009a). In this chapter we perform the same task with the microfauna from Cueva Blanca.

The Modern Rodents

Dozens of owl pellets lay scattered across the surface of Cueva Blanca when it was first discovered. Included in those pellets were 36 reasonably intact crania of rodents; 2 crania of shrews; 127 mandibles of rodents; and 3 mandibles of shrews (Table 10.1). Not surprisingly, the species of rodents from the Cueva Blanca owl pellets were virtually identical to those from Cueva de los Afligidos (Flannery and Wheeler 2009a: Table 16.1). The relative frequencies of those species to one another, however, were different. Such differences probably reflect the fact that Cueva de los Afligidos lies in the *Cassia* facies of Thorn Forest A, while Cueva Blanca lies near the interface of Thorn Forest A (*Quercus* facies) and Thorn Forest B (*Bursera* facies).

As Table 10.1 reveals, the pellets from the surface of Cueva Blanca contained two crania and three mandibles of a small-eared shrew (*Cryptotis* cf. *mexicana*). We are pleased to have this record of shrew, which was unrepresented in our sample from Cueva de los Afligidos.

Our lone representative of the family Heteromyidae was the Mexican spiny pocket mouse (*Liomys irroratus*), which constituted 9.3% of the indigenous wild rodents on the surface of Cueva Blanca. This mouse was three times as common in our Cueva de los Afligidos collection (Flannery and Wheeler 2009a: Table 16.1).

The owl pellets from Cueva de los Afligidos contained eight species of the family Cricetidae. Only six of those species appeared in the Cueva Blanca pellets, possibly because the latter was a smaller and much less well-preserved collection.

Table 10.1. Rodents and shrews from owl pellets on the surface of Cueva Blanca, 1966.

Genus and species	Crania	Mandibles		Percentage of indigenous wild rodents
		Right	Left	
Cryptotis cf. *mexicana*	2	2	1	—
Liomys irroratus	—	6	7	9.3
Oryzomys couesi	1	3	1	4.0
Reithrodontomys spp.	—	24	17	32.0
Reithrodontomys megalotis	6	—	—	—
Reithrodontomys fulvescens	3	—	—	—
Peromyscus maniculatus	4	15	12	20.0
Peromyscus melanophrys	—	—	—	—
Baiomys musculus	17	12	21	28.0
Sigmodon hispidus	4	4	5	6.7
Neotoma mexicana	—	—	—	—
Rattus rattus	1	—	—	—

Coues' rice rat (*Oryzomys couesi*, sometimes lumped with *O. palustris*) constituted 4% of the indigenous wild rodents in the Cueva Blanca pellets. This figure was similar to the rice rat's frequency in the Cueva de los Afligidos collection (6.3%).

The most common rodents in our Cueva Blanca sample were harvest mice (*Reithrodontomys* spp.), represented by a minimum of 24 individuals (32%). This percentage stands in contrast to the Cueva de los Afligidos sample, where harvest mice comprised less than 2% of the local wild rodents. Since harvest mice prefer stands of short grass, we suspect that their higher frequency at Cueva Blanca resulted from owls hunting in the nearby mesquite grassland, which lay only 1.5 kilometers south of the cave.

Owing to poor preservation and missing teeth, only a few of the 41 mandibles of harvest mice could be identified to species. The crania were more diagnostic, and consisted of six western harvest mice (*Reithrodontomys megalotis*) and three fulvous harvest mice (*R. fulvescens*).

Two species of white-footed mice (*Peromyscus spp.*) occurred in the pellets from Cueva de los Afligidos, and one of those species was more common than the other. The deer mouse (*Peromyscus maniculatus*) constituted roughly 10% of the native wild rodents at Cueva de los Afligidos; it was twice as common at Cueva Blanca. The plateau mouse (*P. melanophrys*) made up only 1.1 % of the collection at Cueva de los Afligidos and was entirely absent at Cueva Blanca. As in the case of harvest mice, we attribute the higher frequencies of deer mice at Cueva Blanca to the proximity of mesquite grassland.

One of our biggest surprises at Cueva Blanca was the high frequency of the southern pygmy mouse (*Baiomys musculus*). This tiny mouse, which comprised only 1.9% of the Cueva de los Afligidos collection, made up 28% of the native wild rodents at Cueva Blanca. Since the pygmy mouse seeks out dense grass, it too may reflect the owls' foraging in the mesquite grassland south of Cueva Blanca.

Another surprise was the low frequency of the hispid cotton rat (*Sigmodon hispidus*), which had been the most common native wild rodent in the Cueva de los Afligidos sample (44.7%). Cotton rats were only 6.7% of the Cueva Blanca sample, and we have no easy explanation for this fact.

The Mexican wood rat (*Neotoma mexicana*) did not appear in our Cueva Blanca sample. Since its frequency was relatively low in the much larger Cueva de los Afligidos collection (3.2%), its absence at Cueva Blanca is perhaps not surprising.

Finally, our Cueva Blanca sample contains one cranium of the common black rat (*Rattus rattus*), an Old World commensal rodent inadvertently brought to Mexico by the Spaniards. There were three black rat crania at Cueva de los Afligidos.

The Archaic Rodents

All three of the Archaic strata at Cueva Blanca produced small rodent bones. These remains had the appearance of owl pellet fauna, and tended to occur in clusters below the kinds of rocky ledges where owls roost. Unfortunately, they were not nearly as well preserved as the microfauna from Guilá Naquitz.

Zone E (Early Archaic)

Thirty-two mandibles and one maxilla from Zone E were sufficiently well preserved to identify. The five genera involved were as follows:

Liomys: 1 R. and 1 L. mandible (MNI = 1)
Oryzomys: 4 R. and 2 L. mandibles (MNI = 4)
Peromyscus: 2 L. mandibles (MNI = 2)
Sigmodon: 4 R. and 6 L. mandibles (MNI = 6)
Neotoma: 4 R. and 8 L. mandibles, 1 maxilla (MNI = 8)

Our first impression is that the Zone E rodents (MNI = 21) more closely resemble the sample from Archaic Guilá Naquitz (MNI = 49) than the recent owl pellet rodents from the surface of Cueva Blanca. In Zones E–B1 of Guilá Naquitz, *Sigmodon* was the most common genus, followed by *Neotoma* (Flannery and Wheeler 2009a:242). In Zone E of Cueva Blanca, *Neotoma* was the most common genus, followed by *Sigmodon*. As a pair, these two genera constituted 69.4% of the Archaic rodents from Guilá Naquitz and 66.6% of the Early Archaic rodents from Zone E of Cueva Blanca. The high numbers of wood rats in Zone E of Cueva Blanca may be a function of its great antiquity, since this genus was well represented in the Pleistocene of Oaxaca and Puebla.

Zone D (Late Archaic)

Zone D produced the largest rodent sample of any Archaic level from Cueva Blanca. Included among the identifiable bones were 1 damaged cranium, 3 maxillae, and 47 mandibles (MNI = 29). The list of genera was as follows:

Liomys: 1 damaged cranium, 6 L. mandibles (MNI = 6)
Oryzomys: 1 R. and 2 L. mandibles (MNI = 2)
Peromyscus: 1 R. mandible (MNI = 1)
Sigmodon: 14 R. and 16 L. mandibles, 3 maxillae (MNI = 16)
Neotoma: 3 R. and 4 L. mandibles (MNI = 4)

Once again, *Sigmodon* and *Neotoma* accounted for 68.9% of the rodents in the sample. This time, however, *Sigmodon* was the most common genus of the two, just as it was at Guilá Naquitz.

Zone C (Late Archaic)

The Zone C rodent sample was the smallest from any of Cueva Blanca's Archaic strata, yielding only 15 identifiable mandibles and 2 identifiable maxillae (MNI = 10). The list of genera is as follows:

Liomys: 5 L. mandibles (MNI = 5)
Sigmodon: 3 R. and 3 L. mandibles, 2 maxillae (MNI = 3)
Neotoma: 2 R. and 2 L. mandibles (MNI = 2)

In our Zone C sample, half the minimum individual rodents are either *Sigmodon* or *Neotoma*.

Conclusions

The Archaic rodents from Cueva Blanca, while not as well preserved as those from Guilá Naquitz, seem to have been drawn from the same general environment. Most of the differences between the microfauna in the two sites can be attributed either to differential preservation and sample size, or to the fact that the owls roosting in the two caves were probably not hunting in similar facies of the El Fuerte environment.

11

The Late Archaic Plant Evidence

Kent V. Flannery

Cueva Blanca was not dry enough to provide us with a sample of desiccated Archaic plants. We did, however, manage to glean some information from bits of wood charcoal and grains of pollen. After his initial examination of pollen from Cueva Blanca (Schoenwetter and Smith 2009), the late James Schoenwetter ran further samples, looking exclusively for potential cultivars. Our wood charcoal was identified either by Wilma Wetterstrom of the University of Michigan Laboratory of Ethnobotany or by the staff of the United States Forestry Service. Zone E yielded nothing useful, which limited our results to the Late Archaic.

Zone D

Square E13 of Zone D produced charcoal fragments of the family Ericaceae, probably *Arctostaphylos* sp. (manzanita). This tree was also used as fuel at Guilá Naquitz (Flannery 2009a).

Zone D eventually produced one pollen grain of *Cucurbita pepo*, the same squash we recovered at Guilá Naquitz (B. D. Smith 1997). Fourteen grains from the same stratum were identified by Schoenwetter as *Agave* sp. Two more pollen grains from Zone D were identified as "*Celtis*-Moraceae," and may result from the bringing of desert hackberry fruits to the cave.

Zone C

Square E3 of Zone C produced bits of charcoal from oak (*Quercus* sp.), acacia (*Acacia* sp.), and pine (*Pinus* sp.). Additional charcoal from the same square was assigned to a gymnosperm, possibly the baldcypress (*Taxodium* sp.). Two pollen grains from Zone C were identified as belonging to *Agave* sp.

Conclusions

While admittedly meager, the botanical data from Late Archaic Cueva Blanca suggest a continuation of the pattern seen earlier at Guilá Naquitz. Included are the harvesting of squash, agave, and hackberry as food, and the collection of branches from oak, pine, acacia, manzanita, and baldcypress as fuel.

Part IV

Analysis of the Living Floors

12

Distributional Variability in Zones E–C of Cueva Blanca: A Local Analysis of Grid-Density Data

Charles S. Spencer and Kent V. Flannery

Intrasite spatial analysis was relatively rare before two of Robert Whallon's seminal articles appeared in the 1970s (Whallon 1973, 1974). This type of analysis has since become a major theme in archaeological research, after undergoing a process of critical evaluation, modification, and reformulation (Hietala and Larson 1979; Carr 1984; Hietala 1984a, 1984c; Whallon 1984).

Many of the early attempts at spatial analysis, it is now recognized, involved little more than the wholesale borrowing of techniques from other fields, with little thought given to whether the methods were truly appropriate and pertinent to archaeological data and problems. Whallon himself pointed out that the scatters or clusters of materials ("activity areas") that most intrasite spatial analyses seek to define can be expected to vary widely in terms of "size, shape, density, composition, and internal patterns of covariation or association" (Whallon 1984:243). He argued that we must devise methods of spatial analysis that can identify and exploit these several dimensions of variability. Techniques that place constraints on one or more of these dimensions ought to be avoided.

A particular problem with many analyses has been a lack of congruence, or fit, between the spatial reference frames of the statistical method employed and the distributional patterns themselves. For example, "global" (or site-wide) statistical methods such as factor analysis or the matrix ordering of correlation coefficients based on grid-density data are seen to be generally inappropriate for the analysis of spatial distributions that manifest clustering on a "local" or intrasite scale (Hietala 1984b:45; Whallon 1984:244).

In this chapter we present an analysis of the spatial patterning of debris in the Archaic strata of Cueva Blanca, using an approach that is local in orientation and relatively free of analytical constraints. As such, the method owes a considerable intellectual debt to Whallon (1984), although it differs fundamentally from his approach in that it utilizes grid-density data, i.e., frequencies of items per 1 x 1 m square, while Whallon's approach was applied to individually plotted items. (It should be noted that many Paleolithic archaeologists, dealing with individually plotted items, conduct spatial analysis by refitting pieces of flint that can be traced back to the cores or other large items from which they came.)

The work reported here also represents an extension of the spatial analysis that Spencer conducted on another cave of the Mitla region, Guilá Naquitz (Spencer and Flannery 2009). Although that analysis was carried out in the 1980s, we are gratified to note that it holds up fairly well in terms of the recent reappraisals of intrasite spatial analysis. The primary analytical technique Spencer employed—contour mapping based on input densities—has been singled out by Hietala and

Larson (1979) as well suited to many archaeological problems and data sets. Moreover, since Spencer and Flannery based their interpretations largely upon visual inspection of the maps, there were few computational constraints in effect. And because the spatial framework of the analysis became the contour plots themselves, rather than the site taken as a whole, the study had a local perspective.

At the time, Spencer and Flannery were somewhat dissatisfied with their attempts to assess patterns of spatial covariation among debris categories. The technique Spencer used, overlaying contour maps of different categories, had the advantage of requiring no convoluted computations and their attendant constraints. On the other hand, it was not feasible to evaluate simultaneously the patterns of covariation among all debris categories using this method, and we resorted to presenting overlays of (usually two) contour plots with similar patterning. In doing the analysis for this chapter on Cueva Blanca, the senior author sought to develop a quantitative method for evaluating the patterns of spatial covariation among debris categories that would be computationally straightforward, local in orientation, and tailored to the particular features of the Cueva Blanca data set.

With Cueva Blanca we were faced with 75 square meters of excavated area—substantially more than the 64 square meters excavated at Guilá Naquitz. The debris recovered from Cueva Blanca, however, was less varied and generally lower in density than was the case with Guilá Naquitz. Cueva Blanca had faunal remains and chipped stone artifacts, but no preserved plant remains; hence there is not a single 1 x 1 m square with more than 100 items of any category. By contrast, Guilá Naquitz had high frequencies of preserved plants; in Zone D alone, for example, there was an average of 138 acorns per square, with a maximum of 647 in a single 1 x 1 m square.

The first step in the present analysis involved the creation of a set of basic data files for Cueva Blanca. The original grid designations had to be changed from letter and number combinations to a Cartesian system using only numbers, as shown in Figure 12.1. The frequencies of the various debris categories by 1 x 1 m square were then entered into data files according to the Cartesian grid coordinates for the center of each square. These files were used as input for SURFER, a contour-mapping software package (Golden Software 1987).

SURFER is an interactive, menu-driven package with three major program steps, each of which has a wide range of options. The first step, GRID, transforms the input data into a regular grid that is used as input for the second program step, TOPO, which produces the actual contour map based on the grid and saves it in a form that can be used by the third program step, PLOT, to generate a hard copy version of the map.

In the GRID step, the same options were chosen for all the contour maps of the Cueva Blanca data. For example, though the program will suggest a grid size, Spencer always selected a grid size that reproduced the actual system of meter squares at Cueva Blanca. In addition, in all cases he chose the inverse distance method for creating the grid, which is based on the following equation:

$$Z = \frac{\sum_{i=1}^{n} Z_i / (d_i)^2}{\sum_{i=1}^{n} 1 / (d_i)^2}$$

Where Z_i is a neighboring point, d is distance, and n is the number of Z elements (Golden Software 1987:3:26).

In this method, data points are assigned weights such that the influence of one data point on another decreases with increasing distance from the point being estimated (Golden Software 1987:3:26). Other options, such as matrix smoothing or splining, were never taken with the Cueva Blanca data in the GRID step, the output of which is a grid file that is stored on disk.

The TOPO program step takes the grid file generated by the GRID step and uses it to draw a best-fitting contour map. Again, Spencer tried to be as consistent and conservative as possible in his selection of the many options available. The program always presents a suggested minimum and maximum contour level, as well as a suggested contour interval for the map. In the Cueva Blanca case, where debris densities were usually low, the suggested minimum density was often some fraction of one. This, Spencer felt, was not useful for analysis or interpretation, so he always set the minimum contour level to 1.0 in such cases. He usually did not alter the suggested maximum contour level. Note, however, that he did not generate contour maps for any debris category that had a maximum contour level of less than 1.0. He based this decision on the assumption that such a low-density category might produce spurious results, owing to small sample size.

The contour interval usually required an adjustment, since the value suggested in the TOPO step often resulted in more contour lines than were analytically or aesthetically desirable. Spencer usually set the contour interval to 1.0 or multiples thereof in the higher frequency debris categories, though occasionally he used an interval of 0.5 when that contributed significantly to the clarity of the final map. Other options in TOPO allowed for the addition of labels to the contour lines, a title for the entire map, and the superposition of the excavation boundaries and the site grid on the contour plot. The output of the TOPO step is a plot file, which is stored on disk. The PLOT program step takes the plot file created by the TOPO step and routes it to a designated printer.

A further stage in this study entailed an analysis of the patterns of association among the debris categories for Zones C and D; the very light densities of Zone E, both authors felt, precluded meaningful intercategory analysis. In the first step of this procedure, Spencer superimposed the original grid on the contour plot for each debris category (TOPO will do this as one of its options, as noted earlier). He then defined the extent of the debris scatter using the contour lines, and determined which

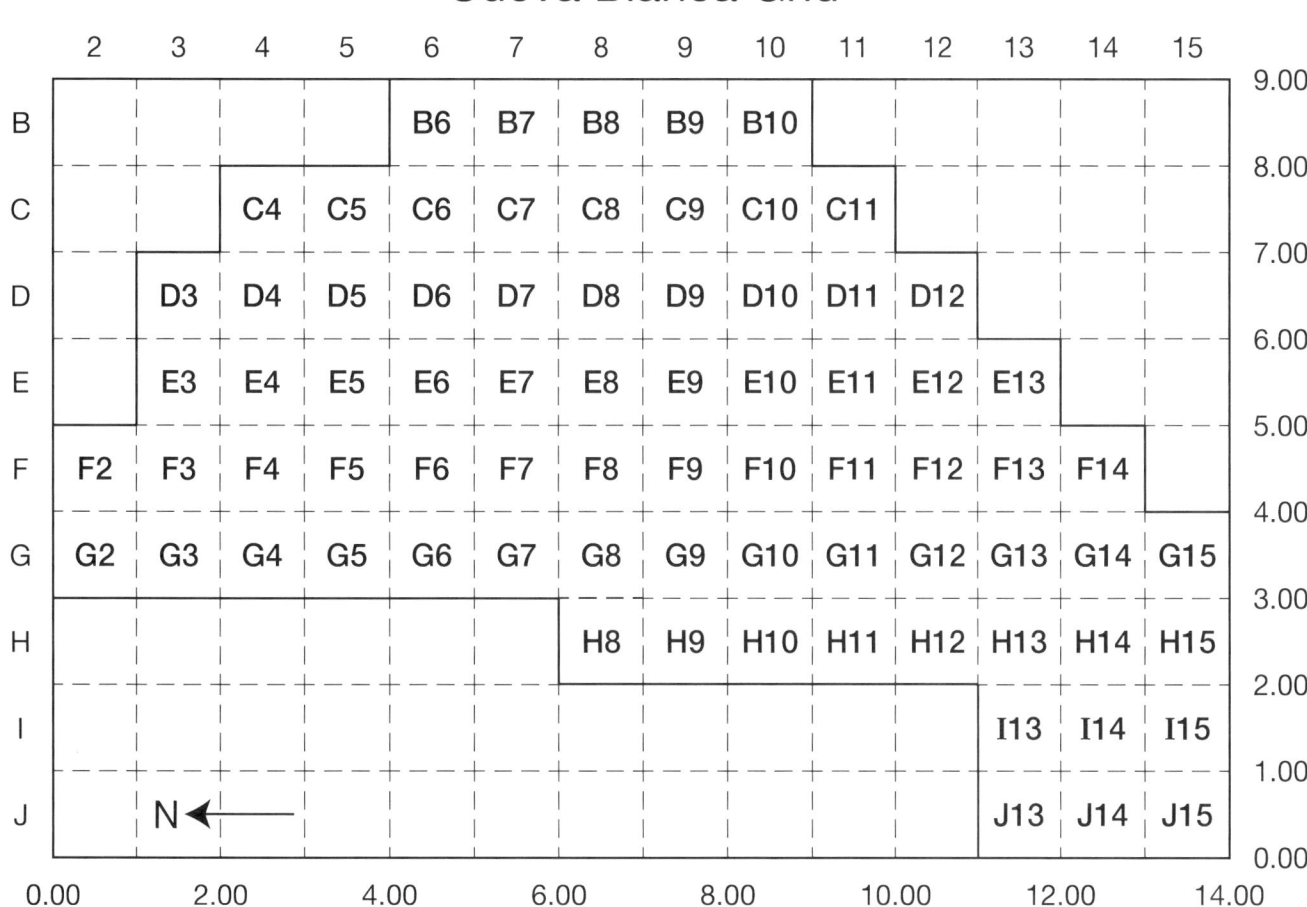

Figure 12.1. Cartesian grid of 126 squares used for the density contour study, with actual excavated squares from Cueva Blanca indicated. The coordinates used for this study appear below and to the right of the grid; the letters and numbers used for the excavation squares appear above and to the left.

grid squares were contained within, or were overlapped by, the contour line of lowest value that defined the cluster. A new file was then created for each debris category, with the values for each grid square recorded as either present or absent, depending upon whether that grid square fell within or outside the debris scatter.

Spencer then computed the Jaccard coefficient of similarity (Doran and Hodson 1975:141) for all pairs of debris categories, producing a matrix of coefficients that could be used in cluster analysis and multidimensional scaling. The Jaccard coefficient between two categories is computed as follows:

$$S_j = a / (a + b + c)$$

Where a = the sum of the positive-positive matches, b = the sum of the positive-negative mismatches, and c = the sum of the negative-positive mismatches.

The Jaccard coefficient, it should be noted, does not utilize the number of negative-negative matches; that is, the empty area within Cueva Blanca that contains neither scatter is not used in the computation of the coefficient. Thus, the Jaccard coefficient is a local procedure, focusing on the scatters themselves and their degree of mutual overlap.

This last stage of Spencer's analysis differs from Whallon's (1984) approach in that Whallon advocated the calculation of a Euclidean distance coefficient based on interpolated values from the contour lines at the original data points (he was analyzing point-plotted data). In the Cueva Blanca case, the low debris frequencies tended to produce maps with few contour lines, resulting in little variability among the Euclidean coefficients. Moreover, since the original data points in the Cueva Blanca case were necessarily all the grid squares, assigning interpolated values to them and then computing Euclidean coefficients would, Spencer felt, have introduced a global dimension to an analysis whose perspective was more appropriately local.

In the next stage of the intercategory analysis, the matrices of Jaccard coefficients for Zone C and Zone D were used as input for cluster analysis and multidimensional scaling. Though these are rather different procedures, they both can be used to discern clustering in the patterns of association among debris categories. If similar clusters are revealed when both procedures are applied to the same matrix, our confidence in these clusters as valid representations of the underlying data structure is enhanced (Cowgill et al. 1984:183). The cluster analyses and multidimensional scaling were carried out using SYSTAT, a comprehensive statistical package for the microcomputer (Wilkinson 1986). The specific linkage option chosen for the cluster analyses was centroid linking (Sokal and Michener 1958). For the multidimensional scaling runs, the method was Kruskal's stress formula 1 (Kruskal 1964a, 1964b); the scalings were always conducted in two dimensions.

Interpreting the Contour Maps

When it came time to interpret the density contour maps for each Archaic zone, Spencer and Flannery joined forces, combining empirical data from the cave with the results of the Cartesian grid analysis and multidimensional scaling. They concluded that the hearths in Zones E and D might have influenced the distribution of items and should therefore be located on their respective grids. They also concluded that since Cueva Blanca faces west, the way in which afternoon sunlight entered the cave might have determined the locations where certain tasks were carried out. Flannery therefore consulted with Matthew P. Linke, the astronomer in charge of the planetarium in the University of Michigan's Ruthven Museum of Natural History.

Linke determined that afternoon sunlight would have penetrated most deeply into the cave from late August (when the angle of the sun was roughly 280°) until mid-November (when the angle was roughly 250°). Which squares received the most light depended on the time of year. On August 21, Squares C9–E9 would have been well lit. During the autumnal equinox, sunlight would have illuminated the center of the chamber. On November 21, Squares C6–E6 would have been well lit. On the other hand, there would never have been a time when Squares F2–G2 or G15–J15 would have received strong sunlight.

Zone E

A prominent landmark of Zone E was Feature 15, a large shallow hearth occupying parts of Squares I13, I14, J13 and J14 (Figure 12.2). This hearth was not located in an area that received strong sunlight; instead, it was placed where the smoke from the hearth would be drawn outside rather than filling the chamber.

Figure 12.3 presents the contour map for total chipped stone tools in Zone E. We see a low-density scatter over a large area, from Squares B6 and E3 in the north to G12 in the southwest. The highest-density peak lies in Squares D8–E9, an area where the afternoon sunlight would have been strongest in late September. When we look at the contour map for notched flakes— the only artifact type present in sufficient numbers to be analyzed—we see one peak in the D8-E9 area and another in Square G12, just east of the Feature 15 hearth (Figure 12.4).

Deer bones were present at low densities per square in Zone E (Figure 12.5). Two minor peaks occurred in Squares D10 and F7, near the epicenter of total tools. Cottontail rabbit bones also showed two peaks, one of which lay immediately northeast of the Feature 15 hearth (Figure 12.6). The other peak was in Squares D9, D10, E9, and E10, overlapping one of the deer bone peaks.

Finally we come to the bird bone from Zone E, which consisted overwhelmingly of songbirds eaten by owls and deposited in the form of owl pellets. The main concentration occupied an oval area in Squares F6, F7, G6, and G7 (Figure 12.7). This scatter, unrelated to the other debris concentrations, was what one would expect to find directly below the rocky ledge where a barn owl chose to roost.

There was, however, a second bird bone peak just northeast of the Feature 15 hearth. This peak overlapped with one of the concentrations of cottontail rabbit bone and therefore might include the bones of at least some birds captured for food.

While the evidence from Zone E is not as abundant as that from the other two Archaic strata, we think we see a pattern similar to that from Zone D (see below). The two atlatl points from Zone E were found in Squares E4 and D9, well within our density contours for total chipped stone tools. Both deer bone peaks also occur in this part of the tool scatter. It is possible, in other words, that the area north of the C11–H11 squares was a work space for men.

If we assume that any women present were in charge of the hearth, their work space might have included one of the chipped stone tool peaks, one of the notched flake peaks, one of the cottontail rabbit bone concentrations, and the lesser of the two bird bone concentrations, all in the southwest quadrant of the cave chamber.

Zone D

Zone D provided us with the largest body of data of any Archaic stratum. Use of space may have been influenced by the presence of Feature 18, a hearth occupying parts of Squares F12, F13, G12, and G13 (Figure 12.8).

The density contours for debitage in Zone D (Figure 12.9) are very informative. There are three main concentrations. The largest and densest peak centers on Squares C7–E7 and C8–E8, an area that would be well lit by the afternoon sun during October and November. Nine of the ten atlatl points found in Zone D occur in this part of the cave (see Figure 6.18), which may have been a men's work area. The second largest concentration centers on Squares I14, I15, J14, and J15, near the southwest

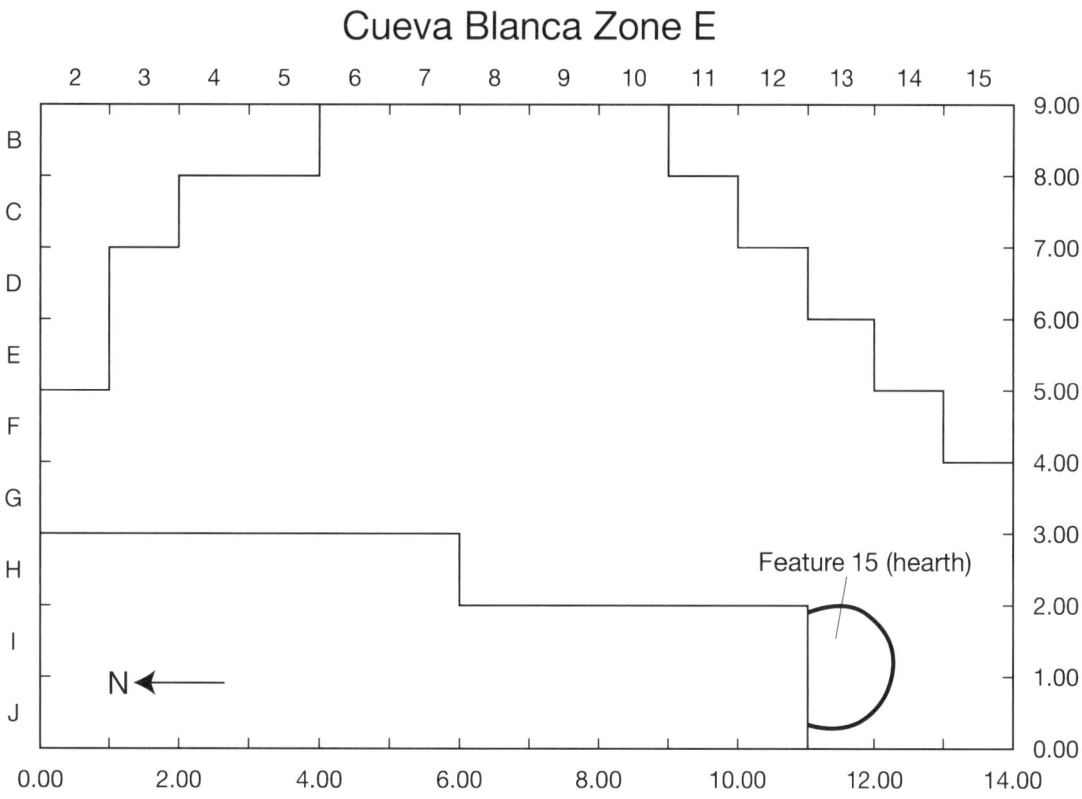

Figure 12.2. Location of Feature 15, a hearth that might have influenced the distribution of items in Zone E.

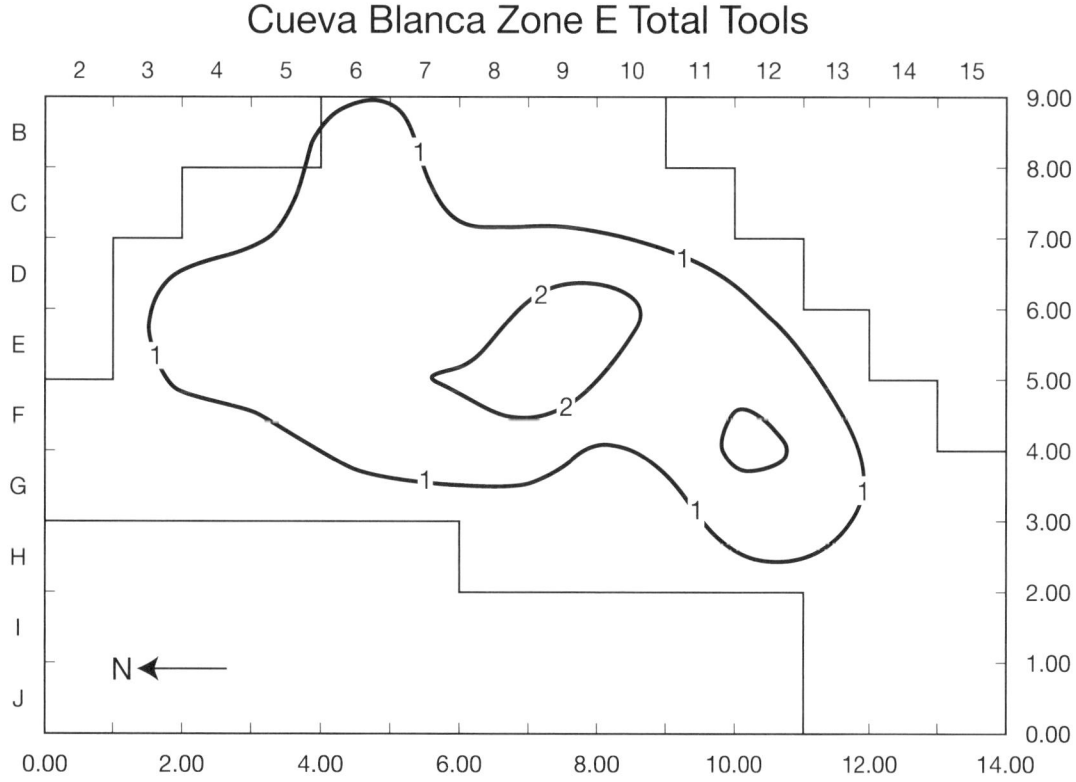

Figure 12.3. Density contours for total tools, Zone E (contour interval = 1).

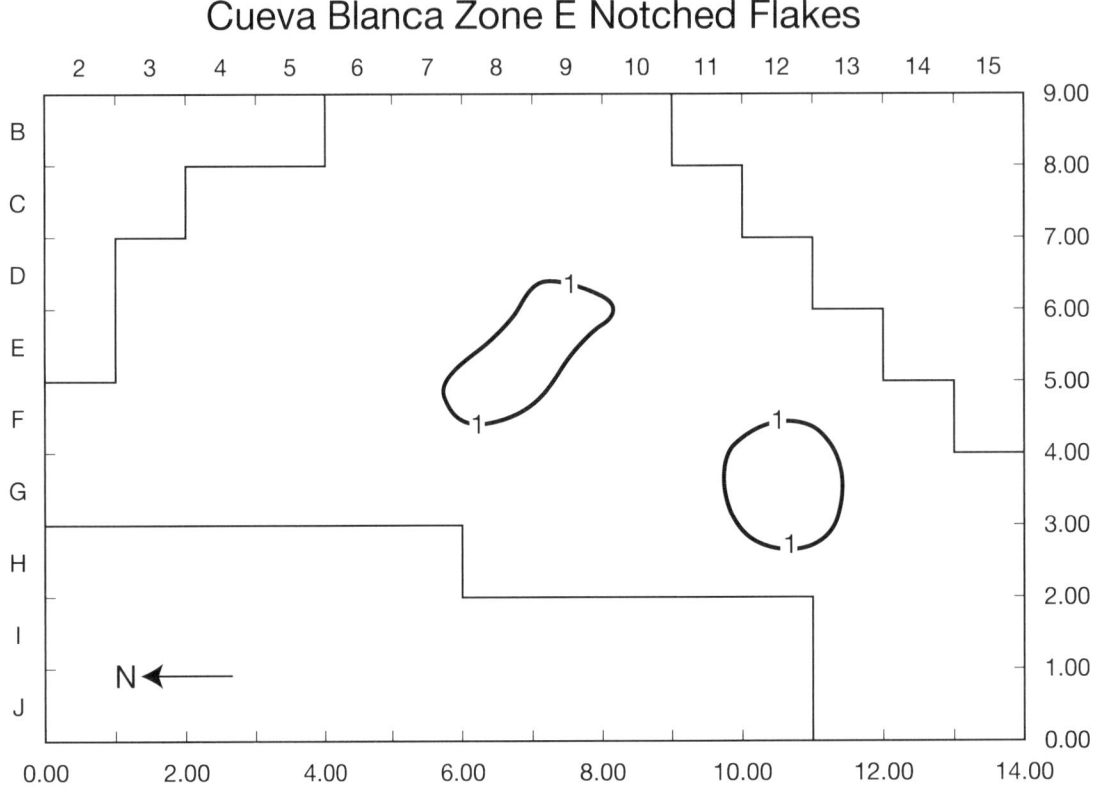

Figure 12.4. Density contours for notched flakes, Zone E (contour interval = 1).

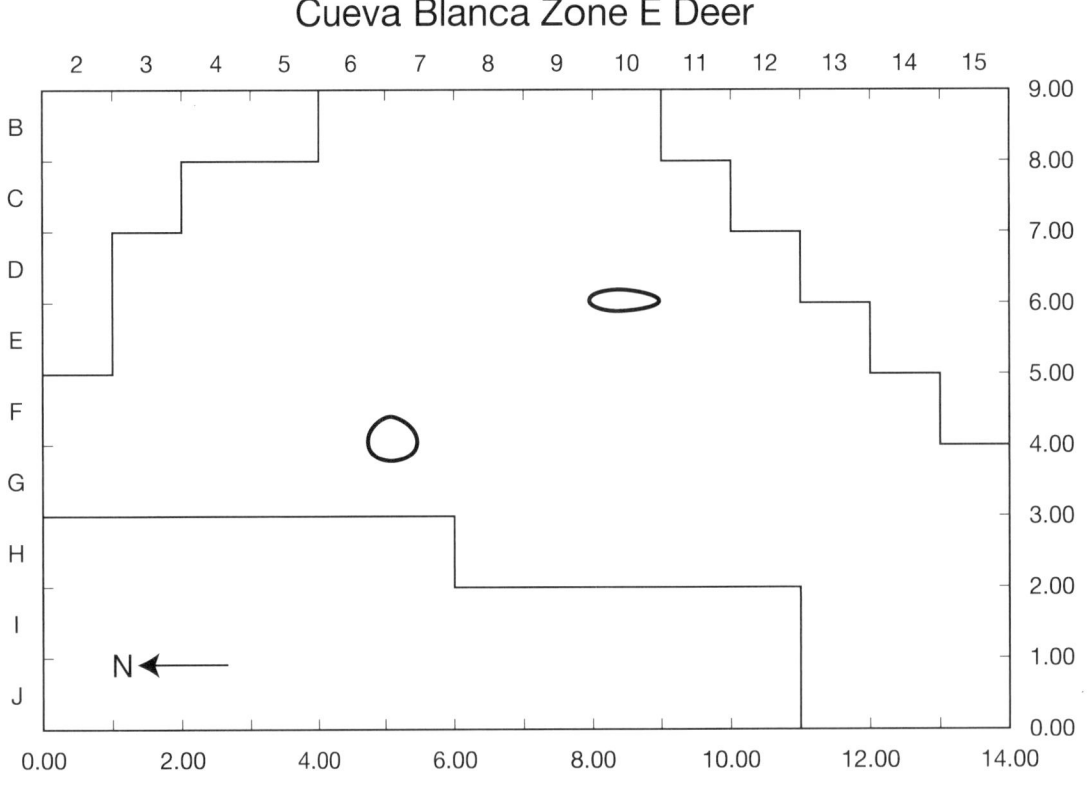

Figure 12.5. Density contours for identified deer bone, Zone E (contour interval = 1).

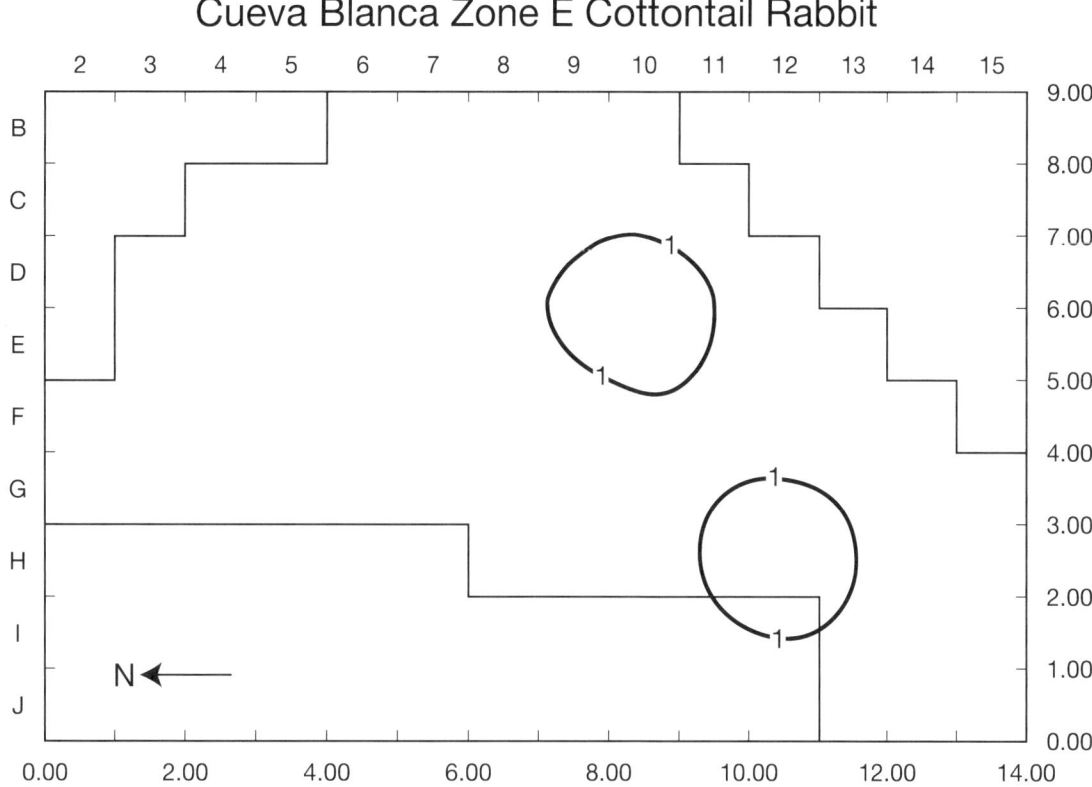

Figure 12.6. Density contours for identified cottontail rabbit bones, Zone E (contour interval = 1).

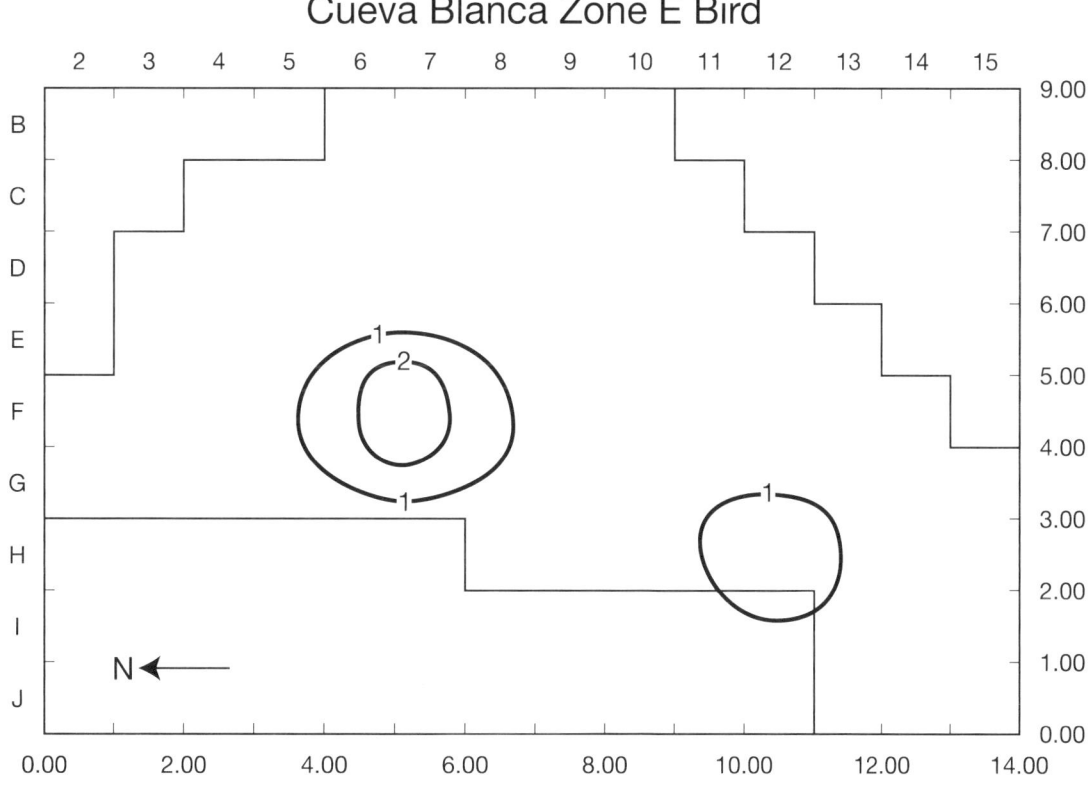

Figure 12.7. Density contours for bird bones, Zone E (contour interval =1).

156　　　　　　　　　　　　　　　　　　　　　Chapter 12

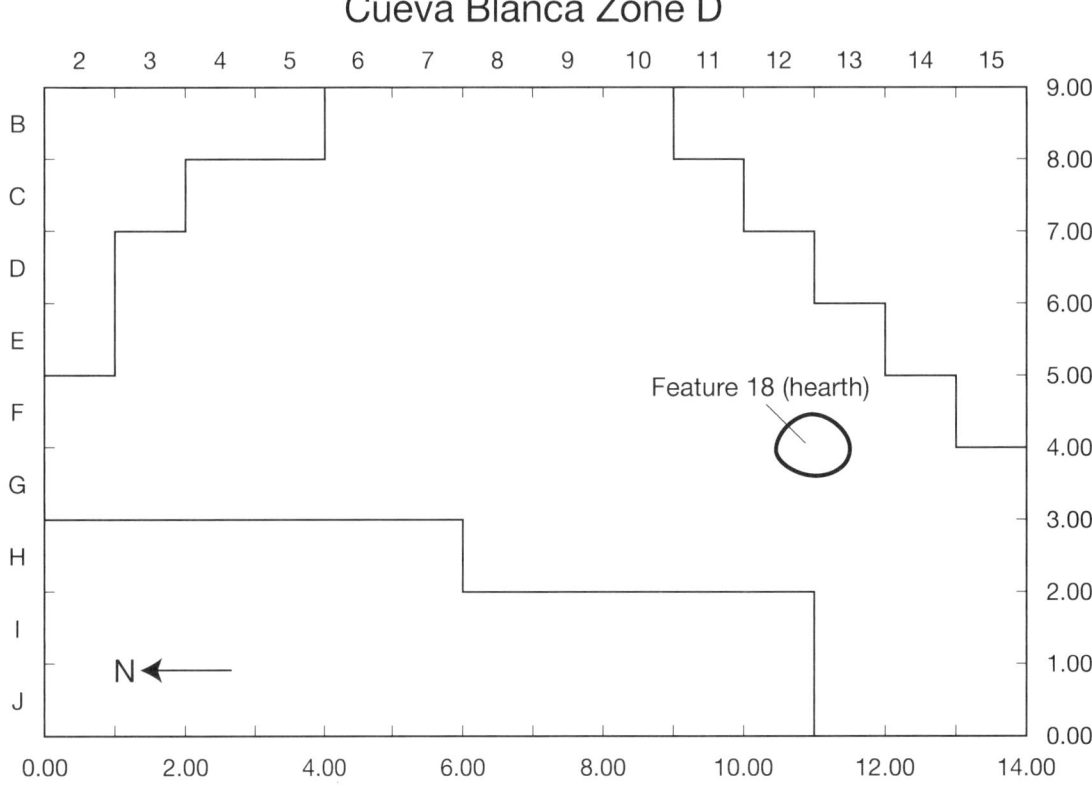

Figure 12.8. Location of Feature 18, a hearth that might have influenced the distribution of items in Zone D.

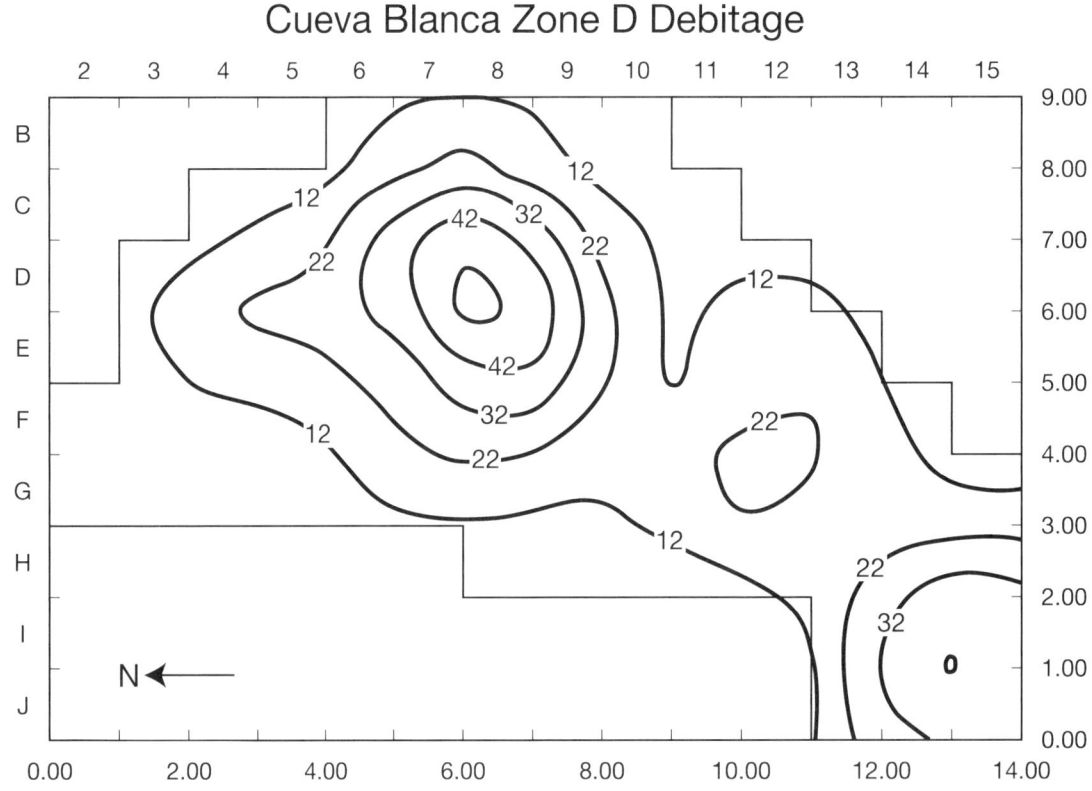

Figure 12.9. Density contours for debitage, Zone D (contour interval = 10).

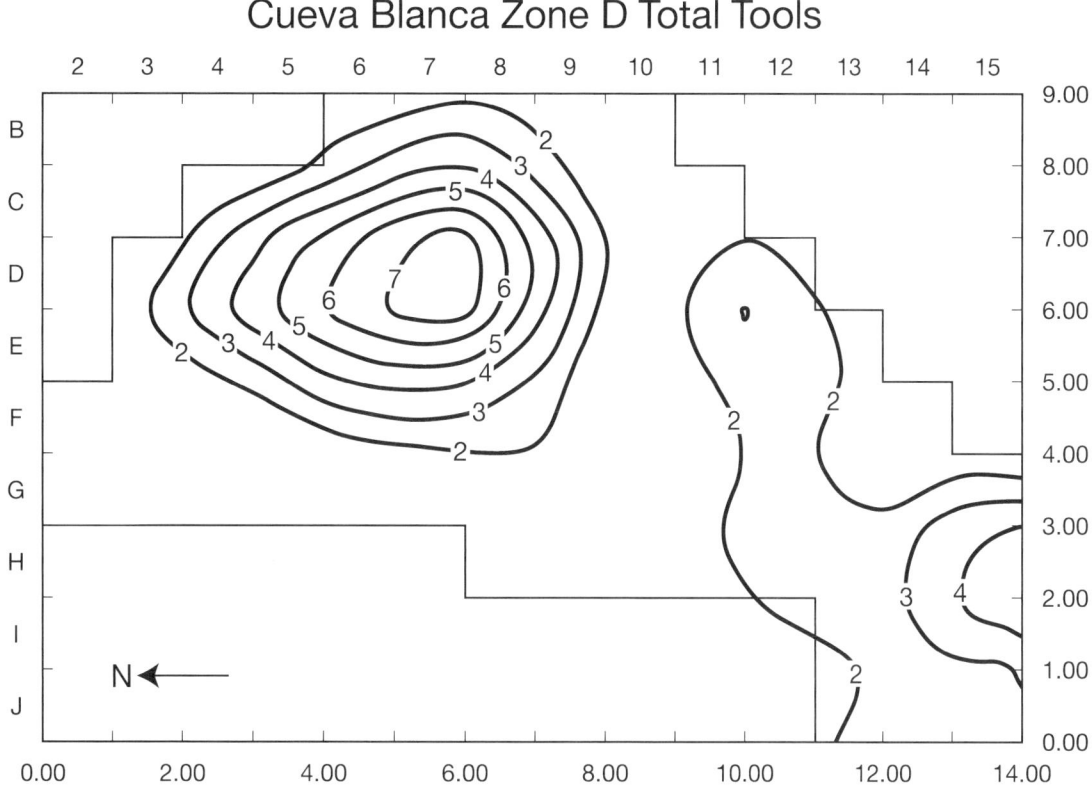

Figure 12.10. Density contours for total tools, Zone D (contour interval = 1).

limit of the excavation. This was an area without strong sunlight, where refuse may have been discarded. The third and smallest concentration of debitage fell in Squares F12–G12, immediately adjacent to the Feature 18 hearth, an area where meals may have been prepared.

The density contours for total chipped stone tools (Figure 12.10) are equally revealing. By far the greatest density of tools occurred in and around Square D7, overlapping with the highest debitage density and the majority of the atlatl points. The southwest quadrant of the excavation was also found to be rich in debitage, but relatively poor in actual tools. This area may have been a "toss zone" (Binford 1984), where unwanted debris was discarded but fewer tools were dropped (see Chapter 14).

Figure 12.11 presents the density contours for steep denticulate scrapers, one of the three tool types present in sufficient numbers to analyze. Essentially, the peak for these scrapers is coextensive with the peak for total chipped stone tools. This area, in the northeast quadrant of the cave chamber, may therefore have included "drop zones" (Binford 1984) for several tool types, including atlatl points and steep denticulate scrapers (see Chapter 14).

The density contours for utilized flakes (Figure 12.12) and notched flakes (Figure 12.13) are informative. Each of these tool types occurs in two concentrations, roughly four meters apart. One peak, not surprisingly, lies in the northeast quadrant of the cave, where so many other tools were concentrated. Both utilized flakes and notched flakes, however, also show modest concentrations in the southwest quadrant of the cave (Squares H14, H15, I14, and I15). In fact, taken together, utilized flakes and notched flakes are almost sufficient to account for the "total tool" presence in the southwest quadrant. We suspect that the individuals in charge of the Feature 18 hearth (possibly women) could have been the source of these tools.

Identified deer bones were concentrated mainly in the same part of the cave where debitage peaked (Figure 12.14); many fewer deer bones were discarded in the southwest corner of the excavation. The situation is different, however, for cottontail rabbit bones (Figure 12.15). In this case there are two large areas of discard, not unlike the distribution for debitage. One concentration peaks near Square D8, the other near J14. Once again we are left with the impression that two groups of agents had staked out their areas of the cave chamber—perhaps men in the northeast, women near the hearth.

The density contours for unidentified small mammal bones (Figure 12.16) present a different picture. Even though these fragments are likely to have come mainly from rabbits, they were not distributed the way the identified cottontail bones were. The most impressive concentration lay in Squares G15–I15, almost resting against the wall of the cave in the southwest corner of the excavation. This is the kind of final resting place

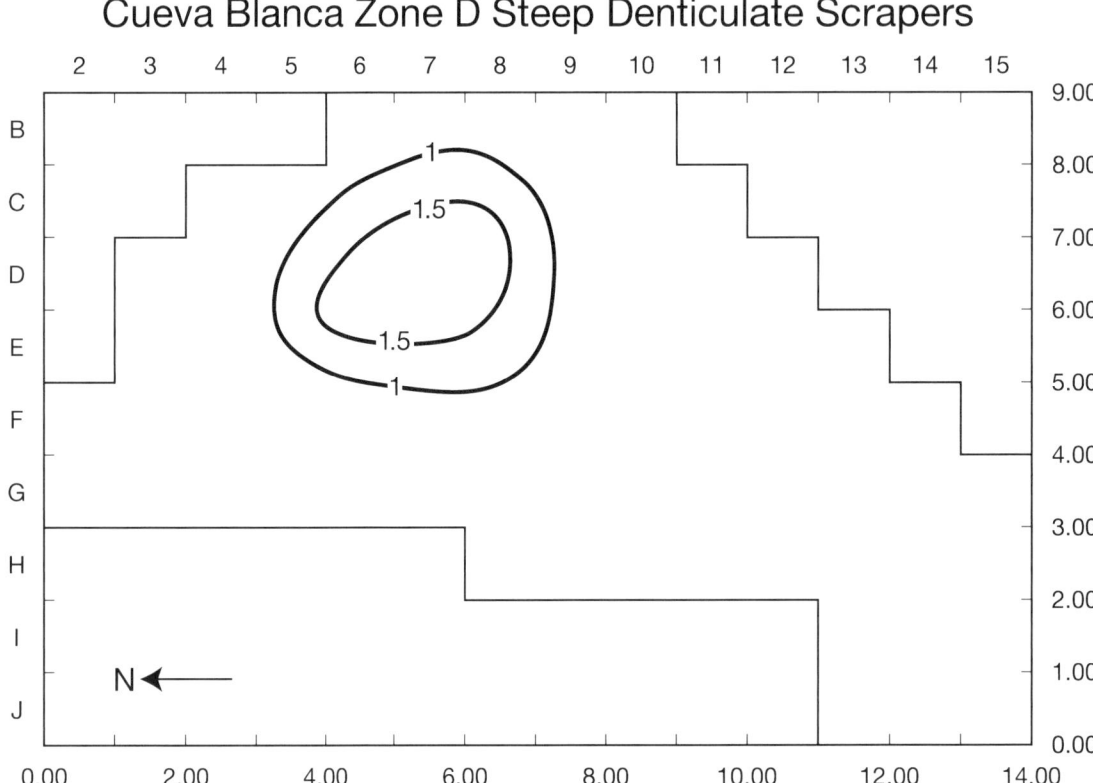

Figure 12.11. Density contours for steep denticulate scrapers, Zone D (contour interval = 0.5).

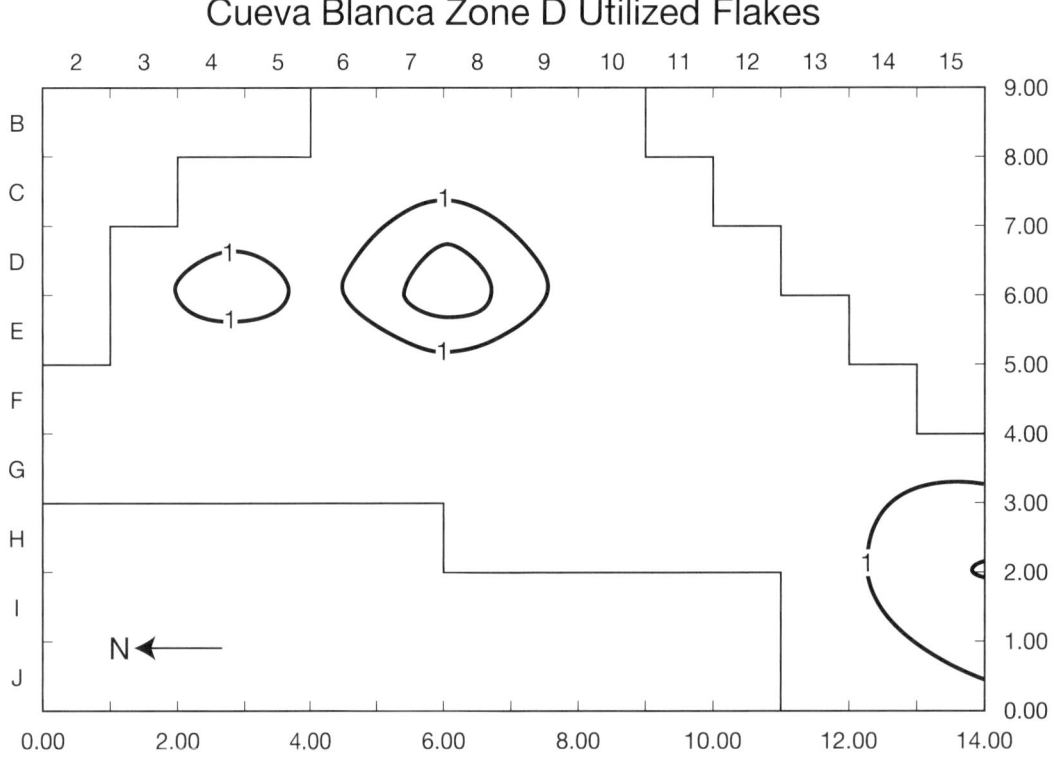

Figure 12.12. Density contours for utilized flakes, Zone D (contour interval = 0.5).

Distributional Variability in Zones E–C of Cueva Blanca 159

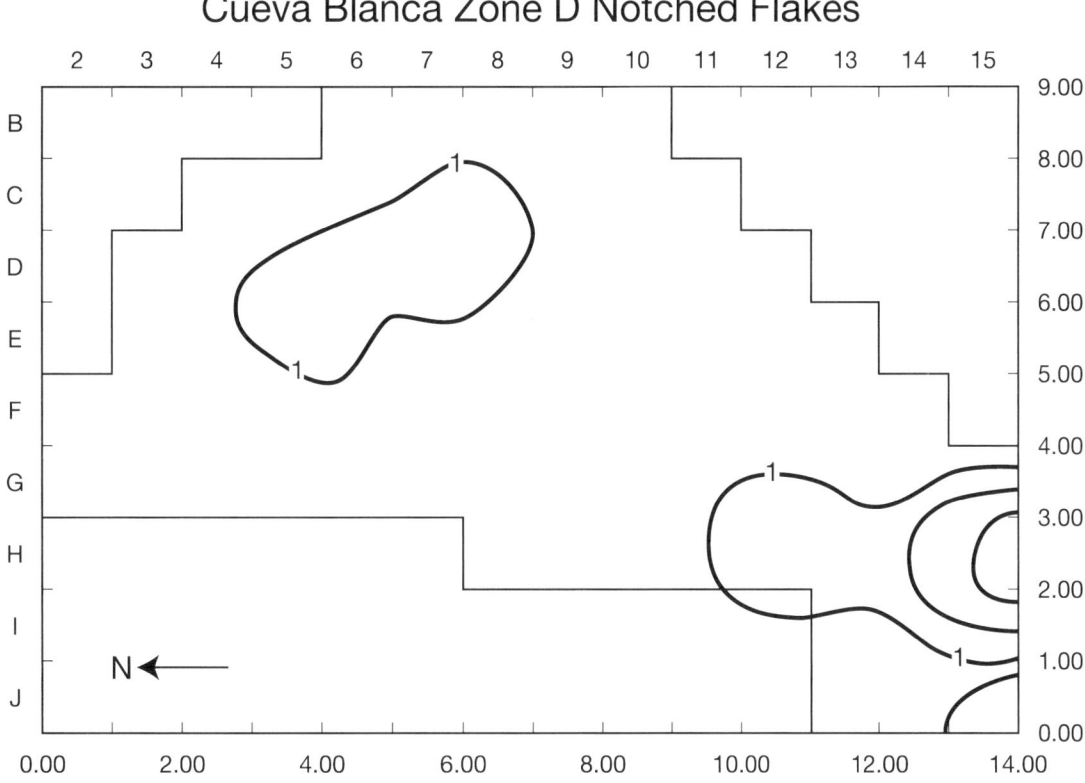

Figure 12.13. Density contours for notched flakes, Zone D (contour interval = 0.5).

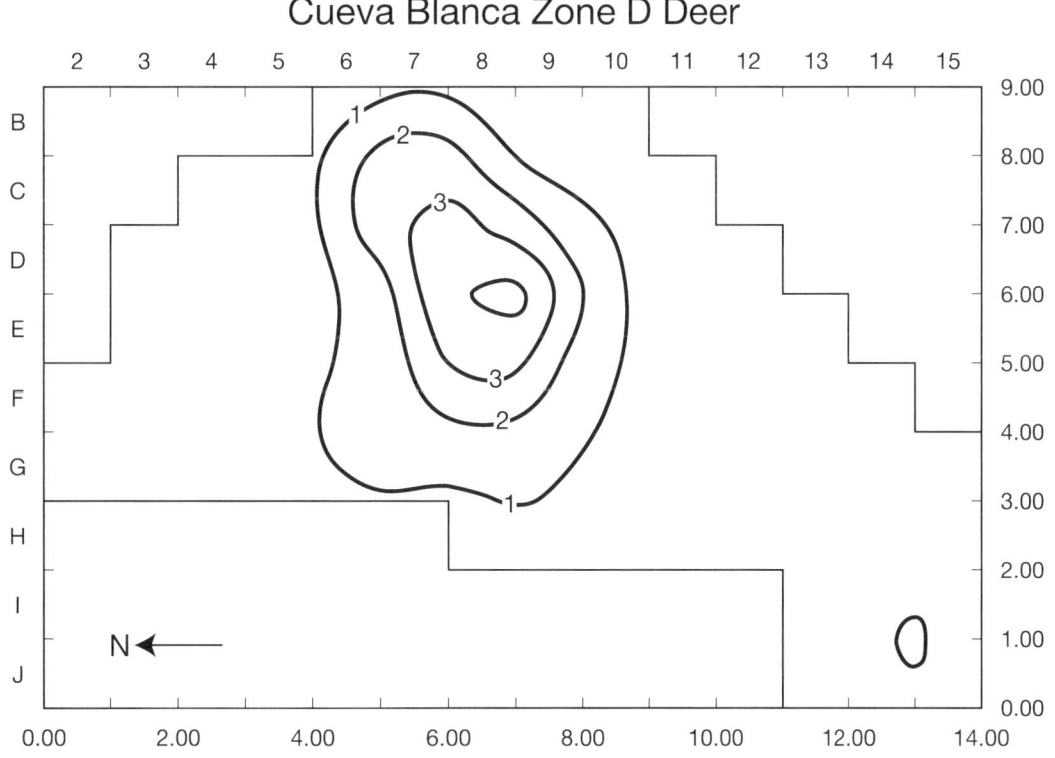

Figure 12.14. Density contours for identified deer bone, Zone D (contour interval = 1).

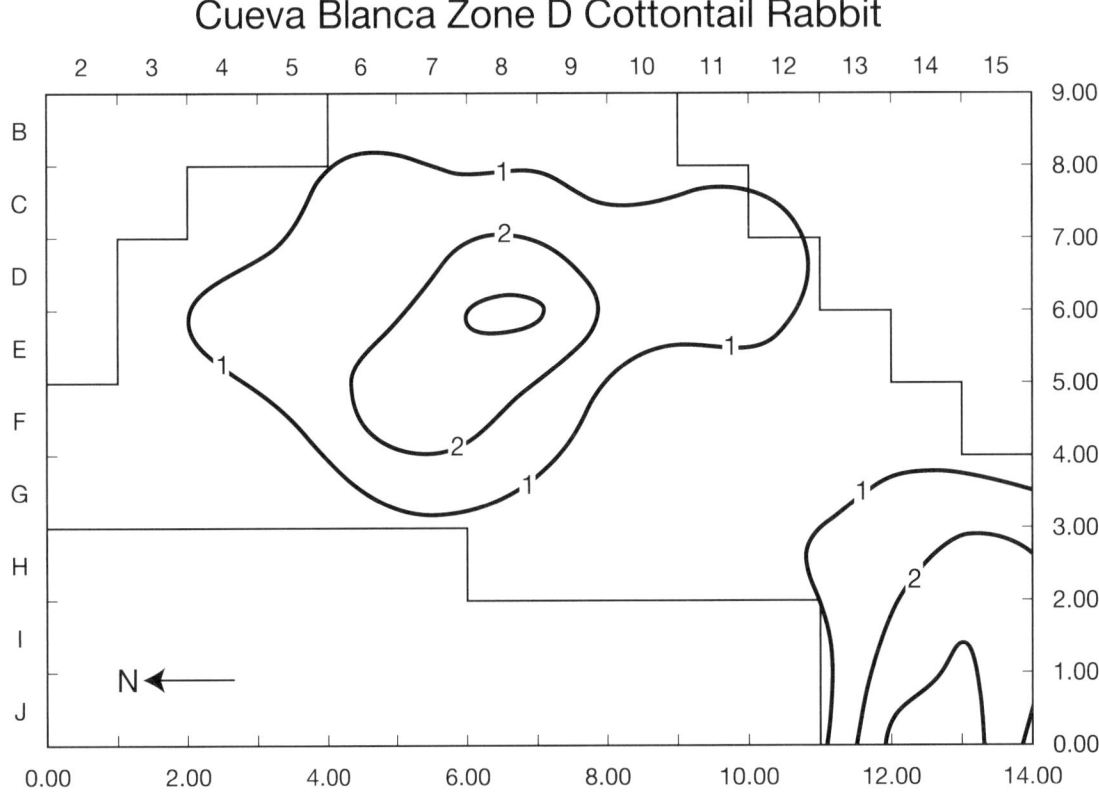

Figure 12.15. Density contours for identified cottontail rabbit bones, Zone D (contour interval = 1).

one might expect for the tiny, unidentifiable scraps resulting from meals.

Finally, we come to the contour densities for bird bone. Since the overwhelming majority of these bones appeared to be from songbirds eaten by owls and deposited in their pellets, we were not surprised to find them all in one concentration surrounding Squares F8–G8 (Figure 12.17). This is directly below a rocky ledge where a barn owl presumably roosted.

Figure 12.18 presents the results of Spencer's multidimensional scaling of eight categories of items recovered from Zone D. As expected, bird bones were not closely related to any other item. Utilized flakes and notched flakes—two simple tools, often shaped more by use than design—were closely related. Cottontail bones and debitage were also closely related, but neither was closely tied to unidentified small mammal bones. This may mean that larger, identifiable cottontail bones were discarded in the same areas as waste flakes, while smaller, unidentifiable bones were discarded with the residue of meals. Finally, while deer bones and steep denticulate scrapers were seemingly associated, that does not necessarily mean that the latter were used to butcher deer. It only means that both items were discarded in the same area of the cave, perhaps having been used by the same individuals.

Our interpretation of Zone D is that the northeast quadrant was a work space for men, while the area between the Feature 18 hearth and Square J15 was a work space for women. The men left behind nine atlatl points of at least four recognizable types; most of the identifiable deer bone; some of the identifiable cottontail bones; most of the steep denticulate scrapers; and some of the utilized flakes and notched flakes. The women left behind some of the utilized flakes and notched flakes; many of the identified cottontail bones; and the bulk of the unidentified small mammal bone. The women may have been in charge of the hearth, but the men (who presumably had to create and repair atlatl points) had access to the most sunlit parts of the cave chamber.

Zone C

Zone C, the youngest of the cave's Archaic strata, presented a different picture from that of Zone D. In the first place, Zone C appears to have had no hearth. In the second place, the atlatl points in that zone were less obviously clustered in one area (see Figure 6.20). Zone C, in other words, does not give the impression of a living floor divided into men's and women's work spaces.

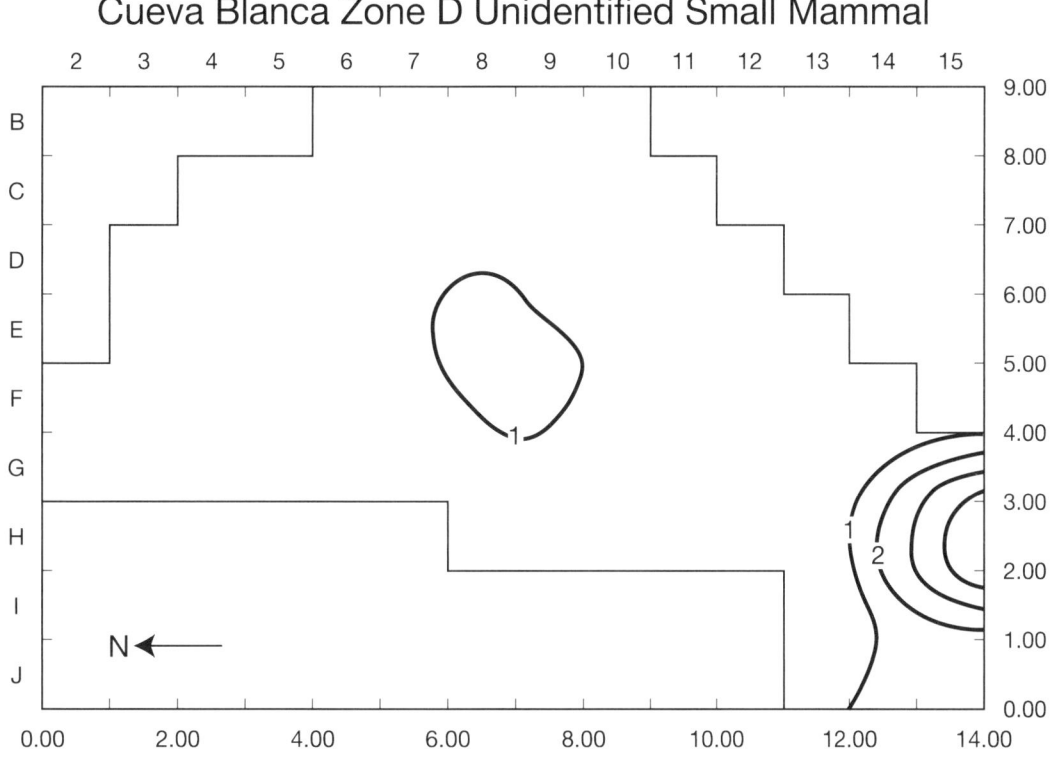

Figure 12.16. Density contours for unidentified fragments of small mammal bone, Zone D (contour interval = 1). It is likely that the vast majority of these fragments belong to rabbits of various species.

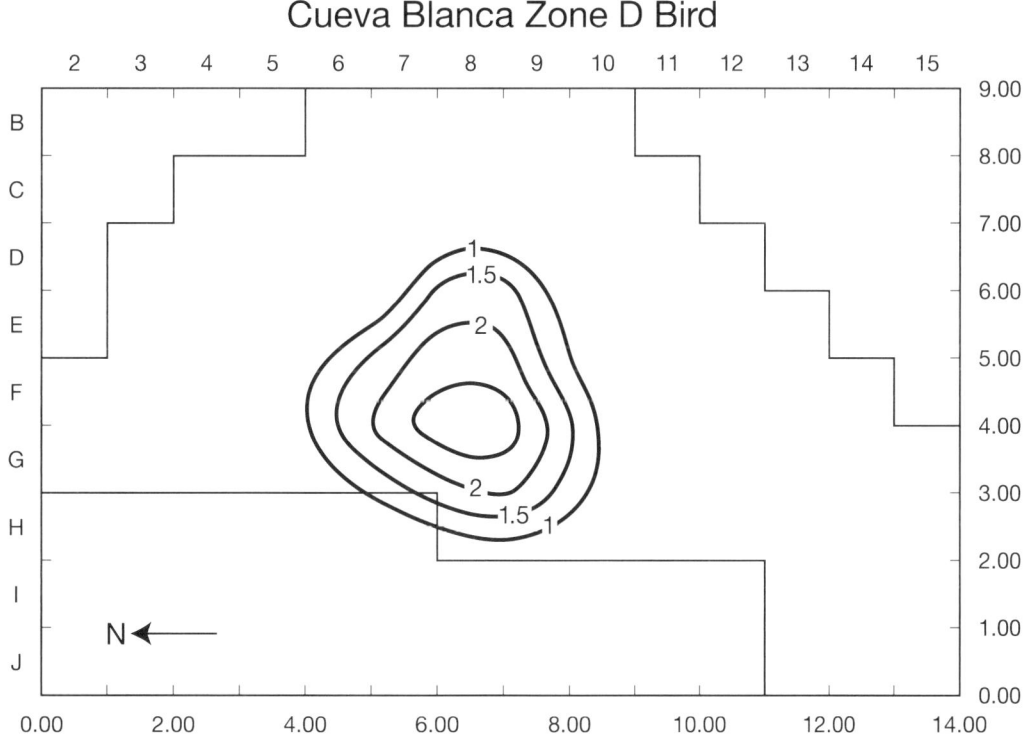

Figure 12.17. Density contours for bird bones, Zone D (contour interval = 0.5). With few exceptions, the bones appear to be from small songbirds eaten by barn owls and deposited in owl pellets.

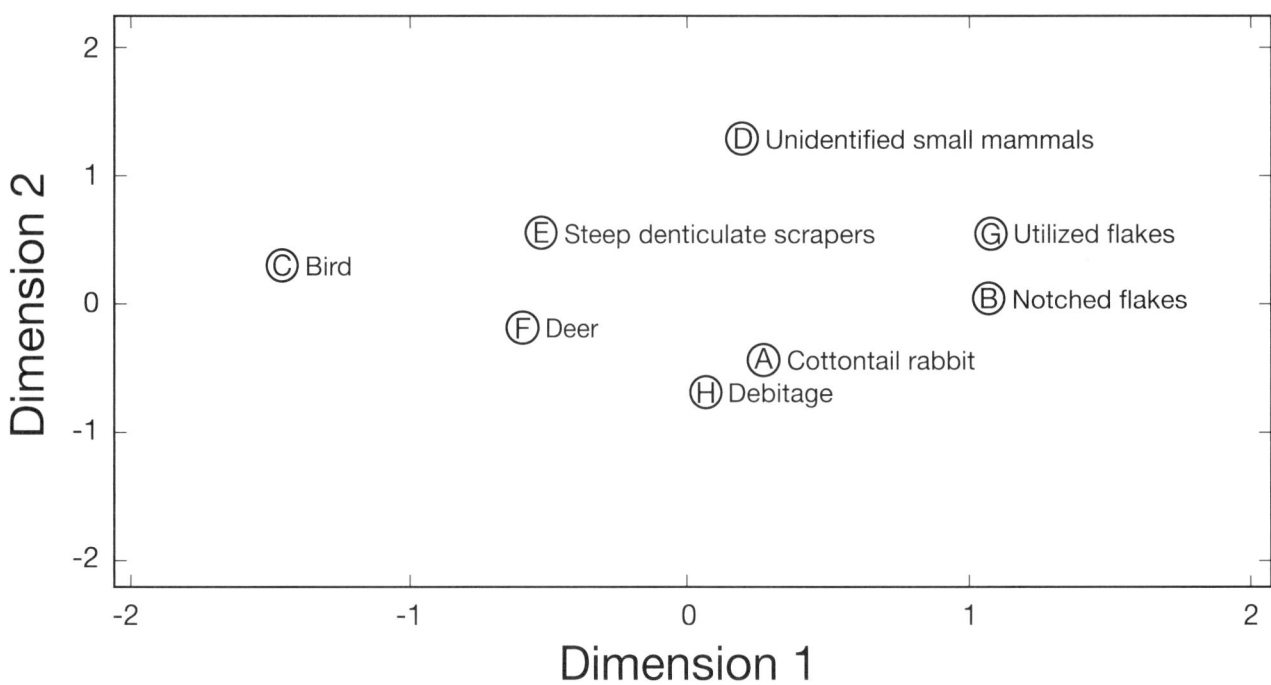

Figure 12.18. Results of multidimensional scaling of eight categories of items found in Zone D.

When one looks at the density contours for debitage in Zone C (Figure 12.19), one sees five small peaks scattered over the area from Square D6 in the northeast to H13 in the southwest. We cannot be sure whether this distribution reflects one visit made by five people, or repeated visits made by a smaller number of people. As for the months when afternoon sunlight would have been the strongest, the debitage peaks are so widely scattered that we can only narrow our estimate down to the period from late September to late November.

The density contours for total tools (Figure 12.20) convey the same impression; there are four modest peaks spread over the whole area from Square D5 to Square H13. The southwest quadrant of the excavation, rather than giving the impression of a separate work space, simply reflects a continuation of the activities in the northeast quadrant.

The density contours for utilized flakes (Figure 12.21) and notched flakes (Figure 12.22) do not alter our impression of Zone C. Utilized flakes display two modest peaks along the E row of squares. Notched flakes display three small peaks along the periphery of the total tool scatter.

The density contours for identified deer bone (Figure 12.23) also imply a use of space different from that of Zone D. Instead of the usual concentration in the northeast quadrant, there are four modest peaks of deer bone scattered across the cave chamber, several of them near peaks of debitage. It is interesting that the two strongest peaks fall in the southwest quadrant, an area that in Zones E and D produced relatively little deer bone.

The density contours for identified cottontail rabbit bones (Figure 12.24) and unidentified small mammal bones (Figure 12.25) are worth comparing. In each case we see two concentrations: a small one centered in the area of Square F7 and a large one filling the southwest corner of the excavation. The majority of the unidentified small mammal bones likely belonged to rabbits, but this is the only living floor on which we have seen their distributions overlap so strongly. In Zone D there were comparable cottontail concentrations in our proposed men's and women's work spaces, but the bulk of the unidentified small mammal bones were concentrated in our suspected women's work space, southwest of the Feature 18 hearth. In Zone C, we cannot make the case for a separate work space where women cooked meals and discarded lots of small, unidentifiable bone fragments.

Finally we come to the density contours for mud turtle bones and scutes (Figure 12.26). What these contours reflect is the fact that someone turned a mud turtle upside down, roasted it over hot coals, and consumed it in the area of Squares E3 and E4. We found no hearth created for this roasting, which might have taken place before the turtle was brought to the cave.

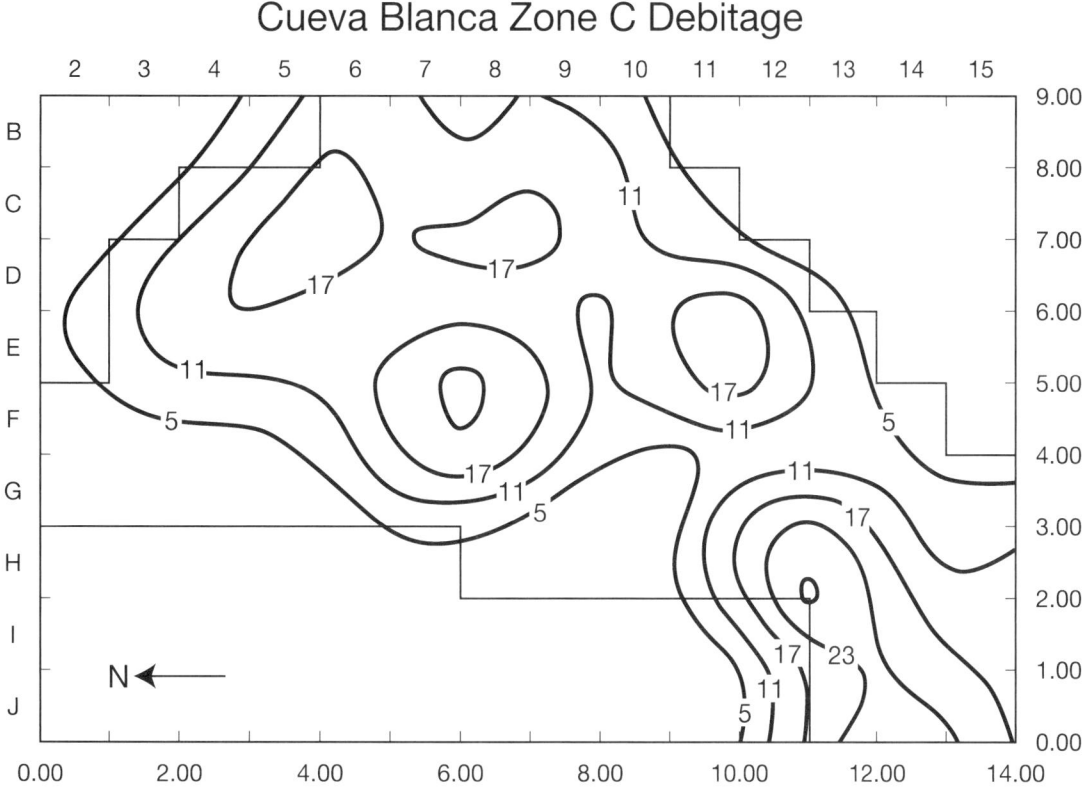

Figure 12.19. Density contours for debitage, Zone C (contour interval = 6).

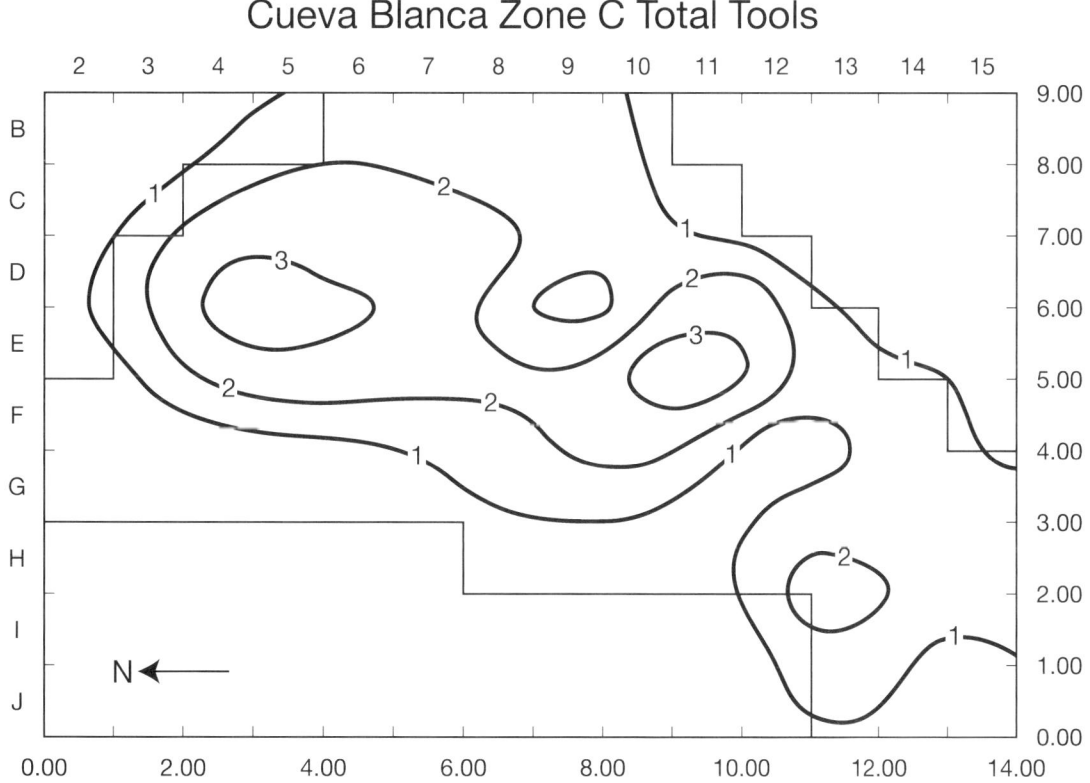

Figure 12.20. Density contours for total tools, Zone C (contour interval = 1).

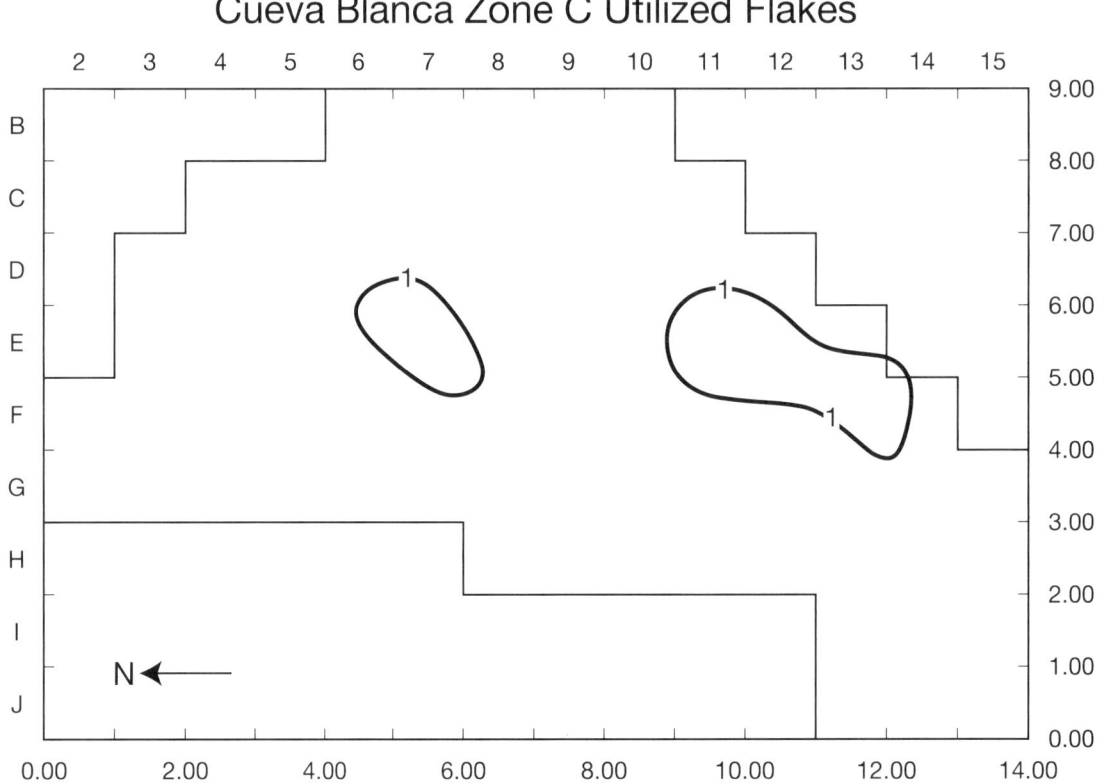

Figure 12.21. Density contours for utilized flakes, Zone C (contour interval = 1).

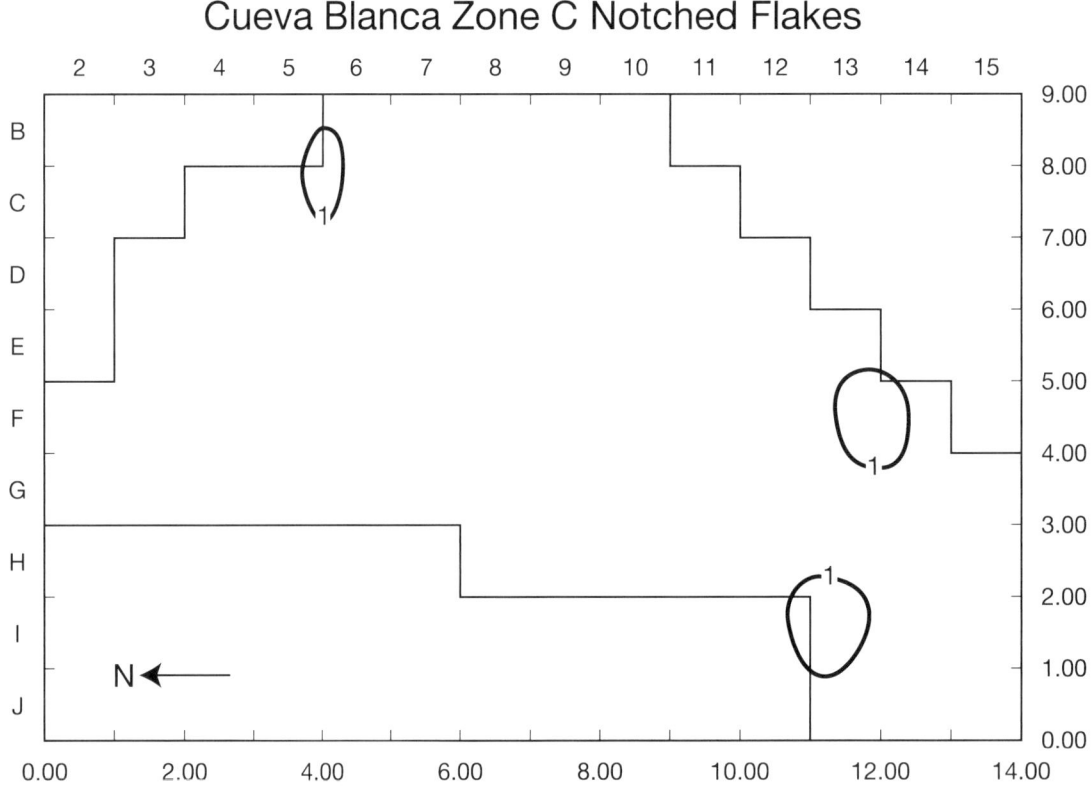

Figure 12.22. Density contours for notched flakes, Zone C (contour interval = 1).

Distributional Variability in Zones E–C of Cueva Blanca

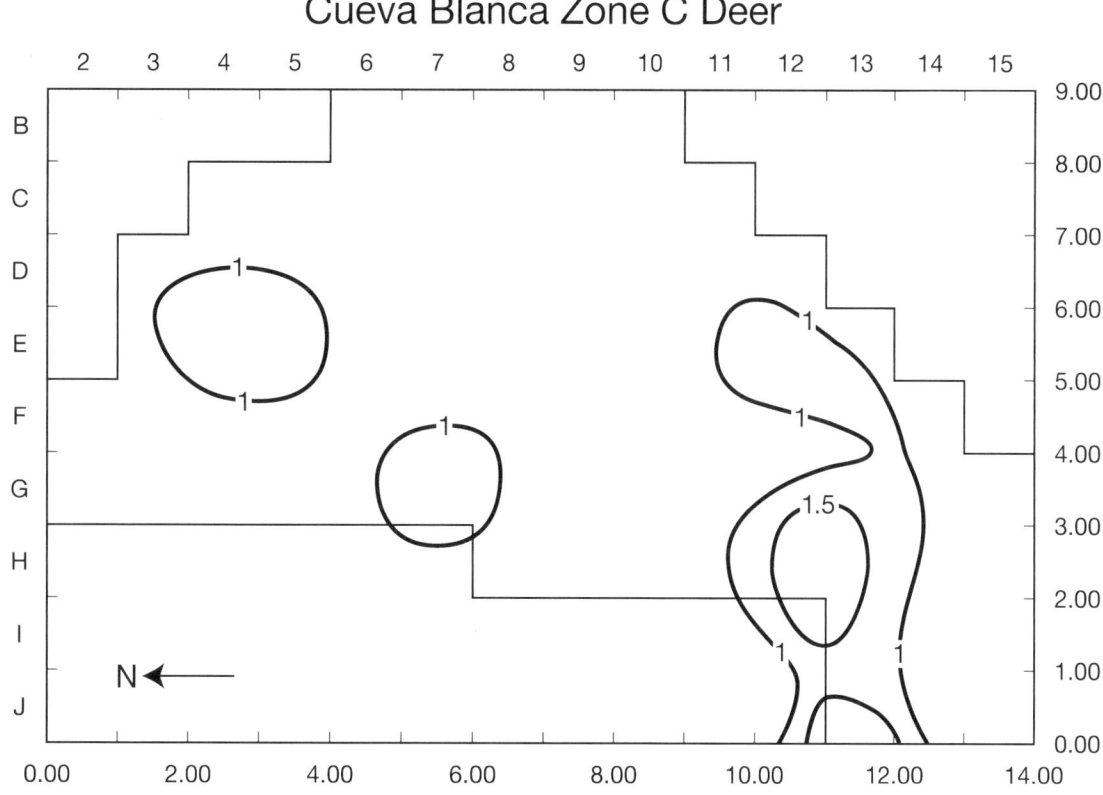

Figure 12.23. Density contours for identified deer bone, Zone C (contour interval = 0.5).

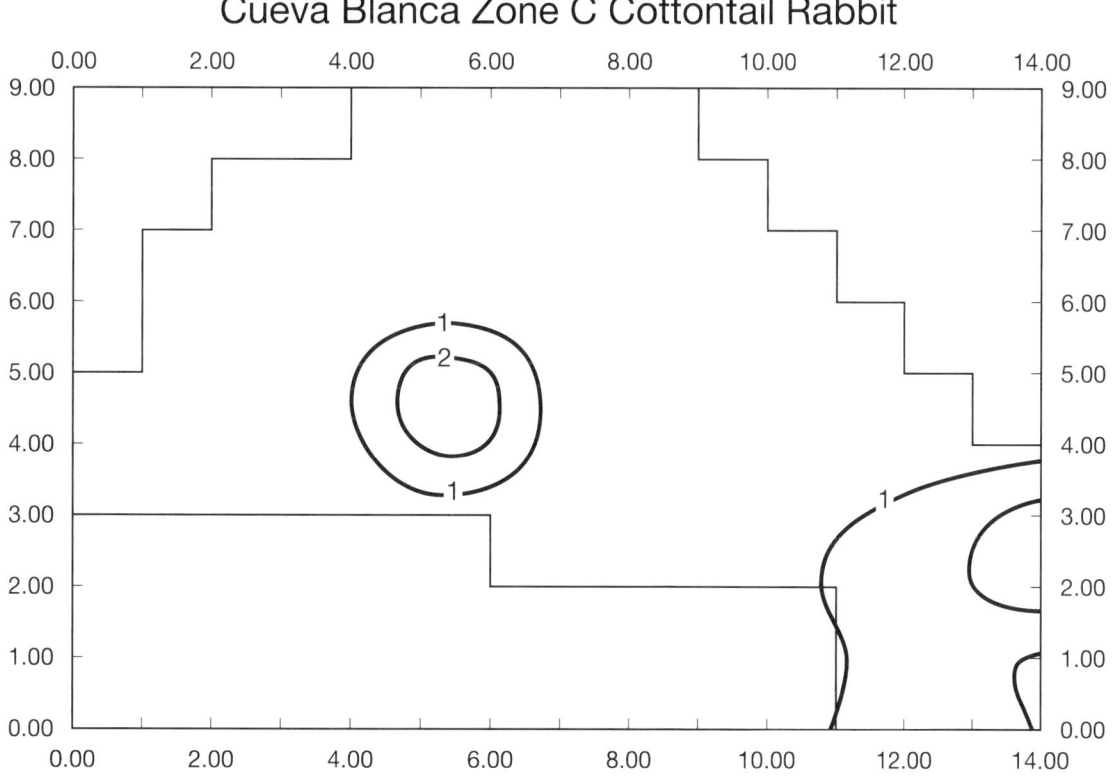

Figure 12.24. Density contours for identified cottontail rabbit bones, Zone C (contour interval = 1).

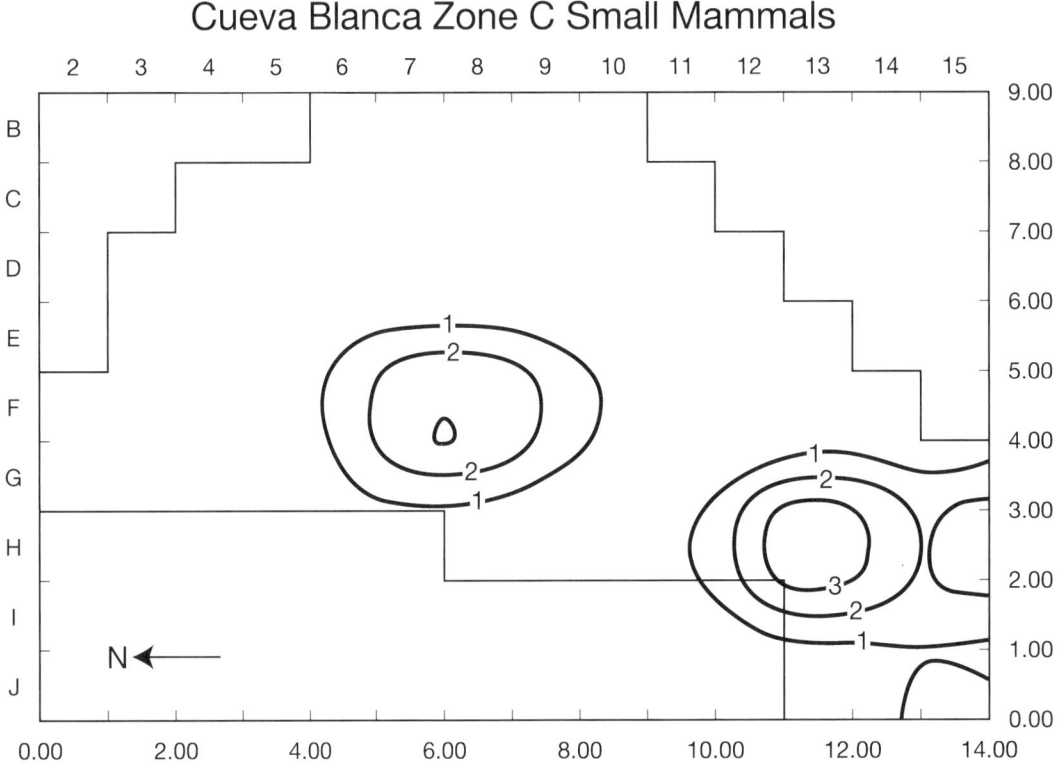

Figure 12.25. Density contours for unidentified fragments of small mammal bone (contour interval = 1). It is likely that the vast majority of these fragments belong to rabbits of various species.

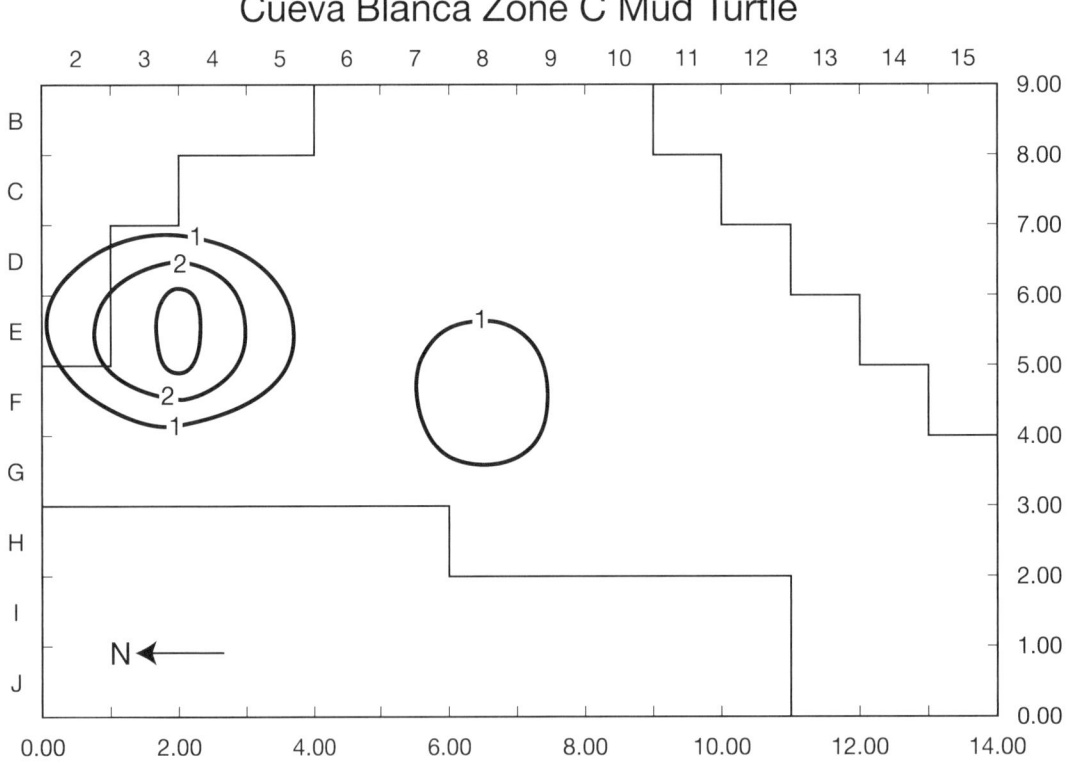

Figure 12.26. Density contours for identified mud turtle bones and scutes, Zone C (contour interval =1).

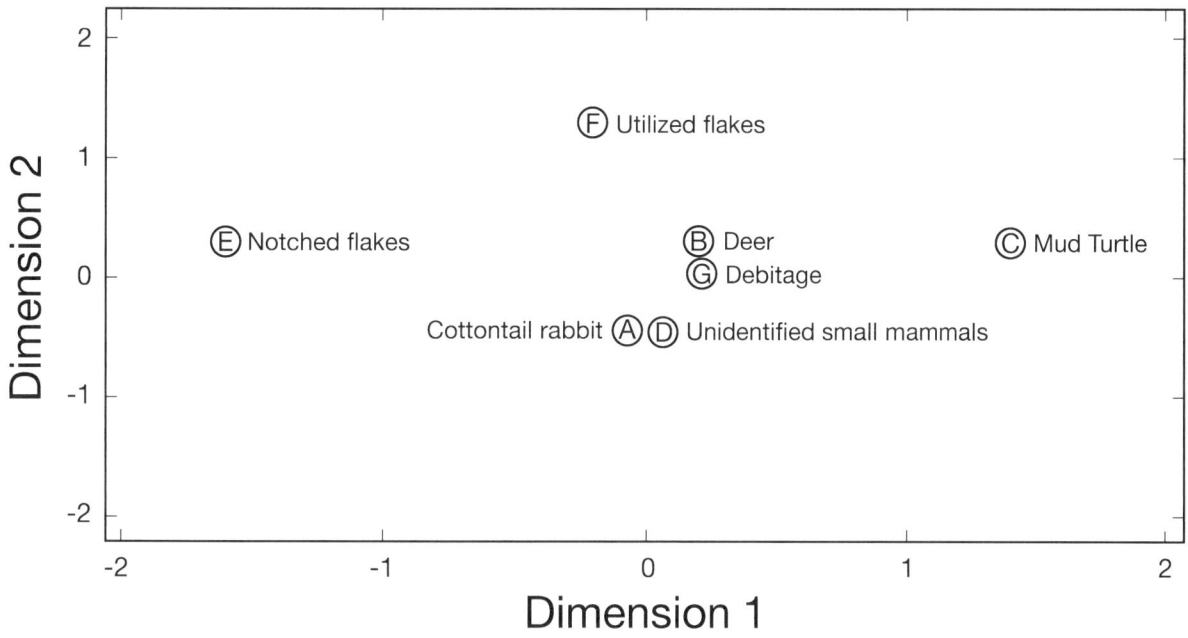

Figure 12.27. Results of multidimensional scaling of seven categories of items found in Zone C.

Fragments from a second mud turtle showed up in Square F8, near the center of the cave.

When one subjects seven categories of items from Zone C to a multidimensional scaling, interesting patterns emerge (Figure 12.27). Mud turtle remains, as expected, are not closely related to anything else, since they resulted from what appears to have been a unique event. Notched flakes, which were seemingly tossed to the margins of the debitage scatter, also do not show a close relationship with anything else—not even with utilized flakes, with which they were closely associated in Zone D.

As for the remaining items, deer bones were closely associated with debitage. Cottontail bones were closely associated with unidentified small mammal bones and lay not far from the debitage and deer bone.

It is instructive to compare the density contours and scaling results of Zones D and C. Zone D can reasonably be seen as having its space divided between a group of men—working in an area with sufficient light for the manufacture, use, and repair of chipped stone tools—and a group of women, who worked (and prepared meals) in the area between the hearth and the mouth of the cave. We cannot propose a similar scenario for Zone C; in fact, it would not surprise us to learn that Zone C was either (1) an all-male camp or (2) a palimpsest created by a series of short-term all-male visits to the cave. Such an interpretation would explain both the absence of a formal hearth and the lack of contrast in activities between the northeast and southwest quadrants of the cave chamber. Simply put, it appears that when no women were present, the men spread out over the entire living floor.

13

The Search for Tool Kits at Cueva Blanca: Two Statistical Approaches

Robert G. Reynolds

In Chapter 12, Spencer and Flannery highlighted work areas in Cueva Blanca by drawing density contours for tools and animal bones. The existence of work areas, of course, implies the existence of tools with which the work was done. In this chapter I initiate the search for possible Archaic tool kits.

Let me begin by acknowledging the inherent difficulty of identifying clear-cut tool kits in Oaxaca's chipped stone industry. As Hole explains in Chapter 5, most of Oaxaca's Archaic tools are expedient rather than standardized. Generalized items, such as utilized flakes, notched flakes, and choppers/knives, could have been used for a variety of tasks and employed by either men or women. It is easy, in fact, to see many of Cueva Blanca's chipped stone items serving in more than one tool kit.

What I have decided to do, therefore, is to focus on two distinctive tools that were almost certainly used for different tasks. There can be little doubt that projectile points were used for hunting animals such as deer and peccary; it is also reasonable to propose that they were used principally by men. Flakes with sheen, on the other hand, likely developed their distinctively glossy edges from being used to cut materials like the tough, fibrous leaf bases of the agave. It is reasonable to propose that women at Cueva Blanca did much of the plant processing, which may have caused the sickle-like edge gloss.

Selecting these two distinctive tools—one for hunting animals, one for processing plants—gives us a starting point in our search for tool kits. Our next step is to ask two questions: (1) Which other tools are positively associated with projectile points and which are negatively associated with them? and (2) Which other tools are positively associated with flakes with sheen and which are negatively associated with them?

Because Cueva Blanca was excavated using a grid of 1 x 1 m squares, an obvious place to start was to ask how often two tool types tended to co-occur in the same square. Like any approach, this one has its weaknesses; because the borders of each square were part of an arbitrary grid, two tools could have been discarded relatively close to one another yet wind up in different squares. At the same time, the density contours presented in Chapter 12 suggest that work areas in the cave were likely to be larger than one or two squares. (The relevance of "drop zones" in defining work areas will be explored in Chapter 14.)

In this chapter I look at artifact co-occurrence using two contrasting statistical techniques: rank-order correlation and cluster analysis (Doran and Hodson 1975, Kintigh 1989). I then look at the extent to which these contrasting approaches produce similar results.

Rank Correlation

The measure of rank correlation I used is referred to as Goodman and Kruskal's gamma (Goodman and Kruskal 1954). The reason I used this measure (rather than Kendall's tau, for example) is that Goodman and Kruskal's gamma works better in situations where there are likely to be ties. In the case of Cueva Blanca, there were likely to be numerous ties because many tool types were represented by zeros or ones in the 1 x 1 m squares of the excavation grid.

Goodman and Kruskal's gamma measures the similarity of the rank orderings of the data when ranked relative to each of two variables (in this case, projectile points and flakes with sheen). Its values range from +1 (perfect positive association) to -1 (perfect negative association). A value of zero represents the absence of association.

In the case of Cueva Blanca, I considered the association between projectile points and any other chipped stone tool type to be significant and positive if its rank order was higher than that between projectile points and debitage; it was considered not to be significant otherwise. I did the same thing when flakes with sheen were involved.

Calculating the G-K gamma begins with G, an estimate of gamma. G depends on two quantities:

1. N_s, the numbers of pairs of cases ranked in the same order on both variables.
2. N_d, the numbers of pairs of cases ranked in reverse order on both variables.

In our study, the variables were projectile points and flakes with sheen, and the pairs of cases were the associations between each of these variables and other tools such as notched flakes, choppers/knives, and so on.

After determining the strength of association of all possible pairs, one next calculates:

$$G = \frac{N_s - N_d}{N_s + N_d}$$

This statistic can be regarded as the maximum likelihood estimator for gamma, where:

$$\gamma = \frac{P_s - P_d}{P_s + P_d}$$

In this case, P_s and P_d are the probabilities that a randomly selected pair of tool types will appear in the same (or opposite) order when ranked in order of their strength of association, relative to both projectile points and flakes with sheen. In other words, in the case of the rank-order tables to follow, G-K gamma values of .9921 or .7376 are not direct measures of the co-occurrence of two tool types in the same square. They are, instead, *the probabilities that a given tool type will be placed in the same rank order*, whether its association with projectile points or flakes with sheen is calculated.

Table 13.1 gives the descriptive statistics of the Cueva Blanca data set. For obvious reasons, my study used only the 1 x 1 m squares in Cueva Blanca that contained artifacts from at least one Archaic living floor.

I began by looking at the largest possible sample—all occupied squares from all three Archaic living floors. Table 13.2 presents the rank-order table for projectile points; Table 13.3 presents the table for flakes with sheen. This step in my research admittedly glossed over any differences among Zones E, D, and C, but I pursued it in order to see whether there were any overall Archaic patterns.

Let us begin with Table 13.2, which shows the relative strength of association of all other chipped stone tools with projectile points. In this figure both G-K gamma and Kendall's tau have been calculated, along with standard error (SE), level of significance, and Spearman's rho, which is a measure of correlation between ranked order variables.

To establish a point of reference we first look to see that the gamma for debitage (all three zones combined) is .7362. That means that both Variety A bifaces (.9921) and end scrapers (.8797) were strongly associated with projectile points. Also associated with points, but somewhat less strongly, were other varieties of bifaces, ovoid scrapers, discoidal cores, and core edges. I was not surprised to find that projectile points were associated with bifaces and scrapers of various kinds. All were tools used for hunting animals or the scraping and cutting of animal byproducts such as hides.

Next, we see that projectile points were negatively associated with choppers/knives, burins, and drills. This suggests that the latter tools were used for tasks other than the ones involving bifaces, end scrapers, and discoidal scrapers.

Let us turn to Table 13.3, which shows the relative strength of association of all other chipped stone tools with flakes with sheen. As a point of reference, we see that debitage was associated with flakes with sheen at a level of .6667. That means that flakes with sheen were most strongly associated with plain blades (.7935), discoidal cores (.7943) and core faces (.8134). This will not be the last time that our analysis shows an association between flakes with sheen and plain blades: two cutting tools. Equally significant is the fact that flakes with sheen were negatively associated with bifaces of Varieties A and B, choppers/knives, ovoid scrapers, end scrapers, burins, and drills.

We can draw two tentative conclusions from these results. First, flakes with sheen and plain blades were frequently used for different tasks (and perhaps by different people) from the previously discussed tool group involving projectile points, bifaces, and scrapers of various types. Second, tools such as (1) choppers/knives and (2) burins and drills were not closely associated with either projectile points or flakes with sheen. The implication is that activities such as (1) chopping or (2)

Table 13.1. The maximum number and average number of chipped stone tools per square in Zones E, D, and C of Cueva Blanca.

Artifact type	MAXIMUM			AVERAGE			STANDARD DEVIATION		
	Zone E	Zone D	Zone C	Zone E	Zone D	Zone C	Zone E	Zone D	Zone C
Projectile points	1.00	2.00	1.00	0.02	0.11	0.07	0.14	0.34	0.26
Biface A	1.00	1.00	0.00	0.01	0.01	0.00	0.10	0.00	0.00
Biface B	1.00	1.00	2.00	0.03	0.03	0.05	0.18	0.18	0.27
Biface C	1.00	1.00	1.00	0.01	0.04	0.01	0.10	0.20	0.10
Choppers/knives	1.00	1.00	1.00	0.01	0.01	0.02	0.00	0.10	0.14
Steep denticulate scrapers	1.00	3.00	2.00	0.07	0.37	0.10	0.26	0.75	0.36
Notched flakes	3.00	6.00	4.00	0.33	0.55	0.40	0.65	1.08	0.85
Utilized flakes	2.00	3.00	5.00	0.12	0.38	0.38	0.36	0.75	0.87
Ovoid scrapers	1.00	1.00	0.00	0.01	0.02	0.00	0.10	0.14	0.00
End scrapers	0.00	2.00	1.00	0.00	0.05	0.02	0.00	0.27	0.14
Sidescrapers/knives	2.00	2.00	1.00	0.10	0.18	0.04	0.36	0.47	0.20
Flakes with sheen	1.00	2.00	1.00	0.03	0.07	0.06	0.18	0.30	0.25
Plain blades	1.00	1.00	2.00	0.04	0.06	0.05	0.20	0.25	0.27
Burins	0.00	1.00	0.00	0.00	0.01	0.00	0.00	0.10	0.00
Drills	0.00	1.00	0.00	0.00	0.01	0.00	0.00	0.10	0.00
Hammerstones	1.00	2.00	2.00	0.01	0.07	0.12	0.10	0.30	0.36
Discoidal cores	0.00	1.00	1.00	0.00	0.02	0.01	0.00	0.14	0.10
Flake cores	2.00	2.00	2.00	0.05	0.20	0.10	0.27	0.45	0.33
Core faces	1.00	2.00	2.00	0.05	0.12	0.08	0.23	0.36	0.32
Core edges	1.00	2.00	1.00	0.02	0.04	0.04	0.14	0.25	0.20
Debitage	35.00	97.00	64.00	4.18	15.75	10.78	7.05	19.32	15.43

Table 13.2. Rank-order table showing the strength of association of all chipped stone tools with projectile points over all squares, Zones E through C.

Variable	Variable	G-K GAMMA	TAU-B	SE	SIGNIF	RHO
Projectile points						
	Biface A	.9921	.2268	.0609	.0002	.2272
	Biface B	.7376	.1811	.0608	.0029	.1817
	Biface C	.7651	.1601	.0609	.0086	.1604
	Choppers/knives	-1.0000	-.0283	.0609	.6487	-.0283
	Steep denticulate scrapers	.7242	.2558	.0599	.0000	.2600
	Notched flakes	.6185	.2195	.0589	.0002	.2273
	Utilized flakes	.6272	.2122	.0593	.0003	.2181
	Ovoid scrapers	.7544	.1126	.0609	.0656	.1128
	End scrapers	.8797	.2610	.0608	.0000	.2618
	Sidescrapers/knives	.7025	.2209	.0604	.0002	.2230
	Retouched blades	-0.	-0.			-0.
	Flakes with sheen	.3855	.0636	.0608	.2972	.0638
	Plain blades	.4344	.0736	.0608	.2273	.0739
	Burins	-1.0000	-.0163	.0609	.8009	-.0163
	Drills	-1.0000	-.0163	.0609	.8009	-.0163
	Pointed pieces	-0.	-0.			-0.
	Polished flakes	-0.	-0.			-0.
	Hammerstones	.5305	.1115	.0607	.0667	.1120
	Discoidal cores	.7741	.1220	.0609	.0459	.1222
	Flake cores	.5733	.1518	.0605	.0121	.1530
	Core faces	.4240	.0854	.0607	.1605	.0858
	Core edges	.7698	.1960	.0608	.0012	.1966
	Core tablets	-0.	-0.			-0.
	Debitage	.7362	.2913	.0534	.0000	.3329

RHO at .0500 = .1195, RHO at .0100 = .1571, Concordance = .1403, F = 3.9171, DF = 288.497, 6923.936, SIGNIF = 0

Strongly associated with projectile points were Variety A bifaces and end scrapers. Somewhat less strongly associated were other varieties of bifaces, ovoid scrapers, discoidal cores, and core edges. Negatively associated with projectile points were choppers/knives, burins, and drills.

slotting and perforating were largely independent of the tasks represented by the projectile point tool group and the flakes with sheen tool group.

Parenthetically, I should say that I am not convinced that items such as core faces and core edges were actually parts of tool kits. It remains to be determined why they were discarded where they were.

Zone E

Let us now move to the rank-order correlations for individual living floors, beginning with Zone E. This living floor had a tool concentration in its northeast quadrant and a hearth (Feature 15) in the southwest (see Figure 12.2).

Table 13.4 indicates the association of all other tools with projectile points. We can take as our reference point the fact that the G-K gamma of debitage with projectile points is .5740. Strongly associated with projectile points were bifaces of Varieties A and B (1.000 to .9545), steep denticulate scrapers (.8636), sidescrapers/knives (.9883), notched flakes (.8611), hammerstones, and core edges. This seems to me to be a plausible group of tools for someone involved in biface manufacture, projectile point manufacture and rejuvenation, and the cutting and scraping of animal byproducts. Negatively associated with projectile points were flakes with sheen (-1.000), Variety C

Table 13.3. Rank-order table showing the strength of association of all chipped stone tools with flakes with sheen over all squares, Zones E through C.

Variable	Variable	G-K GAMMA	TAU-B	SE	SIGNIF	RHO
Flakes with sheen						
	Projectile points	.3855	.0636	.0608	.2972	.0638
	Biface A	-1.0000	-.0148	.0609	.8211	-.0148
	Biface B	-1.0000	-.0474	.0608	.4388	-.0476
	Biface C	.5576	.0726	.0609	.2359	.0727
	Choppers/knives	-1.0000	-.0257	.0609	.6804	-.0257
	Steep denticulate scrapers	.0246	.0040	.0599	.9495	.0041
	Notched flakes	.4733	.1369	.0589	.0201	.1417
	Utilized flakes	.3517	.0855	.0593	.1506	.0877
	Ovoid scrapers	-1.0000	-.0257	.0609	.6804	-.0257
	End scrapers	-1.0000	-.0364	.0608	.5536	-.0366
	Sidescrapers/knives	.2259	.0364	.0604	.5494	.0367
	Retouched blades	-0.	-0.			-0.
	Plain blades	.7935	.2357	.0608	.0001	.2365
	Burins	-1.0000	-.0148	.0609	.8211	-.0148
	Drills	-1.0000	-.0148	.0609	.8211	-.0148
	Pointed pieces	-0.	-0.			-0.
	Polished flakes	-0.	-0.			-0.
	Hammerstones	.4277	.0726	.0607	.2333	.0729
	Discoidal cores	.7943	.1277	.0609	.0366	.1280
	Flake cores	.1365	.0214	.0605	.7259	.0216
	Core faces	.8134	.2848	.0607	.0000	.2864
	Core edges	.6785	.1333	.0608	.0286	.1338
	Core tablets	-0.	-0.			-0.
	Debitage	.6667	.2415	.0534	.0000	.2758

RHO at .0500 = .1195, RHO at .0100 = .1571, Concordance = .1403, F = 3.9171, DF = 288.497, 6923.936, SIGNIF = 0

Strongly associated with flakes with sheen were plain blades, discoidal cores, and core faces. Negatively associated with flakes with sheen were bifaces of Varieties A and B, choppers/knives, ovoid scrapers, end scrapers, burins, and drills.

bifaces, utilized flakes, plain blades, ovoid scrapers, flake cores, and core faces.

We turn next to Table 13.5, which gives us the strength of association of all other tools with flakes with sheen. Strongly associated with flakes with sheen were Variety C bifaces (1.000), plain blades (.9767), and notched flakes (.9754). One function of this group of tools would seem to be cutting activities. Negatively associated with flakes with sheen were projectile points, bifaces of Varieties A and B, steep denticulate scrapers, utilized flakes, ovoid scrapers, hammerstones, flake cores, and core edges.

It is interesting that ovoid scrapers and utilized flakes were not closely associated with either the projectile point tool group or the flakes with sheen tool group. It reminds us that it would be simplistic to think in terms of only two tool kits per living floor.

Overall, the rank-order results from Zone E could be used to support the model of a microband camp in which women maintained a hearth and engaged in a variety of cutting tasks (including the slicing of tough agave leaves), while men engaged in the making of bifaces, the manufacture and rejuvenation of atlatl points, and the cutting and scraping of animal byproducts.

Zone D

We can now move from the Early Archaic to the Late Archaic and consider Zone D. This living floor had a debitage concentration in the northeast and a hearth (Feature 18) in the southwest (see

Table 13.4. Rank-order table showing the strength of association of all chipped stone tools with projectile points over all squares, Zone E.

Variable	Variable	G-K GAMMA	TAU-B	SE	SIGNIF	RHO
Projectile points						
	Biface A	1.0000	.7031	.1060	.0000	.7031
	Biface B	.9545	.3919	.1060	.0002	.3919
	Biface C	-1.0000	-.0160	.1060	.9401	-.0160
	Choppers/knives	-0.	-0.			-0.
	Steep denticulate scrapers	.8636	.2377	.1060	.0266	.2377
	Notched flakes	.8611	.2310	.1036	.0267	.2363
	Utilized flakes	-1.0000	-.0530	.1055	.6340	-.0533
	Ovoid scrapers	-1.0000	-.0160	.1060	.9401	-.0160
	End scrapers	-0.	-0.			-0.
	Sidescrapers/knives	.9883	.5240	.1052	.0000	.5281
	Retouched blades	-0.	-0.			-0.
	Flakes with sheen	-1.0000	-.0280	.1060	.8263	-.0280
	Plain blades	-1.0000	-.0325	.1060	.7890	-.0325
	Burins	-0.	-0.			-0.
	Drills	-0.	-0.			-0.
	Pointed pieces	-0.	-0.			-0.
	Polished flakes	-0.	-0.			-0.
	Hammerstones	1.0000	.7031	.1060	.0000	.7031
	Discoidal cores	-0.	-0.			-0.
	Flake cores	-1.0000	-.0324	.1056	.7890	-.0325
	Core faces	-1.0000	-.0366	.1060	.7569	-.0366
	Core edges	.9773	.4886	.1060	.0000	.4886
	Core tablets	-0.	-0.			-0.
	Debitage	.5740	.1365	.0952	.1561	.1520

RHO at .0500 = .2078, RHO at .0100 = .2730, Concordance = .1135, F = 3.0715, DF = 99.935, 2398.443, SIGNIF = .0000

Strongly associated with projectile points were bifaces of Varieties A and B, steep denticulate scrapers, side scrapers, notched flakes, hammerstones, and core edges. Negatively associated with projectile points were Variety C bifaces, utilized flakes, ovoid scrapers, flakes with sheen, plain blades, flake cores, and core faces.

Figure 12.8). Table 13.6 presents the strength of association of all other tools with projectile points in Zone D. As a point of reference, the G-K gamma for debitage was .6421. Strongly associated with projectile points were bifaces of Varieties B and C (.8935–.8161), ovoid scrapers (.7978), end scrapers (.8182), and discoidal cores (.8333). Once again, this looks like a tool group for the manufacture and use of bifaces, the making and rejuvenating of projectile points, and the scraping of animal byproducts. Negatively associated with projectile points were flakes with sheen (-1.000), choppers/knives, burins and drills, hammerstones, core faces, and core edges.

Table 13.7 gives the strength of association of all other tools with flakes with sheen in Zone D. Positively associated with flakes with sheen were plain blades (.5048), discoidal cores (.8652), core faces, and core edges. All exceeded the G-K gamma for debitage, which was .4455.

Once again, we see that flakes with sheen were associated with other tools for cutting activity (in this case, plain blades). We can only wonder whether the cores and core fragments included in this group are fortuitous, or imply the manufacture of crude blades and flakes by the same agents doing the cutting.

Negatively associated with flakes with sheen were projectile points (-1.000), bifaces of Varieties B and C, choppers/knives, scrapers of three different kinds, notched flakes, hammerstones, flake cores, and burins and drills.

For the second time, we find that (1) choppers/knives and (2) burins and drills were not associated with either the projectile point tool group or the flakes with sheen tool group.

Table 13.5. Rank-order table showing the strength of association of all chipped stone tools with flakes with sheen over all squares, Zone E.

Variable	Variable	G-K GAMMA	TAU-B	SE	SIGNIF	RHO
Flakes with sheen						
	Projectile points	-1.0000	-.0280	.1060	.8263	-.0280
	Biface A	-1.0000	-.0197	.1060	.9018	-.0197
	Biface B	-1.0000	-.0345	.1060	.7731	-.0345
	Biface C	1.0000	.5708	.1060	.0000	.5708
	Choppers/knives	-0.	-0.			-0.
	Steep denticulate scrapers	-1.0000	-.0539	.1060	.6290	-.0539
	Notched flakes	.9754	.3641	.1036	.0004	.3725
	Utilized flakes	-1.0000	-.0653	.1055	.5507	-.0656
	Ovoid scrapers	-1.0000	-.0197	.1060	.9018	-.0197
	End scrapers	-0.	-0.			-0.
	Sidescrapers/knives	.7551	.1884	.1052	.0771	.1899
	Retouched blades	-0.	-0.			-0.
	Plain blades	.9767	.5607	.1060	.0000	.5607
	Burins	-0.	-0.			-0.
	Drills	-0.	-0.			-0.
	Pointed pieces	-0.	-0.			-0.
	Polished flakes	-0.	-0.			-0.
	Hammerstones	-1.0000	-.0197	.1060	.9018	-.0197
	Discoidal cores	-0.	-0.			-0.
	Flake cores	-1.0000	-.0399	.1056	.7299	-.0400
	Core faces	.8242	.2252	.1060	.0358	.2252
	Core edges	-1.0000	-.0280	.1060	.8263	-.0280
	Core tablets	-0.	-0.			-0.
	Debitage	.9308	.2796	.0952	.0032	.3115

RHO at .0500 = .2078, RHO at .0100 = .2730, Concordance = .1135, F = 3.0715, DF = 99.935, 2398.443, SIGNIF = .0000

Strongly associated with flakes with sheen were Variety C bifaces, notched flakes, and plain blades. Negatively associated with flakes with sheen were projectile points, bifaces of Varieties A and B, steep denticulate scrapers, utilized flakes, ovoid scrapers, hammerstones, flake cores, and core edges.

The activities for which these tools were used (chopping, slotting, and perforating) were evidently separate from those of our two contrasting tool groups, the result being that they were discarded elsewhere.

Like Zone E, Zone D can be viewed as a microband campsite where women maintained a hearth and engaged in cutting activities (including the slicing of tough agave leaves), while men manufactured and rejuvenated projectile points and bifaces and engaged in the scraping of animal byproducts. To be sure, the exact mix of tools in Zone D is not identical to that of Zone E, but that is hardly unexpected, given the expedient nature of the tools.

Zone C

Let us turn now to our final Archaic living floor, Zone C. This living floor lacked a hearth, and the density contours drawn by Spencer and Flannery (Chapter 12) make it hard to argue that Zone C was divided into men's and women's work areas.

Table 13.8 gives the strength of association of all other tools with projectile points. As a point of reference, debitage had a G-K gamma value of .7882. Strongly associated with projectile points were end scrapers (.8636), core faces, and core edges. Perhaps most significantly, Zone C differed from Zones E and D in the G-K gamma value of flakes with sheen. In E and D,

Table 13.6. Rank-order table showing the strength of association of all chipped stone tools with projectile points over all squares, Zone D.

Variable	Variable	G-K GAMMA	TAU-B	SE	SIGNIF	RHO
Projectile points						
	Biface A	-0.	-0.			-0.
	Biface B	.8935	.3443	.1055	.0011	.3460
	Biface C	.8161	.2820	.1055	.0077	.2834
	Choppers/knives	-1.0000	-.0351	.1055	.7678	-.0353
	Steep denticulate scrapers	.6491	.2700	.1020	.0081	.2810
	Notched flakes	.4475	.1700	.1015	.0957	.1771
	Utilized flakes	.5848	.2351	.1020	.0213	.2441
	Ovoid scrapers	.7978	.1971	.1055	.0653	.1981
	End scrapers	.8182	.2848	.1050	.0069	.2873
	Sidescrapers/knives	.6467	.2525	.1041	.0155	.2568
	Retouched blades	-0.	-0.			-0.
	Flakes with sheen	-1.0000	-.0882	.1050	.4109	-.0890
	Plain blades	.2991	.0574	.1055	.5979	.0577
	Burins	-1.0000	-.0351	.1055	.7678	-.0353
	Drills	-1.0000	-.0351	.1055	.7678	-.0353
	Pointed pieces	-0.	-0.			-0.
	Polished flakes	-0.	-0.			-0.
	Hammerstones	-1.0000	-.0882	.1050	.4109	-.0890
	Discoidal cores	.8333	.2221	.1055	.0373	.2232
	Flake cores	.6215	.2328	.1045	.0263	.2361
	Core faces	-1.0000	-.1166	.1050	.2730	-.1177
	Core edges	-1.0000	-.0613	.1051	.5752	-.0619
	Core tablets	-0.	-0.			-0.
	Debitage	.6421	.2936	.0908	.0012	.3452

RHO at .0500 = .2078, RHO at .0100 = .2730, Concordance = .1487, F = 4.1929, DF = 94.069, 2257.663, SIGNIF = .0000

Strongly associated with projectile points were bifaces of Varieties B and C, ovoid scrapers, end scrapers, and discoidal cores. Negatively associated with projectile points were flakes with sheen, choppers/knives, burins and drills, hammerstones, and core faces and edges.

such flakes were negatively associated with projectile points; in Zone C, flakes with sheen had a modestly positive association with points (.7753). This suggests that any cutting of tough agave leaves in Zone C was done by the same agents who made and rejuvenated projectile points. Negatively associated with points were bifaces of Varieties B and C, sidescrapers/knives, choppers/knives, and discoidal cores. This could mean that less processing of deer and deer byproducts was carried out in Zone C, perhaps because large sections of deer carcasses were transported to a base camp elsewhere.

Table 13.9 gives the strength of association of all other tools with flakes with sheen. We expected these associations to be different from those in Zones E and D, and our expectations were met. Most notably, flakes with sheen were associated with projectile points (.7753) and sidescrapers/knives (.6875), two items usually found with a different group of tools. Flakes with sheen did show their usual association with plain blades (.6970), and were also found with hammerstones, core faces, and core edges. Negatively associated with flakes with sheen were bifaces of Varieties B and C, steep denticulate scrapers, end scrapers, discoidal cores, and choppers/knives.

In other words, our rank-order correlations show Zone C to be different in certain fundamental ways from Zones E and D. This Late Archaic living floor lacks a hearth and a plausible women's work area, and it does not provide us with convincing evidence for a women's plant-processing tool kit.

Table 13.7. Rank-order table showing the strength of association of all chipped stone tools with flakes with sheen over all squares, Zone D.

Variable	Variable	G-K GAMMA	TAU-B	SE	SIGNIF	RHO
Flakes with sheen						
	Projectile points	-1.0000	-.0882	.1050	.4109	-.0890
	Biface A	-0.	-0.			-0.
	Biface B	-1.0000	-.0494	.1055	.6594	-.0496
	Biface C	-1.0000	-.0574	.1055	.6034	-.0576
	Choppers/knives	-1.0000	-.0282	.1055	.8243	-.0283
	Steep denticulate scrapers	.2203	.0571	.1021	.5845	.0597
	Notched flakes	-.1057	-.0254	.1015	.8101	-.0264
	Utilized flakes	.4514	.1404	.1020	.1726	.1445
	Ovoid scrapers	-1.0000	-.0401	.1055	.7284	-.0403
	End scrapers	-1.0000	-.0571	.1051	.6035	-.0576
	Sidescrapers/knives	-1.0000	-.1124	.1042	.2872	-.1144
	Retouched blades	-0.	-0.			-0.
	Plain blades	.5048	.1046	.1055	.3315	.1051
	Burins	-1.0000	-.0282	.1055	.8243	-.0283
	Drills	-1.0000	-.0282	.1055	.8243	-.0283
	Pointed pieces	-0.	-0.			-0.
	Polished flakes	-0.	-0.			-0.
	Hammerstones	-1.0000	-.0707	.1050	.5137	-.0714
	Discoidal cores	.8652	.2573	.1055	.0158	.2584
	Flake cores	-.0612	-.0115	.1045	.9226	-.0116
	Core faces	.6421	.1901	.1050	.0724	.1919
	Core edges	.7447	.1913	.1051	.0728	.1929
	Core tablets	-0.	-0.			-0.
	Debitage	.4455	.1691	.0908	.0637	.1975

RHO at .0500 = .2078, RHO at .0100 = .2730, Concordance = .1487, F = 4.1929, DF = 94.069, 2257.663, SIGNIF = .0000

Positively associated with flakes with sheen were plain blades, discoidal cores, core faces, and core edges. Negatively associated with flakes with sheen were projectile points, bifaces of Varieties B and C, choppers/knives, notched flakes, scrapers of three different kinds, burins, drills, hammerstones, and flake cores.

Cluster Analysis

While the results of our rank-order correlations were interesting, I was not fully satisfied. I wanted to see if a different form of analysis would yield similar results. My choice for a second approach, using the same data set, was cluster analysis.

"Cluster analysis" is the generic term for a group of algorithms including (1) connectivity-based or hierarchical clustering, (2) distribution-based clustering, (3) density-based clustering, and various other approaches. For several reasons I felt that the most appropriate algorithm was hierarchical clustering, whose results can be expressed in a dendrogram (Doran and Hodson 1975, Whallon 1984, Kintigh 1989).

The specific formula I chose is referred to as Ward's method (Romesburg 1990). It can be described as follows, for the clustering of n objects:

1. The process begins with each item in the data set initially constituting a single group.
2. In each successive step, the procedure selects two clusters which, when merged, produce the smallest value of an index, W, which is called the sum-of-squares index.
3. This process then continues for $n-1$ steps, each time merging the pair that produces the next smallest W value, until all of the n objects have been merged into a single group.

Table 13.8. Rank-order table showing the strength of association of all chipped stone tools with projectile points over all squares, Zone C.

Variable	Variable	G-K GAMMA	TAU-B	SE	SIGNIF	RHO
Projectile points						
	Biface A	-0.	-0.			-0.
	Biface B	-1.0000	-.0624	.1056	.5700	-.0626
	Biface C	-1.0000	-.0308	.1060	.8040	-.0308
	Choppers/knives	-1.0000	-.0438	.1060	.7021	-.0438
	Steep denticulate scrapers	.7204	.2287	.1052	.0306	.2305
	Notched flakes	.6562	.2827	.1024	.0057	.2925
	Utilized flakes	.6474	.2498	.1025	.0149	.2583
	Ovoid scrapers	-0.	-0.			-0.
	End scrapers	.8636	.2377	.1060	.0266	.2377
	Sidescrapers/knives	-1.0000	-.0626	.1060	.5699	-.0626
	Retouched blades	-0.	-0.			-0.
	Flakes with sheen	.7753	.2550	.1060	.0166	.2550
	Plain blades	.6436	.1448	.1056	.1774	.1454
	Burins	-0.	-0.			-0.
	Drills	-0.	-0.			-0.
	Pointed pieces	-0.	-0.			-0.
	Polished flakes	-0.	-0.			-0.
	Hammerstones	.5625	.1575	.1055	.1393	.1583
	Discoidal cores	-1.0000	-.0308	.1060	.8040	-.0308
	Flake cores	.2773	.0532	.1055	.6260	.0534
	Core faces	.8755	.3853	.1055	.0002	.3871
	Core edges	.8837	.3400	.1060	.0013	.3400
	Core tablets	-0.	-0.			-0.
	Debitage	.7882	.3399	.0938	.0003	.3841

RHO at .0500 = .2078, RHO at .0100 = .2730, Concordance = .1313, F = 3.6280, DF = 95.714, 2297.130, SIGNIF = .0000

Strongly associated with projectile points were end scrapers, core faces, and core edges. Even flakes with sheen were modestly associated with points in this zone. Negatively associated with projectile points were bifaces of Varieties B and C, choppers/knives, side scrapers, and discoidal cores.

As for the index, W, it is produced for g groups formed from the clustering of n observations in the following way: it is the sum of the squared differences between each group member and the average value for the group. The within-group sum of squares for the partitioning of n objects into g groups is:

$$W = \sum_{i=1}^{i=g} \sum_{j=1}^{j=n_i} (x_{ij} - \bar{x}_i)^2$$

where X_{ij} is the jth observation in the ith group. Dividing this sum, W, by the number of objects, we get the pooled within-group variance for the given partition or grouping. The pooled within-group variance can be computed for all possible partitions of the n objects.

One of the advantages of using Ward's method is that it favors small clusters (Zupan 1982). Since I expected to get relatively small clusters from the 21 tool categories, Ward's method fits my expectations. I also did not expect to get more than four or five clusters per living floor, given the total number of tool categories. Finally, I felt that the hierarchical nature of the dendrogram produced by Ward's approach was appropriate for an expedient chipped stone assemblage, one in which a given tool could occur in more than one kit, and two kits might occasionally merge into one.

Table 13.9. Rank-order table showing the strength of association of all chipped stone tools with flakes with sheen over all squares, Zone C.

Variable	Variable	G-K GAMMA	TAU-B	SE	SIGNIF	RHO
Flakes with sheen						
	Projectile points	.7753	.2550	.1060	.0166	.2550
	Biface A	-0.	-0.			-0.
	Biface B	-1.0000	-.0574	.1056	.6034	-.0576
	Biface C	-1.0000	-.0283	.1060	.8243	-.0283
	Choppers/knives	-1.0000	-.0403	.1060	.7283	-.0403
	Steep denticulate scrapers	-1.0000	-.0770	.1052	.4761	-.0776
	Notched flakes	.4681	.1478	.1024	.1524	.1530
	Utilized flakes	.2987	.0788	.1025	.4501	.0814
	Ovoid scrapers	-0.	-0.			-0.
	End scrapers	-1.0000	-.0403	.1060	.7283	-.0403
	Sidescrapers/knives	.6875	.1585	.1060	.1412	.1585
	Retouched blades	-0.	-0.			-0.
	Plain blades	.6970	.1650	.1056	.1237	.1657
	Burins	-0.	-0.			-0.
	Drills	-0.	-0.			-0.
	Pointed pieces	-0.	-0.			-0.
	Polished flakes	-0.	-0.			-0.
	Hammerstones	.6667	.2005	.1055	.0592	.2015
	Discoidal cores	-1.0000	-.0283	.1060	.8243	-.0283
	Flake cores	.3628	.0709	.1055	.5129	.0713
	Core faces	.9063	.4265	.1055	.0000	.4286
	Core edges	.6875	.1585	.1060	.1412	.1585
	Core tablets	-0.	-0.			-0.
	Debitage	.6145	.2460	.0938	.0087	.2780

RHO at .0500 = .2078, RHO at .0100 = .2730, Concordance = .1313, F = 3.6280, DF = 95.714, 2297.130, SIGNIF = .0000

It is notable that in Zone C, flakes with sheen were positively associated with projectile points. They were also associated with plain blades, sidescrapers/knives, hammerstones, core faces, and core edges. Negatively associated with flakes with sheen were bifaces of Varieties B and C, choppers/knives, steep denticulate scrapers, end scrapers, and discoidal cores.

Ward's method uses W as a built-in measure of dissimilarity. This required me to decide which statistic to use in order to measure the distance for W in the case of Cueva Blanca. An obvious starting point was the presence or absence of tool types in a given cell (1 x 1 m square). Many of our observations are binary (i.e. the count for a particular tool in a particular cell was often zero or one), so we will suffer very little loss of information by dealing with presence or absence of data here.

In the case of any pair of tool types chosen at random, there are four basic relationships that can occur. When both tools are present in the same square, we call this outcome **a**. When the first tool is present and the second absent, we have outcome **b**. When the first tool is absent and the second present, we have outcome **c**. When both are absent we have outcome **d**. Because Cueva Blanca had large numbers of squares with outcome **d**, I decided to give **d** a weight of zero, so that it would not swamp the impact of **a**, **b**, and **c**. I gave outcomes **b** and **c** the same weight. Finally, I weighted outcome **a** more heavily, because of the significance of finding both tool types in the same square.

I then had to decide whether to use the Jaccard matching coefficient or the Dice coefficient to evaluate outcomes **a**, **b**, and **c** for all tool pairs over all squares. The Jaccard coefficient excludes zero-zero matches (which I wanted to do), but it also assumes an equal weighting among the remaining outcomes (which I did not want to do). I therefore settled on the Dice coefficient, which relaxes the assumption of equal weighting. For the Dice coefficient, the presence of two tool types in the same square is twice as important as the presence of only one of them (Hall 1969). This is the approach I chose.

The Dice coefficient of similarity is defined as follows:

Dice (similarity) = (2*a)/ ((2*a) + b + c)

To get a measure of dissimilarity we subtract the Dice coefficient from 1, as follows:

Dice (dissimilarity) = 1 –((2*a)/((2*a) + b + c))

For a visual representation of how our cluster analysis worked, I refer the reader to Table 13.10. That table presents the dendrogram that resulted when I applied the cluster analysis to all 21 chipped stone categories from all occupied squares of all three Archaic living floors (Zones E, D, and C combined). At the start, each of the 21 categories was considered a cluster in its own right. This was considered STEP 21. The second step that took place was that notched flakes and debitage were merged into a single cluster. This was considered STEP 20. The third step that took place was that steep denticulate scrapers were merged with utilized flakes. This was called STEP 19. This process continued on until STEP 1, at which point all 21 categories had been merged into one large cluster. At every step, the two categories that would produce the minimum variance were merged.

The numbers to the right of the word STEP in Table 13.10 show the progression from STEP 20 to STEP 1. The numbers to the right of the word DISTANCES represent the sums of the squared variances for the two categories being merged at each step of the clustering.

Obviously, I had to decide when a sufficient number of clusters had been produced to inform my analysis. I decided to extract my clusters after STEP 5 of the analysis, and I have drawn a solid vertical line at that point in Table 13.10. This procedure gives us five clusters, each containing four or five tool categories. That seemed appropriate for the Archaic living floors.

As in the case of our earlier rank-order classifications, lumping all three Archaic living floors tends to gloss over any differences among them. However, I did it in order to see whether any general patterns emerged from the whole data set. Let us now look for such patterns.

The first cluster we see in Table 13.10 comprises projectile points, sidescrapers/knives, end scrapers, and bifaces of Varieties A and B. It would not stretch credulity to see this cluster as a men's tool kit, including items for manufacturing bifaces, making and rejuvenating projectile points, and scraping or cutting animal byproducts.

The second cluster was made up of burins, drills, Variety C bifaces, and core edges. This cluster reinforces our earlier conclusion, based on rank-order correlation, that slotting and perforating were activities carried out independent of other tasks.

The third cluster I extracted included flakes with sheen, plain blades, hammerstones, and core faces. This cluster reinforces our earlier discovery, based on rank-order correlation, that plain blades were often associated with flakes with sheen. This potential tool kit might reflect women's activities.

Our fourth cluster comprises choppers/knives, ovoid scrapers, and discoidal cores. It is not immediately clear what activity is represented by this cluster. Finally, our fifth cluster is made up of steep denticulate scrapers, utilized flakes, notched flakes, flake cores, and debitage. While all these items tended to be discarded in the same area, the fact that debitage is part of the cluster suggests that we may be dealing with general refuse rather than a tool kit.

Zone E

Table 13.11 shows the dendrogram that resulted when I conducted a cluster analysis of all the chipped stone tools in Zone E alone. It will be remembered that Zone E had an artifact scatter in its northeast quadrant and a hearth (Feature 15) in the southwest.

The first cluster I extracted consisted of projectile points, hammerstones, and bifaces of Varieties A and B. Not only is this a plausible men's tool kit, it also includes items that were strongly associated in our rank-order analysis of Zone E.

The second cluster comprised flakes with sheen, plain blades, and Variety C bifaces. These three items were also strongly associated in our rank-order correlation analysis of Zone E and would seem to reflect cutting activities. I consider this a potential women's tool kit.

The third cluster I extracted would seem to feature tools for scraping activities of different kinds. Included were steep denticulate scrapers, ovoid scrapers, sidescrapers/knives, core faces, and core edges. While this could constitute a tool kit, I am not sure whether to associate it with male or female activities, and I doubt that the presence of the core fragments is more than fortuitous.

Our final cluster consists of utilized flakes, notched flakes, flake cores, and debitage. This cluster seems to me like general refuse rather than a tool kit.

Zone D

Table 13.12 presents the dendrogram that resulted when I carried out a cluster analysis of the tools in Zone D. This zone featured a living floor with a debitage concentration in the northeast quadrant and a hearth (Feature 18) in the southwest.

The first cluster extracted consisted of projectile points, Variety B bifaces, end scrapers, sidescrapers/knives, and plain blades. Three of these items (projectile points, Variety B bifaces, and end scrapers) had been strongly associated in our rank-order correlation analysis for Zone D; the other components of the cluster are different. In both analyses, what emerges is a plausible men's tool kit.

Table 13.10. Dendrogram resulting from a cluster analysis of chipped stone items from Zones E, D, and C at Cueva Blanca. The point at which clusters were extracted is shown by the solid vertical line.

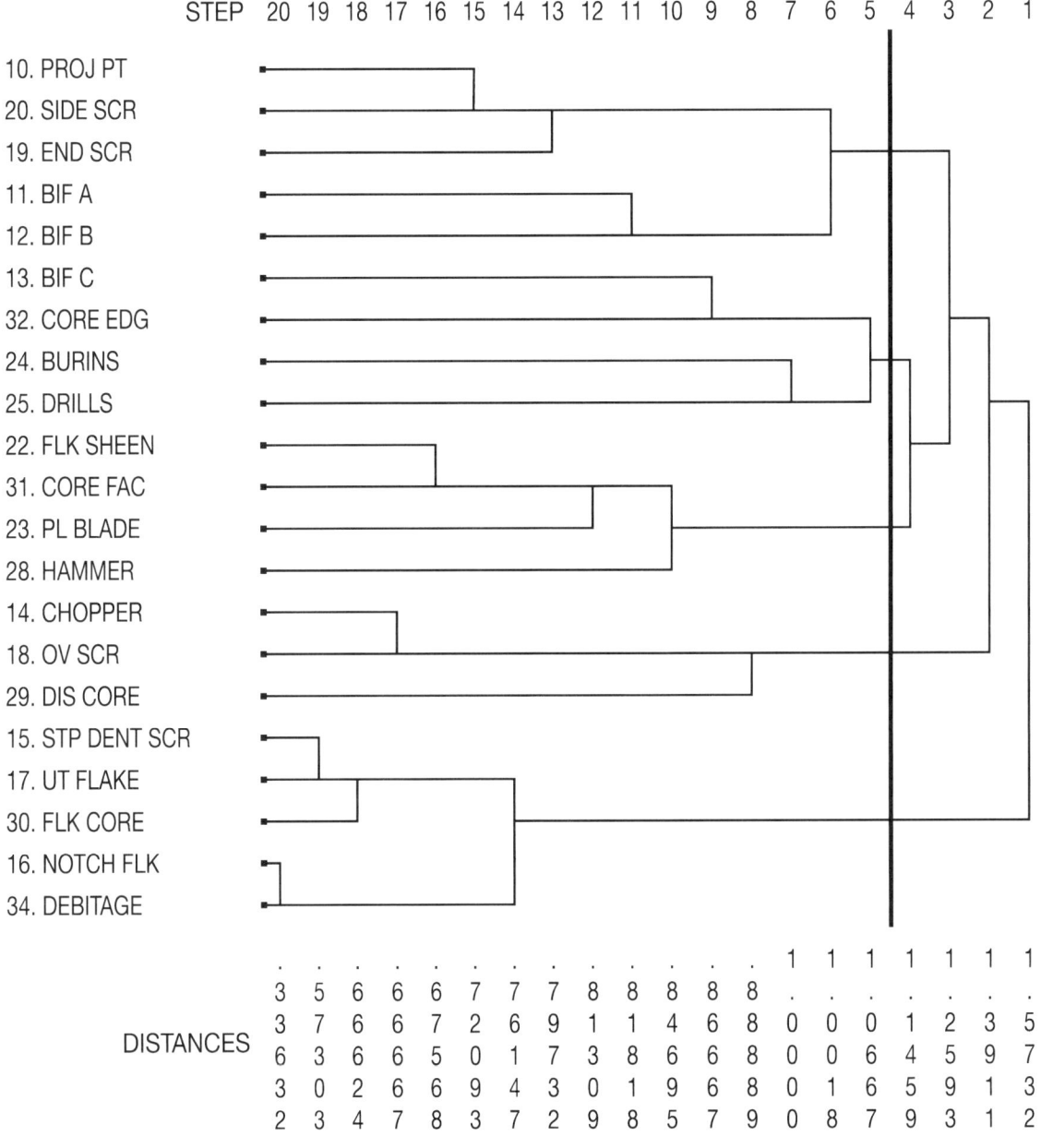

Table 13.11. Dendrogram resulting from a cluster analysis of chipped stone items from Zone E of Cueva Blanca. The point at which clusters were extracted is shown by the solid vertical line.

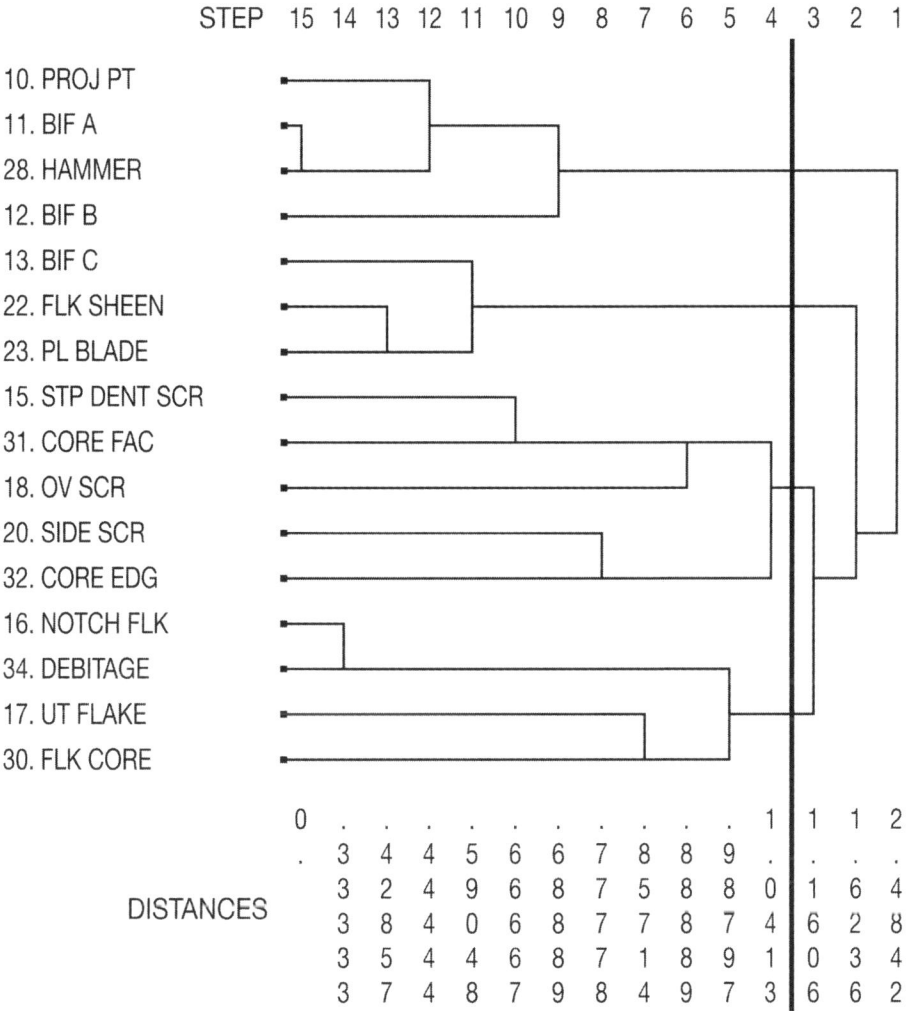

Table 13.12. Dendrogram resulting from a cluster analysis of chipped stone items from Zone D of Cueva Blanca. The point at which clusters were extracted is shown by the solid vertical line.

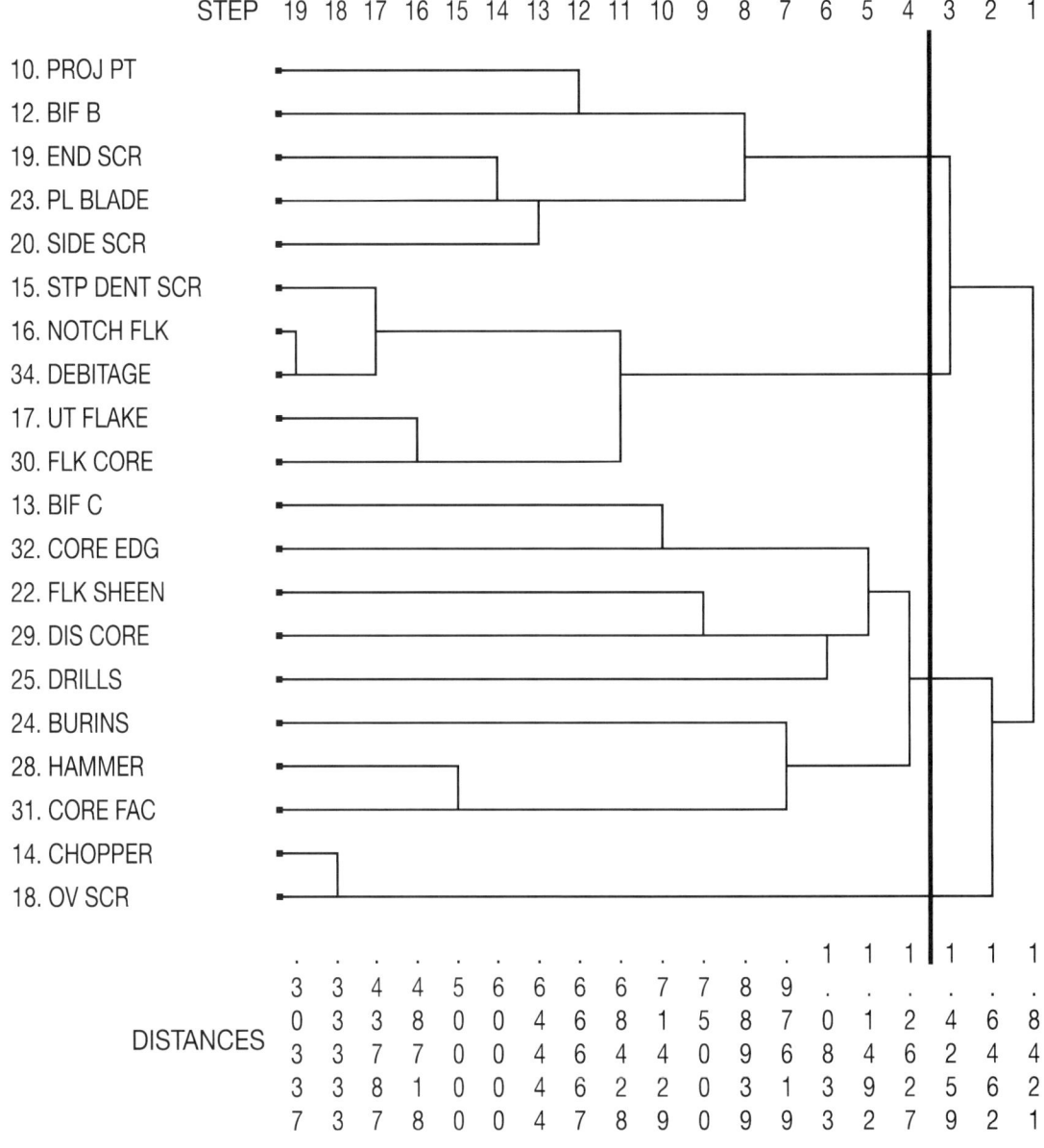

The second cluster I extracted consisted of steep denticulate scrapers, utilized flakes, notched flakes, flake cores, and debitage. Once again, the inclusion of debitage suggests that we may be dealing with refuse rather than an actual tool kit.

Our third cluster is unusually large and could be regarded as consisting of several subclusters. It comprises flakes with sheen, Variety C bifaces, burins and drills, hammerstones, discoidal cores, core faces, and core edges. I note that flakes with sheen were also associated with discoidal cores, core faces, and core edges in our rank-order correlation analysis of Zone D. The other items associated with flakes with sheen are new in this analysis. It is interesting that our cluster analysis links burins and drills to the same agents using flakes with sheen.

Our final cluster from Zone D consists only of choppers/knives and ovoid scrapers. I am uncertain whether or not to consider this small cluster a tool kit.

Zone C

Finally, Table 13.13 presents the dendrogram resulting from my cluster analysis of Zone C. I was understandably interested in seeing whether this living floor, which had no hearth, would yield clusters different from those in Zones E and D.

Our very first cluster indicated that Zone C was, in fact, different. That cluster included projectile points, flakes with sheen, plain blades, core faces, and core edges. In other words, the same agents working with projectile points were apparently also using plain blades and flakes with sheen, items considered parts of different tool kits in Zones E and D. Thus, although the details are different, both our rank-order correlations and cluster analyses show that Zone C contrasted sharply with Zones E and D.

Our second cluster consisted of utilized flakes, notched flakes, hammerstones, flake cores, and debitage. We have seen this group of items before, and it still looks like general refuse rather than a tool kit.

Our third cluster involves sidescrapers/knives and bifaces of Varieties B and C. This cluster, consisting entirely of carefully retouched tools, could be a kit for cutting activities of some kind.

Our fourth and final cluster comprises steep denticulate scrapers, end scrapers, choppers/knives, and discoidal cores. Here is another potential tool kit, consisting largely of carefully retouched tools for scraping and cutting.

Our cluster analysis has therefore led us to the same conclusion as our rank-order correlation: several activities were being carried out by the occupants of Zone C, but we cannot convince ourselves that any of the potential tool kits resulted from women's activities.

Overview

With our rank-order correlations and cluster analyses completed, we can now assess what we have learned about potential Archaic tool kits at Cueva Blanca. Let me begin with a few disclaimers. First, it is clear that no two analytical approaches can be expected to yield exactly the same results. Second, even if there were sets of tools that were regularly used together, we cannot guarantee that their users would always discard them close together on a living floor. Third, even if certain tools were discarded together originally, we have no assurance that they would remain undisturbed over time.

That having been said, our analyses do seem to have revealed a few consistent patterns. In Zones E and D, projectile points seemed often to be associated with bifaces of Varieties A and B, end scrapers, and sidescrapers/knives. In those same zones, flakes with sheen appear to be associated frequently with plain blades and less frequently with bifaces of Variety C. At the same time, tools such as choppers/knives, burins, drills, and steep denticulate scrapers rarely exhibited an association with either of the two groups mentioned above.

Zone C appears to have been different—produced by different formation processes from Zones E and D—regardless of the statistical approach used. Projectile points were still associated with end scrapers, and flakes with sheen were still associated with plain blades, but these two distinctive tools were also positively associated with each other, no matter how the analysis was done.

One of our first conclusions, therefore, is that Archaic tool kits at Cueva Blanca were just as informal and expedient as most of the tool types. On the living floors associated with Zones E and D, where hearths were present and the density contours suggest a division into men's and women's work areas, there are hints of a men's tool kit for the making of bifaces, the manufacture and rejuvenation of projectile points, and the scraping or cutting of animal byproducts. There are also hints of a possible women's tool kit for plant processing, including the repeated cutting of tough agave leaves. In addition, there are hints of tool kits for chopping, slotting, perforating, or steep denticulate scraping that cannot easily be attributed to either gender.

In Zone C, on the other hand, where Spencer and Flannery (Chapter 12) feel that they cannot make a case for women being present, it looks as if men used flakes with sheen and plain blades right along with their customary tools, and they performed many tasks that might have been carried out by women in Zones E and D. I therefore conclude that Archaic tool kits at Cueva Blanca were defined more by the activities for which they served than by the gender of the agents using them.

Table 13.13. Dendrogram resulting from a cluster analysis of chipped stone items from Zone C of Cueva Blanca. The point at which clusters were extracted is shown by the solid vertical line.

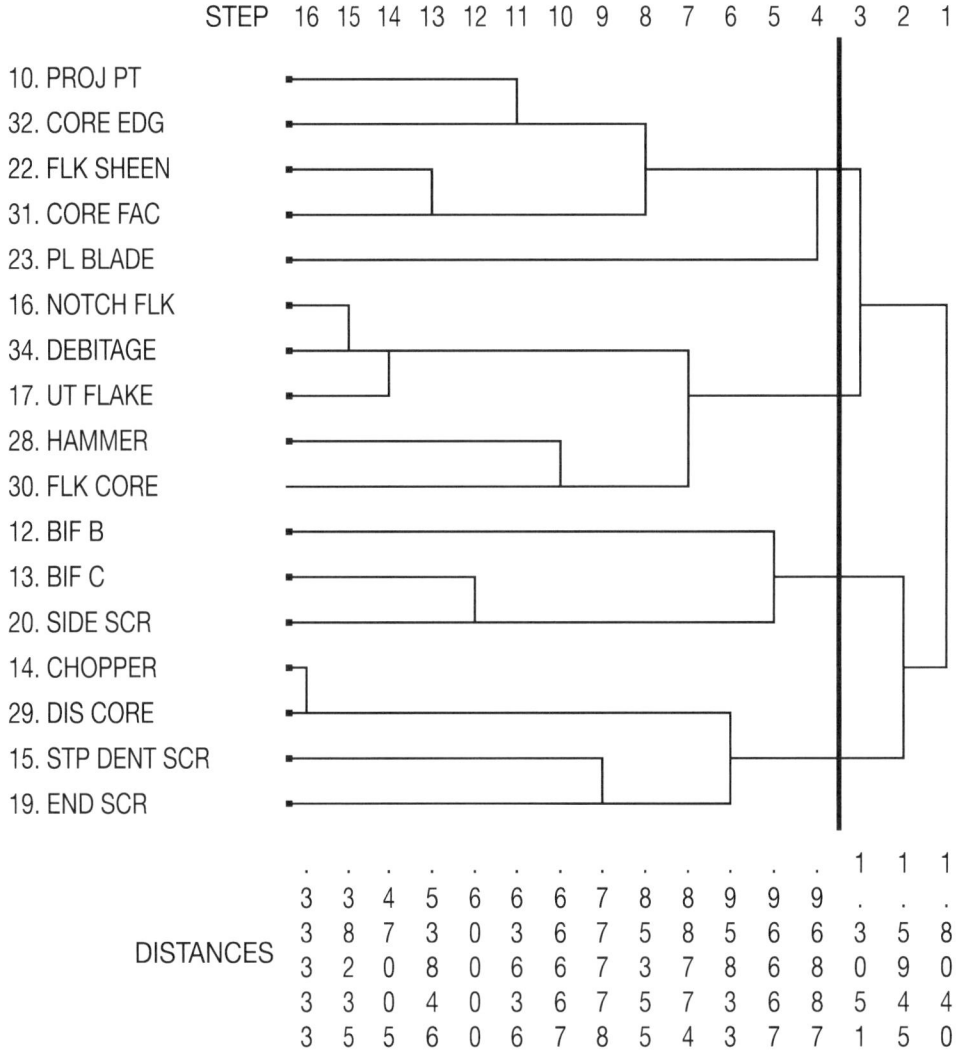

14

The Search for "Drop Zones" at Cueva Blanca: An Approach Drawn from Artificial Intelligence

Robert G. Reynolds

In Chapter 12, Spencer and Flannery drew density contours for various classes of Archaic chipped stone items and animal remains at Cueva Blanca. In the course of their work, they also referred to Binford's (1984) description of "drop zones" and "toss zones" at a Caribou Eskimo hunting camp in Alaska. In this chapter I attempt to identify drop zones on the three Archaic living floors at Cueva Blanca, using an analytical approach drawn from artificial intelligence.

Binford's Model

Binford's model of drop zones and toss zones grew out of his ethnoarchaeological visit to a Nunamiut hunting camp—the Mask site—in Anaktuvuk Pass, Alaska. Binford's work was done at a time when many of his colleagues were engaged in similar studies of hunters and gatherers (Gould 1968; Yellen 1976; Thomas 1983; O'Connell 1987; Carr 1991; Stevenson 1991).

At the Mask site, Binford watched a group of Nunamiut hunters sitting in a semicircle around a campfire. As the men processed the caribou they had hunted, Binford noticed that they tended to drop some tools and bone debris right where they were working; other tools and debris were tossed farther away. Binford used the term "drop zones" for the crescent-shaped areas of nearby refuse; he used the term "toss zones" for the areas where debris was thrown farther away.

Thomas (1983) applied a similar model to the Gatecliff Shelter in Monitor Valley, Nevada. He pointed out that while hunter-gatherers in open-air settings were able to toss debris away in any direction, hunters using a site like Gatecliff were restricted by the walls of the rockshelter. Thomas gave four examples of the directions that debris might be tossed in a cave or rockshelter; in every example, the talus slope outside the shelter was included in the toss zone.

Cueva Blanca is another example of a site where the cave walls would have influenced both dropping and tossing activity. During all three Archaic occupations at Cueva Blanca, it is likely that a great deal of material—especially the larger fragments of animal bone—was tossed onto the cave talus. In the case of Stratigraphic Zones E and D, where hearths were present in the southwest quadrant of the chamber, it seemed possible that men and women might have created their own drop zones and toss zones.[1] Based on the density contours drawn in Chapter 12, my

---

[1] Note that our use of "zone" as a stratigraphic level and Binford's use of "zone" as an area of debris are quite different. We regret any confusion this may cause.

expectations are that we might find men's drop zones in the northeast quadrant of the living floor and women's drop zones near the hearth. When it comes to Zone C, I have no such expectations and will simply see where the analysis leads.

The Computer Vision Model

The approach I used in my search for drop zones is called computer vision. This is a version of artificial intelligence that concerns itself with the computational characterization of the vision process. Its goal is not to mimic the process by which humans acquire visual information, but to identify the basic sequence of steps that need to be performed on a computer in order to arrive at a similar result. Read (1985), Kintigh (1985), and Zubrow (1985) have previously advocated computer vision as an archaeological tool.

The computer vision approach consists of five basic phases (Tanimoto 1995). These are (1) image formation, (2) sensing of the image, (3) preprocessing of the image, (4) segmentation of the image into spatially distinct regions, and (5) interpretation of the scene presented in the image.

In the case of each Archaic living floor at Cueva Blanca, a potential image formed as the cave's occupants dropped or tossed tools and debitage. For our purposes, the granularity of the image will be determined by the fact that the excavators divided each living floor into 1 x 1 m squares (referred to as "cells" in my computer vision analysis). The counts of chipped stone items in each cell make it a unit of image detection, similar to the rods and cones in a human eye. The computer assembles all these cells and "senses" the overall image of each living floor.

Once the initial raw image has been formed, certain preprocessing is done in order to remove "noise" from the image and focus attention on its key aspects. For example, the Monte Albán V pottery kiln that intruded through Squares F2–F5 (see Figure 3.21) was considered "noise," and those cells were excluded from my study. Also excluded was any cell that lacked chipped stone items. A second stage of preprocessing involved the deletion of any artifact category whose numbers were too small to be useful, such as polished flakes and core tablets.

Once the preprocessing had been done, I was called upon to choose a method of image segmentation. My choices were either (1) the gradient method (which assumes that there is a measurable difference between the pixels on the edge of an image and the pixels that comprise the background) or (2) region growing (which assumes that pixels comprising the same object are more similar to each other than to those comprising other objects). I chose region growing for two reasons. The first reason is that this method requires homogeneity or similarity constraints for the forming of each object, and these constraints are similar to the ones I used to determine spatial similarities in artifact discard in Chapter 13. The second reason is that region growing is similar in many respects to a "bottom up" cluster analysis, similar to the one used in our search for tool kits.

The Region-Growing Procedure

Let us now look at the way that the region-growing approach segments an image into objects or regions. Any segmentation of an image represents a set of n nonoverlapping regions $\{R_1, \ldots\ldots, R_n\}$. These regions represent a partitioning of the set of cells into n disjoint collections, the union of which creates the entire image.

A segmentation is a kind of partition that places certain constraints on the combination of cells in each region. In our case, the constraints that need to be satisfied by the cells in each region are as follows:

1. All of the cells present in a given region are connected. That is, for any given cell i in the region, there exists a path to i from any other cell j. This path can be created by crossing either adjacent edges or vertices. For example, given the excavation grid for Cueva Blanca shown in Figure 2.6, cell F7 is edge-adjacent to its neighbors E7, F8, G7, and F6. It is vertex-adjacent to its neighbors E6, E8, G6, and G8. A possible path from C7 to D8 would be written C7–D7–D8. A region is said to be 4-connected if every pair of cells in that region $(x_i$ and $x_j)$ is connected by at least one path crossing adjacent edges only. It is said to be 8-connected if every pair of cells is connected by at least one path crossing adjacent edges and/or vertices. Every 4-connected cell is also 8-connected, but not vice versa. For example, the region formed by cells D9, E9, and E10 is 4-connected, since these cells are linked by a sequence of adjacent edge crossings; it is also 8-connected because E10 could be reached from D9 directly by crossing a vertex, rather than simply crossing adjacent edges from D9 to E9 to E10. On the other hand, the region formed by cells F11, F12, and G10 is 8-connected but not 4-connected, since no path using only adjacent edges is available.
2. All of the cells in a region must satisfy a homogeneity or uniformity constraint. In the Cueva Blanca case, this uniformity constraint is informed by aspects of Binford's drop/toss zone model in terms of certain statistical properties of artifact distributions from cell to cell on each living floor. We will return to this constraint later.
3. If two regions, R_1 and R_2, lie adjacent in the segmented image, and any of the cells present at the union of these regions satisfy the uniformity predicate, the two regions can be merged. For example, the region consisting of cells D9, E9, and E10 lies adjacent to the region consisting of cells G10, F11, and F12. If the larger region that would result from merging these two smaller regions still satisfies our homogeneity or uniformity constraint, then those two smaller regions should not be separated. It is up to the region-growing procedure to enforce this constraint as it merges collections of

cells. As a result of the three constraints above, each region has a continuous physical boundary. The cells within the boundary are all more similar to each other than they are to cells outside the boundary.

The pseudocode for the region-growing procedure is as follows:

    For each row in the image
    Do
    For each cell in each row of the image
    Do
    If the contents of a given cell in a given row satisfy the homogeneity constraint
    Then
    If any of the cells in its 8-connected neighborhood is in a region already
    Then merge each of the existing regions along with the new cell
    Else form a new region consisting of the cell itself

The two **For** loops allow for a "bottom up" systematic scanning of the scene, row by row and cell by cell. Constraint 2 of the segmentation procedure given above is checked for each cell; if it is satisfied, Constraints 1 and 3 are enforced by checking to see if any of the cell's neighbors are homogeneous with it. If a neighboring cell is homogeneous with it, then the cells and their associated regions are merged. This procedure continues until all 75 cells on a living floor have been scanned.

The computer vision procedure used here is a simple one. What provides it with its power is that it is informed *a priori* by the drop/toss zone model. How this occurs will become clear as we look at the Cueva Blanca living floors in detail.

Drop Zone Assumptions

Our assumptions about drop zones are drawn from Binford's description of the Mask site. Our first assumption is that drop zone cells are likely to contain many small items rather than a few large items. This follows from Binford's observation that the Nunamiut let numerous small and unobtrusive items drop nearby, while tossing large obtrusive items farther away.

Our second assumption is that the diversity of items in a drop zone cell is likely to be greater than in a toss zone cell. This follows from the fact that activities such as the manufacture of projectile points from Variety A bifaces, the rejuvenation of damaged projectile points, the manufacture and use of scrapers, and the processing of deer carcasses are likely to produce a variety of remains. Tossing away a large denticulate scraper or a deer femur is less likely to produce such a variety of debris.

I therefore expect drop zone cells to have both a *diversity* characteristic (more types of items) and a *density* characteristic (more items per cell). Let us now look at how those characteristics were measured.

Measuring Diversity

I decided that in order to qualify as a drop zone cell, a given 1 x 1 m square would have to show a variety of chipped stone tools equal to or greater than that of the average square on that living floor. (Since debitage tended to swamp all other categories, I excluded it as a diversity measure.)

In the case of Zone E, a total of 46 cells had at least one item of chipped stone. Among those 46 squares, the average number of actual tools per square was 1.93. If we round this to the nearest whole number (2.0), we can say that an average square contained at least two chipped stone tools. The average number of tool *types* per square was 1.65 (rounded to 2.0).

In the case of Zone D, a total of 58 cells had at least one item of chipped stone. Among those 58 squares, the average number of actual tools per square was 3.78. If we round this to 4.0, we can say that an average square contained at least four chipped stone tools. The average number of tool *types* per square was 2.86 (rounded to 3.0).

In the case of Zone C, a total of 48 cells had at least one item of chipped stone. Among these 48 squares, the average number of actual tools per square was 3.04. If we round this to the nearest whole number (3.0), we can say that an average square contained three chipped stone tools. The average number of tool *types* per square was 2.27 (rounded to 2.0).

Measuring Density

When it came to measuring the density of debris on the Archaic living floors at Cueva Blanca, I decided to include debitage along with actual tool types. Once again, my requirement was that to be considered part of a drop zone, a cell had to contain a number of items equal to or greater than the average for its living floor.

In the case of Zone E, where 46 cells contained at least one item of chipped stone, the average number of items per square was 10.11. I therefore decided that to qualify as average, a square would have to contain at least 10 items of chipped stone.

In the case of Zone D, where 58 cells contained at least one item of chipped stone, the average number of items per square was 28.24. I therefore decided that to qualify as average, a square would have to contain at least 28 items of chipped stone.

In the case of Zone C, where 48 cells contained at least one item of chipped stone, the average number of items per square was 23.27. I therefore decided that to qualify as average, a square would have to contain at least 23 items of chipped stone.

Although I had decided to include debitage in my measure of density, I still wanted to weight actual tools more heavily than debitage in my analysis. I therefore added one more density measure to the mix: the average number of chipped stone tools per cell, which I had already calculated. To be considered average, any square in Zone E would have to contain at least two actual tools; any square in Zone D would have to contain at least four actual tools; and any square in Zone C would have to contain at least three actual tools.

Determining Which Cells Contained the Proper Mix of Artifact Density and Diversity

We come now to the actual procedure through which I determined whether a specific cell might be part of a drop zone. I began by computing each cell's degree of diversity and then its density. The actual steps involved in the computer vision analysis were as follows:

For each cell

Compute the diversity condition (Characteristic 1) as follows:

if
  the cell contains at least one tool type that, based on the cluster analysis in Chapter 13, is not associated with the "general refuse" cluster for that living floor

then
  compute Characteristic 1 by summing the number of chipped stone categories in the cell, excluding debitage. If that value is greater than or equal to the average for that living floor, then set CHAR1 = PASS; otherwise, set CHAR1 = FAIL.

Compute the density condition (Characteristic 2) as follows:

if
  the sum of all occurrences of every chipped stone item in the cell (including debitage) is greater than or equal to the average for that living floor

  then
    set CHAR2a = PASS
  else
    set CHAR2a = FAIL

if
  the sum of all occurrences of all chipped stone tools in the cell (excluding debitage) is greater than the average for that living floor

then

  set CHAR2b = PASS
else
  set CHAR2b = FAIL

Now **compute** the cell state as follows:

if
CHAR1 and CHAR2a and CHAR2b are all PASS

then set CELL_STATE = 7

else
if
  only CHAR1 and CHAR2a are PASS

then
  set CELL_STATE = 6

else
if
  only CHAR1 and CHAR2b are PASS

then
  set CELL_STATE = 5

else
if
  only CHAR1 is PASS

then
  set CELL_STATE = 4

else
if
  only CHAR2a is PASS

then
  set CELL_STATE = 3

else
if
  only CHAR2b is PASS
then
  set CELL_STATE = 2

else
if
  no characteristics are PASS
then
  set CELL_STATE = 1

Based upon these computations, there are seven states into which a given cell (1 x 1 m square) on a given Archaic living floor can be classified. A cell is said to be in State 1 if it satisfies none of the diversity or density conditions; it is in State 2 if it has a sufficient density of chipped stone tools, but lacks diversity. It is in State 3 if it has a sufficient density of items (including debitage), but lacks diversity. It is said to be in State 4 if it displays sufficient artifact diversity, but lacks either density requirement. Cells of States 1–4 are considered to belong to toss zones.

My definition of drop zones is based on cells of States 5–7. State 7 is the ideal, reflecting a cell that satisfies the diversity characteristic and both density measures. Cells of State 6 lack only the density of actual tool types; those of State 5 have the density of actual tool types, but lack the density of items provided when debitage is considered.

For all three Archaic living floors, the majority of cells displayed State 1 and were assigned to toss zones. Barely a quarter of the Archaic cells displayed States 5–7. As for cells of State 7—the ideal drop zone condition—there were only ten in Zone E, eleven in Zone D, and nine in Zone C.

Zone E

Let us now examine the region-growing approach for Zone E. In order to familiarize the reader with the steps involved, we will treat the procedure for Zone E in some detail. Once that procedure has been spelled out, it will not be necessary to give as much detail for Zones D and C.

The algorithm begins by scanning the living floor, starting with cell B6. It checks to see whether any of the characteristics are present in this cell. In this case, they are not, so cell B6 is classified as being in State 1. In our scheme, this means that B6 is part of the toss zone for Zone E. Such a result is not unexpected, because in the case of a square abutting the east wall of the chamber, the cave ceiling would be too low to make that square a good place to work. On the other hand, it might be a convenient place to toss refuse.

The algorithm then continues on to the next cell in that row, B7. This cell also displays State 1, as do all the cells in the B row. The algorithm therefore moves on to the C row. All the cells in that row display State 1 except for cell C6. C6 is classified as being in State 5, since it satisfies Characteristic 1 and Characteristic 2b but not Characteristic 2a.

The algorithm next scans the cells of row D, beginning with D3. This row of squares is distant enough from the east wall of the cave so that the ceiling would have been high enough for any kind of activity. Both cells D9 and D10 display State 7; these are the kinds of cells from which a region can be grown.

The procedure just described continues until the E, F, G, H, I, and J rows have all been scanned. At this point, Zone E displayed ten cells in State 7 and three cells in State 5. All ten of the State 7 cells can be connected by adjacent edges or vertices, and two of the State 5 cells share an adjacent edge with a State 7 cell (Figure 14.1). The image of Zone E therefore contains a 10–12 cell region that could represent either (1) one large drop zone or (2) two modest drop zones that touched each other.

Let us consider the possibility that cells E6–F6–F7–F8–E9–D9 constitute a crescent-shaped drop zone. I presume that the agent or agents producing this drop zone would have been sitting in the area defined by cells D7–D8–E7–E8. Their drop zone would have included a broken contracting-stem atlatl point, nine notched flakes, four sidescrapers/knives, two steep denticulate scrapers, and a Variety C biface. I consider it possible that this was a men's drop zone.

Now let us consider the possibility that cells D10–E11–F12–G12–G13 also constitute a drop zone. Because of their need for sunlight, I presume that the agents or agents responsible for this drop zone would have been sitting immediately to the southeast, facing toward the cave mouth. Their drop zone would have included nine notched flakes, a steep denticulate scraper, a chopper/knife, and an ovoid scraper. I hesitate to assign a gender to the agents who produced this region.

I note that no potential drop zone was found adjacent to the Feature 15 hearth. This could mean that the agent or agents involved with food preparation did not produce the kinds of tool concentrations typical of drop zones. It is significant, however, that one of this living floor's densest concentrations of cottontail rabbit bone occurred near the hearth (see Figure 12.6). These small bone fragments could be post-meal refuse.

Where were the flakes with sheen in Zone E? There were only three in this zone, and they were found in cells E6, F8, and G12. All three, in other words, were incorporated into one of the regions of State 7 cells.

What might our computer vision image tell us about Zone E? Let us begin with a note of caution. One of the most basic mistakes we could make would be to assume that when every tool was discovered, it was still lying exactly where it had been dropped. We know that some tools may well have been moved as the cave's occupants walked around the chamber; all we can hope is that enough of the original pattern survived. We also know that, as mentioned earlier, our impressions of whether or not two tools were found together are partly a function of the 1 x 1 m grid imposed on the chamber.

That having been said, I believe I can see the following patterns. First, there may have been a good deal of spokeshaving activity going on, since our two potential drop zones contained a total of 18 notched flakes between them. This is no surprise, since the density contours in Figure 12.4 showed a considerable scatter of notched flakes in the northeast quadrant of the chamber.

Second, for whatever it may be worth, neither of the two projectile points in Zone E was found in the same cell with a flake with sheen, nor was either found near the Feature 15 hearth.

Zone D

Let us move now to Zone D, a Late Archaic living floor with a sample of tools much larger than the sample from Zone E. Like Zone E, this living floor had a hearth in its southwest quadrant.

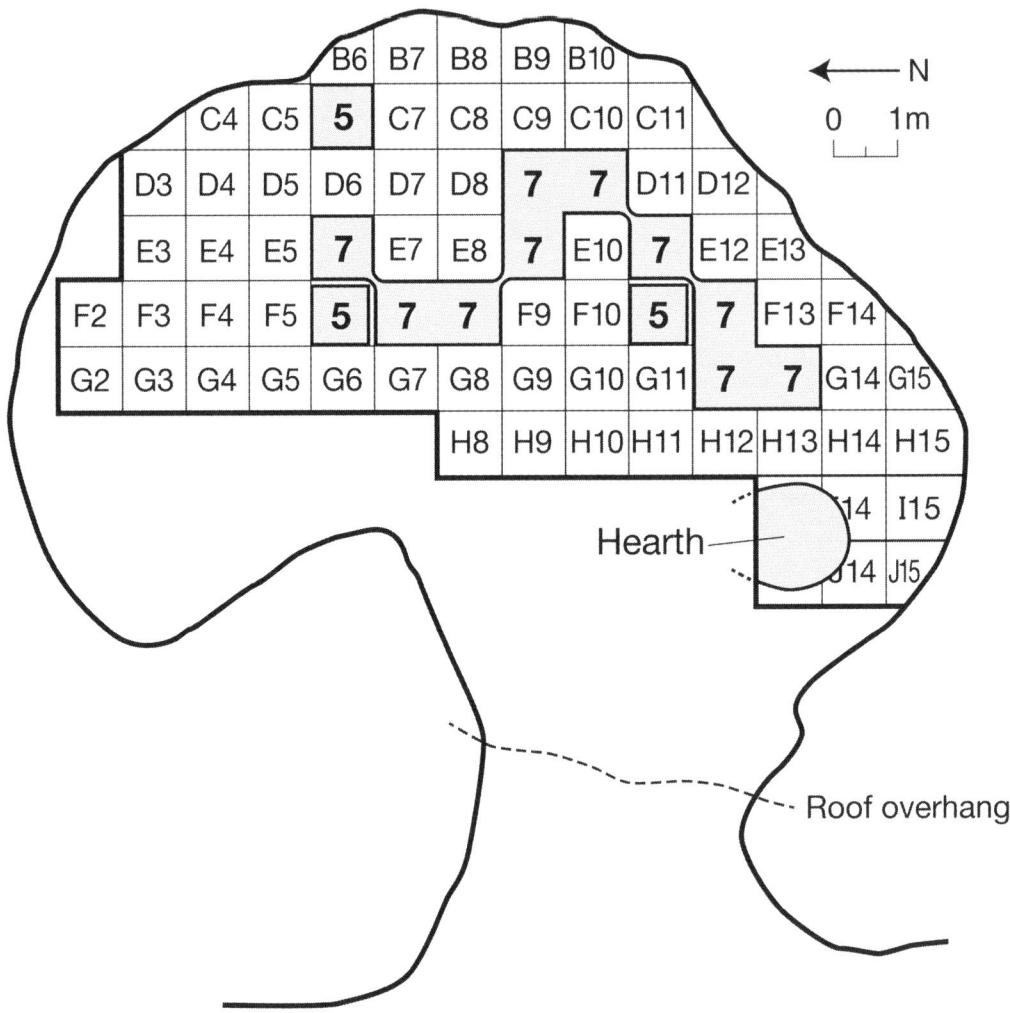

Figure 14.1. Zone E of Cueva Blanca, showing cells in States 5, 6, and 7.

As Figure 14.2 shows, the northeast quadrant of Zone D had great potential for region growing. Seven State 7 cells and seven State 5 cells formed a cluster that may indicate the presence of several drop zones. The most difficult task was deciding where one drop zone ended and another began.

Let us look first at the region composed of cells C7–C8–D7–D8–E8–E9, all of which were in State 7. The tools found in this region included a La Mina point, a Trinidad point, an unclassified atlatl point, three bifaces, 11 steep denticulate scrapers, eight notched flakes, nine utilized flakes, four end scrapers, and two sidescrapers/knives. I would not be surprised to learn that this was a men's drop zone.

Let us look next at the region composed of cells C6–D4–D5–D6–E3–E6–E7, all of which were in State 5. The tools found in this region included a reworked Tilapa point, a Palmillas point, a Trinidad point, a point fragment, three bifaces, 11 steep denticulate scrapers, six notched flakes, seven utilized flakes, four sidescrapers/knives, and two flakes with sheen. This, too, could be a men's drop zone.

In the southwest quadrant of the living floor was a smaller region composed of cells H15–I14–J14, all of which would be classified as State 7. The tools found in this region were as follows: eight notched flakes, six utilized flakes, one damaged Palmillas point, one sidescraper/knife, two steep denticulate scrapers, and three typical Archaic flake cores. It is worth noting that this corner of the cave would have had little or no sunlight for serious work. I therefore suspect that this region was more likely an area for general refuse deposit than a drop zone.

Finally, I note that the hearth (Feature 18) was encircled by a group of three cells displaying State 5. While these cells (F12, G14, and H12) did not form a region, I was curious about their

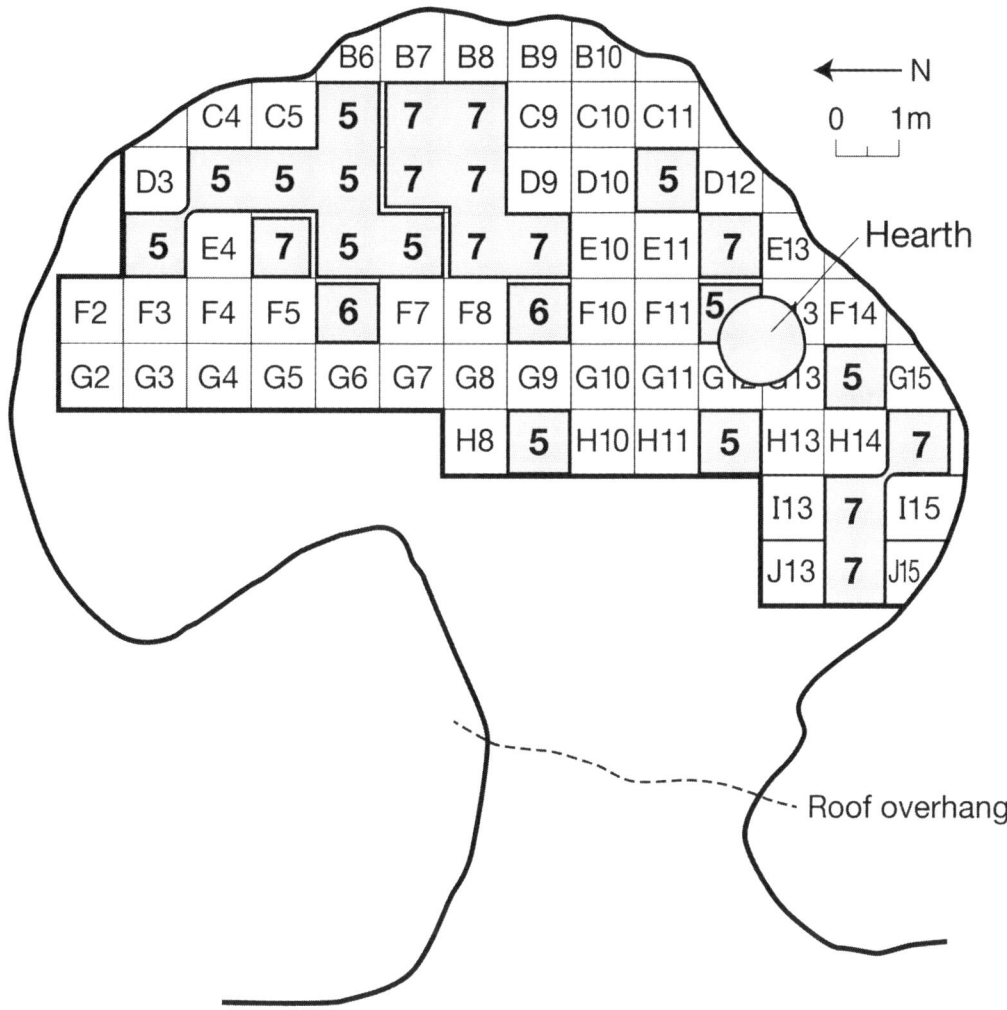

Figure 14.2. Zone D of Cueva Blanca, showing cells in States 5, 6, and 7.

contents because of their proximity to the hearth. Included in those three cells were nine notched flakes, three utilized flakes, three sidescrapers/knives, one drill, and one steep denticulate scraper.

Where were the flakes with sheen in Zone D? Two were in cell E7 and one in E8. These three, in other words, belonged to the State 7 and State 5 regions in the northeast quadrant. One flake with sheen was found in cell I13, only a meter from the hearth; another was in cell I15, near the State 7 region in the southwest quadrant; and the last was in cell G8, outside any of the regions. It would appear that a variety of individuals in Zone D were involved in slicing tough agave leaf bases.

Finally, I note that Zone D contained fragments of two metates, both belonging to types that we suspect were usually used by women (Chapter 7).

Zone C

Finally we come to Zone C, the last of the Archaic living floors. Zone C differed from the earlier two Archaic living floors in having no hearth. Its computer vision pattern was equally different. Instead of dense clusters or crescents in the northeast quadrant of the chamber, Zone C was sprinkled throughout with small regions made up of two to three State 5–7 cells (Figure 14.3). It lacked, in other words, the usual contrast between the northeast and southwest quadrants.

Let us look first at the small regions made up of State 7 cells. We will begin in the northeast with cells C5 and C6. This small region contained four notched flakes, two typical flake cores, a hammerstone, a Variety B biface, and a utilized flake.

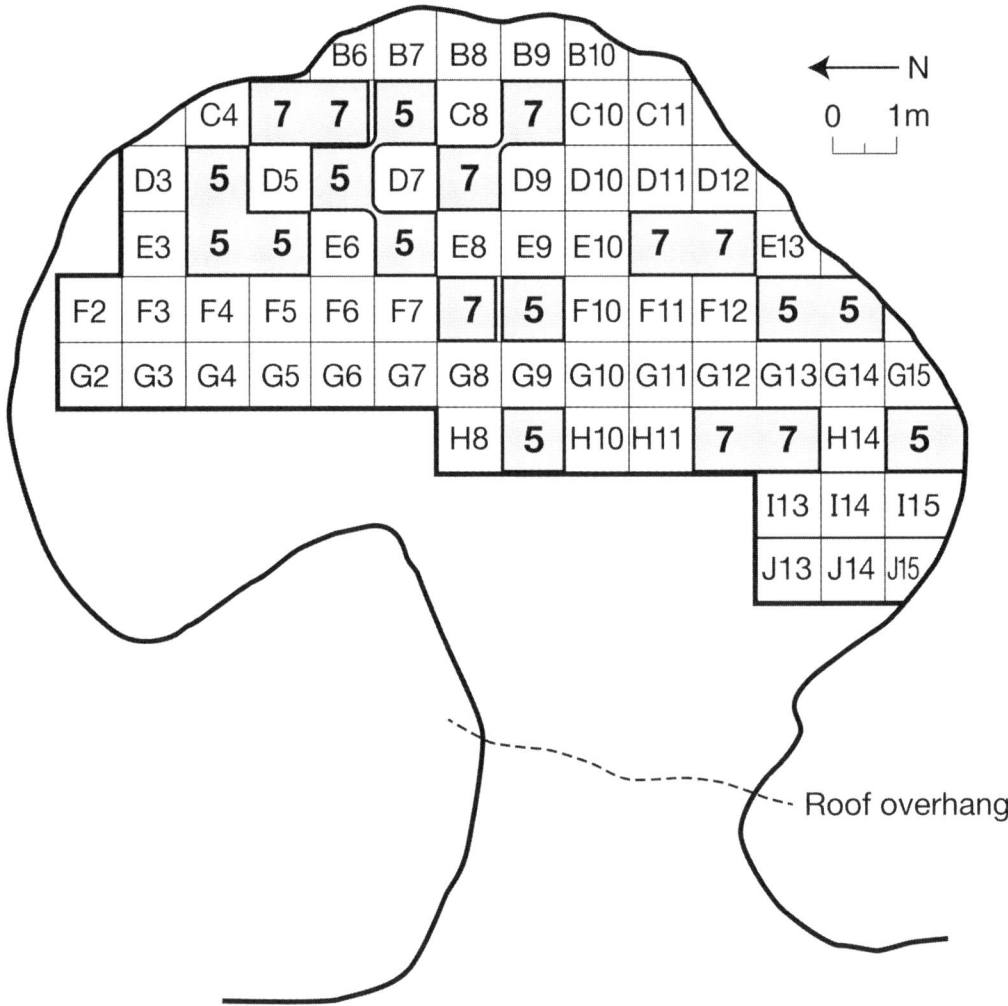

Figure 14.3. Zone C of Cueva Blanca, showing cells in States 5, 6, and 7.

We look next at cells C9 and D8. This region contained a Coxcatlán point, a San Nicolás point, three core fragments, a notched flake, a utilized flake, a flake with sheen, and a steep denticulate scraper. I would not be surprised to learn that this drop zone was produced by male activity.

Moving on to the southern part of the chamber, we look next at cells E11 and E12. This region contained a La Mina point, six utilized flakes, two plain blades, a notched flake, two steep denticulate scrapers, one sidescraper/knife, and a flake with sheen. Once again, I would not be surprised to learn that this was a male drop zone.

Finally we come to our last State 7 region, cells H12 and H13 in the southwest quadrant of the chamber. This region contained a hammerstone, three utilized flakes, two notched flakes, and two plain blades.

Let us turn next to the three regions composed of State 5 cells. One of the largest of these, in the northeast quadrant, consisted of cells C7, D6, and E7. This region contained three hammerstones, three typical flake cores, one discoidal core, four utilized flakes, one flake with sheen, one chopper/knife, and one steep denticulate scraper. The agents who produced this potential drop zone were clearly involved in flint knapping, leaving behind three hammerstones and four cores.

We will look next at cells D4, E4, and E5. This region contained a San Nicolás point, a point fragment, two hammerstones, a typical flake core, two choppers/knives, two end scrapers, two steep denticulate scrapers, four notched flakes, and two utilized flakes. I would not be surprised to learn that the agents producing this potential drop zone were men, and that they were involved in a great deal of primary knapping/core reduction.

We can look now at the final State 5 region—cells F13 and F14—which abutted the south wall of the chamber. This region contained six notched flakes, five utilized flakes, and one plain blade.

Where were the flakes with sheen in Zone C? Interestingly enough, four of the six flakes with sheen had been left in the northeast quadrant of the chamber, and two of them were found in squares containing projectile points.

Spencer and Flannery (Chapter 12) have raised the possibility that there might have been no women present in Zone C. The analysis presented in this chapter reinforces that possibility. This living floor lacks the usual contrast between a men's work area in the northeast and a women's cooking area in the southwest. There were potential drop zones scattered throughout the chamber, and abundant evidence that multiple agents were involved in primary knapping and atlatl point rejuvenation. It also seems likely that the same agents who reworked the atlatl points sometimes produced the flakes with sheen.

It is worth noting that all the ground stone tools in Zone C were one-hand manos (Chapter 7). None of the metate types that we generally associate with women were present.

Conclusions

Our experiment in computer vision has succeeded in producing regions of cells with similar attributes of density and diversity for each of Cueva Blanca's Archaic living floors. I consider it possible that many of these regions were drop zones like those described for the Mask site by Binford. I am aware that an alternative computer program, with different assumptions and different quantitative measures of density and diversity, might well have led to different results. However, the fact that the approach taken here provides support for the conclusions of Spencer and Flannery, who used a completely different approach (Chapter 12), is encouraging.

That having been said, let me draw some possible conclusions. Zones E and D showed us a number of regions that could be men's drop zones. It appears that male agents usually claimed the northeast quadrant of the cave chamber for their work space, where they engaged in atlatl point manufacture and rejuvenation, spokeshaving, and various cutting and scraping activities. I did not find much evidence that the female agents in Zones E and D produced drop zones similar to those left by men; women's presence was indicated mainly by the well-defined hearths in the southwest quadrant of the chamber; certain types of metates; and in some cases, concentrations of small bone fragments that suggested post-meal refuse.

Like Flannery, Hole, and Spencer before me, I found Zone C to be different. This living floor lacked a hearth and had no evidence of metates. Rather than the usual division into a northeast quadrant dedicated to men's activities and a southwest quadrant dedicated to food preparation, Zone C had multiple regions where comparable activities were carried out. I would not be surprised to learn that Zone C's occupants were five or six men, many of whom were involved in primary flaking/core reduction during their use of Cueva Blanca as a hunting camp.

Finally, I conclude that while atlatl points and flakes with sheen were clearly used for different tasks, the latter cannot be seen as used exclusively by women. When no women were present, as seems possible in the case of Zone C, men evidently did their share of tough plant fiber cutting. One such task might have been the conversion of agave fiber into rope.

Part V

Summary and Conclusions

15

The Place of Cueva Blanca in Oaxaca's Archaic Sequence

Kent V. Flannery and Frank Hole

We have described the excavation of Cueva Blanca, the typology of its artifacts, the identification of its animal bones, and several analyses of its living floors. We are now in a position to assess Cueva Blanca's contribution to our understanding of the Archaic sequence in the eastern Valley of Oaxaca. We will proceed through the chronology of the region from early to late, beginning with the Paleoindian period.

The El Fuerte Phase (Paleoindian)

The Paleoindian period in the eastern Valley of Oaxaca is poorly dated. Zone F of Cueva Blanca produced no radiocarbon samples. Its partially fossilized fauna included the Texas gopher tortoise, a species also found in Late Pleistocene levels at Tehuacán. We do have one "Pleistocene-looking" radiocarbon date from Zone E of Guilá Naquitz—12,470 BC ± 60 (Beta-74628)—but that date was run on baldcypress wood that may already have been old when brought to the cave.

Our main justification for creating an El Fuerte phase is the fact that two fluted points have been found within walking distance of Cueva Blanca (see Figure 2.6). That fact suggests that once the right sites have been excavated, there will be a tool assemblage to accompany the Pleistocene fauna from Zone F of Cueva Blanca.

The Paleoindian-Archaic Transition

Key to our understanding of the Paleoindian-Archaic transition is Feature 15 of Cueva Blanca. Stratigraphically, this large shallow hearth appears to have been dug down from Zone E, an Early Archaic living floor.

Perhaps most striking aspect of Feature 15 is that its three radiocarbon dates, if correct, make it older than the currently accepted date of 11,000 years ago (9000 BC) for the end of the last Ice Age (Severinghaus 1998). These dates, given below, suggest that an Archaic tool assemblage existed almost at the moment when the Pleistocene gave way to the Holocene.

SI-511	8960 BC ± 80	(cal.) 11,037–10,745 BC
SI-511R	8780 BC ± 220	(cal.) 11,132–10,090 BC
M-2094	9050 BC ± 400	(cal.) 11,810–9870 BC

The Naquitz Phase (Early Archaic)

Zone E of Cueva Blanca is almost certainly our oldest living floor from the Naquitz phase. Its four radiocarbon dates are as follows:

Beta-82191	7430 BC ± 130	(cal.) 8941–8304 BC
Beta-82189	7880 BC ± 100	(cal.) 9696–9121 BC
Beta-82190	7890 BC ± 90	(cal.) 9675–9136 BC
M-2093	8100 BC ± 350	(cal.) 10,718–8761 BC

We note that the calibrated range of date M-2093 overlaps with that of date M-2094 from Feature 15. These two dates, both run by the same laboratory, reinforce our stratigraphic evidence that the Feature 15 hearth was indeed a part of the Zone E living floor. In fact, all four of the Zone E dates could be used to support the notion that the Archaic had begun before (cal.) 9000 BC in the eastern Valley of Oaxaca.

Guilá Naquitz Cave has produced another 35 radiocarbon dates for the Naquitz phase, making it the most extensively dated period of the Oaxaca Archaic. For the full list of 35 dates, the reader should consult Table 1 of the updated edition of *Guilá Naquitz* (Flannery 2009b). We will only summarize the data here.

Zone E

Zone E of Guilá Naquitz is represented by six radiocarbon assays, one of which produced the aforementioned conventional date of 12,470 BC. For reasons unknown, the remaining five dates are inconsistent, ranging from (cal.) 8995–8495 BC (Beta-74627) to (cal.) 5255–4920 BC (Beta-76873).

Zone D

Zone D produced eight conventional dates, spanning the period 8750 BC ± 350 to 6920 BC ± 80. The two oldest dates, possibly on baldcypress wood, were beyond the calibration curve. The remaining six produced calibrated dates ranging from 9005–8565 BC (Beta-74625) to 8045–7695 BC (Beta-76869). All Zone D dates were based on wood charcoal. Significantly, the plant remains from Zone D indicate that there were still pinyon pines within walking distance of the cave in the ninth millennium BC (C. E. Smith 2009).

Zone C

Zone C produced seven radiocarbon dates, two of which were AMS dates on domestic plants. One conventional date (possibly on baldcypress) was found to be beyond the calibration curve. The other six yielded calibrated dates ranging from 9150–7915 BC (M-2097) to 5330–4360 BC (M-2100). One cultivated squash seed produced a calibrated date of 8035–7920 BC (Beta-100764). A piece of bottle gourd rind produced a calibrated date of 8030–7915 BC (Beta-100762). Clearly, therefore, some agriculture was being practiced in the Valley of Oaxaca by 8000 BC.

Zone B2 + 3

Zone B2 + 3 produced one radiocarbon date (GX-784), whose two-sigma calibrated range was 8235–7565 BC.

Zone B2

Zone B2 produced three radiocarbon dates, two of which were AMS dates on domestic plants. One piece of gourd rind had a calibrated range of 7020–6595 BC (Beta-97237). One squash seed had a calibrated range of 6585–6425 BC (Beta-100763). A piece of wood charcoal from Zone B2 had a calibrated range of 7995–7325 BC (SI-515). Zone B2 also produced eight grains of pollen from maize or teosinte (Schoenwetter and Smith 2009: Table 15.26), raising the interesting possibility of an early cultivar of *Zea*.

At this point we must consider the open-air Archaic site of Gheo-Shih, which has produced dates very close to those of Zone B2 at Guilá Naquitz. Gheo-Shih was a 1.5 hectare macroband camp on good alluvial soil, near the right bank of the Río Mitla (see Figures 1.3 and 1.4). It appears that Gheo-Shih was a favored campsite to which groups of 25–50 persons returned on multiple occasions, presumably during the June-to-September rainy season. At that time they would have been able to plant gourds and squash, while harvesting mesquite pods and hackberry fruits from the river floodplain. Gheo-Shih—like Zone B2 of Guilá Naquitz—also produced grains of *Zea* pollen (Schoenwetter and Smith 2009: Table 15.28).

Area A of Gheo-Shih, excavated by Hole, was found to have two superimposed components. The older component belonged to the Naquitz phase, and has produced two radiocarbon dates. The calibrated two-sigma ranges of these dates (Beta-190316 and Beta-191398) were 7720–7560 BC (Marcus and Flannery 2004).

The Gheo-Shih dates are sufficiently similar to those from Zone B2 of Guilá Naquitz to permit the following scenario: at various times during the eighth millennium BC, foragers in the region spent the rainy season in large camps near the Río Mitla and dispersed during the dry season into small, family-sized camps in the nearby mountains. At one of these microband camps, Zone B2 of Guilá Naquitz, they collected acorns and pinyon nuts (C. E. Smith 2009).

Gheo-Shih also provides us with evidence for two activities that may have been carried out only at macroband camps. First, the occupants of Gheo-Shih cleared a space 20 m by 7 m in extent and lined it with boulders; this feature may have served as a public space for dances, initiations, or athletic competition (see Flannery and Marcus 2015: Figures 2.1–2.3). Second, they spent time making ornaments out of flat river pebbles (Marcus and Flannery 1996: Figure 44).

Significantly, we found no ritual features or evidence of ornament making at Guilá Naquitz. This could mean that during the Naquitz phase, certain ritual and craft activities were carried out largely at macroband camps—that is, at times when the largest number of people were living together.

Zone B1

Zone B1 of Guilá Naquitz produced six AMS dates run on squash and bean specimens. The oldest calibrated date on a squash seed was 6610–6420 BC (Beta-91404). Two runner beans produced calibrated dates of 6460–6260 BC (AA15007) and 6400–6220 BC (AA13336). Our youngest date on a squash peduncle had a two-sigma calibrated range of 6195–5980 BC (Beta-97238). In all, Zone B1 produced six very consistent dates on annual plants, leaving us confident that this living floor was occupied between 6610 and 5980 BC. Zone B1 also produced one grain of *Zea* pollen (Schoenwetter and Smith 2009: Table 15.26).

Zone B

Zone B was the term used in those parts of the cave where no separate Zones B1, B2, and B3 could be distinguished (Flannery 2009a:87–89 and Figure 5.35). Zone B produced five radiocarbon dates, three of which were AMS dates on specimens of squash. Four of the calibrated dates overlapped strongly with those from Zone B1; the oldest of these had a two-sigma range of 6400–6160 BC (Beta-74748) and the youngest a range of 5950–5705 BC (Beta-972540). One squash seed—which we suspect may have been redeposited from Zone C—gave us a suspiciously older date of (cal.) 8085–7955 BC (Beta-100766).

In sum, a total of 44 radiocarbon dates are available for the Naquitz phase: 35 from Guilá Naquitz, seven from Cueva Blanca, and two from Gheo-Shih. Although Guilá Naquitz remains the type site for the phase, Zone E and Feature 15 of Cueva Blanca constitute our oldest Naquitz-phase proveniences.

The available data allow us to suggest that the Naquitz phase began by (cal.) 10,000 BC and lasted until (cal.) 6000 BC. When the phase began, the foragers of the Valley of Oaxaca were still making a few Paleoindian-style leaf-shaped (Lerma?) points, one unfinished example of which was found in Zone E of Guilá Naquitz (Hole 2009: Figures 6.26*a*, 6.27*d*). Zone E of Cueva Blanca produced a fragment of Archaic corner-notched (Palmillas?) point; a similar corner-notched specimen was found at Guilá Naquitz (Hole 2009: Figures 6.27*b*, 6.28*b*).

Zone B1 of Guilá Naquitz, a late Naquitz-phase living floor, produced a possible fragment of Trinidad point (Hole 2009: Figures 6.26*b*, 6.27*a*). Other Archaic point types used during this period include Almagre (Hole 2009: Figures 6.27*c*, 6.28*c*) and Pedernales (Hole 2009: Figures 6.30, 6.31).

The Pedernales point whose distal half was found in Zone B3 of Guilá Naquitz is particularly significant. This point type, which appeared in small numbers toward the end of the Naquitz phase, went on to reach its peak frequency during the subsequent Jícaras phase.

Ground stone tools appeared at the beginning of the Naquitz phase, increasing in quantity and diversity as time went on. One-hand manos were the most widely used ground stone tool. Slab metates were the earliest type of metate used; mortars and basin-shaped metates did not show up until roughly (cal.) 8000 BC (Zones C and B2 of Guilá Naquitz).

No phenotypically domestic plants are known from the beginning of the Naquitz phase; however, an unidentified runner bean was being harvested in quantity as early as Zone E of Guilá Naquitz. Domestic gourds and squash made their first appearance in Zone C of Guilá Naquitz, providing AMS dates of roughly (cal.) 8000 BC. As early as Zone B2 of Guilá Naquitz, there is enough evidence for *Zea* pollen to make us wonder if cultivated teosinte or early maize were present in the region.

Depending on how one views the Zone B1–B3 situation at Guilá Naquitz (see discussion in Flannery 2009a:87–89 and Figure 5.35), at least seven or eight living floors from Naquitz-phase microband camps have been excavated. All appear to have been made, in terms of Binford's (1980) model, by groups who were near the "foraging" end of the spectrum; not one Naquitz-phase living floor suggests that we are dealing with "collectors." To be sure, this could simply mean that we do not as yet have an adequate sample of sites. For the moment, however, we cannot argue that the Early Archaic witnessed any kind of shift toward semipermanent macroband camps and logistically based "collecting."

The Jícaras Phase (Middle Archaic)

The Jícaras phase is believed to have begun at (cal.) 6000 BC and lasted until roughly (cal.) 4000 BC. Unfortunately, it is one of our least thoroughly investigated and radiocarbon dated Archaic phases. Its type site is the macroband camp of Gheo-Shih, whose name means "Río de las Jícaras" or "River of the Gourd Trees" in Spanish. The plant referred to in this case is not the bottle gourd but the tree gourd (*Crescentia cujete*).

The Jícaras phase constitutes the moment in our Archaic sequence when Pedernales points reached their peak frequency. That moment occurred during the laying down of the upper stratigraphic component in Area A at Gheo-Shih. Owing to the erosion of that component over the years, the surface of Gheo-Shih was littered with Pedernales points (Figure 15.1).

Only two radiocarbon dates are available from the Jícaras phase. Both are AMS dates on primitive maize cobs from Guilá Naquitz Cave (Piperno and Flannery 2001). One date had a calibrated two-sigma range of 4340–4220 BC; the other had a range of 4355–4065 BC. Both cobs came from ash lenses that stratigraphically overlay Zone B1. The implication of these ash lenses is that Jícaras phase foragers visited Guilá Naquitz but did not stay long enough to create an actual living floor.

The Blanca Phase (Late Archaic)

We come now to the Blanca phase, for which the type site is Cueva Blanca. To be specific, the phase has been defined primarily on the basis of Zones D and C at that site.

Feature 18

Feature 18 was a hearth that appeared, stratigraphically, to have been created by the occupants of the Zone D living floor. Our

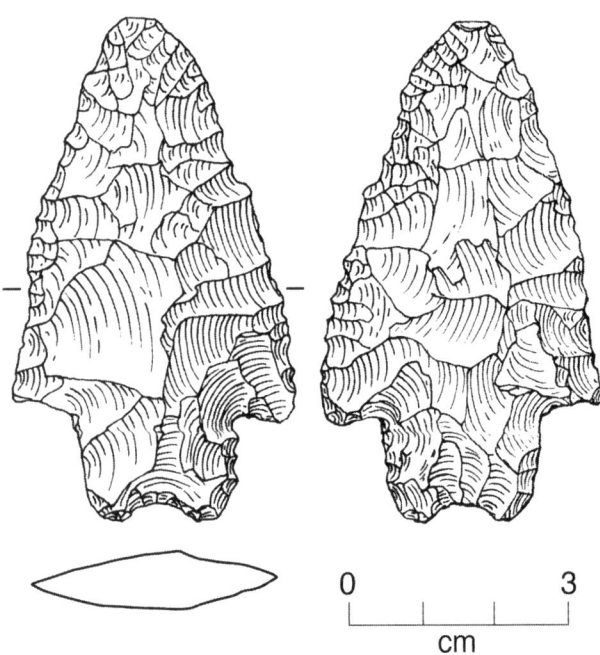

Figure 15.1. A typical Pedernales point from the Mitla region.

lone radiocarbon date for this hearth had a two-sigma range of (cal.) 4330–3915 BC (Gx-0782). This date supports our view that the Blanca phase had begun by (cal.) 4000 BC.

Zone D

Zone D of Cueva Blanca has produced three radiocarbon dates consistent with the date from Feature 18. These dates have two-sigma ranges of (cal.) 3953–3694 BC (Beta-82187), (cal.) 3961–3013 BC (M-2092), and (cal.) 3028–2861 BC (Beta-82186). The four dates just considered support the notion that the Blanca phase spans the fourth millennium BC.

The two remaining dates from Zone D, as described in Chapter 4, came out 4000 years older than the rest. Beta-82188 had a range of (cal.) 8862–8187 BC; SI-512 had a range of (cal.) 9265–8316 BC. The most likely explanation is that the charcoal used for these dates was originally deposited in Zone E and came to be redeposited in Zone D when the occupants of the latter living floor excavated pits, or hearths such as Feature 18.

Zone C

Zone C produced little in the way of useful charcoal for dating the Late Archaic. As reported in Chapter 4, Beta-82185 (cal. 6636–6352 BC) appears to have been based on redeposited charcoal from an earlier level.

Fortunately, when it comes to providing diagnostic artifacts for the Blanca phase we have more to work with. Not a single Pedernales point was recovered from Zones D and C at Cueva Blanca; in other words, one of the most characteristic atlatl points of the Jícaras phase was no longer a popular type. Instead, the Blanca phase featured points of the La Mina, Trinidad, Tilapa, San Nicolás, and Coxcatlán types. The presence of Coxcatlán points, made on nonlocal material, is particularly important because this point is well known from the Abejas phase of the Tehuacán Valley (MacNeish, Nelken-Terner, and Johnson 1967:65). As mentioned in Chapter 4, Johnson and MacNeish (1972:5) suggested that the Abejas phase might have spanned the period 4150–2850 BC in "sidereal" time (an early attempt at calibration). This is very close to the 4330–2861 BC range of our four best calibrated dates from Zone D and Feature 18.

Zones D and C of Cueva Blanca constitute our only two living floors from the Blanca phase. This is admittedly a small sample. We are struck, however, by the fact that only one of these living floors—Zone D—appears to have been created by a family microband like those seen at Guilá Naquitz. Zone C lacks a hearth and does not feature a convincing women's work area. This is true no matter how Zone C is analyzed, whether by density contours (Chapter 12), rank-order tables and cluster analysis (Chapter 13), or a search for "drop zones" (Chapter 14). We cannot rule out the possibility, therefore, that Zone C of Cueva Blanca was created by an all-male task group who came from (and later returned to) a more permanent camp elsewhere. If true, this could signal some movement along Binford's (1980) continuum from "foraging" to "collecting."

One living floor, to be sure, cannot be relied upon to document the moment when this movement along the foraging-collecting continuum first took place. Future researchers in the Mitla region will need a larger sample of Jícaras-phase and Blanca-phase living floors to settle the issue. Among other things, we need additional sites with good plant preservation to reveal the extent to which the evolution of agriculture influenced the foraging-collecting shift.

The Martínez Phase: Terminal Archaic

We currently have no radiocarbon dates for the Martínez phase, which remains the most poorly known and least well dated part of the Archaic sequence. One reason is that we excavated a mere 17 m² of the type site, once we found that only its Postclassic stratum had preservation of organic remains.

The Martínez Rockshelter lies 600 m north of Guilá Naquitz and in the same volcanic tuff cliff. Only the shelter's two lowest stratigraphic levels, Zones C and B, dated to the Archaic, and the preservation in those levels was so poor that we recovered neither plants nor animal bones. Neither zone appeared to be an actual living floor. Instead, the matrix of both zones seemed largely to be the result of natural weathering processes.

It was the uppermost 10 cm of Zone B that we have assigned to the Martínez phase, which we consider the "last gasp" of the Archaic. Several attributes of Upper Zone B suggest that it may represent a transitional period between the Archaic and the Formative. For one thing, Zone B's ground stone artifact assemblage was richer than that of any previous Archaic phase; it included manos, metates, and mortars of several types that resembled Formative tools. Second, Upper Zone B produced stone bowls like those of the Late Archaic in the Tehuacán Valley (MacNeish et al. 1967:117).

MacNeish felt that these stone bowls—some of which appeared to have been used for heating food—showed the need for a fire-resistant cooking vessel prior to the creation of pottery. An alternative possibility, of course, is that some of these labor-intensive vessels were used for consuming ritual beverages, such as pulque or chocolate. Here is a case where future residue analysis may provide answers.

Finally, projectile points became rare in Zone B and we found none in the level assigned to the Martínez phase. This fact is significant because the Early Formative period in both the Valley of Oaxaca and the Central Depression of Chiapas was virtually without chipped stone atlatl points (see discussion in Flannery and Marcus 2005:55–58). It has previously been suggested that Formative societies in this part of Mesoamerica abandoned small-scale, Archaic-style atlatl hunting and went over to large communal deer hunts with nets, slings, and wooden spears (see Lowe 1959:7 for an ethnohistoric example of communal deer hunts from Chiapas).

When did the Martínez phase begin? Johnson and MacNeish (1972:24) have arbitrarily selected a date of 2300 BC for the end of the Abejas phase in the Tehuacán Valley. While we do not necessarily believe that the Tehuacán and Oaxaca sequences are closely correlated, we would not be bothered by a date of (cal.) 2500–2300 BC for the end of the Blanca phase and the start of the Martínez phase. We see the Martínez phase as relatively short, continuing only until the first appearance of Early Formative pottery in the Valley of Oaxaca.

This period—the transition from the Late Archaic to the Formative—is poorly understood not only in Oaxaca, but everywhere in Mesoamerica. Here the contrast with other world regions, such as the Near East, could not be greater. In the Near East, village life began before the first appearance of pottery. Many early villages, such as Ali Kosh (Hole et al. 1969) and Tepe Guran (Mortensen 2014), began in an aceramic or "Pre-pottery Neolithic" era and added ceramics only later. The sequence from Final Paleolithic to Pre-pottery Neolithic is well known, and the latter period can even be subdivided into Pre-pottery Neolithic A, B, and so on.

The only site in the Mexican highlands with stratigraphy comparable to Ali Kosh and Tepe Guran is Zohapilco, on the swampy margins of Lake Chalco in the Basin of Mexico (Niederberger 1976, 1987). Zohapilco has Archaic strata below its Early Formative deposits. No village in the Valley of Oaxaca has a similar sequence.

In Mesoamerica—to return to an analogy used in Chapter 1—we do not yet know whether the transition from Archaic camps to Formative villages was a slow "dial" or a rapid "switch." In fact, at the moment we cannot even prove that the Early Formative villagers in the Valley of Oaxaca were direct descendants of the Late Archaic people who preceded them in the region.

The Importance of Cueva Blanca

MacNeish attempted to work out an Archaic sequence for the Tehuacán Valley by excavating a series of caves in the early 1960s. The University of Michigan attempted to do the same thing for the Oaxaca Valley between 1966 and 1967. In recent years there have been fewer attempts to create comparable multisite Archaic sequences in the southern Mexican highlands. That fact alone made it important for us to bring this site report on Cueva Blanca to completion.

We can think, in addition, of at least six contributions that Cueva Blanca has made to our understanding of Archaic Oaxaca. First, Zone F of Cueva Blanca gives us a look at the fauna available to Late Pleistocene hunters in the Mitla region. Second, the radiocarbon dates from Zone E and Feature 15 suggest that the transition to an Archaic lifeway was underway much earlier than we expected. In fact, those dates raise the possibility that the transition from Paleoindian to Archaic was governed by a "switch" rather than a "dial."

A third factor is that Zones E and D of Cueva Blanca show remarkable similarity to the living floors at Guilá Naquitz. Each features a division into men's and women's work areas, with the women's work area including a hearth. This makes Zone C at Cueva Blanca all the more interesting, since it has neither a hearth nor a convincing women's work area. A fourth contribution of Cueva Blanca, therefore, is the possibility that Zone C documents the shift from foraging to logistically based collecting. Zone C also provides us with evidence that interregional trade in marine shells was underway in the Late Archaic.

A sixth and final contribution would be the relatively large collection of Late Archaic projectile points that Cueva Blanca provided. When we combine the *in situ* Archaic points from Zones E through C with those redeposited in Zones B and A, it gives us the largest collection of points from any cave in the Mitla region. Only Gheo-Shih provided a comparable body of stylistic information.

Let us close with some thoughts about future work on the Archaic of the Valley of Oaxaca. Having tested 10 caves and rockshelters in the Mitla region, we are not confident that there is another Archaic site out there with the extraordinary preservation of Guilá Naquitz. On the other hand, we are impressed by the number of open-air Archaic sites on the former lands of the Hacienda El Fuerte. We believe that every stage of the Archaic is represented at these sites, and that Gheo-Shih is only the tip of the iceberg.

Appendix A

Resumen en español

Soren Frykholm

Cueva Blanca se encuentra en las montañas, a 4 kilómetros al oeste de Mitla, Oaxaca, a una altura de 1813 metros sobre el nivel del mar. Está a menos de 1400 m al este de la cueva de Guilá Naquitz, el sitio donde se han producido las jícaras, las calabazas, los frijoles y los maíces más antiguos de Oaxaca (Flannery 2009a). Desafortunadamente, Cueva Blanca mira hacia el oeste, permitiendo que las lluvias de verano entren en la cámara de la cueva. Como consecuencia, sólo en los niveles posclásicos de la cueva se conservaron restos de plantas.

Tras ser excavada por Kent Flannery y Frank Hole (Capítulo 3), Cueva Blanca resultó tener seis niveles estratigráficos. La Capa F, la más antigua, contenía fauna del Pleistoceno Tardío, incluida la gran tortuga *Gopherus berlandieri*. Esta tortuga de tierra ya no está presente en el sur de México; hoy día se circunscribe a la estepa árida de Chihuahua. Aunque ningún instrumento de pedernal se asociaba a esta fauna del Pleistoceno, se encontró una punta acanalada del tipo Paleoindio a menos de un kilómetro de Cueva Blanca.

La Capa E de la cueva se remonta al Arcaico Temprano (Fase Naquitz) y ha producido fechas de radiocarbono calibradas del 10,718 al 8304 a.C. Los artefactos de este nivel incluían dos puntas de *átlatl*, una de las cuales parece pertenecer al tipo Palmillas (Capítulo 6). La Capa E tenía un hogar con forma de cuenco (Elemento 15), cuyas fechas calibradas de radiocarbono se ubicaron entre los años 11,810 y 9870 a.C.

La Capa D pertenece al Arcaico Tardío (Fase Blanca) y ha producido fechas de radiocarbono calibradas que se ubican entre los años 3953 y 2861 a.C. Este nivel también tenía un hogar con forma de cuenco (Elemento 18), cuyas fechas de radiocarbono calibradas se ubicaron entre el 4330 y el 3915 a.C.

La Capa C también pertenecía al Arcaico Tardío (Fase Blanca), pero carecía de hogares y no produjo fechas de radiocarbono útiles.

En la Fase Blanca había puntas de *átlatl* de los tipos La Mina, Trinidad, Tilapa, San Nicolás, Coxcatlán, Hidalgo, Abasolo y Gary. Las dos puntas de Coxcatlán encontradas en Cueva Blanca parecen haber sido hechas con una materia prima foránea al Valle de Oaxaca, y pudieron haber sido obtenidas por medio del intercambio.

Otros artefactos de la Fase Blanca eran los cantos rodados discoidales usados como manos de molienda, los metates en forma de laja y los metates en forma de cuenco (Capítulo 7). Los ornamentos incluían una concha perforada de molusco marino (*Agaronia testacea*) del Océano Pacífico; ésta es la evidencia más antigua del comercio de conchas marinas en el Valle de Oaxaca (Capítulo 8).

Entre los animales que se consumieron como alimento durante la Fase Blanca se encuentran el venado cola blanca, conejos de dos especies y la tortuga casquito (*Kinosternon integrum*).

Las Capas B y A de Cueva Blanca datan del Posclásico (período Monte Albán V). Durante la ocupación de la Capa B, la cueva fue utilizada como un campamento para asar corazones de agave en un horno de tierra (Elemento 6). Este nivel consistía principalmente en rocas quemadas por el fuego producto de esa actividad.

Durante la deposición de Capa A, una familia extensa utilizó la cueva como una granja, cultivando en seis terrazas agrícolas en el talud de la cueva. Esta familia también construyó un horno de cerámica en la cueva y lo usó para producir ollas de cerámica G3M, un tipo común del período V de Monte Albán. La Capa A produjo una fecha de radiocarbono calibrada que ha sido ubicada entre el 1304 y el 1365 d.C.

Cueva Blanca fue excavada mediante una retícula de 1 x 1 m. Todos los artefactos arcaicos y los huesos de animales fueron registrados y contados dentro de dicha retícula. Esta base de datos proporcionó la información cuadrado-por-cuadrado necesaria para llevar a cabo tres análisis estadísticos por computadora.

Charles Spencer (Capítulo 12) trazó líneas de contorno de densidad para las categorías más numerosas de instrumentos de pedernal y huesos de animales en las Capas E, D y C. Las Capas E y D mostraron patrones espaciales similares. En cada caso, parece que había dos grupos de personas en la cueva, uno que ocupaba el cuadrante noreste, y otro que ocupaba el cuadrante suroeste y cuidaba del hogar. El grupo del cuadrante noreste—presuntamente compuesto de hombres—se dedicaba a la elaboración y reparación de puntas de *átlatl* y al procesamiento de cadáveres de venados. El grupo del cuadrante suroeste—presuntamente compuesto de mujeres—se dedicaba a la preparación de alimentos y al descarte de restos de comida como pequeños huesos de mamíferos no identificables.

La Capa C era diferente. Carecía de hogar, metates y evidencias de actividades femeninas en el cuadrante suroeste de la cueva. Parecía haber sido habitada únicamente por individuos del sexo masculino en este nivel. Estos hombres, en lugar de restringir sus actividades al cuadrante noreste, se extendían por toda la cámara de la cueva.

Es posible, por lo tanto, que entre las Capas D y C, los cazadores y recolectores de la región de Mitla hayan cambiado de un patrón de "forrajeo" (moviéndose a los lugares donde se encontraban los recursos) a un patrón de "recolección" (pasando períodos más prolongados en campamentos grandes, y enviando grupos de varones por períodos cortos a cazar venados). Este modelo fue propuesto originalmente por Binford (1980). En el caso del Valle de Oaxaca, el cambio del "forrajeo" a la "recolección" puede haber estado relacionado con el éxito creciente de la agricultura del Arcaico Tardío, la cual permitió permanecer a estos grupos durante períodos más largos en el suelo aluvial del Río Mitla.

En el Capítulo 13, Robert Reynolds busca *kits* de instrumentos (grupos de instrumentos usados y descartados juntos) en los niveles arcaicos de la cueva. Utiliza dos técnicas estadísticas diferentes: correlaciones ordenadas y análisis de cúmulos. En las Capas E y D, parece que las mismas personas (probablemente hombres) usaron puntas de proyectil, raspadores frontales, raspadores laterales y bifaciales ovoidales para procesar cadáveres de animales, mientras que otros individuos (probablemente mujeres) usaron lascas con bordes lustrosos y navajillas burdas para procesar plantas. Por otro lado, en la Capa C—posiblemente porque no había mujeres—las mismas personas que usaban puntas de proyectil también usaban lascas con borde lustroso.

En el Capítulo 14, Reynolds busca "zonas de arrastre" utilizando las técnicas de "visualización por computadora." "Zona de arrastre" es un término acuñado por Binford (1984) para describir áreas en forma de media luna de escombros densos creados por los cazadores mientras se sientan para procesar las presas de la cacería. En las Capas E y D, Reynolds pudo detectar tales áreas de escombros densos en el cuadrante noreste de la cámara de la cueva, donde trabajaban los hombres. En la Capa C, el patrón era diferente, lo cual llevó a Reynolds a inferir que no había mujeres en la cueva, permitiendo a los hombres extenderse por toda la cámara.

Finalmente, en el Capítulo 15, los autores resumen lo que sabemos acerca de la secuencia arcaica en la región de Mitla. La transición del período Paleoindio a la Fase Arcaica Temprana de Naquitz tuvo lugar en un momento sorprendentemente temprano, quizás entre los años 11,000 y 10,000 a.C. Las jícaras y las calabazas fueron domesticadas hacia el año 8000 a.C., durante la Fase Naquitz. Las mazorcas de maíz aparecieron poco después del 5000 a.C., durante la Fase Jícaras del Arcaico Medio. La Fase Blanca del Arcaico Tardío fue tipificada por las Capas D y C de Cueva Blanca, y la presencia de puntas de Coxcatlán en la Fase Blanca demuestra su contemporaneidad con la Fase Abejas del Valle de Tehuacán, Puebla (MacNeish, Nelken-Terner y Johnson 1967). El Arcaico terminó con la Fase Martínez (2300 a.C. hasta la primera aparición de la cerámica en el Valle de Oaxaca).

References

Alley, Richard B.
    1998   Overview. 10th Annual Symposium on Frontiers of Science, Beckman Center, National Academy of Sciences. Irvine, CA.

Alley, Richard B., Jean Lynch-Stieglitz, and Jeffrey P. Severinghaus
    1999   Global climate change. *Proceedings of the National Academy of Sciences* 96:9987–9988.

Alley, Richard B., D. A. Meese, C. A. Shuman, A. I. Gow, K. C. Taylor, P. M. Grootes, J. W. C. White, M. Ram, E. D. Waddington, P. A. Mayewski, and G. A. Zielinski
    1993   Abrupt increase in Greenland snow accumulation at the end of the Younger Dryas event. *Nature* 362:527–529.

Anderberg, Michael
    1973   *Cluster Analysis for Applications*. New York: Academic Press.

Benz, Bruce F.
    2001   Archaeological evidence of teosinte domestication from Guilá Naquitz, Oaxaca. *Proceedings of the National Academy of Sciences* 98:2104–2106.

Bernal, Juan Pablo, Matthew Lachniet, Malcolm McCulloch, Graham Mortimer, Pedro Morales, and Edith Cienfuegos
    2011   A speleothem record of Holocene climate variability from southwestern Mexico. *Quaternary Research* 75:104–113.

Binford, Lewis R.
    1980   Willow smoke and dogs' tails: Hunter-gatherer settlement systems and archaeological site formation. *American Antiquity* 45(1):4–20.
    1984   Dimensional analysis of behavior and site structure: learning from an Eskimo hunting stand. *American Antiquity* 43(3):330–361.

Bradbury, John P.
    1997   Sources of glacial moisture in Mesoamerica. *Quaternary International* 43/44:97–110.

Bronk Ramsey, Christopher
    2009   Bayesian analysis of radiocarbon dates. *Radiocarbon* 51(1):337–360.

Byers, Douglas S. (editor)
    1967   *The Prehistory of the Tehuacán Valley,* Volume 1: *Environment and Subsistence.* Austin: University of Texas Press.

Carr, Christopher
    1984   The nature of organization of intrasite archaeological records and spatial analytic approaches to their investigation. *Advances in Archaeological Method and Theory* 7:103–222.
    1991   Left in the dust: Contextual information in model-focused archaeology. In *The Interpretation of Archaeological*

Spatial Patterning, edited by Ellen M. Kroll and T. Douglas Price, pp. 221–256. New York: Plenum Press.

Caso, Alfonso, Ignacio Bernal, and Jorge R. Acosta
1967   *La Cerámica de Monte Albán*. Memorias del Instituto de Antropología e Historia, no. 13. México, D. F.

Cowgill, George L., Jeffrey H. Altschul, and Rebecca S. Sload
1984   Spatial analysis of Teotihuacan: a Mesoamerican metropolis. In *Intrasite Spatial Analysis in Archaeology*, edited by Harold J. Hietala, pp. 154–195. Cambridge: Cambridge University Press.

Doran, J. E. and F. R. Hodson
1975   *Mathematics and Computers in Archaeology*. Cambridge, MA: Harvard University Press.

Finsten, Laura, Kent V. Flannery, and Barbara Macnider
1989   Preceramic and cave occupations. In *Monte Albán's Hinterland*, Part II, Volume 1, by Stephen A. Kowalewski, Gary M. Feinman, Laura Finsten, Richard E. Blanton, and Linda M. Nicholas, pp. 39–53. Memoirs No. 23. Museum of Anthropology, University of Michigan, Ann Arbor, MI.

Flannery, Kent V.
1966   The Postglacial "readaptation" as viewed from Mesoamerica. *American Antiquity* 31:800–805.
1967   Vertebrate fauna and hunting patterns. In *The Prehistory of the Tehuacan Valley, vol. 1: Environment and Subsistence*, edited by Douglas S. Byers, pp. 132–177. Austin: University of Texas Press.
2009a *Guilá Naquitz: Archaic Foraging and Early Agriculture in Oaxaca, Mexico* (updated edition). Walnut Creek, CA: Left Coast Press.
2009b Foreword to the updated edition (2009a). In *Guilá Naquitz: Archaic Foraging and Early Agriculture in Oaxaca, Mexico* (updated edition), edited by Kent V. Flannery, pp. xix–xxii. Walnut Creek, CA: Left Coast Press.

Flannery, Kent V. and Joyce Marcus
2003   Urban Mitla and its rural hinterland. In *The Cloud People* (revised edition), edited by Kent V. Flannery and Joyce Marcus, pp. 295–300. Clinton Corners, NY: Percheron Press.
2005   *Excavations at San José Mogote 1: The Household Archaeology*. Memoirs No. 40. Museum of Anthropology, University of Michigan, Ann Arbor, MI.
2015   *Excavations at San José Mogote 2: The Cognitive Archaeology*. Memoirs No. 58. Museum of Anthropology, University of Michigan, Ann Arbor, MI.

Flannery, Kent V. and Jane C. Wheeler
2009a Comparing the preceramic and modern microfauna. In *Guilá Naquitz: Archaic Foraging and Early Agriculture in Oaxaca, Mexico* (updated edition), edited by Kent V. Flannery, pp. 239–246. Walnut Creek, CA: Left Coast Press.
2009b Animal food remains from preceramic Guilá Naquitz. In *Guilá Naquitz: Archaic Foraging and Early Agriculture in Oaxaca, Mexico* (updated edition), edited by Kent V. Flannery, pp. 285–295. Walnut Creek, CA: Left Coast Press.

Flenniken, J. Jeffrey and Anan W. Raymond
1986   Morphological projectile point typology: replication, experimentation, and technological analysis. *American Antiquity* 51(3):603–614.

Frison, George C., Michael Wilson, and Diane J. Wilson
1976   Fossil bison and artifacts from an Early Altithermal Period arroyo trap in Wyoming. *American Antiquity* 41:28–57.

García Moll, Roberto
1977   Análisis de los materiales arqueológicos de la Cueva del Texcal, Puebla. *Colección Científica 56, Arqueología*. México, D.F.: Instituto Nacional de Antropología e Historia, Departamento de Prehistoria.

Golden Software
1987   *SURFER*. Golden Software, Golden, CO.

Goodman, Leo A. and William H. Kruskal
1954   Measures of association for cross classifications. *Journal of the American Statistical Association* 49:732–764.

Gould, Richard A.
1968   Living archaeology: The Ngatatjara of western Australia. *Southwestern Journal of Anthropology* 24(2):101–122.

Hall, A. V.
1969   Avoiding informational distortions in automatic grouping programs. *Systematic Zoology* 18:318–329.

Hietala, Harold
1984a Intrasite spatial analysis: a brief overview. *In Intrasite Spatial Analysis in Archaeology*, edited by Harold Hietala, pp. 1–3. Cambridge: Cambridge University Press.
1984b Variations on a categorical data theme: local and global considerations with Near Eastern Paleolithic applications. *In Intrasite Spatial Analysis in Archaeology*, edited by Harold Hietala, pp. 44–53. Cambridge: Cambridge University Press.
1984c Intrasite spatial analysis: future directions. *In Intrasite Spatial Analysis in Archaeology*, edited by Harold Hietala, pp. 278–280. Cambridge: Cambridge University Press.

Hietala, Harold (editor)
1984   *Intrasite Spatial Analysis in Archaeology*. Cambridge: Cambridge University Press.

Hietala, Harold and Paul Larson
1979   SYMAP analyses in archaeology: intrasite assumptions and a comparison with TREND analysis. *Norwegian Archaeological Review* 12:57–64.

Hole, Frank
2009   Chipped stone tools. In *Guilá Naquitz: Archaic Foraging and Early Agriculture in Oaxaca, Mexico* (updated edition), edited by Kent V. Flannery, pp. 97–139. Walnut Creek, CA: Left Coast Press.

Hole, Frank, Kent V. Flannery, and James A. Neely
1969   *Prehistory and Human Ecology of the Deh Luran Plain*. Memoirs No. 1. Museum of Anthropology, University of Michigan, Ann Arbor, MI.

Holmes, William Henry
   1897   Archaeological studies among the ancient cites of Mexico (Part II): Monuments of Chiapas, Oaxaca, and the Valley of Mexico. *Field Columbian Museum Anthropological Series* 1(1). Chicago.

Johnson, Frederick and Richard S. MacNeish
   1972   Chronometric dating. In *The Prehistory of the Tehuacan Valley, Volume 4: Chronology and Irrigation*, by Richard S. MacNeish, Frederick Johnson, Karl A. Wittfogel, Richard B. Woodbury, James A. Neely, Gorgonio Gil Huerta, and Eva Hunt, pp. 3–55. Austin: University of Texas Press.

Kaplan, Lawrence
   2009   Preceramic *Phaseolus* from Guilá Naquitz. In *Guilá Naquitz: Archaic Foraging and Early Agriculture in Oaxaca, Mexico* (updated edition), edited by Kent V. Flannery, pp. 281–284. Walnut Creek, CA: Left Coast Press.

Kaplan, Lawrence and Thomas F. Lynch
   1999   *Phaseolus* (Fabaceae) in archaeology: AMS radiocarbon dates and their significance for Pre-Columbian agriculture. *Economic Botany* 53:261–272.

Kintigh, Keith W.
   1985   Promise and problems in the study of patterning. *American Archaeology* 5(1):79–80.
   1989   Intrasite spatial analysis: A commentary on major methods. In *Mathematics and Information Science in Archaeology: A Flexible Framework*, edited by Albertus Voorrips, pp. 165–200. Bonn: Holos.

Kirkby, Michael J., Anne V. Whyte, and Kent V. Flannery
   2009   The physical environment of the Guilá Naquitz Cave Group. In *Guilá Naquitz: Archaic Foraging and Early Agriculture in Oaxaca, Mexico* (updated edition), edited by Kent V. Flannery, pp. 43–61. Walnut Creek, CA: Left Coast Press.

Kohler, Timothy A., P. I. Buckland, K. W. Kintigh, R. K. Bocinsky, A. Brin, A. Gillreath-Brown, B. Ludäscher, T. M. McPhillips, R. Opitz, and J. Terstriep
   2018   Paleodata from archaeology. *Pages Magazine* 26:68–69.

Kruskal, Joseph B.
   1964a   Multidimensional scaling by optimizing goodness of fit to a nonmetric hypothesis. *Psychometrika* 29:1–27.
   1964b   Nonmetric multidimensional scaling: a numerical method. *Psychometrika* 29:115–129.

Lachniet, Matthew S., Yemane Asmerom, Juan Pablo Bernal, Victor J. Polyak, and Lorenzo Vazquez-Selem
   2013   Orbital pacing and ocean circulation-induced collapses of the Mesoamerican monsoon over the past 22,000 y. *Proceedings of the National Academy of Sciences* 110:9255–9260.

Lee, Richard B.
   1979   *The !Kung San*. Cambridge: Cambridge University Press.

Lowe, Gareth W.
   1959   *Archaeological Exploration of the Upper Grijalva River, Chiapas, Mexico*. Papers of the New World Archaeological Foundation, no. 2. Provo: Brigham Young University.

Lynch-Stieglitz, Jean
   1998   Oceanic records of abrupt climate change. 10th Annual Symposium on Frontiers of Science, Beckman Center (National Academy of Sciences). Irvine, CA.

MacNeish, Richard S.
   1964   Ancient Mesoamerican civilization. *Science* 143:531–537.
   1972   The evolution of community patterns in the Tehuacán Valley of Mexico and speculations about the cultural processes. In *Man, Settlement, and Urbanism,* edited by Peter J. Ucko, Ruth Tringham, and G. W. Dimbleby, pp. 67–93. London: Gerald Duckworth and Co.

MacNeish, Richard S., Melvin L. Fowler, Angel García Cook, Frederick A. Peterson, Antoinette Nelken-Terner, and James A. Neely
   1967   *The Prehistory of the Tehuacán Valley,* Volume 5: *Excavations and Reconnaissance.* Austin: University of Texas Press.

MacNeish, Richard S., Antoinette Nelken-Terner, and Irmgard W. Johnson
   1967   *The Prehistory of the Tehuacán Valley,* Volume 2: *Nonceramic Artifacts.* Austin: University of Texas Press.

Marcus, Joyce and Kent V. Flannery
   1996   *Zapotec Civilization: How Urban Society Evolved in Mexico's Oaxaca Valley.* New York: Thames and Hudson.
   2004   The coevolution of ritual and society: New ^{14}C dates from ancient Mexico. *Proceedings of the National Academy of Sciences* 101:18257–18261.

Matsuoka, Yoshihiro, Yves Vigouroux, Major M. Goodman, Jesús Sánchez G., Edward Buckler, and John Doebley
   2002   A single domestication for maize shown by multilocus microsatellite genotyping. *Proceedings of the National Academy of Sciences* 99:6080–6084.

Messer, Ellen
   1978   *Zapotec Plant Knowledge: Classification, Uses, and Communication about Plants in Mitla, Oaxaca, Mexico.* In Prehistory and Human Ecology of the Valley of Oaxaca, Volume 5, Part 2, edited by Kent V. Flannery and Richard E. Blanton. Memoirs No. 10. Museum of Anthropology, University of Michigan, Ann Arbor, MI.

Metcalfe, Sarah E.
   2006   Late Quaternary environments of the northern deserts and Central Transvolcanic Belt of Mexico. *Annals of the Missouri Botanical Garden* 93:258–273.

Mortensen, Peder
   2014   Excavations at Tepe Guran: The Neolithic Period. *Acta Iranica* 55. Leuven, Belgium: Peeters.

Moser, Chris L.
   n.d.   A study of the Monte Albán V pottery from Cueva Blanca, Oaxaca. Unpublished manuscript.

Niederberger, Christine
   1976   *Zohapilco: Cinco milenios de ocupación humana en*

un sitio lacustre de la cuenca de México. Mexico City: Instituto Nacional de Antropología e Historia.
1987 *Paléopaysage et Archéologie Pré-urbaine du Bassin de Mexico*, vol. 2. México, D.F.: Centre d'Etudes Mexicaines et Centraméricaines.

O'Connell, James F.
1987 Alyawara site structure and its archaeological implications. *American Antiquity* 52:74–108.

O'Dea, Aaron, Jeremy B. C. Jackson, Helena Fortunato, J. Travis Smith, Luis D'Croz, Kenneth G. Johnson, and Jonathan A. Todd
2007 Environmental change preceded Caribbean extinction by 2 million years. *Proceedings of the National Academy of Sciences* 104:5501–5506.

Payne, Sebastian B.
1985 Zoo-archaeology in Greece: a reader's guide. In *Contributions to Aegean Archaeology: Studies in Honor of William H. McDonald*, edited by N. C. Wilkie and W. D. E. Coulson, pp. 211–244. Dubuque, IA: Kendall/Hunt Publishing Co.

Piperno, Dolores R. and Kent V. Flannery
2001 The earliest archaeological maize (*Zea mays* L.) from highland Mexico: new accelerator mass spectrometry dates and their implications. *Proceedings of the National Academy of Sciences* 98:2101–2103.

Piperno, Dolores R., Anthony J. Ranere, Irene Holst, José Iriarte, and Ruth Dickau
2009 Starch grain and phytolith evidence for early ninth millennium B.P. maize from the central Balsas River Valley, Mexico. *Proceedings of the National Academy of Sciences* 106:5019–5024.

Pires-Ferreira, Jane W.
2003 *Formative Mesoamerican Exchange Networks, with Special Reference to the Valley of Oaxaca*. Memoirs No. 7. Museum of Anthropology, University of Michigan, Ann Arbor, MI.

Read, Dwight
1985 Pattern recognition as a paradigm in the study of patterning. *American Archaeology* 5(1):79–84.

Reimer, Paula J., Edouard Bard, Alex Bayliss, J. Warren Beck, Paul G. Blackwell, Christopher Bronk Ramsey, Caitlin E. Buck, Hai Cheng, R. Lawrence Edwards, Michael Friedrich, Pieter M. Grootes, Thomas P. Guilderson, Haflidi Haflidason, Irka Hajdas, Christine Hatté, Timothy J. Heaton, Dirk J. Hoffmann, Alan G. Hogg, Konrad A. Hughen, H. Felix Kaiser, Bernd Kromer, Sturt W. Manning, Mu Niu, Ron W. Reimer, David A. Richards, E. Marian Scott, John R. Southon, Richard A. Staff, Christian S. M. Turney, and Johannes van der Plicht
2013 IntCal 13 and Marine 13 radiocarbon age calibration curves 0–50,000 years cal BP. *Radiocarbon* 55(4):1869–1887.

Reitz, Elizabeth J. and Elizabeth S. Wing
1999 *Zooarchaeology*. Cambridge: Cambridge University Press.

Reynolds, Robert G.
1995 Learning the parameters for a gradient-based approach to image segmentation using cultural algorithms. *Proceedings of the International IEEE Symposium on Intelligence in Neural and Biological Systems*, pp. 240–247. Los Alamitos, CA: IEEE Computer Society Press.
2009 Multidimensional scaling of four Guilá Naquitz living floors. In *Guilá Naquitz: Archaic Foraging and Early Agriculture in Oaxaca, Mexico* (updated edition), edited by Kent V. Flannery, pp. 385–423. Walnut Creek, CA: Left Coast Press.

Romesburg, H. Charles
1990 *Cluster Analysis for Researchers*. Malabar, Florida: R. E. Krieger.

Rowley-Conwy, Peter and Robert Layton
2011 Foraging and farming as niche construction: stable and unstable adaptations. *Philosophical Transactions: Biological Sciences* 366(1566):849–862. Royal Society of Great Britain and Northern Ireland.

Schiffer, Michael B.
1987 *Formation Processes of the Archaeological Record*. Albuquerque: University of New Mexico Press.

Schoenwetter, James and Landon Douglas Smith
2009 Pollen analysis of the Oaxaca Archaic. In *Guilá Naquitz: Archaic Foraging and Early Agriculture in Oaxaca, Mexico* (updated edition), edited by Kent V. Flannery, pp. 179–237. Walnut Creek, CA: Left Coast Press.

Severinghaus, Jeffrey P.
1998 Abrupt climate change inferred from thermally-fractionated gases in polar ice. 10th Annual Symposium on Frontiers of Science, Beckman Center (National Academy of Sciences). Irvine, CA.

Shafer, Harry J.
1986 *Ancient Texans: Rock Art and Lifeways along the Lower Pecos*. San Antonio: Texas Monthly Press.

Smith, Bruce D.
1997 The initial domestication of *Cucurbita pepo* in the Americas 10,000 years ago. *Science* 276:932–934.
2001 Documenting plant domestication: the consilience of biological and archaeological approaches. *Proceedings of the National Academy of Sciences* 98:1324–1326.
2015 A comparison of niche construction theory and diet breadth models as explanatory frameworks for the initial domestication of plants and animals. *Journal of Archaeological Research* 23(3):215–262.

Smith, C. Earle Jr.
2009 Preceramic plant remains from Guilá Naquitz. In *Guilá Naquitz: Archaic Foraging and Early Agriculture in Oaxaca, Mexico* (updated edition), edited by Kent V. Flannery, pp. 265–274. Walnut Creek, CA: Left Coast Press.

Sokal, Robert R. and Charles D. Michener
1958 A statistical method for evaluating systematic relationships. *University of Kansas Scientific Bulletin* 38:1409–1438.

Spaulding, W. Geoffrey
1989 Environment of the last 18,000 years in extreme southwestern North America. Paper presented at the Texas

A&M Conference on the Archaic of southern Texas and northern Mexico. Lajitas, Texas.

Spencer, Charles S. and Kent V. Flannery
2009 Spatial variation of debris at Guilá Naquitz: a descriptive approach. In *Guilá Naquitz: Archaic Foraging and Early Agriculture in Oaxaca, Mexico* (updated edition), edited by Kent V. Flannery, pp. 331–367. Walnut Creek, CA: Left Coast Press.

Stevenson, Mark G.
1991 Beyond the formation of hearth-associated artifact assemblages. In *The Interpretation of Archaeological Spatial Patterning*, edited by Ellen M. Kroll and T. Douglas Price, pp. 269–299. New York: Plenum Press.

Steward, Julian
1938 Basin-plateau aboriginal sociopolitical groups. *Bureau of American Ethnology Bulletin of the Smithsonian Institution* 120. Washington, D.C.
1955 *Theory of Culture Change*. Urbana, IL: University of Illinois Press.

Tanimoto, Steven
1987 *The Elements of Artificial Intelligence*. Third edition. Rockville, MD: Computer Science Press.

Thomas, David Hurst
1983 *The Archaeology of Monitor Valley: 2. Gatecliff Shelter.* Anthropological Papers of the American Museum of Natural History, Vol. 59, Part 1. New York.

Thomas, Elizabeth Marshall
1959 *The Harmless People*. New York: Vintage Books, A. A. Knopf.

Thoms, Alston V., Laura M. Short, Masahiro Kamiya, and Andrew R. Laurence
2018 Ethnographies and actualistic cooking experiments: Ethnoarchaeological pathways toward understanding earth-oven variability in archaeological records. *Ethnoarchaeology* 10:76–98.

Whalen, Michael E.
2009b Sources of the Guilá Naquitz chipped stone. In *Guilá Naquitz: Archaic Foraging and Early Agriculture in Oaxaca, Mexico* (updated edition), edited by Kent V. Flannery, pp. 141–146. Walnut Creek, CA: Left Coast Press.

Whallon, Robert
1973 Spatial analysis of occupation floors I: Application of dimensional analysis of variance. *American Antiquity* 38:266–278.
1974 Spatial analysis of occupation floors II: The application of nearest neighbor analysis. *American Antiquity* 39:16–34.
1984 Unconstrained clustering for the analysis of spatial distributions in archaeology. In *Intrasite Spatial Analysis in Archaeology,* edited by Harold Hietala, pp. 242–277. Cambridge: Cambridge University Press.
2009 A spatial analysis of four occupation floors at Guilá Naquitz. In *Guilá Naquitz: Archaic Foraging and Early Agriculture in Oaxaca, Mexico* (updated edition), edited by Kent V. Flannery, pp. 369–384. Walnut Creek, CA: Left Coast Press.

Wiessner, Pauline
1977 *Hxaro: A Regional System of Reducing Risk Among the !Kung San*. Ph.D. dissertation, Department of Anthropology, University of Michigan, Ann Arbor, MI.

Wilkinson, Leland
1986 *SYSTAT: The System for Statistics*. Evanston, IL: Systat, Inc.

Williams, Howel and Robert F. Heizer
1965 Geological notes on the ruins of Mitla and other Oaxacan sites, Mexico. *Contributions of the University of California Archaeological Research Facility* 1:41–54.

Winston, Patrick Henry
1984 *Artificial Intelligence*. Reading, MA: Addison-Wesley Publication Co.

Yellen, John E.
1976 Settlement patterns of the !Kung: An archaeological perspective. In *Kalahari Hunter-Gatherers*, edited by Richard B. Lee and Irven DeVore, pp. 47–72. Cambridge, MA: Harvard University Press.

Zubrow, Ezra
1985 The problem of patterns: A frontier in archaeological methodology. *American Archaeology* 5(1):1–3.

Zupan, Jure
1982 *Clustering of Large Data Sets*. Chichester, UK: Research Studies Press.